FRANCES YATES

SELECTED WORKS

FRANCES YATES
Selected Works

FRANCES YATES

Selected Works

Volume III

The Art of Memory

London and New York

First published 1966 by Routledge

Reprinted by Routledge 1999
2 Park Square, Milton Park,
Abingdon, Oxon, OX14 4RN

Simultaneously published in the USA and Canada
by Routledge
270 Madison Ave, New York NY 10016

Reprinted 2001

First issued in paperback 2010

Routledge is an imprint of the Taylor & Francis Group

© 1966 Frances A. Yates

Publisher's note
The publisher has gone to great lengths to ensure the
quality of this reprint but points out that some imperfections
in the original book may be apparent.

British Library Cataloguing in Publication Data
A CIP record of this set is available from the British Library

Library of Congress Cataloging in Publication Data
A catalogue record for this book has been requested

ISBN 978-0-415-22046-0 (hbk) (Volume 3)
ISBN 978-0-415-60605-9 (pbk) (Volume 3)
10 Volumes: ISBN 978-0-415-22043-9 (Set)

Hermetic Silence. From Achilles Bocchius, *Symbolicarum quaestionum . . . libri quinque*, Bologna, 1555. Engraved by G. Bonasone (p. 170)

ARK

FRANCES A. YATES
THE ART OF MEMORY

ARK PAPERBACKS

London, Melbourne and Henley

First published in 1966
ARK Edition 1984
ARK PAPERBACKS is an imprint of
Routledge
2 Park Square, Milton Park,
Abingdon, Oxon, OX14 4RN
270 Madison Ave, New York NY 10016
© Frances A. Yates 1966.

ISBN 0-7448-0020-X

CONTENTS

v

ILLUSTRATIONS

PLATES

ILLUSTRATIONS

FIGURES

ix

PREFACE

THE subject of this book will be unfamiliar to most readers. Few people know that the Greeks, who invented many arts, invented an art of memory which, like their other arts, was passed on to Rome whence it descended in the European tradition. This art seeks to memorise through a technique of impressing 'places' and 'images' on memory. It has usually been classed as 'mnemotechnics', which in modern times seems a rather unimportant branch of human activity. But in the ages before printing a trained memory was vitally important; and the manipulation of images in memory must always to some extent involve the psyche as a whole. Moreover an art which uses contemporary architecture for its memory places and contemporary imagery for its images will have its classical, Gothic, and Renaissance periods, like the other arts. Though the mnemotechnical side of the art is always present, both in antiquity and thereafter, and forms the factual basis for its investigation, the exploration of it must include more than the history of its techniques. Mnemosyne, said the Greeks, is the mother of the Muses; the history of the training of this most fundamental and elusive of human powers will plunge us into deep waters.

My interest in the subject began about fifteen years ago when I hopefully set out to try to understand Giordano Bruno's works on memory. The memory system excavated from Bruno's *Shadows* (Pl. 11) was first displayed in a lecture at the Warburg Institute in May, 1952. Two years later, in January, 1955, the plan of Giulio Camillo's Memory Theatre (see *Folder*) was exhibited, also at a lecture at the Warburg Institute. I had realised by this time that there was some historical connection between Camillo's Theatre, Bruno's and Campanella's systems, and Robert Fludd's Theatre system, all of which were compared, very superficially, at this lecture. Encouraged by what seemed a slight progress, I began to write the history of the art of memory from Simonides onwards. This stage was reflected in an article on 'The Ciceronian Art of Memory' which was published in Italy in the volume of studies in honour of Bruno Nardi (*Medioevo e Rinascimento*, Florence, 1955).

xi

After this there was a rather long halt, caused by a difficulty. I could not understand what happened to the art of memory in the Middle Ages. Why did Albertus Magnus and Thomas Aquinas regard the use in memory of the places and images of 'Tullius' as a moral and religious duty? The word 'mnemotechnics' seemed inadequate to cover the scholastic recommendation of the art of memory as a part of the cardinal virtue of prudence. Gradually the idea began to dawn that the Middle Ages might think of figures of virtues and vices as memory images, formed according to the classical rules, or of the divisions of Dante's Hell as memory places. Attempts to tackle the mediaeval transformation of the classical art were made in lectures on 'The Classical Art of Memory in the Middle Ages' given to the Oxford Mediaeval Society in March, 1958, and on 'Rhetoric and the Art of Memory' at the Warburg Institute in December 1959. Parts of these lectures are incorporated in chapters IV and V.

The greatest problem of all remained, the problem of the Renaissance magical or occult memory systems. Why, when the invention of printing seemed to have made the great Gothic artificial memories of the Middle Ages no longer necessary, was there this recrudescence of the interest in the art of memory in the strange forms in which we find it in the Renaissance systems of Camillo, Bruno, and Fludd? I returned to the study of Giulio Camillo's Memory Theatre and realised that the stimulus behind Renaissance occult memory was the Renaissance Hermetic tradition. It also became apparent that it would be necessary to write a book on this tradition before one could tackle the Renaissance memory systems. The Renaissance chapters in this book depend for their background on my *Giordano Bruno amd the Hermetic Tradition* (London and Chicago, 1964).

I had thought that it might have been possible to keep Lullism out of this book and treat it separately, but it soon became clear that this was impossible. Though Lullism does not come out of the rhetoric tradition, like the classical art of memory, and though its procedures are very different, yet it is, in one of its aspects, an art of memory and as such it becomes conflated and confused with the classical art at the Renaissance. The interpretation of Lullism given in chapter VIII is based on my articles 'The Art of Ramon Lull: An Approach to it through Lull's Theory of the Elements', and 'Ramon Lull and John Scotus

Erigena', *Journal of the Warburg and Courtauld Institutes*, XVII (1954) and XXIII (1960).

There is no modern book in English on the history of the art of memory and very few books or articles on it in any language. When I began, my chief aids were some old monographs in German and the later German studies by H. Hajdu, 1936, and L. Volkmann, 1937 (for full references, see p. 105). In 1960, Paolo Rossi's *Clavis universalis* was published. This book, which is in Italian, is a serious historical study of the art of memory; it prints a good deal of source material, and contains discussions of Camillo's Theatre, of Bruno's works, of Lullism, and much else. It has been valuable to me, particularly for the seventeenth century, though it is on quite different lines from this book. I have also consulted Rossi's numerous articles and one by Cesare Vasoli (references on pp. 105, 184, 194). Other books which have particularly helped me are H. Caplan's edition of *Ad Herennium* (1954); W. S. Howell, *Logic and Rhetoric in England, 1500–1700* (1956); W. J. Ong, *Ramus; Method and the Decay of Dialogue* (1958); Beryl Smalley, *English Friars and Antiquity* (1960).

Though it uses a good deal of earlier work, this book in its present form is a new work, entirely rewritten and expanded in fresh directions during the past two years. Much that was obscure seems to have fallen into better shape, particularly the connections of the art of memory with Lullism and Ramism and the emergence of 'method'. Moreover what is perhaps one of the most exciting parts of the book has become prominent only quite recently. This is the realisation that Fludd's Theatre memory system can throw light on Shakespeare's Globe Theatre. The imaginary architecture of the art of memory has preserved the memory of a real, but long vanished, building.

Like my *Giordano Bruno and the Hermetic Tradition*, the present book is orientated towards placing Bruno in a historical context but also aims at giving a survey of a whole tradition. It particularly endeavours to throw light, through the history of memory, on the nature of the impact which Bruno may have made on Elizabethan England. I have tried to strike out a pathway through a vast subject but at every stage the picture which I have drawn needs to be supplemented or corrected by further studies. This is an immensely rich field for research, needing the collaboration of specialists in many disciplines.

Now that the Memory Book is at last ended, the memory of the late Gertrud Bing seems more poignantly present than ever. In the early days, she read and discussed my drafts, watching constantly over my progress, or lack of progress, encouraging and discouraging by turns, ever stimulating with her intense interest and vigilant criticism. She felt that the problems of the mental image, of the activation of images, of the grasp of reality through images—problems ever present in the history of the art of memory—were close to those which preoccupied Aby Warburg, whom I only knew through her. Whether this book is what she hoped for I can now never know. She did not see even the first three chapters of it which were about to be sent to her when she was taken ill. I dedicate it to her memory, with deep gratitude for her friendship.

My debt to my colleagues and friends of the Warburg Institute, University of London, is, as always, profound. The Director, E. H. Gombrich, has always taken a stimulating interest in my labours and much is owed to his wisdom. I believe that it was he who first put into my hands *L'Idea del Theatro* of Giulio Camillo. There have been many invaluable discussions with D. P. Walker whose specialist knowledge of certain aspects of the Renaissance has been of constant assistance. He read the early drafts and has also read this book in manuscript, kindly checking some of my translations. With J. Trapp there have been talks about the rhetoric tradition, and he has been a mine of bibliographical information. Some iconographical problems were laid before L. Ettlinger.

All the librarians have been endlessly patient with my efforts to find books. And the staff of the photographic collection has shown similar forbearance with my efforts to find photographs.

I am grateful for the comradeship of J. Hillgarth and R. Pring-Mill in Lull studies. And to Elspeth Jaffé, who knows much about arts of memory, for past conversations.

My sister, R. W. Yates, has read the chapters as they were written. Her reactions to them have been a most valuable guide and her clever advice of great help in revisions. With unfailing good humour she has given untiring assistance in countless ways. She has contributed above all to the plans and sketches. She drew the plan of Camillo's Theatre and the sketch of the Globe based on Fludd. The suggested plan of the Globe is very largely her work. We shared together the excitement of the reconstruction of the

Globe out of Fludd during memorable weeks of close collaboration. The book owes to her one of its greatest debts.

I have constantly used the London Library to whose staff I am deeply grateful. And it goes without saying that the same is true of the library of the British Museum and its staff. I am also indebted to the librarians of the Bodleian Library, the Cambridge University Library, the library of Emmanuel College, Cambridge, and of the following libraries abroad: Biblioteca Nazionale, Florence; Biblioteca Ambrosiana, Milan; Bibliothèque Nationale, Paris; Biblioteca Vaticana, Rome; Biblioteca Marciana, Venice.

I am indebted for their kind permissions to reproduce miniatures or pictures in their possession to the Directors of the Biblioteca Nazionale, Florence, of the Badische Landesbibliothek, Karlsruhe, of the Österreichische Nationalbibliothek, Vienna, of the Biblioteca Casanatense, Rome, and the Swiss ownership of the picture by Titian.

FRANCES A. YATES

Warburg Institute,
University of London

Chapter I

THE THREE LATIN SOURCES FOR THE CLASSICAL ART OF MEMORY[1]

AT a banquet given by a nobleman of Thessaly named Scopas, the poet Simonides of Ceos chanted a lyric poem in honour of his host but including a passage in praise of Castor and Pollux. Scopas meanly told the poet that he would only pay him half the sum agreed upon for the panegyric and that he must obtain the balance from the twin gods to whom he had devoted half the poem. A little later, a message was brought in to Simonides that two young men were waiting outside who wished to see him. He rose from the banquet and went out but could find no one. During his absence the roof of the banqueting hall fell in, crushing Scopas and all the guests to death beneath the ruins; the corpses were so mangled that the relatives who came to

---

[1] The English translations of the three Latin sources used are those in the Loeb edition of the classics: the *Ad Herennium* is translated by H. Caplan; the *De oratore* by E. W. Sutton and H. Rackham; Quintilian's *Institutio oratoria* by H. E. Butler. When quoting from these translations I have sometimes modified them in the direction of literalness, particularly in repeating the actual terminology of the mnemonic rather than in using periphrases of the terms.

The best account known to me of the art of memory in antiquity is that given by H. Hajdu, *Das Mnemotechnische Schriftum des Mittelalters*, Vienna, 1936. I attempted a brief sketch of it in my article 'The Ciceronian Art of Memory' in *Medioeve e Rinascimento, Studi in onore di Bruno Nardi*, Florence, 1955, II, pp. 871 ff. On the whole, the subject has been curiously neglected.

take them away for burial were unable to identify them. But Simonides remembered the places at which they had been sitting at the table and was therefore able to indicate to the relatives which were their dead. The invisible callers, Castor and Pollux, had handsomely paid for their share in the panegyric by drawing Simonides away from the banquet just before the crash. And this experience suggested to the poet the principles of the art of memory of which he is said to have been the inventor. Noting that it was through his memory of the places at which the guests had been sitting that he had been able to identify the bodies, he realised that orderly arrangement is essential for good memory.

> He inferred that persons desiring to train this faculty (of memory) must select places and form mental images of the things they wish to remember and store those images in the places, so that the order of the places will preserve the order of the things, and the images of the things will denote the things themselves, and we shall employ the places and images respectively as a wax writing-tablet and the letters written on it.[2]

The vivid story of how Simonides invented the art of memory is told by Cicero in his *De oratore* when he is discussing memory as one of the five parts of rhetoric; the story introduces a brief description of the mnemonic of *places* and *images* (*loci* and *imagines*) which was used by the Roman rhetors. Two other descriptions of the classical mnemonic, besides the one given by Cicero, have come down to us, both also in treatises on rhetoric when memory as a part of rhetoric is being discussed; one is in the anonymous *Ad C. Herennium libri IV*; the other is in Quintilian's *Institutio oratoria*.

The first basic fact which the student of the history of the classical art of memory must remember is that the art belonged to rhetoric as a technique by which the orator could improve his memory, which would enable him to deliver long speeches from memory with unfailing accuracy. And it was as a part of the art of rhetoric that the art of memory travelled down through the European tradition in which it was never forgotten, or not forgotten until comparatively modern times, that those infallible guides in all human activities, the ancients, had laid down rules and precepts for improving the memory.

[2] Cicero, *De oratore*, II, lxxxvi, 351–4.

It is not difficult to get hold of the general principles of the mnemonic. The first step was to imprint on the memory a series of *loci* or places. The commonest, though not the only, type of mnemonic place system used was the architectural type. The clearest description of the process is that given by Quintilian.[3] In order to form a series of places in memory, he says, a building is to be remembered, as spacious and varied a one as possible, the fore-court, the living room, bedrooms, and parlours, not omitting statues and other ornaments with which the rooms are decorated. The images by which the speech is to be remembered—as an example of these Quintilian says one may use an anchor or a weapon—are then placed in imagination on the places which have been memorised in the building. This done, as soon as the memory of the facts requires to be revived, all these places are visited in turn and the various deposits demanded of their custodians. We have to think of the ancient orator as moving in imagination through his memory building *whilst* he is making his speech, draw-ing from the memorised places the images he has placed on them. The method ensures that the points are remembered in the right order, since the order is fixed by the sequence of places in the building. Quintilian's examples of the anchor and the weapon as images may suggest that he had in mind a speech which dealt at one point with naval matters (the anchor), at another with military operations (the weapon).

There is no doubt that this method will work for anyone who is prepared to labour seriously at these mnemonic gymnastics. I have never attempted to do so myself but I have been told of a professor who used to amuse his students at parties by asking each of them to name an object; one of them noted down all the objects in the order in which they had been named. Later in the evening the professor would cause general amazement by repeating the list of objects in the right order. He performed his little memory feat by placing the objects, as they were named, on the window sill, on the desk, on the wastepaper basket, and so on. Then, as Quintilian advises, he revisited those places in turn and demanded from them their deposits. He had never heard of the classical mnemonic but had discovered his technique quite independently. Had he ex-tended his efforts by attaching notions to the objects remembered on the places he might have caused still greater amazement by

[3] *Institutio oratoria*, XI, ii, 17–22.

3

delivering his lectures from memory, as the classical orator delivered his speeches.

Whilst it is important to recognise that the classical art is based on workable mnemotechnic principles it may be misleading to dismiss it with the label 'mnemotechnics'. The classical sources seem to be describing inner techniques which depend on visual impressions of almost incredible intensity. Cicero emphasises that Simonides' invention of the art of memory rested, not only on his discovery of the importance of order for memory, but also on the discovery that the sense of sight is the strongest of all the senses.

> It has been sagaciously discerned by Simonides or else discovered by some other person, that the most complete pictures are formed in our minds of the things that have been conveyed to them and imprinted on them by the senses, but that the keenest of all our senses is the sense of sight, and that consequently perceptions received by the ears or by reflexion can be most easily retained if they are also conveyed to our minds by the mediation of the eyes.[4]

The word 'mnemotechnics' hardly conveys what the artificial memory of Cicero may have been like, as it moved among the buildings of ancient Rome, *seeing* the places, *seeing* the images stored on the places, with a piercing inner vision which immediately brought to his lips the thoughts and words of his speech. I prefer to use the expression 'art of memory' for this process.

We moderns who have no memories at all may, like the professor, employ from time to time some private mnemotechnic not of vital importance to us in our lives and professions. But in the ancient world, devoid of printing, without paper for note-taking or on which to type lectures, the trained memory was of vital importance. And the ancient memories were trained by an art which reflected the art and architecture of the ancient world, which could depend on faculties of intense visual memorisation which we have lost. The word 'mnemotechnics', though not actually wrong as a description of the classical art of memory, makes this very mysterious subject seem simpler than it is.

An unknown teacher of rhetoric in Rome[5] compiled, *circa* 86–82 B.C., a useful text-book for his students which immortalised,

---

[4] *De oratore,* II, lxxxvii, 357.

[5] On the authorship and other problems of the *Ad Herennium,* see the excellent introduction by H. Caplan to the Loeb edition (1954).

not his own name, but the name of the man to whom it was dedicated. It is somewhat tiresome that this work, so vitally important for the history of the classical art of memory and which will be constantly referred to in the course of this book, has no other title save the uninformative *Ad Herennium*. The busy and efficient teacher goes through the five parts of rhetoric (*inventio, dispositio, elocutio, memoria, pronuntiatio*) in a rather dry text-book style. When he comes to memory[6] as an essential part of the orator's equipment, he opens his treatment of it with the words: 'Now let us turn to the treasure-house of inventions, the custodian of all the parts of rhetoric, memory.' There are two kinds of memory, he continues, one natural, the other artificial. The natural memory is that which is engrafted in our minds, born simultaneously with thought. The artificial memory is a memory strengthened or confirmed by training. A good natural memory can be improved by this discipline and persons less well endowed can have their weak memories improved by the art.

After this curt preamble the author announces abruptly, 'Now we will speak of the artificial memory.'

An immense weight of history presses on the memory section of *Ad Herennium*. It is drawing on Greek sources of memory teaching, probably in Greek treatises on rhetoric all of which are lost. It is the only Latin treatise on the subject to be preserved, for Cicero's and Quintilian's remarks are not full treatises and assume that the reader is already familiar with the artificial memory and its terminology. It is thus really the main source, and indeed the only complete source, for the classical art of memory both in the Greek and in the Latin world. Its rôle as the transmitter of the classical art to the Middle Ages and the Renaissance is also of unique importance. The *Ad Herennium* was a well known and much used text in the Middle Ages when it had an immense prestige because it was thought to be by Cicero. It was therefore believed that the precepts for the artificial memory which it expounded had been drawn up by 'Tullius' himself.

In short, all attempts to puzzle out what the classical art of memory was like must be mainly based on the memory section of *Ad Herennium*. And all attempts such as we are making in this book to puzzle out the history of that art in the Western tradition

---

[6] The section on memory is in *Ad Herennium*, III, xvi–xxiv.

5

must refer back constantly to this text as the main source of the tradition. Every *Ars memorativa* treatise, with its rules for 'places', its rules for 'images', its discussion of 'memory for things' and 'memory for words', is repeating the plan, the subject matter, and as often as not the actual words of *Ad Herennium*. And the astonishing developments of the art of memory in the sixteenth century, which it is the chief object of this book to explore, still preserve the 'Ad Herennian' outlines below all their complex accretions. Even the wildest flights of fancy in such a work as Giordano Bruno's *De umbris idearum* cannot conceal the fact that the philosopher of the Renaissance is going through yet once again the old, old business of rules for places, rules for images, memory for things, memory for words.

Evidently, therefore, it is incumbent upon us to attempt the by no means easy task of trying to understand the memory section of *Ad Herennium*. What makes the task by no means easy is that the rhetoric teacher is not addressing us; he is not setting out to explain to people who know nothing about it what the artificial memory was. He is addressing his rhetoric students as they congregated around him *circa* 86–82 B.C., and *they* knew what he was talking about; for *them* he needed only to rattle off the 'rules' which they would know how to apply. We are in a different case and are often somewhat baffled by the strangeness of some of the memory rules.

In what follows I attempt to give the content of the memory section of *Ad Herennium*, emulating the brisk style of the author, but with pauses for reflection about what he is telling us.

The artificial memory is established from places and images (*Constat igitur artificiosa memoria ex locis et imaginibus*), the stock definition to be forever repeated down the ages. A *locus* is a place easily grasped by the memory, such as a house, an intercolumnar space, a corner, an arch, or the like. Images are forms, marks or simulacra (*formae, notae, simulacra*) of what we wish to remember. For instance if we wish to recall the genus of a horse, of a lion, of an eagle, we must place their images on definite *loci*.

The art of memory is like an inner writing. Those who know the letters of the alphabet can write down what is dictated to them and read out what they have written. Likewise those who have learned mnemonics can set in places what they have heard and deliver it from memory. 'For the places are very much like wax tablets or papyrus, the images like the letters, the arrangement and disposition of the images like the script, and the delivery is like the reading.'

If we wish to remember much material we must equip ourselves with a large number of places. It is essential that the places should form a series and must be remembered in their order, so that we can start from any *locus* in the series and move either backwards or forwards from it. If we should see a number of our acquaintances standing in a row, it would not make any difference to us whether we should tell their names beginning with the person standing at the head of the line or at the foot or in the middle. So with memory *loci*. 'If these have been arranged in order, the result will be that, reminded by the images, we can repeat orally what we have committed to the *loci*, proceeding in either direction from any *locus* we please.'

The formation of the *loci* is of the greatest importance, for the same set of *loci* can be used again and again for remembering different material. The images which we have placed on them for remembering one set of things fade and are effaced when we make no further use of them. But the *loci* remain in the memory and can be used again by placing another set of images for another set of material. The *loci* are like the wax tablets which remain when what is written on them has been effaced and are ready to be written on again.

In order to make sure that we do not err in remembering the order of the *loci* it is useful to give each fifth *locus* some distinguishing mark. We may for example mark the fifth *locus* with a golden hand, and place in the tenth the image of some acquaintance whose name is Decimus. We can then go on to station other marks on each succeeding fifth *locus*.

It is better to form one's memory *loci* in a deserted and solitary place for crowds of passing people tend to weaken the impressions. Therefore the student intent on acquiring a sharp and well-defined set of *loci* will choose an unfrequented building in which to memorise places.

Memory *loci* should not be too much like one another, for instance too many intercolumnar spaces are not good, for their resemblance to one another will be confusing. They should be of moderate size, not too large for this renders the images placed

7

on them vague, and not too small for then an arrangement of images will be overcrowded. They must not be too brightly lighted for then the images placed on them will glitter and dazzle; nor must they be too dark or the shadows will obscure the images. The intervals between the *loci* should be of moderate extent, perhaps about thirty feet, 'for like the external eye, so the inner eye of thought is less powerful when you have moved the object of sight too near or too far away'.

A person with a relatively large experience can easily equip himself with as many suitable *loci* as he pleases, and even a person who thinks that he does not possess enough sufficiently good *loci* can remedy this. 'For thought can embrace any region whatsoever and in it and at will construct the setting of some locus.' (That is to say, mnemonics can use what were afterwards called 'fictitious places', in contrast to the 'real places' of the ordinary method.)

Pausing for reflection at the end of rules for places I would say that what strikes me most about them is the astonishing visual precision which they imply. In a classically trained memory the space between the *loci* can be measured, the lighting of the *loci* is allowed for. And the rules summon up a vision of a forgotten social habit. Who is that man moving slowly in the lonely building, stopping at intervals with an intent face? He is a rhetoric student forming a set of memory *loci*.

'Enough has been said of places', continues the author of *Ad Herennium*, 'now we turn to the theory of images.' Rules for images now begin, the first of which is that there are two kinds of images, one for 'things' (*res*), the other for 'words' (*verba*). That is to say 'memory for things' makes images to remind of an argument, a notion, or a 'thing'; but 'memory for words' has to find images to remind of every single word.

I interrrupt the concise author here for a moment in order to remind the reader that for the rhetoric student 'things' and 'words' would have an absolutely precise meaning in relation to the five parts of the rhetoric. Those five parts are defined by Cicero as follows:

> Invention is the excogitation of true things (*res*), or things similar to truth to render one's cause plausible; disposition is the arrangement in order of the things thus discovered; elocution is the accomodation of suitable words to the invented (things); memory

is the firm perception in the soul of things and words; pronunciation is the moderating of the voice and body to suit the dignity of the things and words.[7]

'Things' are thus the subject matter of the speech; 'words' are the language in which that subject matter is clothed. Are you aiming at an artificial memory to remind you only of the order of the notions, arguments, 'things' of your speech? Or do you aim at memorising every single word in it in the right order? The first kind of artificial memory is *memoria rerum*; the second kind is *memoria verborum*. The ideal, as defined by Cicero in the above passage, would be to have a 'firm perception in the soul' of both things and words. But 'memory for words' is much harder than 'memory for things'; the weaker brethren among the author of *Ad Herennium*'s rhetoric students evidently rather jibbed at memorising an image for every single word, and even Cicero himself, as we shall see later, allowed that 'memory for things' was enough.

To return to the rules for images. We have already been given the rules for places, what kind of places to choose for memorising. What are the rules about what kind of images to choose for memorising on the places? We now come to one of the most curious and surprising passages in the treatise, namely the psychological reasons which the author gives for the choice of mnemonic images. Why is it, he asks, that some images are so strong and sharp and so suitable for awakening memory, whilst others are so weak and feeble that they hardly stimulate memory at all? We must enquire into this so as to know which images to avoid and which to seek.

Now nature herself teaches us what we should do. When we see in every day life things that are petty, ordinary, and banal, we generally fail to remember them, because the mind is not being stirred by anything novel or marvellous. But if we see or hear something exceptionally base, dishonourable, unusual, great, unbelievable, or ridiculous, that we are likely to remember for a long time. Accordingly, things immediate to our eye or ear we commonly forget; incidents of our childhood we often remember best. Nor could this be so for any other reason than that ordinary things easily slip from the memory while the striking and the novel stay longer in the mind. A sunrise, the sun's course, a sunset are

---

[7] *De inventione*, I, vii, 9 (translation based on that by H. M. Hubbell in the Loeb edition, but made more literal in reproducing the technical terms *res* and *verba*).

marvellous to no one because they occur daily. But solar eclipses are a source of wonder because they occur seldom, and indeed are more marvellous than lunar eclipses, because these are more frequent. Thus nature shows that she is not aroused by the common ordinary event, but is moved by a new or striking occurrence. Let art, then, imitate nature, find what she desires, and follow as she directs. For in invention nature is never last, education never first; rather the beginnings of things arise from natural talent, and the ends are reached by discipline.

We ought, then, to set up images of a kind that can adhere longest in memory. And we shall do so if we establish similitudes as striking as possible; if we set up images that are not many or vague but active (*imagines agentes*); if we assign to them exceptional beauty or singular ugliness; if we ornament some of them, as with crowns or purple cloaks, so that the similitude may be more distinct to us; or if we somehow disfigure them, as by introducing one stained with blood or soiled with mud or smeared with red paint, so that its form is more striking, or by assigning certain comic effects to our images, for that, too, will ensure our remembering them more readily. The things we easily remember when they are real we likewise remember without difficulty when they are figments. But this will be essential—again and again to run over rapidly in the mind all the original places in order to refresh the images.[8]

Our author has clearly got hold of the idea of helping memory by arousing emotional affects through these striking and unusual images, beautiful or hideous, comic or obscene. And it is clear that he is thinking of human images, of human figures wearing crowns or purple cloaks, bloodstained or smeared with paint, of human figures dramatically engaged in some activity—doing something. We feel that we have moved into an extraordinary world as we run over his places with the rhetoric student, imagining on the places such very peculiar images. Quintilian's anchor and weapon as memory images, though much less exciting, are easier to understand than the weirdly populated memory to which the author of *Ad Herennium* introduces us.

It is one of the many difficulties which confront the student of the history of the art of memory that an *Ars memorativa* treatise, though it will always give the rules, rarely gives any concrete

---

[8] *Ad Herennium*, III, xxii.

application of the rules, that is to say it rarely sets out a system of mnemonic images on their places. This tradition was started by the author of *Ad Herennium* himself who says that the duty of an instructor in mnemonics is to teach the method of making images, give a few examples, and then encourage the student to form his own. When teaching 'introductions', he says, one does not draft a thousand set introductions and give them to the student to learn by heart; one teaches him the method and then leaves him to his own inventiveness. So also one should do in teaching mnemonic images.[9] This is an admirable tutorial principle though one regrets that it prevents the author from showing us a whole set or gallery of striking and unusual *imagines agentes*. We must be content with the three specimens which he describes.

The first is an example of a 'memory for things' image. We have to suppose that we are the counsel for the defence in a law suit. 'The prosecutor has said that the defendant killed a man by poison, has charged that the motive of the crime was to gain an inheritance, and declared that there are many witnesses and accessories to this act.' We are forming a memory system about the whole case and we shall wish to put in our first memory *locus* an image to remind us of the accusation against our client. This is the image.

> We shall imagine the man in question as lying ill in bed, if we know him personally. If we do not know him, we shall yet take some one to be our invalid, but not a man of the lowest class, so that he may come to mind at once. And we shall place the defendant at the bedside, holding in his right hand a cup, in his left, tablets, and on the fourth finger, a ram's testicles. In this way we can have in memory the man who was poisoned, the witnesses, and the inheritance.[10]

The cup would remind of the poisoning, the tablets, of the will or the inheritance, and the testicles of the ram through verbal similarity with *testes*—of the witnesses. The sick man is to be like the man himself, or like someone else whom we know (though not one of the anonymous lower classes). In the following *loci* we

---

[9] *Ibid.*, III, xxiii, 39.

[10] *Ibid.*, III, xx, 33. On the translation of *medico testiculos arietinos tenentem* as 'on the fourth finger a ram's testicles', see the translator's note, Loeb edition, p. 214. The *digitus medicinalis* was the fourth finger of the left hand. Mediaeval readers, unable to understand *medico*, introduced a doctor into the scene; see below, p. 65

would put other counts in the charge, or the details of the rest of the case, and if we have properly imprinted the places and images we shall easily be able to remember any point that we wish to recall.

This, then, is an example of a classical memory image—consisting of human figures, active, dramatic, striking, with accessories to remind of the whole 'thing' which is being recorded in memory. Though everything appears to be explained, I yet find this image baffling. Like much else in *Ad Herennium* on memory it seems to belong to a world which is either impossible for us to understand or which is not being really fully explained to us.

The writer is not concerned in this example with remembering the speeches in the case but with recording the details or 'things' of the case. It is as though, as a lawyer, he is forming a filing cabinet in memory of his cases. The image given is put as a label on the first place of the memory file on which the records about the man accused of poisoning are kept. He wants to look up something about that case; he turns to the composite image in which it is recorded, and behind that image on the following places he finds the rest of the case. If this is at all a correct interpretation, the artificial memory would now be being used, not only to memorise speeches, but to hold in memory a mass of material which can be looked up at will.

The words of Cicero in the *De oratore* when he is speaking of the advantages of the artificial memory may tend to confirm this interpretation. He has just been saying that the *loci* preserve the order of the facts, and the images designate the facts themselves, and we employ the places and images like a wax writing tablet and the letters written on it. 'But what business is it of mine', he continues, 'to specify the value to a speaker and the usefulness and effectiveness of memory? of retaining the information given you when you were briefed and the opinions you yourself have formed? of having all your ideas firmly planted in your mind and all your resources of vocabulary neatly arranged, of giving such close attention to the instructions of your client and to the speech of the opponent you have to answer that they may seem not just to pour what they say into your ears but to imprint it on your mind? Consequently only people with a powerful memory know what they are going to say and for how long they are going to speak and in what style, what points they have already answered and what still remains; and they can also remember from other cases many arguments which they have previously advanced and many which they have heard from other people.'[11]

We are in the presence of amazing powers of memory. And, according to Cicero, these natural powers were indeed aided by training of the type described in *Ad Herennium*.

The specimen image just described was a 'memory for things' image; it was designed to recall the 'things' or facts of the case and the following *loci* of the system would presumably have held other 'memory for things' images, recording other facts about the case or arguments used in speeches by the defence or the prosecution. The other two specimen images given in *Ad Herennium* are 'memory for words' images.

The student wishing to acquire 'memory for words' begins in the same way as the 'memory for things' student; that is to say he memorises places which are to hold his images. But he is confronted with a harder task for far more places will be needed to memorise all the words of a speech than would be needed for its notions. The specimen images for 'memory for words' are of the same type as the 'memory for things' image, that is to say they represent human figures of a striking and unusual character and in striking dramatic situations—*imagines agentes*.

We are setting out to memorise this line of verse:

Iam domum itionem reges Atridae parant[12]
(And now their homecoming the kings, the sons of Atreus are
   making ready)

The line is found only in the quotation of it in *Ad Herennium* and was either invented by the author to exhibit his mnemonic technique or was taken for some lost work. It is to be memorised through two very extraordinary images.

One is 'Domitius raising his hands to heaven while he is lashed by the Marcii Reges'. The translator and editor of the text in the Loeb edition (H. Caplan) explains in a note that 'Rex was the name of one of the most distinguished families of the Marcian gens; the Domitian, of plebeian origin, was likewise a celebrated gens'. The image may reflect some street scene in which Domitius

---

[11] *De oratore*, II, lxxxvii, 355.

[12] *Ad Herennium*, III, xxi, 34. See translator's notes on pp. 216–17 in the Loeb edition.

of the plebeian gens (perhaps bloodstained to make him more memorable) is being beaten up by some members of the distinguished Rex family. It was perhaps a scene which the author himself had witnessed. Or perhaps it was a scene in some play. It was a striking scene in every sense of the word and therefore suitable as a mnemonic image. It was put on a place for remembering this line. The vivid image immediately brought to mind 'Domitius-Reges' and this reminded *by sound resemblance* of 'domum itionem reges'. It thus exhibits the principles of a 'memory for words' image which brings to mind the words which the memory is seeking through their sound resemblance to the notion suggested by the image.

We all know how, when groping in memory for a word or a name, some quite absurd and random association, something which has 'stuck' in the memory, will help us to dredge it up. The classical art is systematising that process.

The other image for memorising the rest of the line is 'Aesopus and Cimber being dressed for the rôles of Agamemnon and Menelaus in *Iphigenaia*'. Aesopus was a well-known tragic actor, a friend of Cicero; Cimber, evidently also an actor, is only mentioned in this text.[13] The play in which they are preparing to act also does not exist. In the image these actors are being dressed to play the parts of the sons of Atreus (Agamemnon and Menelaus). It is an exciting off-stage glimpse of two famous actors being made up (to smear an image with red paint makes it memorable according to the rules) and dressed for their parts. Such a scene has all the elements of a good mnemonic image; we therefore use it to remember 'Atridae parant', the sons of Atreus are making ready. This image immediately gave the word 'Atridae' (though not by sound resemblance) and also suggested 'making ready' for the home-coming through the actors making ready for the stage.

This method for memorising the verse will not work by itself, says the author of *Ad Herennium*. We must go over the verse three or four times, that is learn it by heart in the usual way, and then represent the words by means of images. 'In this way art will supplement nature. For neither by itself will be strong enough, though we must note that theory and technique are much the

[13] Loeb edition, translator's note, p. 217.

14

more reliable.'[14] The fact that we have to learn the poem by heart as well, makes 'memory for words' a little less baffling.

Reflecting on the 'memory for words' images, we note that our author seems now concerned not with the rhetoric students' proper business of remembering a speech, but with memorising verse in poems or plays. To remember a whole poem or a whole play in this way one has to envisage 'places' extending one might almost say for miles within the memory, 'places' past which one moves in reciting, drawing from them the mnemonic cues. And perhaps that word 'cue' does give a clue to how the method might be workable. Did one really learn the poem by heart but set up some places with 'cue' images on them at strategic intervals?

Our author mentions that another type of 'memory for words' symbol has been elaborated by the Greeks. 'I know that most of the Greeks who have written on the memory have taken the course of listing images that correspond to a great many words, so that persons who wished to learn these images by heart would have them ready without expending effort in a search for them.'[15] It is possible that these Greek images for words are shorthand symbols or *notae* the use of which was coming into fashion in the Latin world at this time.[16] As used in mnemonics, this would presumably mean that, by a kind of inner stenography, the shorthand symbols were written down inwardly and memorised on the memory places. Fortunately our author disapproves of this method, since even a thousand of such ready-made symbols would not begin to cover all the words used. Indeed, he is rather lenient about 'memory for words' of any kind; it must be tackled just because it is more difficult than 'memory for things'. It is to be used as an exercise to strengthen 'that other kind of memory, the memory for things, which is of practical use. Thus we may without effort pass from this difficult training to ease in that other memory.'

The memory section closes with an exhortation to hard work.

[14] *Ad Herennium, loc. cit.*

[15] *Ibid.*, III, xxiii, 38.

[16] Cicero is said by Plutarch to have introduced shorthand to Rome; the name of his freedman, Tiro, became associated with the so-called 'Tironian notes'. See *The Oxford Classical Dictionary*, article Tachygraphy; H. J. M. Milne, *Greek Shorthand Manuals*, London, 1934, introduction. There may be some connection between the introduction of Greek mnemonics into the Latin world, reflected in *Ad Herennium*, and the importation of stenography at about the same time.

'In every discipline artistic theory is of little avail without un-remitting exercise, but especially in mnemonics, theory is almost valueless unless made good by industry, devotion, toil, and care. You can make sure that you have as many places as possible and that these conform as much as possible to the rules; in placing the images you should exercise every day.'[17]

We have been trying to understand inner gymnastics, invisible labours of concentration which are to us most strange, though the rules and examples of *Ad Herennium* give mysterious glimpses into the powers and organisation of antique memories. We think of memory feats which are recorded of the ancients, of how the elder Seneca, a teacher of rhetoric, could repeat two thousand names in the order in which they had been given; and when a class of two hundred students or more spoke each in turn a line of poetry, he could recite all the lines in reverse order, beginning from the last one said and going right back to the first.[18] Or we remember that Augustine, also trained as a teacher of rhetoric, tells of a friend called Simplicius who could recite Virgil back-wards.[19] We have learned from our text-book that if we have properly and firmly fixed our memory places we can move along them in either direction, backwards or forwards. The artificial memory may explain the awe inspiring ability to recite backwards of the elder Seneca and of Augustine's friend. Pointless though such feats may seem to us, they illustrate the respect accorded in antiquity to the man with the trained memory.

Very singular is the art of this invisible art of memory. It reflects ancient architecture but in an unclassical spirit, concen-trating its choice on irregular places and avoiding symmetrical orders. It is full of human imagery of a very personal kind; we mark the tenth place with a face like that of our friend Decimus; we see a number of our acquaintances standing in a row; we visualise a sick man like the man himself, or if we did not know him, like someone we do know. These human figures are active and dramatic, strikingly beautiful or grotesque. They remind one more of figures in some Gothic cathedral than of classical art proper. They appear to be completely amoral, their function being solely to give an emotional impetus to memory by their personal

[17] *Ad Herennium*, III, xxiv, 40.
[18] Marcus Annaeus Seneca, *Controversiarum Libri*, Lib. I, Praef. 2.
[19] Augustine, *De anima*, lib. IV. cap. vii.

idiosyncracy or their strangeness. This impression may, however, be due to the fact that we have not been given a specimen image of how to remember, for example, the 'things' justice or temperance and their parts, which are treated by the author of *Ad Herennium* when discussing the invention of the subject matter of a speech.[20] The elusiveness of the art of memory is very trying to its historian.

Though the mediaeval tradition which assigned the authorship of *Ad Herennium* to 'Tullius' was wrong in fact, it was not wrong in its inference that the art of memory was practised and reccmmended by 'Tullius'. In his *De oratore* (which he finished in 55 B.C.) Cicero treats of the five parts of rhetoric in his elegant, discursive, gentlemanly manner—a manner very different from that of our dry rhetoric teacher—and in this work he refers to a mnemonic which is obviously based on the same techniques as those described in *Ad Herennium*.

The first mention of the mnemonic comes in Crassus's speech in the first book in which he says that he does not altogether dislike as an aid to memory 'that method of places and images which is taught in an art.'[21] Later, Anthony tells of how Themistocles refused to learn the art of memory 'which was then being introduced for the first time' saying that he preferred the science of forgetting to that of remembering. Anthony warns that this frivolous remark must not 'cause us to neglect the training of the memory'.[22] The reader is thus prepared for Anthony's later brilliant rendering of the story of the fatal banquet which occasioned the invention of the art by Simonides—the story with which I began this chapter. In the course of the discussion of the art of memory which follows Cicero gives a potted version of the rules.

Consequently (in order that I may not be prolix and tedious on a subject that is well known and familiar) one must employ a large number of places which must be well lighted, clearly set out in order, at moderate intervals apart (*locis est utendum multis, illustribus, explicatis, modicis intervallis*); and images which are active, sharply defined, unusual, and which have the power of speedily

---

[20] *Ad Herennium*, III, iii.
[21] *De oratore*, I, xxxiv, 157.
[22] *Ibid.*, II, lxxiv, 299–300.

encountering and penetrating the psyche (*imaginibus autem agentibus, acribus, insignitis, quae occurrere celeriterque percutere animum possint*).[23]

He has boiled down rules for places and rules for images to a minimum in order not to bore the reader by repeating the text-book instructions which are so well known and familiar.

Next he makes an obscurely worded reference to some extremely sophisticated types of memory for words.

> ... the ability to use these (images) will be supplied by practise which engenders habit, and (by images) of similar words changed and unchanged in case or drawn (from denoting) the part to denot-ing the genus, and by using the image of one word to remind of a whole sentence, as a consummate painter distinguishing the position of objects by modifying their shapes.[24]

He next speaks of the type of memory for words (described as 'Greek' by the author of *Ad Herennium*) which attempts to memo-rise an image for every word, but decides (like *Ad Herennium*) that memory for things is the branch of the art most useful to the orator.

> Memory for words, which for us is essential, is given distinct-ness by a greater variety of images (in contrast to using the image of one word for a whole sentence of which he has just been speak-ing); for there are many words which serve as joints connecting the limbs of a sentence, and these cannot be formed by any use of similitudes—of these we have to model images for constant em-ployment; but a memory for things is the special property of the orator—this we can imprint on our minds by a skilful arrangement of the several masks (*singulis personis*) that represent them, so that we may grasp ideas by means of images and their order by means of places.[25]

The use of the word *persona* of the memory-for-things image is interesting and curious. Does it imply that the memory image heightens its striking effect by exaggerating its tragic or comic aspect, as the actor does by wearing a mask? Does it suggest that the stage was a likely source of striking memory images? Or does the word mean in this context that the memory image is like a known individual person, as the author of *Ad Herennium* advises, but wears that personal mask only to jog the memory?

[23] *Ibid.*, II, lxxxvii, 358.
[24] *Ibid.*, loc. cit.
[25] *Ibid.*, II, lxxxviii, 359.

18

Cicero has provided a highly condensed little *Ars memorativa* treatise bringing in all the points in their usual order. Beginning with the statement, introduced by the Simonides story that the art consists in places and images and is like an inner writing on wax, he goes on to discuss natural and artificial memory, with the usual conclusion that nature can be improved by art. Then follow rules for places and rules for images; then the discussion of memory for things and memory for words. Though he agrees that memory for things is alone essential for the orator he has evidently put himself through a memory for words drill in which images for words move (?), change their cases (?), draw a whole sentence into one word image, in some extraordinary manner which he visualises within, as though it were the art of some consummate painter.

> Nor is it true as unskilled people assert (*quod ab inertibus dicitur*) that memory is crushed beneath a weight of images and even what might have been retained by nature unassisted is obscured: for I have myself met eminent people with almost divine powers of memory (*summos homines et divina prope memoria*), Charmadas at Athens and Metrodorus of Scepsis in Asia, who is said to be still living, each of whom used to say that he wrote down what he wanted to remember in certain places in his possession by means of images, just as if he were inscribing letters on wax. It follows that this practice cannot be used to draw out the memory if no memory has been given by nature, but it can undoubtedly summon it to come forth if it is in hiding.[26]

From these concluding words of Cicero's on the art of memory we learn that the objection to the classical art which was always raised throughout its subsequent history—and is still raised by everyone who is told of it—was voiced in antiquity. There were inert or lazy or unskilled people in Cicero's time who took the common sense view, to which, personally, I heartily subscribe—as explained earlier I am a historian only of the art, not a practitioner of it—that all these places and images would only bury under a heap of rubble whatever little one does remember naturally. Cicero is a believer and a defender. He evidently had by nature a fantastically acute visual memory.

And what are we to think of those eminent men, Charmades and Metrodorus, whom he had met whose powers of memory were

[26] *Ibid.,* II, lxxxviii, 360.

'almost divine'? As well as being an orator with a phenomenal trained memory, Cicero was in philosophy a Platonist, and for the Platonist memory has very special connotations. What does an orator and a Platonist mean when he speaks of memories which are 'almost divine'?

The name of the mysterious Metrodorus of Scepsis will reverberate on many later pages of this book.

Cicero's earliest work on rhetoric was the *De inventione* which he wrote about thirty years earlier than the *De oratore*, at about the same time that the unknown author of *Ad Herennium* was compiling his text book. We can learn nothing new from the *De inventione* about Cicero on the artificial memory for the book is concerned with only the first part of the rhetoric, namely *inventio*, the inventing or composing of the subject matter of a speech, the collection of the 'things' with which it will deal. Nevertheless the *De inventione* was to play a very important part in the later history of the art of memory because it was through Cicero's definitions of the virtues in this work that the artificial memory became in the Middle Ages a part of the cardinal virtue of Prudence.

Towards the end of the *De inventione*, Cicero defines virtue as 'a habit of mind in harmony with reason and the order of nature' a stoic definition of virtue. He then states that virtue has four parts, namely Prudence, Justice, Fortitude, and Temperance. Each of these four main virtues he subdivides into parts of their own. The following is his definition of Prudence and its parts:

> Prudence is the knowledge of what is good, what is bad and what is neither good nor bad. Its parts are memory, intelligence, foresight (*memoria, intelligentia, providentia*). Memory is the faculty by which the mind recalls what has happened. Intelligence is the faculty by which it ascertains what is. Foresight is the faculty by which it is seen that something is going to occur before it occurs.[27]

Cicero's definitions of the virtues and their parts in the *De inventione* were a very important source for the formulation of what afterwards became known as the four cardinal virtues. The definition by 'Tullius' of the three parts of Prudence is quoted by Albertus Magnus and Thomas Aquinas when discussing the virtues in their *Summae*. And the fact that 'Tullius' makes memory a part of Prudence was the main factor in their recommendation

[27] *De inventione*, II, liii, 160 (trans. H. M. Hubbell in the Loeb edition).

of the artificial memory. The argument was beautifully symmetrical, and related to the fact that the Middle Ages grouped the *De inventione* with the *Ad Herennium* as both by Tullius; the two works were known respectively as the First and Second Rhetorics of Tullius. Tullius in his First Rhetoric states that memory is a part of Prudence; Tullius in his Second Rhetoric says that there is an artificial memory by which natural memory can be improved. Therefore the practice of the artificial memory is a part of the virtue of Prudence. It is under memory as a part of Prudence that Albertus and Thomas quote and discuss the rules of the artificial memory.

The process by which the scholastics switched artificial memory from rhetoric to ethics will be discussed more fully in a later chapter.[28] I briefly refer to it here in advance because one wonders whether the prudential or ethical use of artificial memory was entirely invented by the Middle Ages, or whether it too may have had an antique root. The stoics, as we know, attached great importance to the moral control of the fantasy as an important part of ethics. As I mentioned earlier, we have no means of knowing how the 'things' Prudence, Justice, Fortitude, Temperance, and their parts would have been represented in the artificial memory. Would Prudence, for example, have taken on a strikingly beautiful mnemonic form, a *persona* like someone that we know, holding or having grouped round her secondary images to remind of her parts—on the analogy of how the parts of the case against the man accused of poisoning formed a composite mnemonic image?

Quintilian, an eminently sensible man and a very good educator, was the dominating teacher of rhetoric in Rome in the first century A.D. He wrote his *Institutio oratoria* more than a century after Cicero's *De oratore*. In spite of the great weight attaching to Cicero's recommendation of the artificial memory, it would seem that its value is not taken for granted in leading rhetorical circles in Rome. Quintilian says that some people now divide rhetoric into only three parts, on the ground that *memoria* and *actio* are given to us 'by nature not by art'.[29] His own attitude to the artificial memory is ambiguous; nevertheless he gives it a good deal of prominence.

[28] See Chapter III, below.
[29] *Institutio oratoria*, III, iii, 4.

Like Cicero, he introduces his account of it with the story of its invention by Simonides of which he gives a version which is in the main the same as that told by Cicero though with some variant details. He adds that there were a good many versions of the story in Greek authorities and that its wide circulation in his own day is due to Cicero.

This achievement of Simonides appears to have given rise to the observation that it is an assistance to the memory if places are stamped upon the mind, which anyone can believe from experiment. For when we return to a place after a considerable absence, we not merely recognise the place itself, but remember things that we did there, and recall the persons whom we met and even the unuttered thoughts which passed through our minds when we were there before. Thus, as in most cases, art originates from experiment.

Places are chosen, and marked with the utmost possible variety, as a spacious house divided into a number of rooms. Everything of note therein is diligently imprinted on the mind, in order that thought may be able to run through all the parts without let or hindrance. The first task is to secure that there shall be no difficulty in running through these, for that memory must be most firmly fixed which helps another memory. Then what has been written down, or thought of, is noted by a sign to remind of it. This sign may be drawn from a whole 'thing', as navigation or warfare, or from some 'word'; for what is slipping from memory is recovered by the admonition of a single word. However, let us suppose that the sign is drawn from navigation, as, for instance, an anchor; or from warfare, as, for example, a weapon. These signs are then arranged as follows. The first notion is placed, as it were, in the forecourt; the second, let us say, in the atrium; the remainder are placed in order all round the impluvium, and committed not only to bedrooms and parlours, but even to statues and the like. This done, when it is required to revive the memory, one begins from the first place to run through all, demanding what has been entrusted to them, of which one will be reminded by the image. Thus, however numerous are the particulars which it is required to remember, all are linked one to another as in a chorus nor can what follows wander from what has gone before to which it is joined, only the preliminary labour of learning being required.

What I have spoken of as being done in a house can also be done in public buildings, or on a long journey, or in going through a city, or with pictures. Or we can imagine such places for ourselves.

We require therefore places, either real or imaginary, and images

22

or simulacra which must be invented. Images are as words by which we note the things we have to learn, so that as Cicero says, 'we use places as wax and images as letters'. It will be as well to quote his actual words:—'One must employ a large number of places which must be well-lighted, clearly set out in order, at moderate intervals apart, and images which are active, which are sharply defined, unusual, and which have the power of speedily encountering and penetrating the mind. Which makes me wonder all the more how Metrodorus can have found three hundred and sixty places in the twelve signs through which the sun moves. It was doubtless the vanity and boastfulness of a man glorying in a memory stronger by art than by nature.[30]

The perplexed student of the art of memory is grateful to Quintilian. Had it not been for his clear directions about how we are to go through the rooms of a house, or a public building, or along the streets of a city memorising our places, we might never have understood what 'rules for places' were about. He gives an absolutely rational reason as to why the places may help memory, because we know from experience that a place does call up associations in memory. And the system which he describes, using signs like an anchor or a weapon for the 'things', or calling up one word only by such a sign through which the whole sentence would come into mind, seems quite possible and is within the range of our understanding. It is in fact what we should call mnemotechnics. There was then, in antiquity, a practice of which that word can be used in the sense in which we use it.

The peculiar *imagines agentes* are not mentioned by Quintilian though he certainly knew of them since he quotes Cicero's abbreviation of the rules which were themselves based on *Ad Herennium*, or on the kind of memory practice with its strange images which *Ad Herennium* describes. But after quoting Cicero's version of the rules, Quintilian dares to contradict that revered rhetorician very abruptly in the totally different estimate which he gives of Metrodorus of Scepsis. For Cicero, the memory of Metrodorus was 'almost divine.' For Quintilian this man was a boaster and something of a charlatan. And we learn from Quintilian an interesting fact—to be discussed further later—that the divine, or pretentious (according to one's point of view) memory

---

[30] *Ibid.*, XI, ii, 17–22.

system of Metrodorus of Scepsis was based on the twelve signs of the zodiac.

Quintilian's last word on the art of memory is as follows:

> I am far from denying that those devices may be useful for certain purposes, as for example if we have to reproduce many names of things in the order in which we heard them. Those who use such aids place the things themselves in their memory places; they put, for instance, a table in the forecourt, a platform in the atrium, and so on for the rest, and then when they run through the places again they find these objects where they put them. Such a practice may perhaps have been of use to those who, after an auction, have succeeded in stating what object they had sold to each buyer, their statements being checked by the books of the money-takers; a feat which it is alleged was performed by Hortensius. It will however be of less service in retaining the parts of a speech. For notions do not call up images as material things do, and something else has to be invented for them, although even here a particular place may serve to remind us, as, for example, of some conversation which we may have held there. But how can such an art grasp a whole series of connected words? I pass by the fact that there are certain words which it is impossible to represent by any likeness, for example conjunctions. We may, it is true, like short-hand writers, have definite images for everything, and may use an infinite number of places to recall all the words contained in the five books of the second pleading against Verres, and we may even remember them all as if they were deposits placed in safe keeping. But will not the flow of our speech inevitably be impeded by the double task imposed on our memory? For how can our words be expected to flow in connected speech, if we have to look back at separate forms for each individual word? Therefore Charmadas and Metrodorus of Scepsis, to whom I have just referred, of whom Cicero says that they used this method, may keep their systems for themselves; my precepts will be of a simpler kind.[31]

The method of the auctioneer who places images of the actual objects he has sold on memory places is precisely the method used by the professor whose mode of amusing his students we described earlier. This, Quintilian says, will work and may be useful for certain purposes. But the extension of the method to remembering a speech through images for 'things' he thinks is more trouble than it is worth since images for 'things' must all be invented. Even

---

[31] *Ibid.*, XI, ii. 23–6.

in the simple form of the anchor and weapon type of image he seems not to advise it. He says nothing of the fantastic *imagines agentes*, either for things or words. Images for words he interprets as memorising shorthand *notae* on the memory places; this was the Greek method which the author of *Ad Herennium* discarded but which Quintilian thinks that Cicero admired in Charmadas and Metrodorus of Scepsis.

The 'simpler precepts' of memory training which Quintilian would substitute for the art of memory consist mainly in the advocacy of hard and intensive learning by heart, in the ordinary way, of speeches and so on, but he allows that one can sometimes help oneself by simple adaptations of some of the mnemonic usages. One may use privately invented marks to remind one of difficult passages; these signs may even be adapted to the nature of the thoughts. 'Although drawn from the mnemonic system' the use of such signs is not without value. But there is above all one thing which will be of assistance to the student.

> namely to learn a passage by heart from the same tablets on which he has committed it to writing. For he will have certain tracks to guide him in pursuit of memory, and the mind's eye will be fixed not merely on the pages on which the words were written, but on individual lines, and at times he will speak as though he were reading aloud . . . This device bears some resemblance to the mnemonic system which I mentioned above, but, if my experience is worth anything, is at once more expeditious and more effective.

I understand this to mean that this method adopts from the mnemonic system the habit of visualising writing on 'places', but instead of attempting to visualise shorthand *notae* on some vast place system it visualises ordinary writing as actually placed on the tablet or page.

What it would be interesting to know is whether Quintilian envisages preparing his tablet or page for memorisation by adding to it signs, *notae*, or even *imagines agentes* formed according to the rules, to mark the places which the memory arrives at as it travels along the lines of writing.

There is thus a very marked difference between Quintilian's attitude to the artificial memory and that of the author of *Ad Herennium* and of Cicero. Evidently the *imagines agentes*, fantasti-

---

[32] *Ibid.*, XI, ii, 32–3.

cally gesticulating from their places and arousing memory by their emotional appeal, seemed to him as cumbrous and useless for practical mnemonic purposes as they do to us. Has Roman society moved on into greater sophistication in which some intense, archaic, almost magical, immediate association of memory with images has been lost? Or is the difference a temperamental one? Would the artificial memory not work for Quintilian because he lacked the acute visual perceptions necessary for visual memorisation? He does not mention, as Cicero does, that Simonides' invention depended on the primacy of the sense of sight.

Of the three sources for the classical art of memory studied in this chapter, it was not on Quintilian's rational and critical account of it that the later Western memory tradition was founded, nor on Cicero's elegant and obscure formulations. It was founded on the precepts laid down by the unknown rhetoric teacher.

Chapter II

THE ART OF MEMORY IN GREECE: MEMORY AND THE SOUL

THE Simonides story, with its gruesome evocation of the faces of the people sitting in their places at the banquet just before their awful end, may suggest that the human images were an integral part of the art of memory which Greece transmitted to Rome. According to Quintilian, there were several versions of the story extant in Greek sources,[1] and one may perhaps conjecture that it formed the normal introduction to the section on artificial memory in a text-book on rhetoric. There were certainly many such in Greek but they have not come down to us, hence our dependence on the three Latin sources for any conjectures we may make concerning Greek artificial memory.

Simonides of Ceos[2] (*circa* 556 to 468 B.C.) belongs to the pre-Socratic age. Pythagoras might still have been alive in his youth. One of the most admired lyric poets of Greece (very little of his poetry has survived) he was called 'the honey-tongued', Latinised

---

[1] Quintilian says (*Institutio oratoria*, XI, ii, 14–16) that there is disagreement among the Greek sources as to whether the banquet was held 'at Pharsalus, as Simonides himself seems to indicate in a certain passage, and is recorded by Apollodorus, Eratosthenes, Euphorion and Eurypylus of Larissa, or at Crannon, as is stated by Apollas Callimachus, who is followed by Cicero.'

[2] A collection of references to Simonides in ancient literature is brought together in *Lyra Graeca*, edited and translated by J. M. Edmonds, Loeb Classical Library, Vol. II (1924), pp. 246 ff.

as Simonides Melicus, and he particularly excelled in the use of beautiful imagery. Various new departures were credited to this evidently brilliantly gifted and original man. He was said to have been the first to demand payment for poems; the canny side of Simonides comes into the story of his invention of the art of memory which hinges on a contract for an ode. Another novelty is attributed to Simonides by Plutarch who seems to think that he was the first to equate the methods of poetry with those of painting, the theory later succinctly summed up by Horace in his famous phrase *ut pictura poesis*. 'Simonides', says Plutarch, 'called painting silent poetry and poetry painting that speaks; for the actions which painters depict as they are being performed, words describe after they are done.'[3]

It is significant that the comparison of poetry with painting is fathered on Simonides, for this has a common denominator with the invention of the art of memory. According to Cicero, the latter invention rested on Simonides' discovery of the superiority of the sense of sight over the other senses. The theory of the equation of poetry and painting also rests on the supremacy of the visual sense; the poet and the painter both think in visual images which the one expresses in poetry the other in pictures. The elusive relations with other arts which run all through the history of the art of memory are thus already present in the legendary source, in the stories about Simonides who saw poetry, painting and mnemonics in terms of intense visualisation. Looking forward here for one brief moment to our ultimate objective, Giordano Bruno, we shall find that in one of his mnemonic works he treats of the principle of using images in the art of memory under the heads 'Phidias the Sculptor' and 'Zeuxis the Painter', and under those same heads he discusses the theory of *ut pictura poesis*.[4]

Simonides is the cult hero, the founder of our subject, his invention of which is attested not only by Cicero and Quintilian, but also by Pliny, Aelian, Ammianus Marcellinus, Suidas, and others, and also by an inscription. The *Parian Chronicle*, a marble tablet of about 264 B.C. which was found at Paros in the seventeenth century, records legendary dates for discoveries like the invention of the flute, the introduction of corn by Ceres and Triptolemus, the

[3] Plutarch, *Glory of Athens*, 3; cf. R. W. Lee, '*Ut pictura poesis*: The Humanistic Theory of Painting', *Art Bulletin*, XXII (1940), p. 197.
[4] See below, p. 253

publication of Orpheus' poetry; when it comes to historical times the emphasis is on festivals and the prizes awarded at them. The entry which interests us is as follows:

> From the time when the Ceian Simonides son of Leoprepes, the inventor of the system of memory-aids, won the chorus prize at Athens, and the statues were set up to Harmodius and Aristogeiton, 213 years (i.e. 477 B.C.).[5]

It is known from other sources that Simonides won the chorus prize in old age; when this is recorded on the Parian marble the victor is characterised as 'the inventor of the system of memory-aids'.

One must believe, I think, that Simonides really did take some notable step about mnemonics, teaching or publishing rules which, though they probably derived from an earlier oral tradition, had the appearance of a new presentation of the subject. We cannot concern ourselves here with the pre-Simonidean origins of the art of memory; some think that it was Pythagorean; others have hinted at Egyptian influence. One can imagine that some form of the art might have been a very ancient technique used by bards and story-tellers. The inventions supposedly introduced by Simonides may have been symptoms of the emergence of a more highly organised society. Poets are now to have their definite economic place; a mnemonic practised in the ages of oral memory, before writing, becomes codified into rules. In an age of transition to new forms of culture it is normal for some outstanding individual to become labelled as an inventor.

The fragment known as the *Dialexeis*, which is dated to about 400 B.C., contains a tiny section on memory, as follows:

> A great and beautiful invention is memory, always useful both for learning and for life.
> This is the first thing: if you pay attention (direct your mind), the judgment will better perceive the things going through it (the mind).
> Secondly, repeat again what you hear; for by often hearing and saying the same things, what you have learned comes complete into your memory.

---

[5] Quoted as translated in *Lyra Graeca*, II, p. 249. See F. Jacoby, *Die Fragmente der Griechischen Historiker*, Berlin, 1929, II, p. 1000, and *Fragmente, Kommentar*, Berlin, 1930, II, p. 694.

Thirdly, what you hear, place on what you know. For example, Χρύσιππος (Chrysippus) is to be remembered; we place it on χρυσός (gold) and ἵππός (horse). Another example: we place πυριλάμπης (glow-worm) on πύρ (fire) and λάμπειν (shine). So much for names.
For things (do) thus: for courage (place it) on Mars and Achilles; for metal-working, on Vulcan; for cowardice, on Epeus.[6]

Memory for things; memory for words (or names)! Here are the technical terms for the two kinds of artificial memory already in use in 400 B.C. Both memories use images; the one to represent things, the other words; this again belongs to the familiar rules. It is true that rules for places are not given; but the practice here described of placing the notion or word to be remembered actually on the image will recur all through the history of the art of memory, and was evidently rooted in antiquity.

The skeleton outline of the rules of the artificial memory is thus already in existence about half a century after the death of Simonides. This suggests that what he 'invented', or codified, may really have been the rules, basically as we find them in *Ad Herennium*, though they would have been refined and amplified in successive texts unknown to us before they reached the Latin teacher four centuries later.

In this earliest *Ars memorativa* treatise, the images for words are formed from primitive etymological dissection of the word. In the examples given of images for things, the 'things' virtue and vice are represented (valour, cowardice), also an art (metallurgy). They are deposited in memory with images of gods and men (Mars, Achilles, Vulcan, Epeus). Here we may perhaps see in an archaically simple form those human figures representing 'things' which eventually developed into the *imagines agentes*.

The *Dialexeis* is thought to reflect sophist teaching, and its memory section may refer to the mnemonics of the sophist Hippias of Elis,[7] who is said, in the pseudo-Platonic dialogues which satirise him and which bear his name, to have possessed a 'science of memory' and to have boasted that he could recite fifty names after hearing them once, also the genealogies of heroes

[6] H. Diels, *Die Fragmente der Vorsokratiker*, Berlin, 1922, II, p. 345. Cf. H. Gomperz, *Sophistik und Rhetorik*, Berlin, 1912, p. 149, where a German translation is given.
[7] See Gomperz, pp. 179 ff.

and men, the foundations of cities, and much other material.[8] It does indeed sound probable that Hippias was a practioner of the artificial memory. One begins to wonder whether the sophist educational system, to which Plato objected so strongly, may have made a lavish use of the new 'invention' for much superficial memorisation of quantities of miscellaneous information. One notes the enthusiasm with which the sophist memory treatise opens: 'A great and most beautiful invention is memory, always useful for learning and for life.' Was the beautiful new invention of artificial memory an important element in the new success technique of the sophists?

Aristotle was certainly familiar with the artificial memory which he refers to four times, not as an expositor of it (though according to Diogenes Laertius he wrote a book on mnemonics which is not extant[9]) but incidentally to illustrate points under discussion. One of these references is in the *Topics* when he is advising that one should commit to memory arguments upon questions which are of most frequent occurrence:

> For just as in a person with a trained memory, a memory of things themselves is immediately caused by the mere mention of their places (τόποι), so these habits too will make a man readier in reasoning, because he has his premisses classified before his mind's eye, each under its number.[10]

There can be no doubt that these *topoi* used by persons with a trained memory must be mnemonic *loci*, and it is indeed probable that the very word 'topics' as used in dialectics arose through the places of mnemonics. Topics are the 'things' or subject matter of dialectic which came to be known as *topoi* through the places in which they were stored.

In the *De insomnis*, Aristotle says that some people have dreams in which they 'seem to be arranging the objects before them in accordance with their mnemonic system'[11]—rather a warning, one

---

[8] *Greater Hippias*, 285D–286A; *Lesser Hippias*, 368D.

[9] Diogenes Laertius, *Life of Aristotle* (in his *Lives of the Philosophers*, V. 26). The work referred to in the list of Aristotle's works here given, may, however, be the extant *De memoria et reminiscentia*.

[10] *Topica*, 163[b] 24–30 (translated by W. A. Pickard-Cambridge in *Works of Aristotle*, ed. W. D. Ross, Oxford, 1928, Vol. I).

[11] *De insomnis*, 458[b] 20–22 (translated by W. S. Hett in the Loeb volume containing the *De anima*, *Parva naturalia*, etc., 1935).

would think, against doing too much artificial memory, though this is not how he is using the allusion. And in the *De anima* there is a similar phrase: 'it is possible to put things before our eyes just as those do who invent mnemonics and construct images.'[12]

But the most important of the four allusions, and the one which most influenced the later history of the art of memory comes in the *De memoria et reminiscentia*. The great scholastics, Albertus Magnus and Thomas Aquinas, with their proverbially acute minds perceived that the Philosopher in his *De memoria et reminiscentia* refers to an art of memory which is the same as that which Tullius teaches in his Second Rhetoric (the *Ad Herennium*). Aristotle's work thus became for them a kind of memory treatise, to be conflated with the rules of Tullius and which provided philosophical and psychological justifications for those rules.

Aristotle's theory of memory and reminiscence is based on the theory of knowledge which he expounds in his *De anima*. The perceptions brought in by the five senses are first treated or worked upon by the faculty of imagination, and it is the images so formed which become the material of the intellectual faculty. Imagination is the intermediary between perception and thought. Thus while all knowledge is ultimately derived from sense impressions it is not on these in the raw that thought works but after they have been treated by, or absorbed into, the imaginative faculty. It is the image-making part of the soul which makes the work of the higher processes of thought possible. Hence 'the soul never thinks without a mental picture';[13] 'the thinking faculty thinks of its forms in mental pictures';[14] 'no one could ever learn or understand anything, if he had not the faculty of perception; even when he thinks speculatively, he must have some mental picture with which to think.'[15]

For the scholastics, and for the memory tradition which followed them, there was a point of contact between mnemonic theory and the Aristotelian theory of knowledge in the importance assigned by both to the imagination. Aristotle's statement that it is impossible to think without a mental picture is constantly brought in to support the use of images in mnemonics. And Aristotle himself uses the images of mnemonics as an illustration of what he is saying about imagination and thought. Thinking, he says, is something which we can do whenever we choose, 'for it is possible

---

[12] *De anima* 427[b] 18–22 (Hett's translation).   [13] *Ibid.*, 432[a] 17.
[14] *Ibid.*, 431[b] 2.   [15] *Ibid.*, 432[a] 9.

to put things before our eyes just as those do who invent mnemonics and construct images.'[16] He is comparing the deliberate
selection of mental images about which to think with the deliberate
construction in mnemonics of images through which to remember.

The *De memoria et reminiscentia* is an appendix to the *De anima*
and it opens with a quotation from that work: 'As has been said
before in my treatise *On the Soul* about imagination, it is impossible even to think without a mental picture.'[17] Memory, he
continues, belongs to the same part of the soul as the imagination;
it is a collection of mental pictures from sense impressions but with
a time element added, for the mental images of memory are not
from perception of things present but of things past. Since memory
belongs in this way with sense impression it is not peculiar to man;
some animals can also remember. Nevertheless the intellectual
faculty comes into play in memory for in it thought works on the
stored images from sense perception.

The mental picture from sense impression he likens to a kind of
painted portrait, 'the lasting state of which we describe as
memory';[18] and the forming of the mental image he thinks of as a
movement, like the movement of making a seal on wax with a
signet ring. It depends on the age and temperament of the person
whether the impression lasts long in memory or is soon effaced.

> Some men in the presence of considerable stimulus have no
> memory owing to disease or age, just as if a stimulus or a seal were
> impressed on flowing water. With them the design makes no
> impression because they are worn down like old walls in build-
> ings, or because of the hardness of that which is to receive the
> impression. For this reason the very young and the old have poor
> memories; they are in a state of flux, the young because of their
> growth, the old because of their decay. For a similar reason neither
> the very quick nor the very slow appear to have good memories;
> the former are moister than they should be, and the latter harder;
> with the former the picture has no permanence, with the latter it
> makes no impression.[19]

Aristotle distinguishes between memory and reminiscence, or
recollection. Recollection is the recovery of knowledge or sensation

[16] Already quoted above.
[17] *De memoria et reminiscentia*, 449ᵇ 31 (translated, as one of the *Parva Naturalia*, by W. S. Hett in the Loeb volume cited).
[18] *Ibid.*, 450ᵃ 30.
[19] *Ibid.*, 450ᵇ 1–10.

which one had before. It is a deliberate effort to find one's way among the contents of memory, hunting among its contents for what one is trying to recollect. In this effort, Aristotle emphasises two principles, which are connected with one another. These are the principles of what we call association, though he does not use this word, and of order. Beginning from 'something similar, or contrary, or closely connected'[20] with what we are seeking we shall come upon it. This passage has been described as the first formulation of the laws of association through similarity, dissimilarity, contiguity.[21] We should also seek to recover an order of events or impressions which will lead us to the object of our search, for the movements of recollection follow the same order as the original events; and the things that are easiest to remember are those which have an order, like mathematical propositions. But we need a starting-point from which to initiate the effort of recollection.

> It often happens that a man cannot recall at the moment, but can search for what he wants and find it. This occurs when a man initiates many impulses, until at last he initiates that which the object of his search will follow. For remembering really depends upon the potential existence of the stimulating cause . . . But he must seize hold of the starting-point. For this reason some use places (τόπων) for the purposes of recollecting. The reason for this is that men pass rapidly from one step to the next; for instance from milk to white, from white to air, from air to damp; after which one recollects autumn, supposing that one is trying to recollect that season.[22]

What is certain here is that Aristotle is bringing in the places of artificial memory to illustrate his remarks on association and order in the process of recollection. But apart from that the meaning of the passage is very difficult to follow, as editors and annotators admit.[23] It is possible that the steps by which one passes rapidly from milk to autumn—supposing one is trying to recollect that season—may depend on cosmic association of the elements with

[20] Ibid., 451[b] 18-20.
[21] See W. D. Ross, Aristotle, London, 1949, p. 144; and Ross's note on this passage in his edition of the Parva Naturalia, Oxford, 1955, p. 245.
[22] De mem. et rem., 452[a] 8-16.
[23] For a discussion of the passage, see Ross's note in his edition of the Parva naturalia, p. 246.

seasons. Or the passage may be corrupt and fundamentally incomprehensible as it stands.

It is immediately followed by one in which Aristotle is speaking of recollecting through starting at any one point in a series.

> Generally speaking the middle point seems to be a good point to start from; for one will recollect when one comes to this point, if not before, or else one will not recollect from any other. For instance, suppose one were thinking of a series, which may be represented by the letters ABCDEFGH; if one does not recall what is wanted at E, yet one does at H; from that point it is possible to travel in either direction, that is either towards D or towards F. Supposing one is seeking for either G or F, one will recollect on arriving at C, if one wants G or F. If not then on arrival at A. Success is always achieved in this way. Sometimes it is possible to recall what we seek and sometimes not; the reason being that it is possible to travel from the same starting-point in more than one direction; for instance from C we may go direct to F or only to D.[24]

Since the starting-point in a train of recollection has earlier been likened to the mnemonic locus, we may recall in connection with this pretty confusing passage that one of the advantages of the artificial memory was that its possessor could start at any point in his places and run through them in any direction.

The scholastics proved to their own satisfaction that the *De memoria et reminiscentia* provided philosophical justification for the artificial memory. It is however very doubtful whether this is what Aristotle meant. He appears to use his references to the mnemonic technique only as illustrations of his argument.

The metaphor, used in all three of our Latin sources for the mnemonic, which compares the inner writing or stamping of the memory images on the places with writing on a waxed tablet is obviously suggested by the contemporary use of the waxed tablet for writing. Nevertheless it also connects the mnemonic with ancient theory of memory, as Quintilian saw when, in his introduction to his treatment of the mnemonic, he remarked that he did not propose to dwell on the precise functions of memory, 'although

---

[24] *De mem. et rem.*, 452[a] 16–25. For suggested emendations of the baffling series of letters, of which there are many variations in the manuscripts, see Ross's note in his edition of the *Parva naturalia*, pp. 247–8.

many hold the view that certain impressions are made on the mind, analogous to those which a signet ring makes on wax.'[25]

Aristotle's use of this metaphor for the images from sense impressions, which are like the imprint of a seal on wax, has already been quoted. For Aristotle such impressions are the basic source of all knowledge; though refined upon and abstracted by the thinking intellect, there could be no thought or knowledge without them, for all knowledge depends on sense impressions.

Plato also uses the seal imprint metaphor in the famous passage in the *Theaetetus* in which Socrates assumes that there is a block of wax in our souls—of varying quality in different individuals—and that this is 'the gift of Memory, the mother of the Muses'. Whenever we see or hear or think of anything we hold this wax under the perceptions and thoughts and imprint them upon it, just as we make impressions from seal rings.[26]

But Plato, unlike Aristotle, believes that there is a knowledge not derived from sense impressions, that there are latent in our memories the forms or moulds of the Ideas, of the realities which the soul knew before its descent here below. True knowledge consists in fitting the imprints from sense impressions on to the mould or imprint of the higher reality of which the things here below are reflections. The *Phaedo* develops the argument that all sensible objects are referable to certain types of which they are likenesses. We have not seen or learned the types in this life; but we saw them before our life began and the knowledge of them is innate in our memories. The example given is that of referring our sense perceptions of objects which are equal to the Idea of Equality which is innate in us. We perceive equality in equal subjects, such as equal pieces of wood, because the Idea of Equality has been impressed on our memories, the seal of it is latent in the wax of our soul. True knowledge consists in fitting the imprints from sense impressions on to the basic imprint or seal of the Form or Idea to which the objects of sense correspond.[27] In the *Phaedrus*, in which Plato expounds his view of the true function of rhetoric—which is to persuade men to the knowledge of the truth—he again develops the theme that knowledge of the truth and of the soul consists in remembering, in the recollection of the Ideas once seen by all souls

[25] *Institutio oratoria*, XI, ii, 4.
[26] *Theaetetus*, 191 C–D.
[27] *Phaedo*, 75 B–D.

of which all earthly things are confused copies. All knowledge and all learning are an attempt to recollect the realities, the collecting into a unity of the many perceptions of the senses through their correspondencies with the realities. 'In the earthly copies of justice and temperance and the other ideas which are precious to souls there is no light, but only a few, approaching the images through the darkling organs of sense, behold in them the nature of that which they imitate.'[28]

The *Phaedrus* is a treatise on rhetoric in which rhetoric is regarded, not as an art of persuasion to be used for personal or political advantage, but as an art of speaking the truth and of persuading hearers to the truth. The power to do this depends on a knowledge of the soul and the soul's true knowledge consists in the recollection of the Ideas. Memory is not a 'section' of this treatise, as one part of the art of rhetoric; memory in the Platonic sense is the groundwork of the whole.

It is clear that, from Plato's point of view, the artificial memory as used by a sophist would be anathema, a desecration of memory. It is indeed possible that some of Plato's satire on the sophists, for instance their senseless use of etymologies, might be explicable from the sophist memory treatise, with its use of such etymologies for memory for words. A Platonic memory would have to be organised, not in the trivial manner of such mnemotechnics, but in relation to the realities.

The grandiose attempt to do just this, within the framework of the art of memory, was made by the Neoplatonists of the Renaissance. One of the most striking manifestations of the Renaissance use of the art is the Memory Theatre of Giulio Camillo. Using images disposed on places in a neoclassical theatre—that is using the technique of the artificial memory in a perfectly correct way— Camillo's memory system is based (so he believes) on archetypes of reality on which depend secondary images covering the whole realm of nature and of man. Camillo's view of memory is fundamentally Platonic (though Hermetic and Cabalist influences are also present in the Theatre) and he aims at constructing an artificial memory based on truth. 'Now if the ancient orators,' he says, 'wishing to place from day to day the parts of the speech which they had to recite, confided them to frail places as frail things, it

---

[28] *Phaedrus*, 249 E–250 D.

is right that we, wishing to store up eternally the eternal nature of all things which can be expressed in speech . . . should assign to them eternal places.'[29]

In the *Phaedrus*, Socrates tells the following story:

I heard, then, that at Naucratis, in Egypt, was one of the ancient gods of that country, the one whose sacred bird is called the ibis, and the name of the god himself was Theuth. He it was who invented numbers and arithmetic and geometry and astronomy, also draughts and dice, and, most important of all, letters. Now the king of all Egypt at that time was the god Thamus, who lived in a great city of the upper region, which the Greeks call the Egyptian Thebes, and they call the god himself Ammon. To him came Theuth to show his inventions, saying that they ought to be imparted to the other Egyptians. But Thamus asked what use there was in each, and as Theuth enumerated their uses, expressed praise or blame of the various arts which it would take too long to repeat; but when they came to letters, 'This invention, O king,' said Theuth, 'will make the Egyptians wiser and will improve their memories; for it is an elixir of memory and wisdom that I have discovered.' But Thamus replied, 'Most ingenious Theuth, one man has the ability to beget arts, but the ability to judge of their usefulness or harmfulness to their users belongs to another; and now you, who are the father of letters, have been led by your affection to ascribe to them a power the opposite of that which they really possess. For this invention will produce forgetfulness in the minds of those who learn to use it, because they will not practise their memory. Their trust in writing, produced by external characters which are not part of themselves will discourage the use of their own memory within them. You have invented an elixir not of memory but of reminding; and you offer your pupils the appearance of wisdom, not true wisdom, for they will read many things without instruction and will therefore seem to know many things, when they are for the most part ignorant and hard to get along with, since they are not wise, but only appear wise.[30]

It has been suggested that this passage may represent a survival of the traditions of oral memory, of the times before writing had

---

[29] See below p. 138

[30] *Phaedrus*, 274 C–275 B (quoted in the translation by H. N. Fowler in the Loeb edition).

come into common use.[31] But as Socrates tells it, the memories of the most ancient Egyptians are those of truly wise men in contact with the realities. The ancient Egyptian practice of the memory is presented as a most profound discipline.[32] The passage was used by a disciple of Giordano Bruno when propagating in England Bruno's Hermetic and 'Egyptian' version of the artificial memory as an 'inner writing' of mysterious significance.[33]

As the reader will have perceived, it is a part of the plan of this chapter to follow the treatment of memory by the Greeks from the point of view of what will be important in the subsequent history of the art of memory. Aristotle is essential for the scholastic and mediaeval form of the art; Plato is essential for the art in the Renaissance.

And now there comes a name of recurring importance in our history, Metrodorus of Scepsis of whom Quintilian lets fall the remark that he based his memory on the zodiac.[34] Every subsequent user of a celestial memory system will invoke Metrodorus of Scepsis as the classical authority for bringing the stars into memory. Who was Metrodorus of Scepsis?

He belongs to the very late period in the history of Greek rhetoric which is contemporary with the great development of Latin rhetoric. As we have already been informed by Cicero, Metrodorus of Scepsis was still living in his time. He was one of the Greek men of letters whom Mithridates of Pontus, drew to his court.[35] In his attempt to lead the east against Rome, Mithridates affected the airs of a new Alexander and tried to give a veneer of Hellenistic culture to the mixed orientalism of his court. Metrodorus would appear to have been his chief Greek tool in this process. He seems to have played a considerable political, as well as cultural rôle at the court of Mithridates with whom he was for a

[31] See J. A. Notopoulos, 'Mnemosyne in Oral Literature', *Transactions and Proceedings of the American Philological Association*, LXIX (1938), p. 476.

[32] E. R. Curtius (*European Literature in the Latin Middle Ages*, London, 1953, p. 304) takes the passage as a 'typically Greek' disparagement of writing and books as compared with more profound wisdom.

[33] See below, p. 268

[34] See above, p. 23

[35] The chief source for the life of Metrodorus is Plutarch's Life of Lucullus.

time in high favour, though Plutarch hints that he was eventually put out of the way by his brilliant but cruel master.

We know from Strabo that Metrodorus was the author of a work, or works, on rhetoric. 'From Scepsis', says Strabo, 'came Metrodorus, a man who changed from his pursuit of philosophy to political life, and taught rhetoric, for the most part, in his written works; and he used a brand new style and dazzled many.'[36] It may be inferred that Metrodorus' rhetoric was of the florid 'Asianist' type, and it may well have been in his work or works on rhetoric, under memory as a part of rhetoric, that he expounded his mnemonics. The lost works of Metrodorus may have been amongst the Greek works on memory which the author of *Ad Herennium* consulted; Cicero and Quintilian may have read them. But all that we have to build on is Quintilian's statement that Metrodorus 'found three hundred and sixty places in the twelve signs through which the sun moves'. A modern writer, L. A. Post, has discussed the nature of Metrodorus' memory-system, as follows:

> I suspect that Metrodorus was versed in astrology, for astrologers divided the zodiac not only into 12 signs, but also into 36 decans, each covering ten degrees; for each decan there was an associated decan-figure. Metrodorus probably grouped ten artificial back-grounds (*loci*) under each decan figure. He would thus have a series of *loci* numbered 1 to 360, which he could use in his opera-tions. With a little calculation he could find any background (*locus*) by its number, and he was insured against missing a background, since all were arranged in numerical order. His system was there-fore well designed for the performance of striking feats of memory.[37]

Post assumes that Metrodorus used the astrological images as places which would ensure order in memory, just as the normal places memorised in buildings ensured remembering the images on them, and the things or words associated with them, in the right order. The order of the signs, Aries, Taurus, Gemini, and so on gives at once an easily memorised order; and if Metrodorus also had the decan images in memory—three of which go with each

[36] Strabo, *Geography*, XIII, i, 55 (quoted in the translation in the Loeb edition).
[37] L. A. Post, 'Ancient Memory Systems', *Classical Weekly*, New York, XV (1932), p. 109.

sign—he would, as Post says, have an order of astrological images in memory which, if he used them as places, would give him a set of places in a fixed order.

This is a sensible suggestion and there is no reason why an order of astrological images should not be used absolutely rationally as an order of easily remembered and numbered places. This suggestion even may give a clue to what has always struck me as an inexplicable feature of the memory image for remembering the lawsuit given in *Ad Herennium*—namely the testicles of the *ram*. If one has to remember that there were many witnesses in the case through sound resemblance of *testes* with testicles, why need these be the testicles of a ram? Could an explanation of this be that Aries is the first of the signs, and that the introduction of an allusion to a ram in the image to be put on the first place for remembering the lawsuit helped to emphasise the order of the place, that it was the first place? Is it possible that without the missing instructions of Metrodorus and other Greek writers on memory we do not quite understand the *Ad Herennium*.

Quintilian seems to assume that when Cicero says that Metrodorus 'wrote down' in memory all that he wished to remember, this means that he wrote it down inwardly through memorising shorthand signs on his places. If this is right, and if Post is right, we have to envisage Metrodorus writing inwardly in shorthand on the images of the signs and decans which he had fixed in memory as the order of his places. This opens up a somewhat alarming prospect; and the author of *Ad Herennium* disapproves of the Greek method of memorising signs for every word.

The Elder Pliny, whose son attended Quintilian's school of rhetoric, brings together a little anthology of memory stories in his *Natural History*. Cyrus knew the names of all the men in his army; Lucius Scipio, the names of all the Roman people; Cineas repeated the names of all the senators; Mithridates of Pontus knew the languages of all the twenty-two peoples in his domains; the Greek Charmadas knew the contents of all the volumes of a library. And after this list of *exempla* (to be constantly repeated in the memory treatises of after times) Pliny states that the art of memory

was invented by Simonides Melicus and perfected (*consummata*) by Metrodorus of Scepsis who could repeat what he had heard in the very same words.[38]

[38] Pliny, *Natural History*, VII, cap. 24

Like Simonides, Metrodorus evidently took some novel step about the art. It had to do with memory for words, possibly through memorising the *notae* or symbols of shorthand, and was connected with the zodiac. That is all we really know.

Metrodorus's mnemonics need not necessarily have been in any way irrational. Nevertheless a memory based on the zodiac sounds rather awe-inspiring and might give rise to rumours of magical powers of memory. And if he did use the decan images in his system, these were certainly believed to be magical images. The late sophist Dionysius of Miletus, who flourished in the reign of Hadrian, was accused of training his pupils in mnemonics by 'Chaldaean arts'. Philostratus, who tells the story, rebuts the charge,[39] but it shows that suspicions of this kind could attach themselves to mnemonics.

Memory-training for religious purposes was prominent in the revival of Pythagoreanism in late antiquity. Iamblichus, Porphyry, and Diogenes Laertius all refer to this aspect of Pythagoras's teaching, though without any specific reference to the art of memory. But Philostratus in his account of the memory of the leading sage, or Magus, of Neopythagoreanism—Apollonius of Tyana—brings in the name of Simonides.

> Euxemus having asked Apollonius why he had written nothing yet, though full of noble thoughts, and expressing himself so clearly and readily, he replied: 'Because so far I have not practised silence.' From that time on he resolved to be mute, and did not speak at all, though his eyes and his mind took in everything and stored it away in his memory. Even after he had become a centenarian he remembered better than Simonides, and used to sing a hymn in praise of the memory, in which he said that all things fade away in time, but time itself is made fadeless and undying by recollection.[40]

During his travels, Apollonius visited India where he conversed with a Brahmin who said to him: 'I perceive that you have an excellent memory, Apollonius, and that is the goddess whom we most adore.' Apollonius's studies with the Brahmin were very abstruse, and particularly directed towards astrology and divina-

[39] Philostratus and Eunapius, *The Lives of the Sophists* (Life of Dionysius of Miletus), trans. W. C. Wright, Loeb Classical Library, pp. 91–3.
[40] Philostratus, *Life of Apollonius of Tyana*, I, 14; trans. C. P. Ealls, Stanford University Press, 1923, p. 15.

tion; the Brahmin gave him seven rings, engraved with the names of the seven planets, which Apollonius used to wear, each on its own day of the week.[41]

It may have been out of this atmosphere that there was formed a tradition which, going underground for centuries and suffering transformations in the process, appeared in the Middle Ages as the *Ars Notoria*,[42] a magical art of memory attributed to Apollonius or sometimes to Solomon. The practitioner of the *Ars Notoria* gazed at figures or diagrams curiously marked and called 'notae' whilst reciting magical prayers. He hoped to gain in this way knowledge, or memory, of all the arts and sciences, a different 'nota' being provided for each discipline. The *Ars Notoria* is perhaps a bastard descendant of the classical art of memory, or of that difficult branch of it which used the shorthand *notae*. It was regarded as a particularly black kind of magic and was severely condemned by Thomas Aquinas.[43]

The period of the history of the art of memory in ancient times which most nearly concerns its subsequent history in the Latin West is its use in the great age of Latin oratory as reflected in the rules of *Ad Herennium* and their recommendation by Cicero. We have to try to imagine the memory of a trained orator of that period as architecturally built up with orders of memorised places stocked with images in a manner to us inconceivable. We have seen from the examples of memory quoted how greatly the feats of the trained memory were admired. Quintilian speaks of the astonishment aroused by the powers of memory of the orators. And he even suggests that it was the phenomenal development of memory by the orators which attracted the attention of Latin thinkers to the philosophical and religious aspects of memory. Quintilian's words about this are rather striking:

> We should never have realised how great is the power (of memory) nor how divine it is, but for the fact that it is memory which has brought oratory to its present position of glory.[44]

[41] *Ibid.*, III, 16, 41; translation cited, pp. 71, 85–6.
[42] On the *Ars Notoria*, see Lynn Thorndike, *History of Magic and Experimental Science*, II, Chap. 49.
[43] See below, p. 204.
[44] *Institutio oratoria*, XI, ii, 7.

This suggestion that the practical Latin mind was brought to reflect about memory through its development in the most important of careers open to a Roman has perhaps not attracted the attention it deserves. The idea must not be exaggerated, but it is interesting to glance at Cicero's philosophy from this point of view.

Cicero was not only the most important figure in the transfer of Greek rhetoric to the Latin world; but was also probably more important than anyone else in the popularising of Platonic philosophy. In the *Tusculan Disputations,* one of the works written after his retirement with the object of spreading the knowledge of Greek philosophy among his countrymen, Cicero takes up the Platonic and Pythagorean position that the soul is immortal and of divine origin. A proof of this is the soul's possession of memory 'which Plato wishes to make the recollection of a previous life'. After proclaiming at length his absolute adherence to the Platonic view of memory, Cicero's thought runs towards those who have been famous for their powers of memory:

> For my part I wonder at memory in a still greater degree. For what is it that enables us to remember, or what character has it, or what is its origin? I am not inquiring into the powers of memory which, it is said, Simonides possessed, or Theodectes, or the powers of Cineas, whom Pyrrhus sent as ambassador to the Senate, or the powers in recent days of Charmadas, or of Scepsius Metrodorus, who was lately alive, or the powers of our own Hortensius. I am speaking of the average memory of man, and chiefly of those who are engaged in some higher branch of study and art, whose mental capacity it is hard to estimate, so much do they remember.[45]

He then examines the non-Platonic psychologies of memory, Aristotelian and Stoic, concluding that they do not account for the prodigious powers of the soul in memory. Next, he asks what is the power in man which results in all his discoveries and inventions, which he enumerates;[46] the man who first assigned a name to everything; the man who first united the scattered human units and formed them into social life; the man who invented written characters to represent the sounds of the voice in language; the

[45] *Tusculan Disputations,* I, xxiv, 59 (quoted in the translation in the Loeb edition).
[46] *Ibid.,* I, xxv, 62–4.

44

man who marked down the paths of the wandering stars. Earlier still, there were 'the men who discovered the fruits of the earth, raiment, dwellings, an ordered way of life, protection against wild creatures—men under whose civilising and refining influence we have gradually passed on from the indispensable handicrafts to the finer arts.' To the art, for example, of music and its 'due combinations of musical sounds'. And to the discovery of the revolution of the heavens, such as Archimedes made when he 'fastened on a globe the movements of moon, sun, and five wandering stars'. Then there are still more famous fields of labour; poetry, eloquence, philosophy.

> A power able to bring about such a number of important results is to my mind wholly divine. For what is the memory of things and words? What further is invention? (*Quid est enim memoria rerum et verborum? quid porro inventio?*) Assuredly nothing can be apprehended even in God of greater value than this . . . Therefore the soul is, as I say, divine, as Euripides dares say, God . . .[47]

Memory for things; memory for words! It is surely significant that the technical terms of the artificial memory come into the orator's mind when, as philosopher, he is proving the divinity of the soul. That proof falls under the heads of the parts of rhetoric, *memoria* and *inventio*. The soul's remarkable power of remembering things and words is a proof of its divinity; so also is its power of invention, not now in the sense of inventing the arguments or things of a speech, but in the general sense of invention or discovery. The things over which Cicero ranges as inventions represent a history of human civilisation from the most primitive to the most highly developed ages. (The ability to do this would be in itself evidence of the power of memory; in the rhetorical theory, the things invented are stored in the treasure house of memory.) Thus *memoria* and *inventio* in the sense in which they are used in the *Tusculan Disputations* are transposed from parts of rhetoric into divisions under which the divinity of the soul is proved, in accordance with the Platonic presuppositions of the orator's philosophy.

In this work, Cicero probably has in mind the perfect orator, as defined by his master Plato in the *Phaedrus*, the orator who knows the truth and knows the nature of the soul, and so is able to persuade souls of the truth. Or we may say that the Roman

[47] *Ibid.*, I, xxv, 65.

orator when he thinks of the divine powers of memory cannot but also be reminded of the orator's trained memory, with its vast and roomy architecture of places on which the images of things and words are stored. The orator's memory, rigidly trained for his practical purposes, has become the Platonic philosopher's memory in which he finds his evidence of the divinity and immortality of the soul.

Few thinkers have pondered more deeply on the problems of memory and the soul than Augustine, the pagan teacher of rhetoric whose conversion to Christianity is recounted in his *Confessions*. In the wonderful passage on memory in that work one gains, I think, quite strongly the impression that Augustine's was a trained memory, trained on the lines of the classical mnemonic.

> I come to the fields and spacious palaces of memory (*campos et lata praetoria memoriae*), where are the treasures (*thesauri*) of innumerable images, brought into it from things of all sorts perceived by the senses. There is stored up, whatever besides we think, either by enlarging or diminishing, or any other way varying those things which the sense hath come to; and whatever else hath been committed and laid up, which forgetfulness hath not yet swallowed up and buried. When I enter there, I require instantly what I will to be brought forth, and something instantly comes; others must be longer sought after, which are fetched, as it were out of some inner receptacle; others rush out in troops, and while one thing is desired and required, they start forth, as who should say, 'Is it perchance I?' These I drive away with the hand of my heart from the face of my remembrance; until what I wish for be unveiled, and appear in sight, out of its secret place. Other things come up readily, in unbroken order, as they are called for; those in front making way for the following; and as they make way, they are hidden from sight, ready to come when I will. All which takes place when I recite a thing by heart.[48]

Thus opens the meditation on memory, with, in its first sentence, the picture of memory as a series of buildings, 'spacious palaces', and the use of the word 'thesaurus' of its contents, recalling the orator's definition of memory as 'thesaurus of inventions and of all the parts of rhetoric'.

In these opening paragraphs, Augustine is speaking of the images from sense impressions, which are stored away in the 'vast court'

[48] *Confessions*, X, 8 (Pusey's translation).

46

of memory (*in aula ingenti memoriae*), in its 'large and boundless chamber' (*penetrale amplum et infinitum*). Looking within, he sees the whole universe reflected in images which reproduce, not only the objects themselves, but even the spaces between them with wonderful accuracy. Yet this does not exhaust the capacity of memory, for it contains also

> all learnt of the liberal sciences and as yet unforgotten; removed as it were to some inner place, which is as yet no place: nor are they the images thereof, but the things themselves.[49]

And there are also preserved in memory the affections of the mind.

The problem of images runs through the whole discourse. When a stone or the sun is named, the things themselves not being present to the sense, their images are present in memory. But when 'health', 'memory', 'forgetfulness' are named are these present to the memory as images or not? He seems to distinguish as follows between memory of sense impressions and memory of the arts and of the affections:

> Behold in the plains, and caves, and caverns of my memory, innumerable and innumerably full of innumerable kinds of things, either as images, as all bodies; or by actual presence, as the arts; or by certain notions and impressions, as the affections of the mind, which, even when the mind doth not feel, the memory retaineth, while yet whatsoever is in the memory is also in the mind—over all these do I run, I fly; I dive on this side and that, as far as I can, and there is no end.[50]

Then he passes deeper within to find God in the memory, but not as an image and in no place.

> Thou hast given this honour to my memory to reside in it; but in what quarter of it Thou residest, that I am considering. For in thinking on Thee, I have passed beyond such parts of it as the beasts also have, for I found Thee not there among the images of corporeal things; and I came to those parts to which I have committed the affections of my mind, nor found Thee there. And I entered into the very seat of my mind . . . neither wert Thou there . . . And why seek I now in what place thereof Thou dwellest, as if there were places therein? . . . Place there is none; we go forward and backward and there is no place . . .[51]

[49] *Ibid.*, X, 9.   [50] *Ibid.*, X, 17.   [51] *Ibid.*, X, 25–6.

It is as a Christian that Augustine seeks God in the memory, and as a Christian Platonist, believing that knowledge of the divine is innate in memory. But is not this vast and echoing memory in which the search is conducted that of a trained orator? To one who saw the buildings of the antique world in their fullest splendour, not long before their destruction, what a choice of noble memory places would have been available! 'When I call back to mind some arch, turned beautifully and symmetrically, which, let us say, I saw at Carthage', says Augustine in another work and in another context, 'a certain reality that had been made known to the mind through the eyes, and transferred to the memory, causes the imaginary view.'[52] Moreover the refrain of 'images' runs through the whole meditation on memory in the *Confessions*, and the problem of whether notions are remembered with, or without, images would have been raised by the effort to find images for notions in the orator's mnemonic.

The transition from Cicero, the trained rhetorician and religious Platonist, to Augustine, the trained rhetorician and Christian Platonist, was smoothly made, and there are obvious affinities between Augustine on memory and Cicero on memory in the *Tusculan Disputations*. Moreover Augustine himself says that it was the reading of Cicero's lost work the *Hortensius* (called by the name of that friend of Cicero's who excelled in memory) which first moved him to serious thoughts about religion, which 'altered my affections, and turned my prayers to Thyself, O Lord'.[53]

Augustine is not discussing or recommending the artificial memory in those passages which we have quoted. It is merely almost unconsciously implied in his explorations in a memory which is not like our own in its extraordinary capacity and organisation. The glimpses into the memory of the most influential of the Latin Fathers of the Church raise speculations as to what a Christianised artificial memory might have been like. Would human images of 'things' such as Faith, Hope, and Charity, and of other virtues and vices, or of the liberal arts, have been 'placed' in such a memory, and might the places now have been memorised in churches?

These are the kind of questions which haunt the student of this most elusive art all through its history. All that one can say is that

[52] *De Trinitate*, IX, 6, xi.
[53] *Confessions*, III, 4.

48

these indirect glimpses of it vouchsafed to us before it plunges, with the whole of ancient civilisation, into the Dark Ages, are seen in rather a lofty context. Nor must we forget that Augustine conferred on memory the supreme honour of being one of the three powers of the soul, Memory, Understanding, and Will, which are the image of the Trinity in man.

Chapter III

THE ART OF MEMORY IN
THE MIDDLE AGES

LARIC sacked Rome in 410, and the Vandals conquered North Africa in 429. Augustine died in 430, during the siege of Hippo by the Vandals. At some time during this terrible era of collapse, Martianus Capella wrote his *De nuptiis Philologiae et Mercurii*, a work which preserved for the Middle Ages the outline of the ancient educational system based on the seven liberal arts (grammar, rhetoric, dialectic, arithmetic, geometry, music, astronomy). In his account of the parts of rhetoric, Martianus gives under memory a brief description of the artificial memory. He thus handed on the art to the Middle Ages firmly lodged in its correct niche in the scheme of the liberal arts.

Martianus belonged to Carthage where were the great rhetoric schools in which Augustine had taught before his conversion. The *Ad Herennium* was certainly known in North African rhetorical circles; and it has been suggested that the treatise had a late revival in North Africa whence it spread back to Italy.[1] It was known to Jerome who mentions it twice and attributes it to 'Tullius',[2] like the Middle Ages. However, knowledge of the artificial memory would not depend for rhetorically educated Christian Fathers, like Augustine and Jerome, or for the pagan Martianus Capella, on knowledge of this actual text. Its techniques were no

[1] F. Marx, introduction to the edition of *Ad Herennium*, Leipzig, 1894, p. I; H. Caplan, introduction to the Loeb edition of *Ad Herennium*, p. xxxiv.

[2] *Apologia adversus libros Rufini* I, 16; *In Abdiam Prophetam* (Migne, *Pat. lat.*, XXIII, 409; XXV, 1098).

doubt known to all rhetoric students, as they had been in Cicero's time, and would have reached Martianus through living contact with normal ancient civilised life, not yet completely obliterated by the barbarian tides.

Reviewing in order the five parts of rhetoric, Martianus comes in due course to its fourth part, which is *memoria*, about which he speaks as follows:

Now order brings in the precepts for memory which is certainly a natural (gift) but there is no doubt that it can be assisted by art. This art is based on only a few rules but it requires a great deal of exercise. Its advantage is that it enables words and things to be grasped in comprehension quickly and firmly. Not only those matters which we have invented ourselves have to be retained (in memory) but also those which our adversary brings forward in the dispute. Simonides, a poet and also a philosopher, is held to have invented the precepts of this art, for when a banqueting-hall suddenly collapsed and the relatives of the victims could not recognise (the bodies), he supplied the order in which they were sitting and their names which he had recorded in memory. He learned from this (experience) that it is order which sustains the precepts of memory. These (precepts) are to be pondered upon in well-lighted places (*in locis illustribus*) in which the images of things (*species rerum*) are to be placed. For example (to remember) a wedding you may hold in mind a girl veiled with a wedding-veil; or a sword, or some other weapon, for a murderer; which images as it were deposited (in a place) the place will give back to memory. For as what is written is fixed by the letters on the wax, so what is consigned to memory is impressed on the places, as on wax or on a page; and the remembrance of things is held by the images, as though they were letters.

But, as said above, this matter requires much practise and labour, whence it is customarily advised that we should write down the things which we wish easily to retain, so that if the material is lengthy, being divided into parts it may more easily stick (in memory). It is useful to place *notae* against single points which we wish to retain. (When memorising, the matter) should not be read out in a loud voice, but meditated upon with a murmur. And it is obviously better to exercise the memory by night, rather than by day, when silence spreading far and wide aids us, so that the attention is not drawn outward by the senses.

There is memory for things and memory for words, but words are not always to be memorised. Unless there is (plenty of) time for meditation, it will be sufficient to hold the things themselves in memory, particularly if the memory is not naturally good.[3]

We can recognise clearly enough the familiar themes of the artificial memory here, though it is a very compressed account. Rules for places are reduced to one only (well-lighted); rules for striking, *imagines agentes* are not given, though one of the specimen images is human (the girl in the wedding dress); the other (the weapon) is of the Quintilian type. No one could practise the art from instructions as slight as these, but enough is said to make recognisable what is being talked about if the description in *Ad Herennium* were available, as it was in the Middle Ages.

Martianus, however, seems most to recommend the Quintilian method of memorising through visualising the tablet, or the page of manuscript, on which the material is written—divided into clearly defined parts and with some marks or *notae* on it at special points—which is to be committed to memory in a low murmur. We see him intent on his carefully prepared pages and hear him faintly disturbing the silence of the night with his muttering.

The sophist Hippias of Elis was regarded in antiquity as the originator of the system of general education based on the liberal arts;[4] Martianus Capella knew them in their latest Latin form, just before the collapse of all organised education in the break up of the ancient world. He presents his work on them in a romantic and allegorical form which made it highly attractive to the Middle Ages. At the 'nuptials of Philology and Mercury' the bride received as a wedding present the seven liberal arts personified as women. Grammar was a severe old woman, carrying a knife and file with which to remove children's grammatical errors. Rhetoric was a tall and beautiful woman, wearing a rich dress decorated with the figures of speech and carrying weapons with which to wound her adversaries. The personified liberal arts conform remarkably well to the rules for images in the artificial memory—strikingly ugly or beautiful, bearing with them secondary images to remind of their parts like the man in the lawsuit image. The mediaeval student, comparing his *Ad Herennium* with Martianus on the artificial memory, might have thought that he was being intro-

[3] Martianus Capella, *De nuptiis Philologiae et Mercurii*, ed. A Dick, Leipzig, 1925, pp. 268–70.
[4] See Curtius, *European Literature in the Latin Middle Ages*, p. 36.

duced to the correct classical memory images for those 'things', the liberal arts.

In the barbarised world, the voices of the orators were silenced. People cannot meet together peacefully to listen to speeches when there is no security. Learning retreated into the monasteries and the art of memory for rhetorical purposes became unnecessary, though Quintilianist memorising of a prepared written page might still have been useful. Cassiodorus, one of the founders of monasticism, does not mention the artificial memory in the rhetoric section of his encyclopaedia on the liberal arts. Nor is it mentioned by Isidore of Seville or the Venerable Bede.

One of the most poignant moments in the history of Western civilisation is Charlemagne's call to Alcuin to come to France to help to restore the educational system of antiquity in the new Carolingian empire. Alcuin wrote a dialogue 'Concerning Rhetoric and the Virtues' for his royal master, in which Charlemagne seeks instruction on the five parts of rhetoric. When they reach memory, the conversation is as follows:

Charlemagne. What, now, are you to say about Memory, which I deem to be the noblest part of rhetoric?

Alcuin. What indeed unless I repeat the words of Marcus Tullius that 'Memory is the treasure-house of all things and unless it is made custodian of the thought-out things and words, we know that all the other parts of the orator, however distinguished they may be, will come to nothing'.

Charlemagne. Are there not other precepts which tell us how it can be obtained or increased.

Alcuin. We have no other precepts about it, except exercise in memorising, practice in writing, application to study, and the avoidance of drunkenness which does the greatest possible injury to all good studies . . .[5]

The artificial memory has disappeared! Its rules have gone, replaced by 'avoid drunkenness'! Alcuin had few books at his disposal; he compiled his rhetoric from two sources only, Cicero's

[5] W. S. Howell, *The Rhetoric of Charlemagne and Alcuin* (Latin text, English translation and introduction), Princeton and Oxford, 1941, pp. 136–9.

De inventione and the rhetoric of Julius Victor, with a little help from Cassiodorus and Isidore.[6] Of these, only Julius Victor mentions the artificial memory and he only in passing and slightingly.[7] Hence Charlemagne's hope that there might be other precepts for memory was doomed to disappointment. But he was told about the virtues, Prudence, Justice, Fortitude, and Temperance. And when he asked how many parts Prudence has he got the correct answer: 'Three; *memoria, intelligentia, providentia.*'[8] Alcuin was of course using Cicero's *De inventione* on the virtues; but he did not seem to know the second horse of the chariot, the *Ad Herennium*, which was to carry the artificial memory to great heights as a part of Prudence.

Alcuin's lack of knowledge of *Ad Herennium* is rather curious because it is mentioned as early as 830 by Lupus of Ferrières and several ninth-century manuscripts of it exist. The earliest manuscripts are not complete; they lack parts of the first book which is not the book which contains the memory section. Complete manuscripts are extant dating from the twelfth century. The popularity of the work is attested by the unusually large numbers of manuscripts that have come down to us; the majority of these date from the twelfth to the fourteenth centuries when the vogue for the work would seem to have been at its height.[9]

All the manuscripts ascribe the work to 'Tullius' and it becomes associated with the genuinely Ciceronian *De inventione*; the habit of associating the two works in the manuscripts was certainly established by the twelfth century.[10] The *De inventione*—described as the 'First Rhetoric' or the 'Old Rhetoric' is given first, and is

[6] See Howell's introduction, pp. 22 ff.

[7] 'For the obtaining of memory many people bring in observations about places and images which do not seem to me to be of any use' (Carolus Halm, *Rhetores latini*, Leipzig, 1863, p. 440).

[8] Alcuin, *Rhetoric, ed. cit.*, p. 146.

[9] See the introductions by Marx and Caplan to their editions of *Ad Herennium*. An admirable study of the diffusion of *Ad Herennium* is made in an unpublished thesis by D. E. Grosser, *Studies in the influence of the Rhetorica ad Herennium and Cicero's De inventione*, Ph.D. thesis, Cornell University, 1953. I have had the advantage of seeing this thesis in microfilm, for which I here express my gratitude.

[10] Marx, *op. cit.*, pp. 51 ff. The association of *Ad Herennium* with *De inventione* in the manuscript tradition is studied in the thesis by D. E. Grosser, referred to in the preceding note.

immediately followed by the *Ad Herennium* as the 'Second Rhetoric' or the 'New Rhetoric'.[11] Many proofs could be given as to how this classification was universally accepted. Dante, for example, is obviously taking it for granted when he gives 'prima rhetorica' as the reference for a quotation from *De inventione*.[12] The powerful alliance between the two works was still in operation when the first printed edition of *Ad Herennium* appeared at Venice in 1470; it was published together with the *De inventione*, the two works being described on the title-page in the traditional way as *Rhetorica nova et vetus*.

The importance of this association for the understanding of the mediaeval form of the artificial memory is very great. For Tullius in his First Rhetoric gave much attention to ethics and to the virtues as the 'inventions' or 'things' with which the orator should deal in his speech. And Tullius in his Second Rhetoric gave rules as to how the invented 'things' were to be stored in the treasure-house of memory. What were the things which the pious Middle Ages wished chiefly to remember? Surely they were the things belonging to salvation or damnation, the articles of the faith, the roads to heaven through virtues and to hell through vices. These were the things which it sculptured in places on its churches and cathedrals, painted in its windows and frescoes. And these were the things which it wished chiefly to remember by the art of memory, which was to be used to fix in memory the complex material of mediaeval didactic thought. The word 'mnemotechnics', with its modern associations is inadequate as a description of this process, which it is better to call the mediaeval transformation of a classical art.

It is of great importance to emphasise that the mediaeval artificial memory rested, so far as I know, entirely on the memory section of *Ad Herennium* studied without the assistance of the other two sources for the classical art. It might be untrue to say that the other two sources were entirely unknown in the Middle Ages; the *De oratore* was known to many mediaeval scholars, particularly

---

[11] Curtius (*Op. cit.*, p. 153) compares the 'old' and 'new' pairing of the two rhetorics with similar correspondences between *Digestum vetus* and *novus*, Aristotle's *Metaphysica vetus* and *nova*, all ultimately suggested by the Old and New Testaments.

[12] *Monarchia*, II, cap. 5, where he is quoting from *De inv.*, I, 38, 68; Cf. Marx, *Op. cit.*, p. 53.

in the twelfth century,[13] though probably in incomplete copies; it may, however, be unsafe to say that the complete text was unknown until the discovery at Lodi in 1422.[14] The same is true of Quintilian's *Institutio*; it was known in the Middle Ages though in incomplete copies; probably the passage on the mnemonics would not have been accessible before Poggio Bracciolini's much advertised find of a complete text at St. Gall in 1416.[15] However, though the possibility should not be excluded that a few chosen spirits here and there in the Middle Ages might have come across Cicero and Quintilian on the mnemonics,[16] it is certainly true to say that these sources did not become generally known in the memory tradition until the Renaissance. The mediaeval student, puzzling over rules for places and images in *Ad Herennium*, could not turn to the clear description of the mnemotechnical process given by Quintilian; nor did he know Quintilian's cool discussion of its advantages and disadvantages. For the mediaeval student, the rules of *Ad Herennium* were the rules of Tullius, who must be obeyed even if one did not quite understand him. His only other

[13] It was known to Lupus of Ferrières in the ninth century; see C. H. Beeson, 'Lupus of Ferrières as Scribe and Text Critic', *Mediaeval Academy of America*, 1930, pp. I ff.

[14] On the transmission of *De oratore*, see J. E. Sandys, *History of Classical Scholarship*, I, pp. 648 ff.; R. Sabbadini, *Storia e critica di testi latini*, pp. 101 ff.

[15] On the transmission of Quintilian, see Sandys, *Op. cit.*, I, pp. 655 ff.; Sabbadini, *Op. cit.*, p. 381; Priscilla S. Boskoff, 'Quintilian in the Late Middle Ages', *Speculum*, XXVII (1952), pp. 71 ff.

[16] One of these might have been John of Salisbury whose knowledge of the classics was exceptional and who was familiar with Cicero's *De oratore* and Quintilian's *Institutio* (see H. Liebeschütz, *Mediaeval Humanism in the Life and Writings of John Salisbury*, London, Warburg Institute, 1950, pp. 88 ff.)

In the *Metalogicon* (Lib. I, cap. XI) John of Salisbury discusses 'art' and repeats some of the phrases used in the classical sources when introducing the artificial memory (he is quoting from *De oratore* and perhaps also from *Ad Herennium*) but he does not mention places and images nor give the rules about these. In a later chapter (Lib. IV. cap. XII) he says that memory is a part of Prudence (of course quoting *De inventione*) but has nothing about artificial memory here. John of Salisbury's approach to memory appears to me to be different from the main mediaeval 'Ad Herennian' tradition and closer to what was later to be Lull's view of an art of memory. Lull's *Liber ad memoriam confirmandam* (on which see below pp. 191 ff.) seems to echo some of the terminology of the *Metalogicon*.

available sources would have been Martianus Capella with his incomprehensibly potted version of the rules in a setting of allegory.

Albertus Magnus and Thomas Aquinas certainly knew no other source for the rules than the work which they refer to as 'the Second Rhetoric of Tullius'. That is to say, they knew only the *Ad Herennium* on the artificial memory, and they saw it, through a tradition already well established in the earlier Middle Ages, in the context of the 'First Rhetoric of Tullius', the *De inventione* with its definitions of the four cardinal virtues and their parts. Hence it comes about that the scholastic *ars memorativa* treatises—those by Albertus Magnus and Thomas Aquinas—do not form part of a treatise on rhetoric, like the ancient sources. The artificial memory has moved over from rhetoric to ethics. It is under memory as a part of Prudence that Albertus and Thomas treat of it; and this in itself, surely, is an indication that mediaeval artificial memory is not quite what we should call 'mnemotechnics', which, however useful at times, we should hesitate to class as a part of one of the cardinal virtues.

It is very unlikely that Albertus and Thomas invented this momentous transference. Much more probably the ethical or prudential interpretation of artificial memory was already there in the earlier Middle Ages. And this is indeed strongly indicated by the peculiar contents of a pre-scholastic treatise on memory at which we will glance before coming to the scholastics, for it gives us a glimpse of what mediaeval memory was like before the scholastics took it up.

As is well known, in the earlier Middle Ages the classical rhetoric tradition took the form of the *Ars dictaminis*, an art of letter writing and of style to be used in administrative procedure. One of the most important centres of this tradition was at Bologna, and in the late twelfth and early thirteenth centuries the Bolognese school of *dictamen* was renowned throughout Europe. A famous member of this school was Boncompagno da Signa, author of two works on rhetoric the second of which, the *Rhetorica Novissima*, was written at Bologna in 1235. In his study of Guido Faba, another member of the Bolognese school of *dictamen* of about the same period, E. Kantorowicz has drawn attention to the vein of mysticism which runs through the school, its tendency to place rhetoric in a cosmic setting, to raise it to a 'sphere of quasi-holiness in order to compete with theology'.[17] This tendency is very marked in the *Rhetorica Novissima* in which supernatural origins are suggested, for example, for *persuasio* which must exist in the heavens for without it Lucifer would not have been able to persuade the angels to fall with him. And metaphor, or *transumptio*, must without doubt have been invented in the Earthly Paradise.

Going through the parts of rhetoric in this exalted frame of mind, Boncompagno comes to memory, which he states belongs not only to rhetoric but to all arts and professions, all of which have need of memory.[18] The subject is introduced thus:

> *What memory is.* Memory is a glorious and admirable gift of nature by which we recall past things, we embrace present things, and we contemplate future things through their likeness to past things.
> *What natural memory is.* Natural memory comes solely from the gift of nature, without aid of any artifice.
> *What artificial memory is.* Artificial memory is the auxiliary and assistant of natural memory . . . and it is called 'artificial' from 'art' because it is found artificially through subtlety of mind.[19]

The definition of memory may suggest the three parts of Prudence; the definitions of natural and artificial memory are certainly echoes of the opening of the memory section of *Ad Herennium,* which was well known in the *Ars dictaminis* tradition. We seem to detect here a prefiguration of the scholastics on prudence and the artificial memory, and we wait to hear how Boncompagno will give the memory rules.

We wait in vain, for the matter which Boncompagno treats under memory seems to have little connection with the artificial memory as expounded in *Ad Herennium.*

Human nature, so he informs us, has been corrupted from its original angelic form through the fall and this has corrupted memory. According to 'philosophic discipline' the soul before it came into the body knew and remembered all things, but since its infusion into the body its knowledge and memory are confused; this opinion must, however, be immediately rejected because it is contrary to 'theological teaching.' Of the four humours, the

[17] E. H. Kantorowicz, 'An "Autobiography" of Guido Faba', *Mediaeval and Renaissance Studies*, Warburg Institute, I (1943), pp. 261–2.
[18] Boncompagno, *Rhetorica Novissima*, ed. A. Gaudentio, *Bibliotheca Iuridica Medii Aevi*, II, Bologna, 1891, p. 255.
[19] *Ibid.*, p. 275.

sanguine and the melancholic are the best for memory; melancholics in particular retain well owing to their hard and dry constitution. It is the author's belief that there is an influence of the stars on memory; how this works, however, is known only to God and we must not enquire too closely into it.[20]

Against the arguments of those who say 'that natural memory cannot be assisted by artificial aids' it can be urged that there are many mentions in the scriptures of artificial aids to memory; for example, the cock-crow reminded Peter of something, and this was a 'memory sign'. This is only one of these alleged 'memory signs' in the Scriptures of which Boncompagno gives a long list.[21]

But by far the most striking feature of Boncompagno's memory section is that he includes in it, as connected with memory and artificial memory, the memory of Paradise and Hell.

> *On the memory of Paradise.* Holy men . . . firmly maintain, that the divine majesty resides on the highest throne before which stand the Cherubim, Seraphim, and all the orders of angels. We read, too, that there is ineffable glory and eternal life . . . Artificial memory gives no help to man for these ineffable things . . .
>
> *On the memory of the infernal regions.* I remember having seen the mountain which in literature is called Etna and in the vulgar Vulcanus, whence, when I was sailing near it, I saw sulphurous balls ejected, burning and glowing; and they say that this goes on all the time. Whence many hold that there is the mouth of Hell. However, wherever Hell may be, I firmly believe that Satan, the prince of Demons, is tortured in that abyss together with his myrmidons.
>
> *On certain heretics who assert that Paradise and Hell are matters of opinion.* Some Athenians who studied philosophical disciplines and erred through too much subtlety, denied the resurrection of the body . . . Which damnable heresy is imitated by some persons today . . . We however believe without doubting the Catholic faith, AND WE MUST ASSIDUOUSLY REMEMBER THE INVISIBLE JOYS OF PARADISE AND THE ETERNAL TORMENTS OF HELL.[22]

No doubt connected with the primary necessity of remembering Paradise and Hell, as the chief exercise of memory, is the list of virtues and vices which Boncompagno gives, which he calls 'memorial notes which we may call directions or signacula, through which we may frequently direct ourselves in the paths of

[20] *Ibid.*, pp. 275–6.　　[21] *Ibid.*, p. 277.　　[22] *Ibid.*, p. 278.

'remembrance'. Amongst such 'memorial notes' are the following:

> ... wisdom, ignorance, sagacity, imprudence, sanctity, perversity, benignity, cruelty, gentleness, frenzy, astuteness, simplicity, pride, humility, audacity, fear, magnanimity, pusillanimity . . .[23]

Though Boncompagno is a somewhat eccentric figure, and should not be taken as entirely representative of his time, yet certain considerations lead one to think that such a pietistic and moralised interpretation of memory, and what it should be used for, may be the background against which Albertus and Thomas formulated their careful revisions of the memory rules. It is extremely probable that Albertus Magnus would have known of the mystical rhetorics of the Bolognese school, for one of the most important of the centres established by Dominic for the training of his learned friars was at Bologna. After becoming a member of the Dominican Order in 1223, Albertus studied at the Dominican house in Bologna. It is unlikely that there should have been no contact between the Dominicans at Bologna and the Bolognese school of *dictamen*. Boncompagno certainly appreciated the friars, for in his *Candelabrium eloquentiae* he praises the Dominican and Franciscan preachers.[24] The memory section of Boncompagno's rhetoric therefore perhaps foreshadows the tremendous extension of memory training as a virtuous activity which Albertus and Thomas (who was of course trained by Albertus) recommend in their *Summae*. Albertus and Thomas, it may be suggested, would have taken for granted—as something taken for granted in an earlier mediaeval tradition—that 'artificial memory' is concerned with remembering Paradise and Hell and with virtues and vices as 'memorial notes'.

Moreover we shall find that in later memory treatises which are certainly in the tradition stemming from the scholastic emphasis on artificial memory, Paradise and Hell are treated as 'memory places', in some cases with diagrams of those 'places' to be used in 'artificial memory'.[25] Boncompagno also foreshadows other characteristics of the later memory tradition, as will appear later.

We should therefore be on our guard against the assumption that when Albertus and Thomas so strongly advocate the exercise

[23] *Ibid.*, p. 279.
[24] See R Davidsohn, *Firenze ai tempi di Dante.* Florence, 1929, p. 44.
[25] See below, pp. 94–5, 108–11, 115–16, 122 (Pl. 7).

of 'artificial memory' as a part of Prudence, they are necessarily talking about what we should call a 'mnemotechnic'. They may mean, amongst other things, the imprinting on memory of images of virtues and vices, made vivid and striking in accordance with the classical rules, as 'memorial notes' to aid us in reaching Heaven and avoiding Hell.

The scholastics were probably giving prominence to, or re-handling and re-examining, already existing assumptions about 'artificial memory' as an aspect of their rehandling of the whole scheme of the virtues and vices. This general revision was made necessary by the recovery of Aristotle whose new contributions to the sum of knowledge which had to be absorbed into the Catholic framework were as important in the field of ethics as in other fields. The *Nicomachean Ethics* complicated the virtues and vices and their parts, and the new evaluation of Prudence by Albertus and Thomas is part of their general effort to bring virtues and vices up to date.

What was also strikingly new was their examination of the precepts of the artificial memory in terms of the psychology of Aristotle's *De memoria et reminiscentia*. Their triumphant conclusion that Aristotle confirmed the rules of Tullius put the artificial memory on an altogether new footing. Rhetoric is in general graded rather low in the scholastic outlook which turns its back on twelfth-century humanism. But that part of rhetoric which is the artificial memory leaves its niche in the scheme of the liberal arts to become, not only a part of a cardinal virtue but a worth-while object of dialectical analysis.

We now turn to the examination of Albertus Magnus and Thomas Aquinas on the artificial memory.

The *De bono* of Albertus Magnus is, as its title states, a treatise 'on the good', or on ethics.[26] The core of the book is formed by the sections on the four cardinal virtues of Fortitude, Temperance, Justice, and Prudence. These virtues are introduced by the definitions given of them in the First Rhetoric of Tullius, and their parts or subdivisions are also taken from the *De inventione*. Other authorities, both Scriptural, patristic, and pagan—Augustine,

[26] Albertus Magnus, *De bono*, in *Opera omnia*, ed. H. Kühle, C. Feckes, B. Geyer, W. Kübel, Monasterii Westfalorum in aedibus Aschendorff, XXVIII (1951), pp. 82 ff.

Boethius, Macrobius, Aristotle—are of course cited as well, but the four sections of the book on the four virtues depend for their structure and main definitions on the *De inventione*. Albertus seems almost as anxious to bring the ethics of the New Aristotle into line with those of the Tullius of the First Rhetoric as with those of the Christian fathers.

When discussing the parts of Prudence, Albertus states that he will follow the divisions made by Tullius, Macrobius, and Aristotle, beginning with those given by

> Tullius at the end of the First Rhetoric where he says that the parts of Prudence are *memoria, intelligentia, providentia*.[27]

We shall first enquire, he continues, what memory is, which Tullius alone makes a part of Prudence. Secondly, we shall enquire what is the *ars memorandi* of which Tullius speaks. The ensuing discussion falls under these two heads, or *articuli*.

The first *articulus* gets rid of the objections which could be made to the inclusion of memory in Prudence. These are mainly two (though drawn up under five heads). First, that memory is in the sensitive part of the soul, whereas Prudence is in the rational part. Answer: reminiscence as defined by the Philosopher (Aristotle) is in the rational part, and reminiscence is the kind of memory which is a part of Prudence. Secondly, memory as a record of past impressions and events is not a habit, whereas Prudence is a moral habit. Answer: memory can be a moral habit when it is used to remember past things with a view to prudent conduct in the present, and prudent looking forward to the future.

Solution. Memory as reminiscence and memory used to draw useful lessons from the past is a part of Prudence.[28]

The second *articulus* discusses 'the *ars memorandi* which Tullius gives in the Second Rhetoric'. It draws up twenty-one points in the course of which rules for places and images are quoted verbatim from *Ad Herennium*, with comments and criticisms. The solution goes through the twenty-one points, solves the problems, abolishes all criticisms, and confirms the rules.[29]

The discussion opens with the definition of natural and artificial memory. The artificial memory, it is now stated, is both a habit and belongs to the rational part of the soul, being concerned with what

---

[27] *Ibid.*, p. 245.   [28] *Ibid.*, pp. 245–6.   [29] *Ibid.*, pp. 246–52.

Aristotle calls reminiscence. 'What he [Tullius] says of artificial memory which is confirmed by induction and rational precept . . . belongs not to memory but to reminiscence, as Aristotle says in the book *De memoria et reminiscentia*.'[30] Thus we have at the start the conflation of Aristotle on reminiscence with *Ad Herennium* on memory training. So far as I know, Albertus was the first to make this conflation.

Then come the precepts, beginning, of course, with rules for places. Discussing the phrase in *Ad Herennium* describing good memory places as standing out 'breviter, perfecte, insigniter aut natura aut manu', Albertus asks how can a place be at the same time both 'brevis' and perfectus'? Tullius seems to be contradicting himself here.[31] The solution is that by a 'brevis' place Tullius means that it should not 'distend the soul' by carrying it through 'imaginary spaces as a camp or city'.[32] One deduces from this that Albertus himself advises the use of only 'real' memory places, memorised in real buildings, not the erection of imaginary systems in memory. Since he has mentioned in the previous solution that 'solemn and rare' memory places are the most 'moving',[33] perhaps one can further deduce that the best kind of building in which to form memory places would be a church.

Again, what does Tullius mean by saying that the places should be memorable 'aut natura aut manu'?[34] Tullius should have defined what he means by this which he nowhere does. The solution is that a place memorable by nature is, for example, a field; a place memorable by hand is a building.[35]

The five rules for choosing places are now quoted, namely (1) in quiet spots to avoid disturbance of the intense concentration needed for memorising; (2) not too much alike, for example not too many identical intercolumniations; (3) neither too large nor too small; (4) neither too brightly lighted nor too obscure; (5) with intervals between them of moderate extent, about thirty feet.[36] It is objected that these precepts do not cover current memory practice, for 'Many people remember through dispositions of places contrary to those described'.[37] But the solution is that Tullius means

---

[30] Point 3, *ibid.*, p. 246.   [31] Point 8, *ibid.*, p. 247.
[32] Solution, point 8, *ibid.*, p. 250.   [33] Solution, point 7, *ibid., loc. cit.*
[34] Point 10, *ibid.*, p. 247.   [35] Solution, point 10, *ibid.*, p. 251.
[36] Point 11, *ibid.*, p. 247.   [37] Point 15, *ibid.*, p. 247.

to say that though different people will choose different places—some a field, some a temple, some a hospital—according to what 'moves' them most; yet the five precepts hold good, whatever the nature of the place-system chosen by the individual.[38]

As a philosopher and theorist on the soul, Albertus has to stop and ask himself what he is doing. These places which are to be so strongly imprinted on memory are corporeal places (*loca corporalia*)[39] therefore in the imagination which receives the corporeal forms from sense impression, therefore not in the intellectual part of the soul. Yes, but we are talking not of memory but of reminiscence which uses the *loca imaginabilia* for rational purposes.[40] Albertus needs to reassure himself about this before he can go on recommending an art which seems to be forcing the lower power of imagination up into the higher rational part of the soul.

And before he comes, as he is about to do, to precepts for images, the second arm of the artificial memory, he has to clear up another knotty point. As he has said in his *De anima* (to which he here refers), memory is the thesaurus not of the forms or images alone (as is the imagination) but also of the *intentiones* drawn from these by the estimative power. In the artificial memory, therefore, does one need extra images to remind of the *intentiones*?[41] The answer, fortunately, is in the negative, for the memory image includes the *intentio* within itself.[42]

This hair-splitting has its momentous side, for it means that the memory image gains in potency. An image to remind of a wolf's form will also contain the *intentio* that the wolf is a dangerous animal from which it would be wise to flee; on the animal level of memory, a lamb's mental image of a wolf contains this *intentio*.[43] And on the higher level of the memory of a rational being, it will mean that an image chosen, say, to remind of the virtue of Justice will contain the *intentio* of seeking to acquire this virtue.[44]

---

[38] Solution, point 15, *ibid.*, p. 251.

[39] Point 12, *ibid.*, p. 247.

[40] Solution, point 12, *ibid.*, p. 251.

[41] Point 13, *ibid.*, p. 247.

[42] Solution, point 13, *ibid.*, p. 251.

[43] This example is given by Albertus when discussing *intentiones* in his *De anima*; see Albertus Magnus, *Opera omnia*, ed. A. Borgnet, Paris, 1890, V, p. 521.

[44] This is my deduction; this example is not given by Albertus.

Now Albertus turns to the precepts for 'the images which are to be put in the said places'. Tullius says that there are two kinds of images, one for things, the other for words. Memory for things seeks to remind of notions only by images; memory for words seeks to remember every word by means of an image. What Tullius advises would seem to be an impediment rather than a help to memory; first, because one would need as many images as there are notions and words and this multitude would confuse memory; secondly because metaphors represent a thing less accurately than the description of the actual thing itself (*metaphorica minus repraesentant rem quam propria*). But Tullius would have us translate the *propria* into *metaphorica* for the purpose of remembering, saying, for example, that to remember a law-suit in which a man is accused of having poisoned another man for an inheritance, there being many witnesses to his guilt, one should place in memory, images of a sick man in bed, the accused man standing by it holding a cup and a document, and a doctor holding the testicles of a ram. (Albertus has interpreted *medicus*, the fourth finger, as a doctor and so introduced a third person into the scene.) But might it not have been easier to remember all this through the actual facts (*propria*) rather than through these metaphors (*metaphorica*)?[45]

We salute Albertus Magnus across the ages for having had worries about the classical art of memory so like our own. But his solution entirely reverses this criticism on the grounds (1) that images are an aid to memory; (2) that many *propria* can be remembered through a few images; (3) that although the *propria* give more exact information about the thing itself, yet the *metaphorica* 'move the soul more and therefore better help the memory'.[46]

He next struggles with the memory-for-words images of Domitius being beaten up by the Reges, and of Aesop and Cimber dressing up for their parts in the play of *Iphigeneia*.[47] His task was even harder than ours because he was using a corrupt text of *Ad Herennium*. He seems to have had in mind two highly confused images of someone being beaten by the sons of Mars, and of

[45] Point 16, *De bono, ed. cit.*, pp. 247–8.
[46] Solution, points 16 and 18, *ibid.*, p. 251.
[47] Point 17, *ibid.*, p. 248.

Aesop and Cimber and the wandering Iphigeneia.[48] He tries as best he can to make these fit the line to be remembered, but remarks pathetically, 'These metaphorical words are obscure and not easy to remember.' Nevertheless—such was his faith in Tullius— he decides in the solution that *metaphorica* like these are to be used as memory images, for the wonderful moves the memory more than the ordinary. And this was why the first philosophers expressed themselves in poetry, because, as the Philosopher says (referring to Aristotle in the *Metaphysics*), the fable, which is composed of wonders, moves the more.[49]

What we are reading is very extraordinary indeed. For scholasticism in its devotion to the rational, the abstract, as the true pursuit of the rational soul, banned metaphor and poetry as belonging to the lower imaginative level. Grammar and Rhetoric which dealt with such matters had to retreat before the rule of Dame Dialectic. And those fables about the ancient gods with which poetry concerned itself were highly reprehensible morally. To move, to excite the imagination and the emotions with *metaphorica* seems a suggestion utterly contrary to the scholastic puritanism with its attention severely fixed on the next world, on Hell, Purgatory, and Heaven. Yet, though we are to practise the artificial memory as a part of Prudence, its rules for images are letting in the metaphor and the fabulous for their moving power.

And now the *imagines agentes* make their appearance, quoted in full from Tullius.[50] Remarkably beautiful or hideous, dressed in crowns and purple garments, deformed or disfigured with blood or mud, smeared with red paint, comic or ridiculous, they stroll mysteriously, like players, out of antiquity into the scholastic treatise on memory as a part of Prudence. The solution emphasises

---

[48] Albertus was using a text in which *itionem* (in the line of poetry to be memorised) was read as *ultionem* (vengeance); and which instead of *in altero loco Aesopum et Cimbrum subornari ut ad Iphigeniam in Agamemnonem et Menelaum—hoc erit 'Atridae parant'* read *in altero loco Aesopum et Cimbrum subornari vagantem Iphigeniam, hoc erit 'Atridae parant'*. Marx's notes to his edition of *Ad Herennium* (p. 282) show that some manuscripts have such readings.

[49] Solution, point 17, *De bono*, ed. cit., p. 251. Cf. Aristotle, *Metaphysics*, 982^b 18–19.

[50] Point 20, *De bono*, ed. cit., p. 248.

that the reason for the choice of such images is that they 'move strongly' and so adhere to the soul.[51]

The verdict in the case for and against the artificial memory, which has been conducted in strict accordance with the rules of scholastic analysis, is as follows:

> We say that the *ars memorandi* which Tullius teaches is the best and particularly for the things to be remembered pertaining to life and judgment (*ad vitam et iudicium*), and such memories (i.e. artificial memories) pertain particularly to the moral man and to the speaker (*ad ethicum et rhetorem*) because since the act of human life (*actus humanae vitae*) consists in particulars it is necessary that it should be in the soul through corporeal images; it will not stay in memory save in such images. Whence we say that of all the things which belong to Prudence the most necessary of all is memory, because from past things we are directed to present things and future things, and not the other way round.[52]

Thus the artificial memory achieves a moral triumph; it rides with Prudence in a chariot of which Tullius is the driver, whipping up his two horses of the First and Second Rhetorics. And if we can see Prudence as a striking and unusual corporeal image—as a lady with three eyes, for example, to remind of her view of things past, present, and future—this will be in accordance with the rules of the artificial memory which recommends the *metaphorica* for remembering the *propria*.

As we have realised from *De bono*, Albertus relies much on Aristotle's distinction between memory and reminiscence in his arguments in favour of the artificial memory. He had carefully studied the *De memoria et reminiscentia* on which he wrote a commentary and had perceived in it what he thought were references to the same kind of artificial memory as that described by Tullius. And it is true, as we saw in the last chapter, that Aristotle does refer to the mnemonic to illustrate his arguments.

In his commentary on the *De memoria et reminiscentia*,[53] Albertus goes through his 'faculty psychology' (more fully described in his *De anima* and developed, of course, out of Aristotle and Avicenna) by which sense impressions pass by various stages

[51] Solution, point 20, *ibid.*, p. 252.

[52] *Ibid.*, p. 249. These are the first words of the Solution.

[53] Albertus Magnus, *De memoria et reminiscentia*, *Opera omnia*, ed. Borgnet, IX, pp. 97 ff.

67

from *sensus communis* to *memoria* being gradually dematerialised in the process.[54] He develops Aristotle's distinction between memory and reminiscence into a division between memory, which although more spiritual than the preliminary faculties is still in the sensitive part of the soul, and reminiscence which is in the intellectual part, though still retaining traces of the corporeal forms. The process of reminiscence therefore demands that the thing which it is sought to recall should have passed beyond the successive faculties of the sensitive part of the soul and should have reached the domain of the distinguishing intellect, with reminiscence. At this point, Albertus introduces the following astonishing allusion to the artificial memory:

> Those wishing to reminisce (i.e. wishing to do something more spiritual and intellectual than merely to remember) withdraw from the public light into obscure privacy: because in the public light the images of sensible things (*sensibilia*) are scattered and their movement is confused. In obscurity, however, they are unified and are moved in order. This is why Tullius in the *ars memorandi* which he gives in the Second Rhetoric prescribes that we should imagine and seek out dark places having little light. And because reminiscence requires many images, not one, he prescribes that we should figure to ourselves through many similitudes, and unite in figures, that which we wish to retain and remember (*reminisci*). For example, if we wish to record what is brought against us in a law-suit, we should imagine some ram, with huge horns and testicles, coming towards us in the darkness. The horns will bring to memory our adversaries, and the testicles the dispositions of the witnesses.[55]

This ram gives one rather a fright! How has it managed to break loose from the lawsuit image to career dangerously around on its own in the dark? And why has the rule about places being not too dark and not too light been combined with the one about memorising in quiet districts,[56] to produce this mystical obscurity and retirement in which the *sensibilia* are unified and their underlying order perceived? If we were in the Renaissance instead of in the

[54] For an account of the faculty psychology of Albertus, see M. W. Bundy, *The Theory of Imagination in Classical and Mediaeval Thought*, University of Illinois Studies, XII (1927), pp. 187 ff.

[55] Borgnet, IX, p. 108.

[56] Both these rules were quoted correctly by Albertus in *De bono*, ed. cit., p. 247.

Middle Ages, we might wonder whether Albertus thought that the ram was Aries, the sign of the zodiac, and was using magical images of the stars to unify the contents of memory. But perhaps he had merely been doing too much memory work in the night, when silence spreads far and wide, as advised by Martianus Capella, and his worries about the lawsuit image began to take strange forms!

Another feature of Albertus' commentary on the *De memoria et reminiscentia* is his allusion to the melancholy temperament and memory. According to the normal theory of humours, melancholy, which is dry and cold, was held to produce good memories, because the melancholic received the impressions of images more firmly and retained them longer than persons of other temperaments.[57] But it is not of ordinary melancholy that Albertus is speaking in what he says of the type of melancholy which is the temperament of *reminiscibilitas*. The power of reminiscence, he says, will belong above all to those melancholics of whom Aristotle speaks 'in the book of the *Problemata*' who have a *fumosa et fervens* type of melancholy.

> Such are those who have an accidental melancholy caused by an adustation with the sanguine and choleric (temperaments). The phantasmata move such men more than any others, because they are most strongly imprinted in the dry of the back part of the brain: and the heat of the *melancholia fumosa* moves these (*phantasmata*). This mobility confers reminiscence which is investigation. The conservation in the dry holds many (*phantasmata*) out of which it (reminiscence) is moved.[58]

Thus the temperament of reminiscence is not the ordinary dry-cold melancholy which gives good memory; it is the dry-hot melancholy, the intellectual, the inspired melancholy.

Since Albertus insists so strongly that the artificial memory

[57] On melancholy as the temperament of good memory, see R. Klibansky, E. Panofsky, F. Saxl, *Saturn and Melancholy*, Nelson, 1964, pp. 69, 337. The stock definition is given by Albertus in *De bono (ed. cit.*, p. 240): 'the goodness of memory is in the dry and the cold, wherefore melancholics are called the best for memory.' Cf. also Boncompagno on melancholy and memory, above p. 59

[58] Borgnet, IX, p. 117. On Albertus Magnus and the 'inspired' melancholy of the Pseudo-Aristotelian *Problemata*, see *Saturn and Melancholy*, pp. 69 ff.

belongs to reminiscence, would his *ars reminiscendi* therefore be a prerogative of inspired melancholics ? This would seem to be the assumption.

Early biographers of Thomas Aquinas say that he had a phenomenal memory. As a boy at school in Naples he committed to memory all that the master said, and later he trained his memory under Albertus Magnus at Cologne. 'His collection of utterances of the Fathers on the Four Gospels prepared for Pope Urban was composed of what he had *seen*, not *copied*, in various monasteries' and his memory was said to be of such capacity and retentive power that it always retained everything that he read.[59] Cicero would have called such a memory 'almost divine'.

Like Albertus, Aquinas treats of the artificial memory under the virtue of Prudence in the *Summa Theologiae*. Like Albertus, too, he also wrote a commentary on Aristotle's *De memoria et reminiscentia* in which there are allusions to the art of Tullius. It will be best to look first at the allusions in the commentary since these help to explain the precepts for memory in the *Summa*.

Aquinas introduces what he has to say about Aristotle on memory and reminiscence[60] with a reminder of the First Rhetoric on memory as a part of Prudence. For he opens the commentary with the remark that the philosopher's statement in his *Ethics* that reason which is peculiar to man is the same as the virtue of Prudence, is to be compared with the statement of Tullius that the parts of Prudence are *memoria, intelligentia, providentia*.[61] We are on familiar ground and wait expectantly for what is sure to come. It is led up to by analysis of the image from sense impression as the ground of knowledge, the material on which intellect works. 'Man cannot understand without images (*phantasmata*); the image is a similitude of a corporeal thing, but understanding is of universals which are to be abstracted from particulars.'[62] This formulates the fundamental position of the theory of knowledge of both Aristotle and Aquinas. It is constantly repeated on the early

[59] E. K. Rand, *Cicero in the Courtroom of St. Thomas Aquinas*, Milwaukee, 1946, pp. 72–3.

[60] Edition used, Thomas Aquinas, *In Aristotelis libros De sensu et sensato, De memoria et reminiscentia commentarium,* ed. R. M. Spiazzi, Turin-Rome, 1949, pp. 85 ff.

[61] *Ibid.*, p. 87.

[62] *Ibid.*, p. 91.

pages of the commentary: 'Nihil potest homo intelligere sine phantasmate.'[63] What then is memory? It is in the sensitive part of the soul which takes the images of sense impressions; it therefore belongs to the same part of the soul as imagination, but is also *per accidens* in the intellectual part since the abstracting intellect works in it on the phantasmata.

> It is manifest from the preceding to what part of the soul memory belongs, that is to say to the same (part) as phantasy. And those things are *per se* memorable of which there is a phantasy, that is to say, the sensibilia. But the intelligibilia are *per accidens* memorable, for these cannot be apprehended by man without a phantasm. And thus it is that we remember less easily those things which are of subtle and spiritual import; and we remember more easily those things which are gross and sensible. And if we wish to remember intelligible notions more easily, we should link them with some kind of phantasms, as Tullius teaches in his Rhetoric.[64]

It has come, the inevitable reference to Tullius on the artificial memory in the Second Rhetoric. And these phrases, curiously overlooked by modern Thomists but very famous and forever quoted in the old memory tradition, give the Thomist justification for the use of images in the artificial memory. It is as a concession to human weakness, to the nature of the soul, which will take easily and remember the images of gross and sensible things but which cannot remember 'subtle and spiritual things' without an image. Therefore we should do as Tullius advises and link such 'things' with images if we wish to remember them.

In the later part of his commentary, Aquinas discusses the two main points of Aristotle's theory of reminiscence, that it depends on association and order. He repeats from Aristotle the three laws of association, giving examples, and he emphasises the importance of order. He quotes Aristotle on mathematical theorems being easy to remember through their order; and on the necessity of finding a

[63] *Ibid.*, p. 92. The commentary should be read in conjunction with the psychology expounded in Aquinas' commentary on the *De anima*. Aquinas was using the Latin translation of Aristotle by William of Moerbeke in which Aristotle's statements are rendered as *Numquam sine phantasmate intelligit anima* or *intelligere non est sine phantasmate*. An English translation of the Latin translation which Aquinas used is given in *Aristotle's 'De anima' with the Commentary of St. Thomas Aquinas*, trans. Kenelm Foster and Sylvester Humphries, London, 1951.

[64] Aquinas, *De mem. et rem.*, ed. cit., p. 93.

starting-point in memory from which reminiscence will proceed through an associative order until it finds what it is seeking. And at this point, where Aristotle himself refers to the τόποι of Greek mnemonics, Aquinas brings in the *loci* of Tullius.

> It is necessary for reminiscence to take some starting-point, whence one begins to proceed to reminisce. For this reason, some men may be seen to reminisce from the places in which something was said or done, or thought, using the place as it were as the starting-point for reminiscence; because access to the place is like a starting-point for all those things which were raised in it. Whence Tullius teaches in his Rhetoric that for easy remembering one should imagine a certain order of places upon which images (*phantasmata*) of all those things which we wish to remember are distributed in a certain order.[65]

The places of the artificial memory are thus given a rational grounding in Aristotelian theory of reminiscence based on order and association.

Aquinas thus continues Albertus' conflation of Tullius with Aristotle, but more explicitly and in a more carefully thought out way. And we are at liberty to imagine the places and images of the artificial memory as in some way the 'sensible' furniture of a mind and a memory directed towards the intelligible world.

But Aquinas does not make the hard and fast distinction between memory in the sensitive part, and reminiscence (including the artificial memory as an art of reminiscence) in the intellectual part of the soul on which Albertus had insisted. Reminiscence is indeed peculiar to man, whereas animals also have memory, and its method of proceeding from a starting-point can be likened to the method of the syllogism in logic, and 'syllogizare est actus rationis'. Nevertheless the fact that men in trying to remember strike their heads and agitate their bodies (Aristotle had mentioned this) shows that the act is partly corporeal. Its superior and partly rational character is due—not to its being in no way in the sensitive part—but to the superiority of the sensitive part in man, to that in animals, because man's rationality is used in it.

This caution means that Aquinas does not fall into the trap, into which Albertus is beginning to fall, of regarding the artificial

[65] *Ibid.*, p. 107. Immediately following this passage, Aquinas gives an interpretation of the Aristotle passage on transition from milk, to white, to air, to autumn (see above, p. 34) as illustrating the laws of association.

memory with superstitious awe. There is nothing comparable in Aquinas to Albertus's transformation of a memory image into a mysterious vision in the night. And although he, too, alludes to memory and melancholy, he does not refer to the melancholy of the *Problemata*, nor assume that this 'inspired' type of melancholy belongs to reminiscence.

In the second portion of the second part—the *Secunda Secundae* —of the *Summa*, Aquinas treats of the four cardinal virtues. As Albertus had done he takes his definitions and naming of these virtues from the *De inventione*, always called the Rhetoric of Tullius. To quote E. K. Rand on this, 'He (Aquinas) begins with Cicero's definition of the virtues and treats them in the same order . . . His titles are the same, Prudentia (not Sapientia), Justitia, Fortitudo, Temperantia.'[66] Like Albertus Aquinas is using many other sources for the virtues but the *De inventione* provides his basic framework.

In discussing the parts of Prudence,[67] he mentions the first three parts which Tullius gives; then the six parts assigned to it by Macrobius; then one other part mentioned by Aristotle but not by his other sources. He takes as his basis the six parts of Macrobius; adds to these *memoria* given as a part by Tullius; and *solertia* mentioned by Aristotle. He thereupon lays down that Prudence has eight parts, namely, *memoria, ratio, intellectus, docilitas, solertia* (skill), *providentia, circumspectio, cautio*. Of these, Tullius alone gave *memoria* as a part, and the whole eight parts can really be subsumed under Tullius' three of *memoria, intelligentia, providentia*.

He begins his discussion of the parts with *memoria*.[68] He must first of all decide whether memory is a part of Prudence. The arguments against are:

(1) Memory is in the sensitive part of the soul says the Philosopher. Prudence is in the rational part. Therefore memory is not a part of Prudence.
(2) Prudence is acquired by exercise and experience; memory is in us by nature. Therefore memory is not a part of Prudence.
(3) Memory is of the past; Prudence of the future. Therefore memory is not a part of Prudence.

[66] Rand, *Op. cit.*, p. 26.
[67] *Summa Theologiae*, II, II, quaestio XLVIII, *De partibus Prudentiae*.
[68] Quaestio XLIX, *De singulis Prudentiae partibus*: articulus I, *Utrum memoria sit pars Prudentiae*.

73

BUT AGAINST THIS THERE IS THAT TULLIUS PUTS MEMORY AMONG THE PARTS OF PRUDENCE.

To agree with Tullius, the above three objections are answered:

(1) Prudence applies universal knowledge to particulars, which are derived from sense. Therefore much belonging to the sensitive part belongs to Prudence, and this includes memory.
(2) As Prudence is both a natural aptitude but increased by exercise so also is memory. 'For Tullius (and another authority) says in his Rhetoric that memory is not only perfected from nature, but also has much of art and industry.'
(3) Prudence uses experience of the past in providing for the future. Therefore memory is a part of Prudence.

Aquinas is partly following Albertus but with differences; as we should expect, he does not rest the placing of memory in Prudence on a distinction between memory and reminiscence. On the other hand, he states even more clearly than Albertus that it is the artificial memory, the memory exercised and improved by art, which is one of the proofs that memory is a part of Prudence. The words quoted on this are a paraphrase of *Ad Herennium* and are introduced as deriving from 'Tullius (alius auctor)'. The 'other authority' probably refers to Aristotle, whose advice on memory is assimilated to that given by 'Tullius' in the memory rules as formulated by Thomas Aquinas.

It is in his reply to the second point that Aquinas gives his own four precepts for memory which are as follows:

Tullius (and another authority) says in his Rhetoric that memory is not only perfected from nature but also has much of art and industry: and there are four (points) through which a man may profit for remembering well.

(1) The first of these is that he should assume some convenient similitudes of the things which he wishes to remember; these should not be too familiar, because we wonder more at unfamiliar things and the soul is more strongly and vehemently held by them; whence it is that we remember better things seen in childhood. It is necessary in this way to invent similitudes and images because simple and spiritual intentions slip easily from the soul unless they are as it were linked to some corporeal similitudes, because human cognition is stronger in regard to the sensibilia. Whence the memorative (power) is placed in the sensitive (part) of the soul.

(2) Secondly it is necessary that a man should place in a considered order those (things) which he wishes to remember, so that from one remembered (point) progress can easily be made to the next. Whence the Philosopher says in the book *De memoria*: 'some men can be seen to remember from places. The cause of which is that they pass rapidly from one (step) to the next.'

(3) Thirdly, it is necessary that a man should dwell with solicitude on, and cleave with affection to, the things which he wishes to remember; because what is strongly impressed on the soul slips less easily away from it. Whence Tullius says in his Rhetoric that 'solicitude conserves complete figures of the simulachra'.

(4) Fourthly, it is necessary that we should meditate frequently on what we wish to remember. Whence the Philosopher says in the book *De memoria* that 'meditation preserves memory' because, as he says 'custom is like nature. Thence, those things which we often think about we easily remember, proceeding from one to another as though in a natural order.'

Let us consider with care Thomas Aquinas's four precepts for memory. They follow in outline the two foundations of the artificial memory, places and images.

He takes images first. His first rule echoes *Ad Herennium* on choosing striking and unusual images as being the most likely to stick in memory. But the images of the artificial memory have turned into 'corporeal similitudes' through which 'simple and spiritual intentions' are to be prevented from slipping from the soul. And he gives again here the reason for using 'corporeal similitudes' which he gives in the Aristotle commentary, because human cognition is stronger in regard to the sensibilia, and therefore 'subtle and spiritual things' are better remembered in the soul in corporeal forms.

His second rule is taken from Aristotle on order. We know from his Aristotle commentary that he associated the 'starting-point' passage, which he here quotes, with Tullius on places. His second rule is therefore a 'place' rule though arrived at through Aristotle on order.

His third rule is very curious, for it is based on a misquotation of one of the rules for places in *Ad Herennium*, namely that these should be chosen in deserted regions 'because the crowding and passing to and fro of people confuse and weaken the impress of the images while solitude keeps their outlines sharp (*solitudo conservat*

75

integras simulacrorum figuras).[69] Aquinas quotes this as *sollicitudo conservat integras simulacrorum figuras*, turning 'solitude' into 'solicitude', turning the memory rule which advised solitary districts in which to make the effort of memorising places in order to avoid distraction from the mnemonic effort, into 'solicitude'. It might be said that it comes to the same thing, since the object of the solitude was to be solicitous about memorising. But I do *not* think that it comes to the same thing, because Aquinas' 'solicitude' involves 'cleaving with affection' to the things to be remembered, introducing a devotional atmosphere which is entirely absent from the classical memory rule.

Aquinas' mistranslation and misunderstanding of the place rule is all the more interesting because we had a similar kind of misunderstanding of place rules in Albertus, who turned the 'not too dark or too light' and the 'solitude' place rules into some kind of mystical retirement.

The fourth rule is from Aristotle's *De memoria* on frequent meditation and repetition, advice which is also given in *Ad Herennium*.

To sum up, it would seem that Thomas' rules are based on the places and images of the artificial memory, but that these have been transformed. The images chosen for their memorable quality in the Roman orator's art have been changed by mediaeval piety into 'corporeal similitudes' of 'subtle and spiritual intentions'. The place rules may also have been somewhat misunderstood. It seems that the mnemotechnical character of the place rules, chosen for their dissimilarity, clear lighting, in quiet districts, all with a view to helping memorisation, may not have been fully realised by either Albertus or Thomas. They interpret the place rules also in a devotional sense. And, particularly in Thomas, one gains the impression that the important thing is order. His corporeal similitudes would perhaps be arranged in a regular order, a 'natural' order, not according to the studied irregularity of the rules, the meaning of which—in the case of *solitudo-sollicitudo*—he has transformed with devotional intensity.

How then are we to think of a scholastic artificial memory, a memory following to some extent the rules of Tullius but transforming these with moralising and pietistic intentions? What

---

[69] *Ad Herennium*, III, xix, 31. See above p. 7.

becomes of the strikingly beautiful and strikingly hideous *imagines agentes* in such a memory? The immediately pre-scholastic memory of Boncompagno suggests an answer to this question, with its virtues and vices as 'memorial notes' through which we are to direct ourselves in the paths of remembrance, reminding of the ways to Heaven and to Hell. The *imagines agentes* would have been moralised into beautiful or hideous human figures as 'corporeal similitudes' of spiritual intentions of gaining Heaven or avoiding Hell, and memorised as ranged in order in some 'solemn' building.

As I said in the first chapter, it is a great help to us in reading the memory section of *Ad Herennium* to be able to refer to Quintilian's clear description of the mnemotechnical process—the progress round the building choosing the places, the images remembered on the places for reminding of the points of the speech The mediaeval reader of *Ad Herennium* did not have that advantage. He read those queer rules for places and images without the assistance of any other text on the classical art of memory, and, moreover, in an age when the classical art of oratory had disappeared, was no longer practised. He read the rules, not in association with any living practice of oratory, but in close association with the teaching of Tullius on ethics in the First Rhetoric. One can see how misunderstandings might have arisen. And there is even the possibility, as already suggested, that an ethical, or didactic, or religious use of the classical art might have arisen much earlier, might have been used in some early Christian transformation of it of which we know nothing but which might have been handed on to the early Middle Ages. It is therefore probable that the phenomenon which I call 'the mediaeval transformation of the classical art of memory' was not invented by Albertus and Thomas but was already there long before they took it up with renewed zeal and care.

The scholastic refurbishing of the art and strong recommendation of it marks a very important point in its history, one of the great peaks of its influence. And one can see how it belongs into the general picture of thirteenth-century effort as a whole. The aim of the learned Dominican friars, of whom Thomas and Albertus were such notable representatives, was to use the new Aristotelian learning to preserve and defend the Church, and absorb it into the Church, to re-examine the existing body of learning in its light.

The immense dialectical effort of Thomas was, as everyone knows, directed towards answering the arguments of the heretics. He it was who turned Aristotle from a potential enemy into an ally of the Church. The other great scholastic effort of incorporating the Aristotelian ethics into the already existing virtue and vice system is not so much studied in modern times but may have seemed equally, if not more, important to contemporaries. The parts of the virtues, their incorporation into the existing Tullian scheme, their analysis in the light of Aristotle on the soul—all this is as much a part of the *Summa Theologiae*, a part of the effort to absorb the Philosopher, as are the more familiar aspects of Thomist philosophy and dialectics.

Just as the Tullian virtues needed overhauling with Aristotelian psychology and ethics, so would the Tullian artificial memory need such an overhaul. Perceiving the references to the art of memory in the *De memoria et reminiscentia*, the friars made that work the basis of their justification of the Tullian places and images through re-examining the psychological *rationale* of places and images with the help of Aristotle on memory and reminiscence. Such an effort would be parallel to their new examination of the virtues in the light of Aristotle. And the two efforts were closely linked because the artificial memory was actually a part of one of the cardinal virtues.

It has sometimes been a matter for surprised comment that the age of scholasticism, with its insistence on the abstract, its low grading of poetry and metaphor, should also be an age which saw an extraordinary efflorescence of imagery, and of new imagery, in religious art. Searching for an explanation of this apparent anomaly in the works of Thomas Aquinas, the passage in which he justifies the use of metaphor and imagery in the Scriptures has been quoted. Aquinas has been asking the question why the Scriptures use imagery since 'to proceed by various similitudes and representations belongs to poetry which is the lowest of all the doctrines'. He is thinking of the inclusion of poetry with Grammar, the lowest of the liberal arts, and enquiring why the Scriptures use this low branch of knowledge. The reply is that the Scriptures speak of spiritual things under the similitude of corporeal things 'because it is natural to man to reach the intelligibilia through the sensibilia because all our knowledge has its beginning in sense.'[70]

[70] *Summa theologiae*, I, I, quaestio I, articulus 9.

This is a similar argument to that which justifies the use of images in the artificial memory. It is extremely curious that those in search of scholastic justification of the use of imagery in religious art should have missed the elaborate analyses of why we may use images in memory given by Albertus and Thomas.

Something has been left out all along the line and it is Memory. Memory which not only had immense practical importance for the men of ancient times, but also a religious and ethical importance. Augustine, the great Christian rhetor, had made Memory one of the three powers of the soul, and Tullius—that Christian soul before Christianity—had made it one of the three parts of Prudence. And Tullius had given advice as to how to make 'things' memorable. I make so bold as to suggest that Christian didactic art which needs to set forth its teaching in a memorable way, which must show forth impressively the 'things' which make for virtuous and unvirtuous conduct, may owe more than we know to classical rules which have never been thought of in this context, to those striking *imagines agentes* which we have seen trooping out of the rhetoric text book into a scholastic treatise on ethics.

The high Gothic cathedral, so E. Panofsky has suggested, resembles a scholastic summa in being arranged according to 'a system of homologous parts and parts of parts'.[71] The extraordinary thought now arises that if Thomas Aquinas memorised his own *Summa* through 'corporeal similitudes' disposed on places following the order of its parts, the abstract *Summa* might be corporealised in memory into something like a Gothic cathedral full of images on its ordered places. We must refrain from too much supposition, yet it remains an undoubted fact that the *Summa* contained, in an unnoticed part of it, justification and encouragement for the use of imagery, and the creation of new imagery, in its recommendation of the artificial memory.

On the walls of the Chapter House of the Dominican convent of Santa Maria Novella in Florence, there is a fourteenth-century fresco (Pl. I) glorifying the wisdom and virtue of Thomas Aquinas. Thomas is seated on a throne surrounded by flying figures representing the three theological and the four cardinal virtues. To right and left of him sit saints and patriarchs and

[71] E. Panofsky, *Gothic Architecture and Scholasticism*, Latrobe, Pennsylvania, 1951, p. 45.

beneath his feet are the heretics whom he has crushed by his learning.

On the lower level, placed in niches or stalls, are fourteen female figures symbolising the vast range of the saint's knowledge. The seven on the right represent the liberal arts. Beginning on the extreme right is the lowest of the seven, Grammar; next to her is Rhetoric; then Dialectic, then Music (with the organ), and so on. Each of the arts has a famous representative of it sitting in front of her; in front of Grammar sits Donatus; in front of Rhetoric is Tullius, an old man with a book and upraised right hand; in front of Dialectic is Aristotle, in a large hat and with a forked white beard; and so on for the rest of the arts. Then come seven other female figures which are supposed to represent theological disciplines or the theological side of Thomas's learning, though no systematic attempt has been made to interpret them; in front of them sit representatives of these branches of learning, bishops and others, who again have not been fully identified.

Obviously the scheme is far from being entirely original. What could be less novel than the seven virtues? The seven liberal arts with their representatives was an ancient theme (the reader may think of the famous porch at Chartres), the seven additional figures symbolic of other disciplines, with representatives, is merely an extension of it. Nor would the mid-fourteenth-century designers of the scheme have wished to be original. Thomas is defending and supporting the traditions of the Church, using his vast learning to that end.

After our study of the mediaeval Tullius in this chapter we may look with renewed interest at Tullius, sitting modestly with Rhetoric in his right place in the scheme of things, rather low down in the scale of the liberal arts, only one above Grammar, and below Dialectic and Aristotle. Yet he is, perhaps, more important than he seems? And the fourteen female figures sitting in order in their places, as in a church, do they symbolise not only the learning of Thomas but also his method of remembering it? Are they, in short, 'corporeal similitudes', formed partly out of well known figures, the liberal arts, adapted to a personal use, and partly of newly invented figures?

I leave this only as a question, a suggestion, emphasising only that the mediaeval Tullius is a character of considerable importance in the scholastic scheme of things. Certainly he is a character

1 The Wisdom of Thomas Aquinas, Fresco by Andrea da Firenze, Chapter House of Santa Maria Novella, Florence (pp. 79–80)

of major importance for the mediaeval transformation of the classical art of memory. And though one must be extremely careful to distinguish between art proper and the art of memory, which is an invisible art, yet their frontiers must surely have overlapped. For when people were being taught to practise the formation of images for remembering, it is difficult to suppose that such inner images might not sometimes have found their way into outer expression. Or, conversely, when the 'things' which they were to remember through inner images were of the same kind as the 'things' which Christian didactic art taught through images, that the places and images of that art might themselves have been reflected in memory, and so have become 'artificial memory'.

2 Justice and Peace
Fresco by Ambrogio Lorenzetti
(Detail), Palazzo Pubblico,
Siena (p. 92)

Chapter IV

⟡⟡

MEDIAEVAL MEMORY AND THE FORMATION OF IMAGERY

⟡⟡

THE tremendous recommendation of the art of memory, in the form of corporeal similitudes ranged in order, by the great saint of scholasticism was bound to have far reaching results. If Simonides was the inventor of the art of memory, and 'Tullius' its teacher, Thomas Aquinas became something like its patron saint. The following are a few examples, culled from a much larger mass of material, of how the name of Thomas dominated memory in later centuries.

In the middle of the fifteenth century, Jacopo Ragone wrote an *Ars memorativa* treatise; the opening words of its dedication to Franceso Gonzaga are: 'Most illustrious Prince, the artificial memory is perfected through two things, namely *loci* and *imagines*, as Cicero teaches and as is confirmed by St. Thomas Aquinas.'[1] Later in the same century, in 1482, there appeared at Venice an early and beautiful specimen of the printed book; it was a work on rhetoric by Jacobus Publicius which contained as an appendix the first printed *Ars memorativa* treatise. Though this book looks like a Renaissance product it is full of the influence of Thomist artificial memory; the rules for images begin with the words: 'Simple and spiritual intentions slip easily from the memory unless joined to corporeal similitudes.'[2] One of the fullest and most widely cited of

[1] Jacopo Ragone, *Artificialis memoriae regulae*, written in 1434. Quoted from the manuscript in the British Museum, Additional 10, 438, folio 2 *verso*.

[2] Jacobus Publicius, *Oratoriae artis epitome*, Venice, 1482 and 1485; ed. of 1485, sig. G 4 *recto*.

the printed memory treatises is the one published in 1520 by Johannes Romberch, a Dominican. In his rules for images, Romberch remarks that 'Cicero in *Ad Herennium* says that memory is not only perfected from nature but also has many aids. For which St. Thomas gives a reason in II, II, 49 (i.e. in this section of the *Summa*) where he says that spiritual and simple intentions slip easily from the soul unless they are linked with certain corporeal similitudes.'[3] Romberch's rules for places are based on Thomas's conflation of Tullius with Aristotle, for which he quotes from Thomas's commentary on the *De memoria et reminiscentia*.[4] One would expect that a Dominican, like Romberch, would base himself on Thomas, but the association of Thomas with memory was widely known outside the Dominican tradition. The *Piazza Universale*, published by Tommaso Garzoni in 1578, is a popularisation of general knowledge; it contains a chapter on memory in which Thomas Aquinas is mentioned as a matter of course among the famous teachers of memory.[5] In his *Plutosofia* of 1592, F. Gesualdo couples Cicero and St. Thomas together on memory.[6] Passing on into the early seventeenth century we find a book, the English translation of the Latin title of which would be 'The Foundations of Artificial Memory from Aristotle, Cicero, and Thomas Aquinas.'[7] At about the same time a writer who is defending the artificial memory against attacks upon it, reminds of what Cicero, Aristotle, and St. Thomas have said about it, emphasising that St. Thomas in II, II, 49 has called it a part of Prudence.[8] Gratarolo in a work which was Englished in 1562 by William Fulwood as *The Castel of Memory* notes that Thomas Aquinas advised the use of places in memory,[9] and this was quoted from Fulwood in an *Art of Memory* published in 1813.[10]

[3] J. Romberch, *Congestorium artificiosa memorie*, ed. of Venice, 1533, p. 8.

[4] *Ibid.*, p. 16 etc.

[5] T. Garzoni, *Piazza universale*, Venice, 1578, Discorso LX.

[6] F. Gesualdo, *Plutosofia*, Padua, 1592, p. 16.

[7] Johannes Paepp, *Artificiosae memoriae fundamenta ex Aristotele, Cicerone, Thomae Aquinatae, aliisque praestantissimis doctoribus*, Lyons, 1619.

[8] Lambert Schenkel, *Gazophylacium*, Strasburg, 1610, pp. 5, 38 etc.; (French version) *Le Magazin de Sciences*, Paris, 1623, pp. 180 etc.

[9] W. Fulwood, *The Castel of Memorie*, London, 1562, sig. Gv, 3 *recto*.

[10] Gregor von Feinaigle, *The New Art of Memory*, third edition, London, 1813, p. 206.

Thus a side of Thomas Aquinas who was venerated in the ages of Memory was still not forgotten even in the early nineteenth century. It is a side of him which, so far as I know, is never mentioned by modern Thomist philosophers. And though books on the art of memory are aware of II, II, 49 as an important text in its history,[11] no very serious enquiry has been undertaken into the nature of the influence of the Thomist rules for memory.

What were the results of the momentous recommendation by Albertus and Thomas of their revisions of the memory rules as a part of Prudence? An enquiry into this should begin near the source of the influence. It was in the thirteenth century that the scholastic rules were promulgated, and we should expect to find their influence at their greatest strength beginning at once and carrying on in strength into the fourteenth century. I propose in this chapter to raise the question of what was the nature of this immediate influence and where we should look for its effects. I cannot hope to answer it adequately, nor do I aim at more than sketching possible answers, or rather possible lines of enquiry. If some of my suggestions seem daring, they may at least provoke thought on a theme which has hardly been thought about at all. This theme is the rôle of the art of memory in the formation of imagery.

The age of scholasticism was one in which knowledge increased. It was also an age of Memory, and in the ages of Memory new imagery has to be created for remembering new knowledge. Though the great themes of Christian doctrine and moral teaching remained, of course, basically the same, they became more complicated. In particular the virtue-vice scheme grew much fuller and was more strictly defined and organised. The moral man who wished to choose the path of virtue, whilst also remembering and avoiding vice, had more to imprint on memory than in earlier simpler times.

The friars revived oratory in the form of preaching, and

---

[11] For example, H. Hajdu, *Das Mnemotechnische Schrifttum des Mittelalters*, Vienna, Amsterdam, Leipzig, 1936, pp. 68 ff.; Paolo Rossi, *Clavis Universalis*, Milan-Naples, 1960, pp. 12 ff. Rossi discusses Albertus and Thomas on memory in their *Summae* and in their Aristotle commentaries. His treatment is much the best hitherto available, but he does not examine the *imagines agentes* nor raise the question of how these were interpreted in the Middle Ages.

preaching was indeed the main object for which the Dominican Order, the Order of Preachers, was founded. Surely it would have been for remembering sermons, the mediaeval transformation of oratory, that the mediaeval transformation of the artificial memory would have been chiefly used.

The effort of Dominican learning in the reform of preaching is parallel to the great philosophical and theological effort of the Dominican schoolmen. The *Summae* of Albertus and Thomas provide the abstract philosophical and theological definitions, and in ethics the clear abstract statements, such as the divisions of the virtues and vices into their parts. But the preacher needed another type of *Summae* to help him, *Summae* of examples and similitudes[12] through which he could easily find corporeal forms in which to clothe the spiritual intentions which he wished to impress on the souls and memories of his hearers.

The main effort of this preaching was directed towards inculcating the articles of the Faith, together with a severe ethic in which virtue and vice are sharply outlined and polarised and enormous emphasis is laid on the rewards and punishments which await the one and the other in the hereafter.[13] Such was the nature of the 'things' which the orator-preacher would need to memorise.

The earlist known quotation of Thomas's memory rules is found in a summa of similitudes for the use of preachers. This is the *Summa de exemplis ac similitudinibus rerum* by Giovanni di San Gimignano, of the Order of Preachers, which was written early in the fourteenth century.[14] Though he does not mention Thomas by name, it is an abbreviated version of the Thomist memory rules which San Gimignano quotes.

> There are four things which help a man to remember well.
> The first is that he should dispose those things which he wishes to remember in a certain order.
> The second is that he should adhere to them with affection.

---

[12] Many such collections for the use of preachers were compiled; see J. T. Welter, *L'exemplum dans la littérature religieuse et didactique du Moyen Age*, Paris-Toulouse, 1927.

[13] See G. R. Owst, *Preaching in Mediaeval England*, Cambridge, 1926.

[14] See A. Dondaine, 'La vie et les œuvres de Jean de San Gimignano', *Archivum Fratrum Praedicatorum*, II (1939), p. 164. The work must be later than 1298 and is probably earlier than 1314. It was enormously popular (see *ibid.*, pp. 160 ff.).

The third is that he should reduce them to unusual similitudes.
The fourth is that he should repeat them with frequent meditation.[15]

We have to make clear to ourselves a distinction. In a sense, the
whole of San Gimignano's book with its painstaking provision of
similitudes for every 'thing' which the preacher might have to
treat is based on the memory principle. To make people remember
things, preach them to them in 'unusual' similitudes for these will
stick better in memory than the spiritual intentions will do, unless
clothed in such similitudes. Yet the similitude spoken in the
sermon is not strictly speaking the similitude used in artificial
memory. For the memory image is invisible, and remains hidden
within the memory of its user, where, however, it can become the
hidden generator of externalised imagery.

The next in date to quote the Thomist memory rules is Bartolomeo da San Concordio (1262–1347) who entered the Dominican
Order at an early age and spent most of his life at the convent in
Pisa. He is celebrated as the author of a legal compendium, but
what interests us here is his *Ammaestramenti degli antichi*,[16] or
'teachings of the ancients' about the moral life. It was written
early in the fourteenth century, before 1323.[17] Bartolomeo's
method is to make an improving statement and then support it with
a string of quotations from the ancients and the Fathers. Though
this gives a discursive, almost an early humanist, flavour to his
treatise, its groundwork is scholastic; Bartolomeo is moving among
the Aristotelian ethics guided by the ethic of Tullius in the *De
inventione* after the manner of Albertus and Thomas. Memory is
the subject of one set of quotations, and the art of memory of
another; and since the immediately following sections of the book
are recognisably concerned with *intelligentia* and *providentia*, it is
certainly of *memoria* as a part of Prudence that the devout Dominican author is thinking.

One gains the impression that this learned friar is close to the

[15] Giovanni di San Gimignano, *Summa de exemplis ac similitudinibus
rerum*, Lib. VI, cap. xlii.
[16] I have used the edition of Milan, 1808. The first edition was at
Florence in 1585. The edition of Florence, 1734, edited by D. M. Manni
of the Academia della Crusca, influenced later editions. See below, p. 88,
note 20.
[17] It could be almost exactly contemporary with San Gimignano's
Summa, and not later than that work.

well-head of an enthusiasm for artificial memory which is spreading through the Dominican Order. His eight rules for memory are mainly based on Thomas, and he is using both 'Tommaso nella seconda della seconda' (i.e. *Summa Theologiae*, II, II, 49) and 'Tommaso d'Aquino sopra il libro de memoria' (i.e. Thomas's commentary on the *De memoria et reminiscentia*). That he does not call him Saint Thomas is the evidence that the book was written before the canonisation in 1323. The following are Bartolomeo's rules which I translate, though leaving the sources in the original Italian:

> (On order).
> *Aristotile in libro memoria.* Those things are better remembered which have order in themselves. Upon which Thomas comments: Those things are more easily remembered which are well ordered, and those which are badly ordered we do not easily remember. Therefore those things which a man wishes to retain, let him study to set them in order.
> *Tommaso nella seconda della seconda.* It is necessary that those things which a man wishes to retain in memory he should consider how to set out in order, so that from the memory of one thing he comes to another.
> (On similitudes).
> *Tommaso nella seconda della seconda.* Of those things which a man wishes to remember, he should take convenient similitudes, not too common ones, for we wonder more at uncommon things and by them the mind is more strongly moved.
> *Tommaso quivi medesimo* (i.e. *loc. cit.*). The finding out of images is useful and necessary for memory; for pure and spiritual intentions slip out of memory unless they are as it were linked to corporeal similitudes.
> *Tullio nel terzo della nuova Rettorica.* Of those things which we wish to remember, we should place in certain places images and similitudes. And Tullius adds that the places are like tablets, or paper, and the images like letters, and placing the images is like writing, and speaking is like reading.[18]

Obviously, Bartolomeo is fully aware that Thomas's recommendation of order in memory is based on Aristotle, and that his recommendation of the use of similitudes and images is based on *Ad*

---

[18] Bartolomeo da San Concordio, *Ammaestramenti degli antichi*, IX, viii (*ed. cit.*, pp. 85–6).

Herennium, refered to as 'Tullius in the third book of the New Rhetoric'.

What are we, as devout readers of Bartolomeo's ethical work intended to do? It has been arranged in order with divisions and sub-divisions after the scholastic manner. Ought we not to act prudently by memorising in their order through the artificial memory the 'things' with which it deals, the spiritual intentions of seeking virtues and avoiding vices which it arouses? Should we not exercise our imaginations by forming corporeal similitudes of, for example, Justice and its sub-divisions, or of Prudence and her parts? And also of the 'things' to be avoided, such as Injustice, Inconstancy, and the other vices examined? The task will not be an easy one, for we live in new times when the old virtue-vice system has been complicated by the discovery of new teachings of the ancients. Yet surely it is our duty to remember these teachings by the ancient art of memory. Perhaps we shall also more easily remember the many quotations from ancients and Fathers by memorising these as written on or near the corporeal similitudes which we are forming in memory.

That Bartolomeo's collection of moral teachings of the ancients was regarded as eminently suitable for memorisation is confirmed by the fact that in two fifteenth-century codices[19] his work is associated with a 'Trattato della memoria artificiale'. This treatise passed into the printed editions of the *Ammaestramenti degli antichi* in which it was assumed to be by Bartolomeo himself.[20] This was an error for the 'Trattato della memoria artificiale' is not an original work but an Italian translation of the memory section of *Ad Herennium* which has been detached from the Italian translation of the rhetoric made, probably by Bono Giamboni, in the thirteenth century.[21] In this translation, known as the *Fiore di Rettorica*, the memory section was placed at the end of the work,

[19] J.I. 47 and Pal. 54, both in the Bibliotheca Nazionale at Florence. Cf. Rossi, *Clavis universalis*, pp. 16–17, 271–5.

[20] The first to print the 'Trattato della memoria artificiale' with the *Ammaestramenti* was Manni in his edition of 1734. Subsequent editors followed his error of assuming that the 'Trattato' is by Bartolomeo; it was printed after the *Ammaestramenti* in all later editions (in the edition of Milan, 1808, it is on pp. 343–56).

[21] The two rhetorics (*De inventione* and *Ad Herennium*) were amongst the earliest classical works to be translated into Italian. A free translation of the parts of the first Rhetoric (*De inventione*) was made by Dante's

and so was easily detachable. Possibly it was so placed through the influence of Boncompagno, who stated that memory did not belong to rhetoric alone but was useful for all subjects.[22] By placing the memory section at the end of the Italian translation of the rhetoric it became easily detachable, and applicable to other subjects, for example to ethics and the memorising of virtues and vices. The detached memory section of *Ad Herennium* in Giamboni's translation, circulating by itself,[23] is an ancestor of the separate *Ars memorativa* treatise.

A remarkable feature of the *Ammaestramenti degli antichi*, in view of its early date, is that it is in the vulgar tongue. Why did the learned Dominican present his semi-scholastic treatise on ethics in Italian ? Surely the reason must be that he was addressing himself to laymen, to devout persons ignorant of Latin who wanted to know about the moral teachings of the ancients, and not primarily to clerics. With this work in the *volgare* became associated Tullius on memory, also translated into the *volgare*.[24] This suggests that the artificial memory was coming out into the world, was being recommended to laymen as a devotional exercise. And this tallies

---

[22] This is my suggestion. It is however recognised that there is an influence of the Bolognese school of *dictamen* on the early translations of the rhetorics; see Maggini, *Op. cit.*, p. I.

[23] It is to be found by itself in the fifteenth-century Vatican manuscript Barb. Lat. 3929, f. 52, where a modern note wrongly attributes it to Brunetto Latini.

There is much confusion about Brunetto Latini and the translations of the rhetorics. The facts are that he made a free version of *De inventione* but did not translate *Ad Herennium*. But he certainly knew of the artificial memory to which he refers in the third book of the *Trésor*: 'memore artificiel que l'en aquiert par ensegnement des sages' (B. Latini, *Li Livres dou Tresor*, ed. F. J. Carmody, Berkeley, 1948, p. 321).

[24] This association is only found in two codices which are both of the fifteenth century. The earliest manuscript of the *Ammaestramenti* Bibl. Naz., II. II. 319, dated 1342) does not contain the 'Trattato'.

---

teacher, Brunetto Latini. A version of the Second Rhetoric (*Ad Herennium*) was made between 1254 and 1266 by Guidotto of Bologna, with the title *Fiore di Rettorica*. This version omits the section on memory. But another translation, also called *Fiore di Rettorica*, was made at about the same time by Bono Giamboni, and this does contain the memory section, placed at the end of the work.

On the Italian translations of the two rhetorics, see F. Maggini, *I primi volgarizzamenti dei classici latini*, Florence, 1952.

with the remark of Albertus, when he is concluding triumphantly in favour of the *Ars memorandi* of Tullius, that the artificial memory pertains both 'to the moral man and to the speaker'.[25] Not only the preacher was to use it but any 'moral man' who, impressed by the preaching of the friars, wished at all costs to avoid the vices which lead to Hell and to reach Heaven through the virtues.

Another ethical treatise which was certainly intended to be memorised by the artificial memory is also in Italian. This is the *Rosaio della vita*,[26] probably by Matteo de' Corsini and written in 1373. It opens with some rather curious mystico-astrological features but consists mainly of long lists of virtues and vices, with short definitions. It is a mixed collection of such 'things' from Aristotelian, Tullian, patristic, Scriptural, and other sources. I select a few at random—Wisdom, Prudence, Knowledge, Credulity, Friendship, Litigation, War, Peace, Pride, Vain Glory. An *Ars memorie artificialis* is provided to be used with it, opening with the words 'Now that we have provided the book to be read it remains to hold it in memory.'[27] The book provided is certainly the *Rosaio della vita* which is later mentioned by name in the text of the memory rules, and we thus have certain proof that the memory rules were here intended to be used for memorising lists of virtues and vices.

The *Ars memorie artificialis* provided for memorising the virtues and vices of the *Rosaio* is closely based on *Ad Herennium* but with expansions. The writer calls 'natural places' those which are memorised in the country, as trees in fields; 'artificial places' are those memorised in buildings, as a study, a window, a coffer, and the like.[28] This shows some real understanding of places as used in the mnemotechnic. But the technique would be being used with the moral and devotional purpose of memorising corporeal similitudes of virtues and vices on the places.

There is probably some connection between the *Rosaio* and the *Ammaestramenti degli antichi*; the former might almost be an

[25] See above, p. 67.

[26] A. Matteo de' Corsini, *Rosaio della vita*, ed. F. Polidori, Florence, 1845.

[27] The *Ars memorie artificialis* which is to be used for memorising the *Rosaio della vita* has been printed by Paolo Rossi, *Clavis universalis*, pp. 272–5.

[28] Rossi, *Clavis*, p. 272.

abridgement or a simplification of the latter. And the two works and the memory rules associated with them are found in the same two codices.[29]

These two ethical works in Italian, which we may envisage laymen labouring to memorise by the artificial memory, open up the possibility that tremendous efforts after the formation of imagery may have been going on in the imaginations and memories of many people. The artificial memory begins to appear as a lay devotional discipline, fostered and recommended by the friars. What galleries of unusual and striking similitudes for new and unusual virtues and vices, as well as for the well known ones, may have remained forever invisible within the memories of pious and possibly artistically gifted persons! The art of memory was a creator of imagery which must surely have flowed out into creative works of art and literature.

Though always bearing in mind that an externalised visual representation in art proper must be distinguished from the invisible pictures of memory—the mere fact of external representation so distinguishes it—it can be a new experience to look at some

[29] The contents of Pal. 54 and of J.1. 47 (which are identical, except that some works of St. Bernard are added at the end of J.1. 47) are as follows:—

(1) The *Rosaio della vita*.
(2) The *Ttattato della memoria artificiale* (that is, Bono Giamboni's translation of the memory section of *Ad Herennium*).
(3) The Life of Jacopone da Todi.
(4) The *Ammaestramenti degli antichi*.
(5) The *Ars memorie artificiali* beginning 'Poi che hauiamo fornito il libro di leggere resta di potere tenere a mente' and later mentioning the *Rosaio della vita* as the book to be remembered.

In other codices the *Rosaio della vita* is found with one or both of the two tracts on memory but without the *Ammaestramenti* (see for example Riccardiana 1157 and 1159).

Another work which may have been thought suitable for memorisation is the ethical section of Brunetto Latini's *Trésor*. The curious volume entitled *Ethica d'Aristotele, ridotta, in compendio da ser Brunetto Latini* published at Lyons by Jean de Tournes in 1568 was printed from an old manuscript volume, otherwise lost. It contains eight items amongst which are the following: (1) An *Ethica* which is the ethical section from the *Trésor* in Italian translation; (4) A fragment which appears to be an attempt to put the vices with which the *Ethica* ends into images; (7) The *Fiore di Rettorica*, i.e., Bono Giamboni's translation of *Ad Herennium*, with the memory section at the end, in a very corrupt version.

early fourteenth-century works of art from the point of view of memory. See for example the row of virtuous figures (Pl. 2) in Lorenzetti's presentation of Good and Bad Government (commissioned between 1337 and 1340) in the Palazzo Communale at Siena.[30] On the left sits Justice, with secondary figures illustrating her 'parts', after the manner of a composite memory, image. On the couch, to the right, sits Peace (and Fortitude, Prudence, Magnanimity, Temperance, not here reproduced). On the bad side of the series (not here reproduced), with the diabolical horned figure of Tyranny, sit the hideous forms of tyrannical vices, whilst War, Avarice, Pride, and Vain Glory hover like bats over the grotesque and dreadful crew.

Such images, of course, have most complex derivations, and such a picture can be studied in many ways, by iconographers, historians, art historians. I would tentatively suggest yet another approach. There is an argument behind this picture about Justice and Injustice, the themes of which are set out in order and clothed in corporeal similitudes. Does it not gain in meaning after our attempts to imagine the efforts of Thomist artificial memory to form corporeal similitudes for the moral 'teachings of the ancients'? Can we see in these great monumental figures a striving to regain the forms of classical memory, of those *imagines agentes*—remarkably beautiful, crowned, richly dressed, or remarkably hideous and grotesque—moralised by the Middle Ages into virtues and vices, into similitudes expressive of spiritual intentions?

With yet greater daring, I now invite the reader to look with the eyes of memory at those figures sacred to art historians, Giotto's virtues and vices (probably painted about 1306) in the Arena Capella at Padua (Pl. 3). These figures are justly famous for the variety and animation introduced into them by the great artist, and for the way in which they stand out from their backgrounds, giving an illusion of depth on a flat surface which was altogether new. I would suggest that both features may owe something to memory.

The effort to form similitudes in memory encouraged variety and individual invention, for did not Tullius say that everyone must form his memory images for himself? In a renewed return to the text of `Ad Herennium` aroused by the scholastic insistence on

[30] On the iconography of this picture, see N. Rubinstein, 'Political Ideas in Sienese Art', *Journal of the Warburg and Courtauld Institutes*, XXI (1958), pp. 198–227.

artificial memory, the dramatic character of the images recommended would appeal to an artist of genius, and this is what Giotto shows so brilliantly in, for example, the movement of Charity (Pl. 3a), with her attractive beauty, or in the frenzied gestures of Inconstancy. Nor has the grotesque and the absurd as useful in a memory image been neglected in Envy (Pl. 3b) and Folly. And the illusion of depth depends on the intense care with which the images have been placed on their backgrounds, or, speaking mnemonically, on their *loci*. One of the most striking features of classical memories as revealed in *Ad Herennium* is the sense of space, depth, lighting in the memory suggested by the place rules; and the care taken to make the images stand out clearly on the *loci*, for example in the injunction that places must not be too dark, or the images will be obscured, nor too light lest the dazzle confuse the images. It is true that Giotto's images are regularly placed on the walls, not irregularly as the classical directions advise. But the Thomist emphasis on regular order in memory had modified that rule. And Giotto has interpreted the advice about variety in *loci* in his own way, by making all the painted backgrounds of the pictures different from one another. He has, I would suggest, made a supreme effort to make the images stand out against the carefully variegated *loci*, believing that in so doing he is following classical advice for making memorable images.

WE MUST ASSIDUOUSLY REMEMBER THE INVISIBLE JOYS OF PARADISE AND THE ETERNAL TORMENTS OF HELL, says Boncompagno with terrible emphasis in the memory section of his rhetoric, giving lists of virtues and vices as 'memorial notes . . . through which we may frequently direct ourselves in the paths of remembrance'.[31] The side walls of the Arena Capella on which the virtues and vices are painted frame the Last Judgment on the end wall which dominates the little building. In the intense atmosphere aroused by the friars and their preaching, in which Giotto was saturated, the images of the virtues and vices take on an intense significance, and to remember them, and to take warning by them in time, is a matter of life and death importance. Hence the need to make truly memorable images of them in accordance with the rules of artificial memory. Or rather, the need to make truly memorable corporeal similitudes of them infused with spiritual intentions, in accordance

[31] See above, p. 59

with the purpose of artificial memory as interpreted by Thomas Aquinas.

The new variety and animation of Giotto's images, the new way in which they stand out from their backgrounds, their new spiritual intensity—all these brilliant and original features could have been stimulated by the influences of scholastic artificial memory and its powerful recommendation as a part of Prudence.

That the remembering of Paradise and Hell, such as Boncompagno emphasised under memory, lay behind the scholastic interpretation of artificial memory is indicated by the fact that later memory treatises in the scholastic tradition usually include remembering Paradise and Hell, frequently with diagrams of those places, as belonging to artificial memory. We shall meet examples of this in the next chapter where some of the diagrams are reproduced.[32] I mention here, however, because of their bearing on the period under discussion, the remarks of the German Dominican Johannes Romberch, on this subject. As already mentioned, Romberch's memory rules are based on those of Thomas Aquinas and as a Dominican he was naturally in the Thomist memory tradition.

In his *Congestorium artificiose memorie* (first edition in 1520), Romberch introduces remembering Paradise, Purgatory, and Hell. Hell, he says, is divided into many places which we remember with inscriptions on them.

> And since the orthodox religion holds that the punishments of sins are in accordance with the nature of the crimes, here the Proud are crucified . . . there the Greedy, the Avaricious, the Angry, the Slothful, the Envious, the Luxurious (are punished) with sulphur, fire, pitch, and that kind of punishments.[33]

This introduces the novel idea that the places of Hell, varied in accordance with the nature of the sins punished in them, could be regarded as variegated memory *loci*. And the striking images on those places would be, of course, the images of the damned. We may now look with the eyes of memory at the fourteenth-century painting of Hell in the Dominican church of Santa Maria Novella (Pl. 8a). Hell is divided into places with inscriptions on them

[32] See below, pp. 108–11, 115–16, 122 (Pl. 7).
[33] Johannes Romberch, *Congestorium artificiose memorie*, ed. of Venice, 1533, p. 18.

(just as Romberch recommends) stating the sins being punished in each, and containing the images to be expected in such places. If we were to reflect this picture in memory, as a prudent reminder, should we be practising what the Middle Ages would call artificial memory? I believe so.

When Ludovico Dolce made an Italian translation (published in 1562) of Romberch's treatise, he made a slight expansion of the text at the point where Romberch is treating of the places of Hell, as follows:

> For this (that is for remembering the places of Hell) the ingenious invention of Virgil AND DANTE will help us much. That is for distinguishing the punishments according to the nature of the sins. Exactly.[34]

That Dante's *Inferno* could be regarded as a kind of memory system for memorising, Hell and its punishments with striking images on orders of places, will come as a great shock, and I must leave it as a shock. It would take a whole book to work out the implications of such an approach to Dante's poem. It is by no means a crude approach, nor an impossible one. If one thinks of the poem as based on orders of places in Hell, Purgatory, and Paradise, and as a cosmic order of places in which the spheres of Hell are the spheres of Heaven in reverse, it begins to appear as a summa of similitudes and exempla, ranged in order and set out upon the universe. And if one discovers that Prudence, under many diverse similitudes, is a leading symbolic theme of the poem,[35] its three parts can be seen as *memoria*, remembering vices and their punishments in Hell, *intelligentia*, the use of the present for penitence and acquisition of virtue, and *providentia*, the looking forward to Heaven. In this interpretation, the principles of artificial memory, as understood in the Middle Ages, would stimulate the intense visualisation of many similitudes in the intense effort to hold in memory the scheme of salvation, and the complex network of virtues and vices and their rewards and punishments—the effect of a prudent man who uses memory as a part of Prudence.

---

[34] L. Dolce, *Dialogo nel quale si ragiona del modo di accrescere et conservar la memoria* (first edition 1562), ed. of Venice, 1586, p. 15 *verso*.

[35] This can be worked out from the similitudes of Prudence given in San Gimignano's *Summa*. I hope to publish a study of this work as a guide to the imagery of the *Divine Comedy*.

The *Divine Comedy* would thus become the supreme example of the conversion of an abstract summa into a summa of similitudes and examples, with Memory as the converting power, the bridge between the abstraction and the image. But the other reason for the use of corporeal similitudes given by Thomas Aquinas in the *Summa*, besides their use in memory, would also come into play, namely that the Scriptures use poetic metaphors and speak of spiritual things under the similitudes of corporeal things. If one were to think of the Dantesque art of memory as a mystical art, attached to a mystical rhetoric, the images of Tullius would turn into poetic metaphors for spiritual things. Boncompagno, it may be recalled, stated in his mystical rhetoric that metaphor was invented in the Earthly Paradise.

These suggestions as to how the cultivation of images in devout uses of the art of memory could have stimulated creative works of art and literature still leave unexplained how the mediaeval art could be used as a mnemonic in a more normal sense of the word. How, for example, did the preacher memorise the points of a sermon through it? Or how did a scholar memorise through it texts which he desired to hold in memory? An approach to this problem has been provided by Beryl Smalley in her study of English friars in the fourteenth century,[36] in which she draws attention to a curious feature in the works of John Ridevall (Franciscan) and Robert Holcot (Dominican), namely their descriptions of elaborate 'pictures' which were not intended to be represented but which they were using for purposes of memorisation. These invisible 'pictures' provide us with specimens of invisible memory images, held within the memory, not intended to be externalised, and being used for quite practical mnemonic purposes.

For example, Ridevall describes the image of a prostitute, blind, with mutilated ears, proclaimed by a trumpet (as a criminal), with a deformed face, and full of disease.[37] He calls this 'the picture of Idolatry according to the poets'. No source is known for such an image and Miss Smalley suggests that Ridevall invented it. No doubt he did, as a memory image which follows the rules in being strikingly hideous and horrible and which is being used to

[36] Beryl Smalley, *English Friars and Antiquity in the Early Fourteenth Century*, Oxford, 1960.
[37] Smalley, *English Friars*, pp. 114–15.

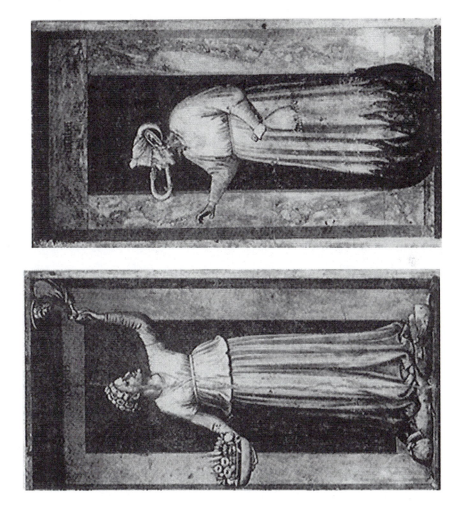

3a LEFT Charity
3b RIGHT Envy
Frescoes by Giotto, Arena
Capella, Padua (pp. 92-4)

remind of points about the sin of Idolatry; which is painted as a harlot because idolaters leave the true God to fornicate with idols; who is shown as blind and deaf because she sprang from flattery which blinds and deafens its objects; who is proclaimed as a criminal because evil doers hope to obtain forgiveness by worshipping idols; who has a sad and disfigured face because one of the causes of idolatry is inordinate grief; who is diseased because idolatry is a kind of unregulated love. A mnemonic verse sums up the features of the image:

> Mulier notata, oculis orbata,
> aure mutilata, cornu ventilata,
> vultu deformata et morbo vexata.

This seems unmistakably identifiable as a memory image, designed to stir memory by its strikingness, not intended to be represented save invisibly in memory (the memorisation of it being helped by the mnemonic verse), used for the genuine mnemonic purpose of reminding of the points of a sermon about idolatry.

The 'picture' of idolatry comes in the introduction to Ridevall's *Fulgentius metaforalis*, a moralisation of the mythology of Fulgentius designed for the use of preachers.[38] This work is very well known, but I wonder whether we have fully understood how the preachers were to use these unillustrated 'pictures'[39] of the pagan gods. That they belong within the sphere of mediaeval artificial memory is strongly suggested by the fact that the first image to be described, that of Saturn, is said to represent the virtue of Prudence, and he is soon followed by Juno as *memoria*, Neptune as *intelligentia*, and Pluto as *providentia*. We have been thoroughly trained to understand that memory as a part of Prudence justifies the use of the artificial memory as an ethical duty. We have been taught by Albertus Magnus that poetic metaphors, including the fables of the pagan gods, may be used in memory for their 'moving' power.[40] Ridevall is, it may be suggested, instructing the preacher

---

[38] J. Ridevall, *Fulgentius Metaforalis*, ed. H. Liebeschütz, Leipzig, 1926. Cf. J. Seznec, *The Survival of the Pagan Gods*, trans. B. Sessions, Bollingen Series, 1953, pp. 94–5.

[39] Though the work was eventually illustrated (see Seznec, Pl. 30) this was not originally intended (see Smalley, pp. 121–3).

[40] See above, p. 66.

4a Temperance, Prudence   4b Justice, Fortitude
From a Fourteenth-Century Italian manuscript, Vienna National
Library (MS. 2639) (pp. 99-100).

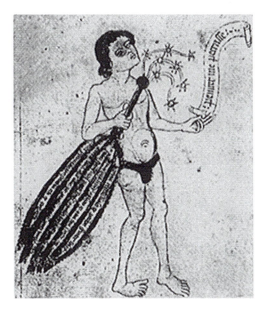

4c Penance
From a Fifteenth-Century
German manuscript,
Biblioteca Casanatense,
Rome (MS. 1404) (p. 98)

how to use 'moving' inner memory images of the gods to memorise a sermon on the virtues and their parts. Each image, like the one of Idolatry, has attributes and characteristics, carefully described and memorised in a mnemonic verse, which serve to illustrate—or rather, as I think, to memorise—points in a discourse on the virtue concerned.

Holcot's *Moralitates* are a collection of material for the use of preachers in which the 'picture' technique is lavishly used. Efforts to find the sources of these 'pictures' have failed, and no wonder, for it is clear that, as in the case of Ridevall's similar efforts, they are invented memory images. Holcot often gives them what Miss Smalley calls a 'sham antique' flavour, as in the 'picture' of Penance.

> The likeness of Penance, which the priests of the goddess Vesta painted, according to Remigius. Penance used to be painted in the form of a man, his whole body naked, who held a five-thonged scourge in his hand. Five verses or sentences were written on it.[41]

The inscriptions about Penance on the five-thonged scourge are then given, and this use of inscriptions on, and surrounding, his images is characteristic of Holcot's method. The 'picture' of Friendship, for example, a youth strikingly attired in green, has inscriptions about Friendship on it and around it.[42]

None of the numerous manuscripts of the *Moralitates* are illustrated; the 'pictures' which they describe were not meant for external representation; they were invisible memory images. However, Saxl did find some representations of Holcot's images in two fifteenth-century manuscripts, including a representation of his 'Penance' (Pl. 4c).[43] When we see the man with the scourge with the inscriptions on it, we recognise the technique of an image with writing on it as something fairly normal in mediaeval manuscripts. But the point is that we ought not to be seeing this image represented. It was an invisible memory image. And this suggests to me that the memorising of words or sentences as placed or written on the memory images was perhaps what the Middle Ages understood by 'memory for words'.

[41] Smalley, p. 165.
[42] *Ibid.*, pp. 174, 178–80.
[43] F. Saxl, 'A Spiritual Encyclopaedia of the Later Middle Ages', *Journal of the Warburg and Courtauld Institutes*, V (1942), p. 102, Pl. 23a.

Another very curious use of memory images is described by Holcot. He places such images, in imagination, on the pages of a Scriptural text, to remind him of how he will comment on the text. On a page of the prophet Hosea he imagines the figure of Idolatry (which he has borrowed from Ridevall) to remind him of how he will expand Hosea's mention of that sin.[44] He even places on the text of the prophet an image of Cupid, complete with bow and arrows![45] The god of love and his attributes are, of course, moralised by the friar, and the 'moving' pagan image is used as a memory image for his moralising expansion of the text.

The preference of these English friars for the fables of the poets as memory images, as allowed by Albertus Magnus, suggests that the artificial memory may be a hitherto unsuspected medium through which pagan imagery survived in the Middle Ages.

Though directions for placing a memory 'picture' on a text are given, these friars do not seem to indicate how their composite memory images for remembering sermons are to be placed. As I have suggested earlier, the Middle Ages seem to have modified the 'Ad Herennian' place rules. The emphasis of the Thomist rules is on order, and this order is really the order of the argument. Provided the material has been placed in order, it is to be memorised in this order through orders of similitudes. To recognise Thomist artificial memory, therefore, we do not necessarily have to seek for figures on places differentiated after the classical manner; such figures can be on a regular order of places.

An Italian illustrated manuscript of the early fourteenth century shows representations of the three theological and the four cardinal virtues seated in a row; also the figures of the seven liberal arts similarly seated.[46] The victorious virtues are shown as dominating

[44] Smalley, pp. 173–4.
[45] *Ibid.*, p. 172.
[46] Vienna National Library, ms. 2639, f. 33 *recto* and *verso*. For a discussion of these miniatures, which may reflect a lost fresco at Padua, see Julius von Schlosser, 'Giusto's Fresken in Padua und die Vorläufen der Stanza della Segnatura', *Jahrbuch der Kunsthistorischen Sammlungen der Allerhöchsten Kaiserhauses*, XVII (1896), pp. 19 ff. They are related to those illustrating a mnemonic poem on the virtues and the liberal arts in a manuscript at Chantilly (see L. Dorez, *La canzone delle virtu e delle scienze*, Bergamo, 1894). There is another copy of them in Bibl. Naz., Florence, II, I, 27.

the vices, which crouch before them. The liberal arts have representatives of those arts seated before them. As Schlosser has pointed out, these seated figures of virtues and liberal arts are reminiscent of the row of theological disciplines and liberal arts in the glorification of St. Thomas in the fresco of the Chapter House of Santa Maria Novella (Pl. 1). Reproduced here (Pl. 4a, b) are the figures of the four cardinal virtues as shown in this manuscript. Someone has been using these figures to memorise the parts of the virtues as defined in the *Summa Theologiae*.[47] Prudence holds a circle, symbol of time, within which are written the eight parts of this virtue as defined by Thomas Aquinas. Besides Temperance is a complicated tree on which are written the parts of Temperance as set out in the *Summa*. The parts of Fortitude are written on her castle and the book which Justice holds contains definitions of that virtue. The figures and their attributes have been elaborated in order to hold—or to memorise—all this complicated material.

The iconographer will see in these miniatures many of the normal attributes of the virtues. The art historian puzzles over their possible reflection of a lost fresco at Padua and over the relationship which they seem to have to the row of figures symbolising theological disciplines and liberal arts in the glorification of St. Thomas in the Chapter House of Santa Maria Novella. I invite the reader to look at them as *imagines agentes*, active and striking, richly dressed and crowned. The crowns symbolise, of course, the victory of the virtues over the vices, but these enormous crowns are surely also rather memorable. And when we see that sections on the virtues of the *Summa Theologiae* are being memorised through the inscriptions (as Holcot memorised the sentences about Penance on the scourge of his memory image) we ask ourselves whether these figures are something like Thomist artificial memory—or as close to it as an external representation can be to an inner invisible and personal art.

Orders of figures expressive of the classifications of the *Summa* and of the whole mediaeval encyclopaedia of knowledge (the liberal arts, for example) ranged in order in a vast memory and having written on them the material relating to them, might be the foundation of some phenomenal memory. The method would be not unlike that of Metrodorus of Scepsis who is said to have written

[47] Schlosser points out (p. 20) that the inscriptions on the figures record the parts of the virtues as defined in the *Summa*.

on the order of the images of the zodiac all that he wanted to remember. Such images would be both artistically potent corporeal similitudes arousing spiritual intentions, and yet also genuinely mnemonic images, used by a genius with an astounding natural memory and intense powers of inner visualisation. Other techniques more closely approximating to the memorising of differentiated places in buildings may also have been used in combination with this method. But one is inclined to think that the basic Thomist method may have been orders of images with inscriptions on them memorised in the order of the carefully articulated argument.[48]

So might the vast inner memory cathedrals of the Middle Ages have been built.

Petrarch is surely the person with whom we should expect a transition from mediaeval to Renaissance memory to begin. And the name of Petrarch was constantly cited in the memory tradition as that of an important authority on the artificial memory. It is not surprising that Romberch, the Dominican, should cite in his memory treatise the rules and formulations of Thomas; but what does surprise us is that he should also mention Petrarch as an authority, sometimes in association with Thomas. When discussing the rules for places, Romberch states that Petrarch has warned that no perturbation must disturb the order of the places. To the rule that places must not be too large nor too small, but proportionate to the image which they are to contain, it is added that Petrarch 'who is imitated by many' has said that places should be of medium size.[49] And on the question of how many places we should employ, it is stated that:

> Divus Aquinas counsels the use of many places in II, II, 49, whom many afterwards followed, for example Franciscus Petrarcha . . .[50]

This is very curious, for Thomas says nothing about how many places we should use in II, II, 49. and, further, there is no extant work by Petrarch giving rules for the artificial memory with the detailed advice about places which Romberch attributes to him.

Perhaps through the influence of Romberch's book, Petrarch's

[48] See further below, pp. 120–1.
[49] Romberch, *Congestorium,* pp. 27 *verso*–28.
[50] *Ibid.,* pp. 19 *verso*–20.

name is continually repeated in sixteenth-century memory treatises. Gesualdo speaks of 'Petrarch whom Romberch follows on memory'.[51] Garzoni includes Petrarch among the famous 'Professors of Memory'.[52] Henry Cornelius Agrippa after giving the classical sources for the art of memory, mentions as the first of the modern authorities, Petrarch.[53] In the early seventeenth century, Lambert Schenkel states that the art of memory was 'avidly revived' and 'diligently cultivated' by Petrarch.[54] And the name of Petrarch is even mentioned in the article on Memory in Diderot's Encyclopaedia.[55]

There must therefore have been a side of Petrarch for which he was admired in the ages of memory but which has been totally forgotten by modern Petrarchan scholars—a situation parallel to the modern neglect of Thomas on memory. What was the source in Petrarch's works which gave rise to this tenacious tradition? It is, of course, possible that Petrarch wrote some *Ars memorativa* treatise which has not come down to us. It is not, however, necessary to suppose this. The source is to be found in one of Petrarch's extant works which we have not read, understood, and memorised as we ought to have done.

Petrarch wrote a book called 'Things to be Remembered' (*Rerum memorandarum libri*), probably about 1343 to 1345. This title is suggestive, and when it transpires that the chief of the 'things' to be remembered is the virtue of Prudence under her three parts of *memoria, intelligentia, providentia,* the student of artificial memory knows that he is on familiar ground. The plan of the work, only a fraction of which was executed, is based on the definitions in Cicero's *De inventione* of Prudence, Justice, Fortitude, and Temperance.[56] It opens with 'preludes to virtue', which are leisure, solitude, study, and doctrine. Then comes Prudence and her parts, beginning with *memoria*. The sections on Justice and Fortitude are missing, or were never written; of the section on

[51] Gesualdo, *Plutosofia*, p. 14.
[52] Garzoni, *Piazza universale*, Discorso LX.
[53] H. C. Agrippa, *De vanitate scientiarum*, 1530, cap. X, 'De arte memorativa'.
[54] Lambert Schenkel, *Gazophylacium*, Strasburg, 1610, p. 27.
[55] In Diodati's note to the entry 'Mémoire' in the edition of Lucca, 1767, X, p. 263. See Rossi, *Clavis*, p. 294.
[56] F. Petrarca, *Rerum memorandarum libri*, ed. G. Billanovich, Florence, 1943, Introduction, pp. cxxiv–cxxx.

Temperance, only a fragment of one of its parts appears. The books on the virtues would probably have been followed by books on the vices.

It has, I believe, never been noticed that there is a strong resemblance between this work and Bartolomeo de San Concordio's 'Teachings of the Ancients'. The *Ammaestramenti degli antichi* begins with exactly the same 'preludes to virtue', then reviews the Ciceronian virtues in a discursive and expanded manner, then comes to the vices. This would have been the plan of Petrarch's book, had he completed it.

There is an even more significant resemblance—namely that both Bartolomeo and Petrarch refer under *memoria* to the artificial memory. Bartolomeo, as we saw, gave the Thomist memory rules under that heading. Petrarch makes his allusions to the art by introducing examples of men of antiquity famed for good memories and associating these with the classical art. His paragraph on the memories of Lucullus and Hortensius begins thus:—'Memory is of two kinds, one for things, one for words.'[57] He tells of how the elder Seneca could recite backwards and repeats from Seneca the statement that the memory of Latro Portius was 'good both by nature and by art'.[58] And of the memory of Themistocles he repeats the story told by Cicero in *De oratore* of how Themistocles refused to learn the 'artificial memory' because his natural memory was so good.[59] Petrarch would of course have known that Cicero in this work does not approve the attitude of Themistocles, and describes how he himself uses the artificial memory.

I suggest that these references to artificial memory in a work in which the parts of Prudence and other virtues are the 'things to be remembered' would be enough to class Petrarch as belonging to the memory tradition,[60] and to class the *Rerum memorandarum libri* as an ethical treatise designed for memorisation, like the *Ammaestramenti degli antichi*. And this is probably what Petrarch himself intended. In spite of the humanist flavour of the work, and the use of *De oratore* rather than solely *Ad Herennium* on the artificial memory, Petrarch's book comes straight out of scholasticism with its pious use of artificial memory as a part of Prudence.

---

[57] *Ibid.*, p. 44.   [58] *Ibid.*, p. 45.   [59] *Ibid.*, p. 60.

[60] Though the *Rerum memorandarum libri* is the most obvious of Petrarch's works to be interpreted as referring to artificial memory, it is possible that others were so interpreted.

What were they like, the corporeal similitudes, the invisible 'pictures' which Petrarch would have placed in memory for Prudence and her parts? If, with his intense devotion to the ancients he chose pagan images to use in memory, images which would 'move' him strongly because of his classical enthusiasms, he would have had behind him the authority of Albertus Magnus.

One wonders whether the virtues rode through Petrarch's memory in chariots, with the famous 'examples' of them marching in their train as in the *Trionfi*.

The attempt made in this chapter to evoke mediaeval memory can be, as I said at the beginning, but partial and inconclusive, consisting of hints for further exploration by others of an immense subject rather than in any sense a final treatment. My theme has been the art of memory in relation to the formation of imagery. This inner art which encouraged the use of the imagination as a duty must surely have been a major factor in the evocation of images. Can memory be one possible explanation of the mediaeval love of the grotesque, the idiosyncratic? Are the strange figures to be seen on the pages of manuscripts and in all forms of mediaeval art not so much the revelation of a tortured psychology as evidence that the Middle Ages, when men had to remember, followed classical rules for making memorable images? Is the proliferation of new imagery in the thirteenth and fourteenth centuries related to the renewed emphasis on memory by the scholastics? I have tried to suggest that this is almost certainly the case. That the historian of the art of memory cannot avoid Giotto, Dante, and Petrarch is surely evidence of the extreme importance of this ubject.

From the point of view of this book, which is mainly concerned with the later history of the art, it is fundamental to emphasise that the art of memory came out of the Middle Ages. Its profoundest roots were in a most venerable past. From those deep and mysterious origins it flowed on into later centuries, bearing the stamp of religious fervour strangely combined with mnemotechnical detail which was set upon it in the Middle Ages.

Chapter V

THE MEMORY TREATISES

FOR the period with which the last two chapters have been concerned the actual material on the artificial memory is scanty. For the period on which we are now entering, the fifteenth and sixteenth centuries, the contrary is the case. The material becomes too abundant and selection has to be made from the great mass of the memory treatises[1] if our story is not to be overwhelmed in too much detail.

Of the manuscripts of *Ars memorativa* treatises which I have seen, and I have examined a good many in libraries in Italy, France, and England, none is earlier than the fifteenth century. Some of these may, of course, be copies of earlier originals. For example, the treatise attributed to Thomas Bradwardine, Archbishop of Canterbury, of which two fifteenth-century copies exist,[2] must have been written in the fourteenth century, since Bradwardine died in

---

[1] The main modern works in which material on the memory treatises will be found are: H. Hajdu, *Das Mnemtechnische Schrifftum des Mittelalters*, Vienna, 1936; Ludwig Volkmann, 'Ars Memorativa', *Jahrbuch der Kunsthistorischen Sammlungen in Wien*, N. F., Sonderheft 30, Vienna, 1929, pp. 111–203 (the only illustrated work on the subject); Paolo Rossi, 'Immagini e memoria locale nei secoli XIV e XV', *Rivista critica di storia della filosofia*, Facs. II (1958), pp. 149–191, and 'La costruzione delle immagini nei trattati di memoria artificiale del Rinascimento', in *Umanesimo e Simbolismo*, ed. E. Castelli, Padua, 1958, pp. 161–78 (both these articles publish in appendices some manuscript *Ars memorativa* treatises); Paolo Rossi, *Clavis universalis*, Milan, 1960 (also prints manuscript *Ars memorativa* treatises in appendices and in quotations in the text).

[2] British Museum, Sloane 3744, ff. 7 *verso*–9 *recto*; Fitzwilliam Museum, Cambridge, McClean Ms. 169, ff. 254–6.

1349. In 1482, the first of the printed memory treatises appears, inaugurating what was to be a popular genre throughout the sixteenth and early seventeenth centuries. Practically all memory treatises, whether manuscript or printed, follow the 'Ad Herennian' plan, rules for places, rules for images, and so on. The problem is to decide how the rules are being interpreted.

In treatises which are in the main line of descent from the scholastic tradition, the interpretations of artificial memory studied in the last chapter survive. Such treatises also describe mnemotechnic techniques of a classical character which are more mechanical than the use of the 'corporeal similitudes' and which, almost certainly, also go back to earlier mediaeval roots. Besides the types of memory treatises in the main line of descent from the scholastic tradition, there are other types, possibly having a different provenance. Finally, the memory tradition in this period undergoes changes, due to the influence of humanism and the development of Renaissance types of memory.

The subject is therefore a very involved one, the problems of which cannot be finally sorted out until full collection and systematic examination of all the material has been made. My purpose in this chapter is to suggest the complexity of the memory tradition, and to draw out from it certain themes, both of survival and change, which seem to me important.

One type of memory treatise may be called the 'Democritus' type from the peculiarity that such treatises assign the invention of the art of memory to Democritus and not to Simonides. In their rules for images, such treatises do not mention the striking human figures of *Ad Herennium* but concentrate on Aristotelian laws of association. Nor do they usually mention Thomas Aquinas nor quote the Thomist formulations of the rules. A good example of this type is the one by Lodovico da Pirano,[3] a Franciscan, who was teaching at Padua from about 1422 and had some knowledge of

[3] Lodovico da Pirano's treatise has been printed, with an introduction, by Baccio Ziliotto, 'Frate Lodovico da Pirano e le sue *regulae memoriae artificialis*', *Atti e memorie della società istriana di archeologia e storia patria*, XLIX, (1937), pp. 189–224. Ziliotto prints the treatise from the version in Marciana, VI, 274, which does not contain the curious diagrams of the rows of towers to be used for 'multiplication of places' which is given in other manuscripts of the treatise, for example in Marciana, XIV, 292, ff. 182 ff., and in the Vatican manuscript Lat. 5347, ff. 1 ff. Only Marciana VI, 274 names Lodovico da Pirano as the author. Cf. F. Tocco,

Greek. A possible source for the deviations from the main medi-aeval tradition of the Democritus type of treatise—I put this forward only as a hypothesis—might be the influx of Byzantine influence in the fifteenth century. The artificial memory was certainly known in Byzantium,[4] where it might have been in touch with Greek traditions lost in the West. Whatever its sources may be, the teachings of the 'Democritus' type of treatise become merged with other types in the general agglomeration of the memory tradition.

A feature of earlier treatises is long lists of objects, often begin-ning with a 'paternoster' and followed by familiar objects, such as an anvil, a helmet, a lantern, a tripod, and so on. One such list is given by Lodovico da Pirano and they are to be found in the type of treatise with the incipit 'Ars memorie artificialis, pater reuerende' of which there are many copies.[5] The reverend father addressed is advised to use such objects in the artificial memory. They are, I believe, as it were prefabricated memory images to be memorised on sets of places. This is almost certainly an old mediaeval tradition for similar miscellanies of objects, said to be useful in memory, are given by Boncompagno in the thirteenth century.[6] One can see such images in action in the illustrations to Romberch's book, showing an abbey and its associated buildings (Pl. 5a) and sets of objects to be memorised in the courtyard, library, and chapel of the abbey

[4] A Greek translation of the memory section of *Ad Herennium* exists, made perhaps by Maximus Planudes (early fourteenth century) or by Theodore of Gaza (fifteenth century). See H. Caplan's introduction to the Loeb edition of *Ad Herennium*, p. xxvi.

[5] Place and image rules from a 'pater reuerende' treatise are quoted by Rossi, *Clavis*, pp. 22–3. The image rules emphasise that images must be like people we know. Rossi does not quote the lists of memory objects, a typical example of which is, however, to be found in Pirano's treatise, printed by Ziliotto in the article cited. Several other manuscripts contain-ing the 'Pater reuerende' treatise might be added to those mentioned in Rossi's note (*Clavis*, p. 22).

[6] Boncompagno, *Rhetorica Novissima*, ed. A. Gaudentio, *Bibliotheca Iuridica Medii Aevi*, 11, Bologna, 1891, pp. 277–8.

Le opere latine di Giordano Bruno, Florence, 1889, pp. 28 ff.; Rossi, *Clavis*, pp. 31–2.

Another treatise which mentions Democritus is the one by Luca Braga, written at Padua in 1477, of which there is a copy in the British Museum, Additional 10,438, ff. 19 ff. Braga does, however, also mention Simonides and Thomas Aquinas.

(Pl. 5b). Each fifth place is marked with a hand and each tenth place with a cross, in accordance with the instructions given in *Ad Herennium* for distinguishing the fifth and tenth places. Obviously there is an association here with the five fingers. As Memory moved along the places, these were ticked off on the fingers.

Romberch is fully in the scholastic tradition in his theory of images as 'corporeal similitudes'. That he includes in his treatise this more mechanical type of memorising, with memory objects as images, suggests that this was in use in earlier times, and understood as artificial memory as well as the loftier types which used the spiritualised human images. What Romberch describes as being practised in the abbey is a fully classical and mnemotechnical, use of the art, though probably mainly used for religious purposes, possibly for memorising the repetition of psalms or prayers.

Amongst manuscript treatises which are in the scholastic tradition, are those by Jacopo Ragone,[7] and by Matthew of Verona,[8] a Dominican. An anonymous treatise,[9] probably also by a Dominican, gives a most solemn description of how to remember the whole order of the universe and the roads to Heaven and Hell by the artificial memory.[10] Parts of this treatise are almost identical with similar matters given by Romberch, the Dominican, in his printed treatise. Such printed treatises came out of a manuscript tradition leading back into the Middle Ages.

It is rare for a memory treatise, either manuscript or printed, to give an illustration of a human figure used as a memory image. This would be, of course, in accordance with the precepts of the

[7] On Ragone's treatise see Rossi, *Clavis*, pp. 19–22, and the article by M. P. Sheridan, 'Jacopo Ragone and his Rules for Artificial Memory', in *Manuscripta* (published by St. Louis University Library), 1960, pp. 131 ff. The copy of Ragone's treatise in the British Museum (Additional, 10,438) contains a drawing of a palazzo which is to be used for forming memory places.

[8] Marciana, XIV, 292, ff. 195 *recto–209 recto*.

[9] Marciana VI, 238, ff. 1 ff. 'De memoria artificiali'. This important and interesting treatise may be earlier than the fifteenth century, the date of this copy. The writer is emphatic that the art is to be used for devout meditations and spiritual consolations; he will use, he says, in his art only 'devout images' and 'sacred histories' not fables or 'vana phantasmata' (f. 1 *recto* ff.). He seems to regard images of saints with their attributes as memory images to be memorised by the devout on memory *loci* (f. 7 *verso*).

[10] *Ibid.*, f. 1 *recto* ff.

author of *Ad Herennium* who tells the student that he must form his own images. An exception to this is the crude attempt in a Vienna manuscript of the mid-fifteenth century[11] to depict a row of memory images. Volkmann has reproduced these figures without attempting to explain what they mean or how they are being used, except that they are 'artificial memory'. This is indeed proved by the inscription on the last figure: 'Ex locis et imaginibus ars memorativa constat Tullius ait.'[12] The series is headed by a lady who is almost certainly Prudence;[13] the other figures also probably represent virtues and vices. The figures are no doubt meant to be remarkably beautiful or remarkably hideous (one is a devil) in accordance with the rules; unfortunately the artist has made them all remarkably hideous. That the discourse being memorised through these figures is concerned with roads to Heaven and Hell is shown by the appearance of Christ in the centre with the mouth of Hell beneath his feet.[14] On the figures and around them are many subsidiary images which are probably intended to be 'memory for words' images. At any rate we are told that both 'things' and 'words' may be remembered through these figures, which may represent a debased survival of mediaeval artificial memory through inscriptions on the figures.

This manuscript also shows plans of memory rooms, marked with five places, four in the corners and one in the centre, on which images are to be memorised. Such diagrams of memory rooms can be seen in other manuscripts and in printed treatises. The regular arrangement of the places in such memory rooms (not chosen for their unlikeness to one another and irregularity, as advised in the classical rules) was, I believe, a normal interpretation of places, both in the Middle Ages and in later times.

[11] Vienna National Library, Codex 5395; see Volkmann, *article cited*, pp. 124–131, Pls. 115–124.

[12] *Ibid.*, p. 128, Pl. 123.

[13] *Ibid.*, Pl. 113. Besides being (supposedly) remarkably beautiful and crowned, this lady follows another memory rule in being made to resemble persons known to the practitioner of the artificial memory. The face of this memory image, says the writer of the treatise, may be remembered as like 'Margaretha, Dorothea, Appolonia, Lucia, Anastasia, Agnes, Benigna, Beatrix or any virgin known to you, as Anna, Martha, Maria, Elizabeth etc.' *Ibid.*, p. 130. One of the male figures (Pl. 116) is labelled 'Brueder Ottell', presumably an inmate of the monastery whom one of his colleagues is using in his memory system!

[14] *Ibid.*, Pl. 119.

The *Oratoriae artis epitome* by Jacobus Publicius was printed at Venice in 1482;[15] the rhetoric has attached to it, as an appendix, an *Ars memorativa*. This beautiful little printed book will surely, we may expect, take us out into a new world, the world of the revived interest in classical rhetoric of the advancing Renaissance. But is Publicius so very modern? The position of his memory section at the end of the rhetoric, reminds us of the position of the memory section in the thirteenth-century *Fiore di Rettorica*, at the end and detachable. And the mystical introduction to the *Ars memorativa* is somewhat reminiscent of thirteenth-century mystical rhetorics of the Boncompagno type.

If the keenness of the mind is lost, so Publicius informs us in this introduction, through being enclosed within these earthly confines, the following 'new precepts' will help towards its release. The 'new precepts' are the rules for places and images. Publicius's interpretation of these includes the construction of 'ficta loca', or imaginary places, which are none other than the spheres of the universe—the spheres of the elements, planets, fixed stars, and higher spheres—topped by 'Paradisus', all of which is shown on a diagram (Fig. 1). In his rules for images which begin 'Simple and spiritual intentions slip easily from the memory unless joined to a corporeal similitude' he follows Thomas Aquinas. He dwells on the 'Ad Herennian' strikingness demanded of memory images, that they should have ridiculous movements, amazing gestures, or be filled with overpowering sadness or severity.[16] Unhappy Envy as described by Ovid with her livid complexion, black teeth, and snakey hair, is a good example of what a memory image should be.

Far from introducing us to a modern world of revived classical rhetoric, Publicius's memory section seems rather to transport us back into a Dantesque world in which Hell, Purgatory, and Paradise are remembered on the spheres of the universe, a Giottesque world with its sharpened expressiveness of virtue and vice memory figures. To use Ovid's Envy as a moving memory image from the poets is not a surprising new classical feature but belongs into the earlier memory tradition as interpreted by Albertus Magnus. In short, this first printed memory treatise is not a symptom of the revival of the classical art of memory as part of the Renais-

---

[15] Second edition, Venice, 1485.
[16] Ed. of Venice, 1485, Sig. G 8 *recto* Cf. Rossi, *Clavis*, p. 38.

sance revival of rhetoric; it comes straight out of the mediaeval tradition.

It is significant that this work, which looks so Renaissance and Italianate in its printed form, was known to an English monk many years before it was printed. A manuscript in the British Museum which Volkmann discovered was written in 1460 by

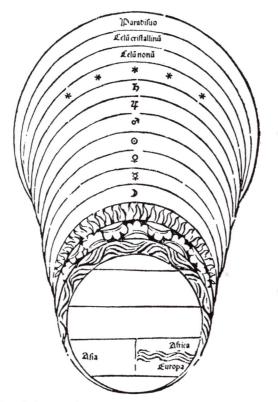

Fig. 1 The Spheres of the Universe as a Memory System. From J. Publicius, *Oratoriae artis epitome*, 1482

Thomas Swatwell, probably a monk of Durham; it is a copy of the *Ars oratoria* of Jacobus Publicius.[17] The English monk has carefully transcribed the memory section, ingeniously developing some of Publicius's fantasies in the quietness of his cloister.[18]

[17] B. M. Additional 28,805; cf. Volkmann, pp. 145 ff.
[18] One of the English monk's memory diagrams (reproduced by Volkmann, Pl. 145) is probably magical.

Nevertheless, the times are changing, the humanists are gaining a better understanding of the civilisation of classical antiquity; classical texts are circulating in printed editions. The student of rhetoric now has many more texts at his disposal than those First and Second Rhetorics on which the alliance of the artificial memory with Prudence had been built. In 1416, Poggio Bracciolini had discovered a complete text of Quintilian's *Institutio oratoria* which had its *editio princeps* at Rome in 1470, soon followed by other editions. As I have emphasised earlier, of the three Latin sources for the classical art of memory, it is Quintilian who gives the clearest account of the art as a mnemotechnic. In Quintilian the art could now be studied as a lay mnemotechnic, quite divorced from the associations which had grown up around the 'Ad Herennian' rules in their progress through the Middle Ages. And the way would be open for an enterprising person to teach the art of memory in a new way, as a success technique. The ancients, who knew everything, knew how to train the memory, and the man with a trained memory has an advantage over others which will help him get on in a competitive world. There will be a demand for the artificial memory of the ancients as now better understood. An enterprising person saw an opportunity here and seized it. His name was Peter of Ravenna.

The *Phoenix, sive artificiosa memoria* (first edition at Venice in 1491) by Peter of Ravenna became the most universally known of all the memory text books. It went through many editions in many countries,[19] was translated,[20] included in the popular general knowledge hand-book by Gregor Reisch,[21] copied by enthusiasts from the printed editions.[22] Peter was a tremendous self-advertiser which helped to boost his methods, but his fame as a memory teacher was probably largely due to the fact that he brought the mnemotechnic out into the lay world. People who wanted an art

[19] Amongst these are those of Bologna, 1492; Cologne, 1506, 1608; Venice, 1526, 1533; Vienna, 1541, 1600; Vicenza, 1600.

[20] The English translation is by Robert Copland, *The Art of Memory that is otherwise called the Phoenix*, London, *circa* 1548. See below, p. 260

[21] Gregor Reisch, *Margarita philosophica*, first edition 1496, many later editions. Peter of Ravenna's art of memory is in Lib. III, Tract. II, cap. XXIII.

[22] Cf. Rossi, *Clavis*, p. 27, note. To the manuscript copies of Ravenna's work mentioned by Rossi may be added those in Vat. Lat. 5347, f. 60, and in Paris, Lat. 8747, f. 1.

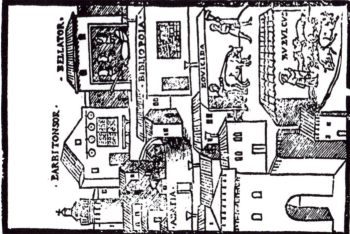

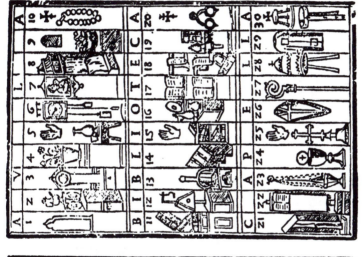

5a LEFT Abbey Memory
System
5b Images to be used in the
Abbey Memory System
From Johannes Romberch,
*Congestorium Artificiose
Memorie*, ed. of Venice, 1533
(p. 117)

of memory to help them practically, and not in order to remember Hell, could turn to the *Phoenix* of Peter of Ravenna.

Peter gives practical advice. When discussing the rule that memory *loci* are to be formed in quiet places he says that the best type of building to use is an unfrequented church. He describes how he goes round the church he has chosen three or four times, committing the places in it to memory. He chooses his first place near the door; the next, five or six feet further in; and so on. As a young man he started with one hundred thousand memorised places, but he has added many more since then. On his travels, he does not cease to make new places in some monastery or church, remembering through them histories, or fables, or Lenten sermons. His memory of the Scriptures, of canon law, and many other matters is based on this method. He can repeat from memory the whole of the canon law, text and gloss (he was a jurist trained at Padua); two hundred speeches or sayings of Cicero; three hundred sayings of the philosophers; twenty thousand legal points.[23] Peter probably was one of those people with very good natural memories who had so drilled themselves in the classical technique that they really could perform astonishing feats of memory. I think that one can definitely see an influence of Quintilian in Peter's account of his vast number of places, for it is Quintilian alone, of the classical sources who says that one may form memory places when on journeys.

On images, Peter makes use of the classical principle that memory images should if possible resemble people we know. He gives the name of a lady, Juniper of Pistoia, who was dear to him when young and whose image he finds stimulates his memory! Possibly this may have something to do with Peter's variation on the classical lawsuit image. To remember that a will is not valid without seven witnesses, says Peter, we may form an image of a scene in which 'the testator is making his will in the presence of two witnesses, and then a girl tears up the will'.[24] As with the classical lawsuit image, we are baffled as to why such an image, even if Juniper is the destructive girl, should help Peter remember his simple point about witnesses.

Peter laicised and popularised memory and emphasised the

[23] Petrus Tommai (Peter of Ravenna), *Foenix*, ed. of Venice, 1491, sigs. b iii-b iv.
[24] *Ibid.*, sig. c iii *recto*.

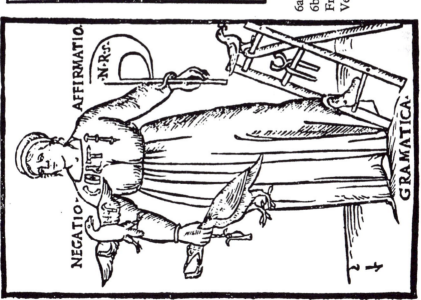

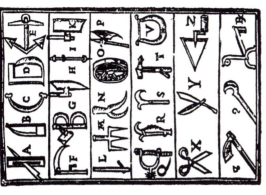

6a Grammar as a Memory Image
6b and c Visual Alphabets used for the Inscriptions on Grammar
From Johannes Romberch, *Congestorium Artificiose Memorie*, ed. of
Venice, 1533 (pp. 119–20)

purely mnemotechnical side. Nevertheless there is a good deal of unexplained confusion and curious detail in Peter's mnemonics, indicating that he is not altogether detached from the mediaeval tradition. His books become absorbed in the general memory tradition as it rolls on its way. Most subsequent writers on memory mention him, not excluding Romberch, the Dominican, who cites 'Petrus Ravennatis' as an authority as well as Tullius and Quintilian, or Thomas Aquinas and Petrarch.

I do not attempt to survey here the whole tribe of the printed memory treatises. Many of them will be referred to in later chapters, as occasion arises. Some treatises teach what I shall hereafter call 'the straight mnemotechnic', perhaps better understood after the recovery of Quintilian. In many, the mnemotechnic is closely entangled with surviving influences of the mediaeval uses of the art. In some there are traces of infiltration of mediaeval forms of magic memory, such as the *Ars notoria* into the art.[25] In some there are influences from the Renaissance Hermetic and occult transformation of the art, which will be the subject of most of the rest of this book.

But it is important that we should look here more particularly at what memory treatises by Dominicans were like in the sixteenth century, since the main strand, descending from the scholastic emphasis on memory, is in my opinion the most important strand in the history of the subject. The Dominicans were naturally at the centre of this tradition, and in Johannes Romberch, a German, and Cosmas Rosselius, a Florentine, we have two Dominicans who wrote books on memory, small in format but packed with detail, apparently intended to make the Dominican art of memory generally known. Romberch says that his book will be useful to theologians, preachers, confessors, jurists, advocates, doctors, philosophers, professors of the liberal arts, and ambassadors. Rossellius makes a similar statement. Romberch's book was published near the beginning of the sixteenth century; Rossellius's near its end. Together they span the century, as influential memory teachers who are frequently quoted. In fact, Publicius, Peter of Ravenna,

[25] Possible examples of this are Jodocus Weczdorff, *Ars memorandi nova secretissima, circa,* 1600, and Nicolas Simon aus Weida, *Ludus artificialis oblivionis,* Leipzig, 1510. Frontispieces and diagrams from these heavily magical works are reproduced by Volkmann, Pls. 168–71.

Romberch, and Rossellius may be said to be the leading names amongst writers on memory.

The *Congestorium artificiose memorie* (1520)[26] of Johannes Romberch is well named, for it is a strange congestion of memory material. Romberch knows all the three classical sources, not only *Ad Herennium* but also Cicero's *De oratore* and Quintilian. By his frequent citation of the name of Petrarch,[27] he absorbs the poet into the Dominican memory tradition; Peter of Ravenna and others are also drawn into the congestion. But his basis is Thomas Aquinas whose formulations, both in the *Summa* and in the Aristotle commentary he quotes on nearly every other page.

The book is in four parts; the first introductory, the second on places, the third on images; the fourth part outlines an encyclopaedic memory system.

Romberch envisages three different types of place systems, as all belonging to artificial memory.

The first type uses the cosmos as a place system, as illustrated in his diagram (Fig. 2). Here we see the spheres of the elements, of the planets, of the fixed stars, and above them the celestial spheres and those of the nine orders of angels. What are we to remember on these cosmic orders ? Marked on the lower part of the diagram we see the letters 'L.PA; L.P; PVR; IN' These stand for the places of Paradise, of the Earthly Paradise, of Purgatory, and of Hell.[28] In Romberch's view, remembering places such as these belong to artificial memory. He calls such realms 'imaginary places' (*ficta loca*). For the invisible things of Paradise we are to form places in memory in which we put the choirs of angels, the seats of the blessed, Patriarchs, Prophets, Apostles, Martyrs. The same is to be done for Purgatory and Hell, which are 'common places' or inclusive places, which are to be ordered into many particular places, to be remembered in order with inscriptions on them. The places of Hell which contain images of sinners being punished in them in accordance with the nature of their sins, as explained in the memorised inscriptions.[29]

---

[26] I use the edition of Venice, 1533. Romberch may be more agreeably studied in Lodovico Dolce's Italian translation, on which see below, pp. 163–4, and above p. 95.

[27] Romberch, pp. 2 *verso*, 12 *verso*, 14 *recto*, 20 *recto*, 26 *verso* etc.

[28] *Ibid.*, pp. 17 *recto* ff., 31 *recto* ff.

[29] *Ibid.*, p. 18 *recto* and *verso*. See above p. 94.

This type of artificial memory may be called the Dantesque type, not because the Dominican treatise is influenced by the *Divine Comedy*, but because Dante was influenced by such an interpretation of artificial memory, as suggested in the last chapter.

As another type of place system, Romberch envisages using the signs of the zodiac as giving an easily memorised order of places. He gives the name of Metrodorus of Scepsis as the authority on

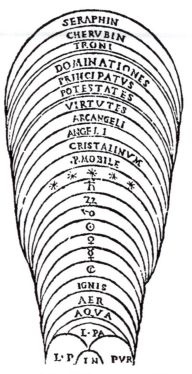

Fig. 2 The Spheres of the Universe as a Memory System. From J. Romberch, *Congestorium artificiose memorie*, ed. of 1533

this.[30] He found the information about the zodiacal memory system of Metrodorus of Scepsis in Cicero's *De oratore* and in Quintilian. He adds that, if a more extended star-order for memory is needed, it is useful to turn to the images given by Hyginus of all the constellations of the sky.[31]

[30] *Ibid.*, pp. 25 *recto* ff.   [31] *Ibid.*, p. 33 *verso.*

He does not state what kind of material he envisages as being memorised on the images of the constellations. In view of the predominantly theological and didactic nature of his approach to memory, one might guess that the constellation order as a place system was to be used by preachers for remembering the order of their sermons on virtues and vices in Heaven and Hell.

His third type of place system is the more normally mnemotechnical method of memorising real places on real buildings,[32] as on the abbey and its associated buildings illustrated by a cut (Pl. 5a). The images which he is using on places in this building (Pl. 5b) are those of 'memory objects' of the type already referred to. Here we are on the ground of 'the straight mnemotechnic' and from the instructions about memorising places in buildings given in this part of the book, the reader could have learned the use of the art as a straight mnemotechnic, of the more mechanical type described by Quintilian. Though even here there are curious and non-classical elaborations about 'alphabetical orders'. It helps to have lists of animals, birds, names, arranged in alphabetical order to use with this system.

Amongst Romberch's additions to the place rules, is one which is not original to him; Peter of Ravenna gives it and it may go back much earlier. A memory *locus* which is to contain a memory image must not be larger than a man can reach;[33] this is illustrated by a cut of a human image on a *locus* (Fig. 3), reaching upwards and sideways to demonstrate the right proportions of the *locus* in relation to the image. This rule grows out of the artistic feeling for space, lighting, distance, in memory in the classical place rules, of which we earlier suggested an influence on Giotto's painted *loci*. It evidently applies to human images, not to memory objects as images, and may imply a similar kind of interpretation of the place rules (that is to make the images placed in regular orders stand out from their backgrounds).

On images,[34] Romberch retails the classical rules on striking images with many elaborations and with much quotation from Thomas on corporeal similitudes. As usual the memory images are not illustrated nor are they very clearly described. We have to construct our own from the rules.

[32] *Ibid.*, pp. 35 *recto* ff.
[33] *Ibid.*, p. 28 *verso*.
[34] *Ibid.*, pp. 39 *verso* ff.

There are however some illustrations in this section of the book but they are 'visual alphabets'. Visual alphabets are ways of representing letters of the alphabet by images. These are formed in various ways; for example with pictures of objects whose shape resemble letters of the alphabet (Pl. 6b), as compasses or a ladder for A; or a hoe for N. Another way is through pictures of animals or birds arranged in the order of the first letter of their names (Pl. 6c), as A for *Anser*, goose, B for *Bubo*, owl. Visual alphabets are very common in the memory treatises and they almost certainly come out of an old tradition. Boncompagno speaks of an 'imaginary alphabet' which is to be used for remembering names.[35] Such

Fig. 3 Human Image on a Memory *Locus*. From Romberch, *Congestorium artificiose memorie*, ed. of 1533

alphabets are frequently described in the manuscript treatises. Publicius's is the first printed treatise to illustrate them;[36] there-after they are a normal feature of most printed memory treatises. Volkmann has reproduced a number of them from various

[35] Boncompagno, *Rhetorica novissima, ed. cit.*, p. 278, 'De alphabeto imaginario'.
[36] Publicius's 'objects' alphabet, on which one of Romberch's is based, is reproduced by Volkmann, Pl. 146.

treatises,[37] but without discussing what their origin may be or for what purposes they were intended to be used.

The visual alphabet probably comes out of endeavours to understand *Ad Herennium* on how proficients in artificial memory write in images in their memories. According to the general principles of artificial memory we should put everything that we want to fix in memory into an image. Applied to the letters of the alphabet, this would mean that they are better remembered if put into images. The notion as worked out in the visual alphabets is of infantile simplicity, like teaching a child to remember C through the picture of a Cat. Rossellius, apparently in perfect seriousness, suggests that we should remember the word AER through the images of an Ass an Elephant, and a Rhinoceros![38]

A variation on the visual alphabet, suggested, I believe, by the words of *Ad Herennium* on remembering a number of our acquaintances standing in a row, is formed by arranging persons known to the practitioner of artificial memory in alphabetical order of their names. Peter of Ravenna gives a splendid example of this method in use when he states that to remember the word ET he visualises Eusebius standing in front of Thomas; and he has only to move Eusebius back behind Thomas to remember the word TE![39]

The visual alphabets illustrated in the memory treatises, were I believe, intended to be used for making inscriptions in memory. In fact, this can be proved from the example illustrated in the third part of Romberch's book of a memory image covered with inscriptions in visual alphabets (Pl. 6a). This is one of the very rare cases in which a memory image is illustrated; and the image turns out to be the familiar figure of old Grammatica, the first of the liberal arts, with some of her familiar attributes, the scalpel and the ladder. She is here, not only the well-known personification of the liberal art of Grammar, but a memory image being used to remember material about grammar through inscriptions on her. The inscription across her chest and the images near or on her are derived from Romberch's visual alphabets, both the 'objects'

---

[37] Volkmann, Pls. 146–7, 150–1, 179–88, 194, 198. Another device was to form images for numbers from objects; examples from Romberch, Rossellius, Porta, are reproduced by Volkmann, Pls. 183–5, 188, 194.

[38] Cosmas Rossellius, *Thesaurus artificiosae memoriae*, Venice, 1579, p. 119 *verso*.

[39] Petrus Tommai (Peter of Ravenna) *Foenix*, ed. cit., sig. c i *recto*.

ones and the 'birds' one which he is using in combination. He explains that he is memorising in this way the answer to the question as to whether Grammar is a common or a particular science; the reply involves the use of the terms *predicatio, applicatio, continentia*.[40] *Predicatio* is memorised by the bird beginning with a P (a *Pica* or pie) which she holds, and its associated objects from the object alphabet. *Applicatio* is remembered by the *Aquila*[41] and associated objects on her arm. *Continentia* is remembered by the inscription on her chest in the 'objects' alphabet (see the objects representing C, O, N, T, in the 'objects' alphabet, Pl. 6b).

Though devoid of aesthetic charm, Romberch's Grammar is of importance to the student of artificial memory. She proves the point that personifications, such as the familiar figures of the liberal arts, when reflected in memory, become memory images. And that inscriptions are to be made in memory on such figures for memorising material about the subject of the personification. The principle exemplified in Romberch's Grammar could be applied to all other personifications, such as those of the virtues and vices, when used as memory images. This is what we suspected in the last chapter when we realised that the inscriptions about Penance on the scourge of Holcot's memory image of Penance were probably 'memory for words'. And when we thought that the inscriptions recording the parts of the cardinal virtues, as defined in the *Summa* of Thomas Aquinas, on the images of these virtues, were perhaps also 'memory for words'. The images themselves recall the memory of the 'things' and the inscriptions memorised on them are 'memory for words' about the 'things'. Or so I would suggest.

Romberch's Grammar, here undoubtedly being used as a memory image, shows the method in action, with the added refinement that the inscriptions are made (so it is supposed) more memorable by being made not in ordinary writing, but in images for the letters from visual alphabets.

The discussion about how to memorise Grammar, her parts and arguments about her, comes in the last part of Romberch's book in which he outlines an extremely ambitious programme for committing all the sciences, theological, metaphysical, moral, as well as

[40] Romberch, pp. 82 *verso*–83 *recto*.
[41] If Romberch had stuck to his own 'birds' alphabet, the A bird should have been an *Anser* (see Pl. 6c); but the text (p. 83 *recto*) states that the bird on Grammar's arm is an *Aquila*.

the seven liberal arts, to memory. The method used about Grammar (the complexity of which I have greatly reduced in the description given above) may, he says, be used for all the sciences, and all the liberal arts. For Theology, for example, we may imagine a perfect and excellent theologian; he will have on his head images of *cognitio, amor, fruitio*; on his members, *essentia divina, actus, forma, relatio, articuli, precepta, sacramenta*, and all that pertains to Theology.[42] Romberch then proceeds to set out in columns the parts and subdivisions of Theology, Metaphysics (including philosophy and moral philosophy), Law, Astronomy, Geometry, Arithmetic, Music, Logic, Rhetoric, and Grammar. For the memorisation of all of these subjects, images are to be formed with associated images and inscriptions. Each subject is to be placed in a memory room.[43] The image-forming instructions given are very complicated, and the memorising of most abstract metaphysical themes, and even of logical arguments, is envisaged. One has the impression that Romberch is presenting in some highly abbreviated and no doubt decayed and debased form (the use of the visual alphabets would be among the debasements) a system used by some mighty mind in the past and which has come down to him by tradition in the Dominican Order. In view of the perpetual quotation from Thomas Aquinas on corporeal similitudes and order in Romberch's book, the possibility arises that we may have in this late Dominican memory treatise some distant echo of the memory system of Thomas Aquinas himself.

Looking back at the fresco in the Chapter House of Santa Maria Novella, our eye rests once more on the fourteen corporeal similitudes, seven of the liberal arts and seven other figures added to represent Thomas's knowledge of much loftier spheres of learning. After our study of the memory system in Romberch, in which memory figures are formed for the highest sciences, as well as for the liberal arts, in some stupendous attempt to hold a vast summa of knowledge in memory through series of images, we may wonder whether it is not something of this kind which is represented by the figures of the fresco. The guess made on an earlier page of this book that those figures may not only symbolise the extent of Thomas's learning but may also allude to his method of memorising it by the art of memory, as he understands it, may now have received some confirmation from Romberch.

[42] Romberch, p. 84 *recto*.   [43] *Ibid.*, p. 81 *recto*.

The *Thesaurus artificiosae memoriae* of Cosmas Rossellius was published at Venice in 1579. Its author described on the title page as a Florentine and a member of the Order of Preachers. The book is on similar lines to Romberch's and the main types of interpretation of artificial memory are discernible in it.

The Dantesque type is given great prominence. Rossellius divides Hell into eleven places, as illustrated in his diagram of Hell as a memory place system (Pl. 7a). In its centre is a horrible well, led up to by steps on which are the places of punishment of Heretics, Jewish Infidels, Idolaters, and Hypocrites. Around it are seven other places adapted to the seven deadly sins punished in them. As Rossellius cheerfully observes 'the variety of punishments, inflicted in accordance with the diverse nature of the sins, the different situations of the damned, their varying gestures, will much help memory and give many places.'[44]

The place of Paradise (Pl. 7b) is to be imagined as surrounded with a wall sparkling with gems. In its centre is the Throne of Christ; ranged in order below are the places of the celestial hierarchies, of Apostles, Patriarchs, Prophets, Martyrs, Confessors, Virgins, Holy Hebrews and the innumerable concourse of the saints. There is nothing at all unusual about Rosellius's Paradise, except that it is classed as 'artificial memory'. With art and exercise and vehement imagination we are to imagine these places. We are to imagine the Throne of Christ so that it may most move the sense and excite the memory. We may imagine the orders of spirits as painters paint them.[45]

Rossellius also envisages the constellations as memory place systems, of course mentioning Metrodorus of Scepsis in connection with a zodiacal place system.[46] A feature of Rossellius's book are the mnemonic verses given to help memorise orders of places, whether orders of places in Hell, or the order of the signs of the zodiac. These verses are by a fellow Dominican who is also an Inquisitor. These 'carmina' by an Inquisitor give an impressive air of great orthodoxy to the artificial memory.

Rossellius describes the making of 'real' places in abbeys, churches and the like. And discusses human images as places on which subsidiary images are to be remembered. Under images, he

[44] Rossellius, *Thesaurus*, p. 2 *verso*.
[45] *Ibid.*, p. 33 *recto*.
[46] *Ibid.*, p. 22 *verso*.

gives general rules, and a visual alphabet of the same type as those in Romberch.

The student of artificial memory who used such books as these could learn the 'straight mnemotechnic' from them in the descriptions of how to memorise 'real' places in buildings. But he would learn it in the context of survivals of the mediaeval tradition, of places in Paradise and Hell, of the 'corporeal similitudes' of Thomist memory. But whilst echoes of the past survive in the treatises, they belong to their own later times. The interweaving of Petrarch's name into the Dominican memory tradition is suggestive of increasing humanist influence. And whilst new influences are making themselves felt, there is at the same time a deterioration going on in the memory tradition. The memory rules become more and more detailed; alphabetical lists and visual alphabets encourage trivial elaborations. Memory, one often feels in reading the treatises, has degenerated into a kind of cross-word puzzle to beguile the long hours in the cloister; much of their advice can have had no practical utility; letters and images are turning into childish games. Yet this kind of elaboration may have been very congenial to Renaissance taste with its love of mystery. If we did not know the mnemonic explanation of Romberch's Grammar, she might seem like some inscrutable emblem.

The art of memory in these later forms would still be acting as the hidden forger of imagery. What scope for the imagination would be offered in memorising Boethius's *Consolation of Philosophy*,[47] as advised in a fifteenth-century manuscript! Would the Lady Philosophy have come to life during this attempt, and begun to wander, like some animated Prudence, through the palaces of memory? Perhaps an artificial memory gone out of control into wild imaginative indulgence might be one of the stimuli behind such a work as the *Hypnerotomachia Polyphili*, written by a Dominican before 1500,[48] in which we meet, not only with Petrarchan triumphs and curious archaeology, but also with Hell, divided into places to suit the sins and their punishments, with explanatory inscriptions on them. This suggestion of artificial memory as a part of Prudence makes one wonder whether the

[47] The Vienna codex 5393, quoted Volkmann, p. 130.
[48] It has been established that the author of this work, Francesco Colonna, was a Dominican; see M. T. Casella and G. Pozzi, *Francesco Colonna, Biografia e Opere*, Padua, 1959, I, pp. 10 ff.

mysterious inscriptions so characteristic of this work may owe something to the influence of visual alphabets and memory images, whether, that is to say, the dream archaeology of a humanist mingles with dream memory systems to form the strange fantasia.

Amongst the most characteristic types of Renaissance cultivation of imagery are the emblem and the *impresa*. These phenomena have never been looked at from the point of view of memory to which they clearly belong. The *impresa*, in particular, is the attempt to remember a spiritual intention through a similitude; the words of Thomas Aquinas define it exactly.

The memory treatises are rather tiresome reading, as Cornelius Agrippa suggests in his chapter on the vanity of the art of memory.[49] This art, he says, was invented by Simonides and perfected by Metrodorus of Scepsis of whom Quintilian says that he was a vain and boastful man. Agrippa then rattles off a list of modern memory treatises which he describes as 'an unworthy catalogue by obscure men' and anyone whose fate it has been to wade through large numbers of such works may endorse his words. These treatises cannot recapture the workings of the vast memories of the past, for the conditions of their world, in which the printed book has arrived, have destroyed the conditions which made such memories possible. The schematic layouts of manuscripts, designed for memorisation, the articulation of a summa into its ordered parts, all these are disappearing with the printed book which need not be memorised since copies are plentiful.

In Victor Hugo's *Notre Dame de Paris*, a scholar, deep in meditation in his study high up in the cathedral, gazes at the first printed book which has come to disturb his collection of manuscripts. Then, opening the window, he gazes at the vast cathedral, silhouetted against the starry sky, crouching like an enormous sphinx in the middle of the town. 'Ceci tuera cela', he says. The printed book will destroy the building. The parable which Hugo develops out of the comparison of the building, crowded with images, with the arrival in his library of a printed book might be applied to the effect on the invisible cathedrals of memory of the past of the spread of printing. The printed book will make such huge built up memories, crowded with images, unnecessary. It

---

[49] *De vanitate scientiarum*, cap. X.

will do away with habits of immemorial antiquity whereby a 'thing' is immediately invested with an image and stored in the places of memory.

A severe blow to the art of memory as understood in the Middle Ages was dealt by modern humanist philological scholarship. In 1491, Raphael Regius brought the new critical techniques to bear on *Ad Herennium* and suggested Cornificius as the author.[50] Shortly before, Lorenzo Valla had taken up this question, putting the whole weight of his great reputation as a philological scholar against the attribution of this work to Cicero.[51] The wrong attribution lingered for a time in the printed editions,[52] but gradually it became generally known that *Ad Herennium* is not by Cicero.

This broke up the old alliance between the First and Second Rhetorics of Tullius. It remained true that Tullius was really the author of *De inventione*, the First Rhetoric, where he had really said that memory is a part of Prudence; but the neat sequel, that Tullius teaches in the Second Rhetoric that memory can be trained by the artificial memory dropped off, since Tullius was not the author of the Second Rhetoric. The importance for the memory tradition descending from the Middle Ages of the wrong attribution is shown by the fact that the discovery of the humanist philologists is consistently ignored by writers in that tradition. Romberch always attributes his quotations from *Ad Herennium* to Cicero[53] so does Rossellius.[54] Nothing shows more clearly that Giordano Bruno came out of the Dominican memory tradition than the fact that this ex-friar, in a work on memory published in 1582, firmly ignores humanist critical scholarship by introducing a quotation from *Ad Herennium* with the words, 'Hear what Tullius says'.[55]

---

[50] Raphael Regius, *Ducenta problemata in totidem institutionis oratoriae Quintiliani depravationes*, Venice, 1491. Included in this is an essay on 'Utrum ars rhetorica ad Herennium Ciceroni falso inscribatur'. Cf. Marx's introduction to his edition of *Ad Herennium*, p. lxi. Cornificius has frequently been a candidate for the authorship, though not now accepted; see Caplan's introduction to the Loeb edition, pp. ix ff.

[51] L. Valla, *Opera*, ed. of Bâle, 1540, p. 510; cf. Marx, *loc. cit.;* Caplan, *loc. cit.*

[52] See above, p. 55.

[53] Romberch, pp. 26 *verso*, 44 *recto*, etc.

[54] Rossellius, preface, p. 1 *verso* etc.

[55] G. Bruno, *Opere latine*, II (i), p. 251.

With the revival of lay oratory in the Renaissance, we should expect to find a renewed cult of the art of memory as a lay technique, divested of mediaeval associations. Remarkable feats of memory were admired in the Renaissance, as in antiquity; a new lay demand for the art as a mnemonic technique arose; and memory writers like Peter of Ravenna arose to supply that demand. We catch an amusing glimpse of a humanist orator preparing a speech to be memorised by the art in a letter of Albrecht Dürer to his friend Willibald Pirckheimer:

> A chamber must have more than four corners which is to contain all the gods of memory. I am not going to cram my head full of them; that I leave to you; for I believe that however many chambers there might be in the head, you would have something in each of them. The Margrave would not grant an audience long enough![56]

For the Renaissance imitator of Cicero as an orator, the loss of *Ad Herennium* as a genuinely Ciceronian work did not necessarily weaken his belief in the artificial memory, for in the much admired *De Oratore* Cicero refers to the artificial memory and states that he himself practises it. The cult of Cicero as orator could thus encourage renewed interest in the art, now understood in the classical sense as a part of rhetoric.

Nevertheless, whilst social conditions demanding much speech-making and good memory in speakers, were operating towards an increased demand for mnemonic aids, there were other forces in Renaissance humanism which were unfavourable to the art of memory. Important among these was the intensive study of Quintilian by humanist scholars and educators. For Quintilian does not wholeheartedly recommend the artificial memory. His account of the art makes it very clear as a straight mnemotechnic, but he treats of it in a rather superior and critical tone of voice, unlike Cicero's enthusiasm in the *De oratore*, very different from the unquestioning acceptance of it in *Ad Herennium*, and worlds away from the devout mediaeval faith in the places and images of Tullius. A sensible modern humanist, even though he knows that Cicero himself recommends this curious art, will be inclined to listen to the moderate and rational voice of Quintilian, who,

[56] *Literary Remains of Albrecht Dürer*, ed. W. M. Conway, Cambridge, 1899, pp. 54–5 (letter dated September, 1506). I owe this reference to O. Kurz.

though he thinks that places and images may be of some use for some purposes, on the whole recommends more straightforward methods of memorising.

> Though I do not deny that memory can be helped by places and images, yet the best memory is based on three most important things, namely study, order, and care.[57]

The quotation is from Erasmus; but behind the words of the great critical scholar we can hear those of Quintilian. The distinctly cool and Quintilianist attitude of Erasmus to the artificial memory develops in later leading humanist educators into a strong disapproval of it. Melanchthon forbids students to use any mnemotechnical devices and enjoins learning by heart in the normal way as the sole art of memory.[58]

We have to remember that for Erasmus, confidently emerging into a brave new world of modern humanist scholarship, the art of memory would wear a mediaeval look. It belonged to the ages of barbarism; its methods in decay were an example of those cobwebs in monkish minds which new brooms must sweep away. Erasmus did not like the Middle Ages, a dislike which developed into violent antagonism in the Reformation, and the art of memory was a mediaeval and a scholastic art.

Thus, in the sixteenth century, the art of memory might appear to be on the wane. The printed book is destroying age-old memory habits. The mediaeval transformation of the art, though still living on and in some demand as the treatises testify, may have lost its ancient force and be dwindling into curious memory games. Modern trends in humanist scholarship and education are luke warm about the classical art, or increasingly hostile to it. Though little books on How to Improve Your Memory are popular, as they still are, the art of memory may be moving out of the great nerve centres of the European tradition and becoming marginal.

Nevertheless, far from waning, the art of memory had actually

---

[57] Erasmus, *De ratione studii*, 1512 (in the Froben edition of the *Opera*, 1540, 1, p. 466). Cf. Hajdu, p. 116; Rossi, *Clavis*, p. 3.
Needless to say, Erasmus was strongly against all magical short cuts to memory, against which he warns his godson in the Colloquy on *Ars Notoria*; see *The Colloquies of Erasmus*, translated by Craig R. Thompson, Chicago University Press, 1965, pp. 458–61.

[58] F. Melanchthon, *Rhetorica elementa*, Venice, 1534, p. 4 *verso* Cf. Rossi, *Clavis*, p. 89.

entered upon a new and strange lease of life. For it had been taken up into the main philosophical current of the Renaissance, the Neoplatonic movement inaugurated by Marsilio Ficino and Pico della Mirandola in the late fifteenth century. Renaissance Neoplatonists were not so averse to the Middle Ages as were some humanists, and they did not join in the depreciation of the ancient art of memory. Mediaeval scholasticism had taken up the art of memory, and so did the main philosophical movement of the Renaissance, the Neoplatonic movement. Through Renaissance Neoplatonism, with its Hermetic core, the art of memory was once more transformed, this time into a Hermetic or occult art, and in this form it continued to take a central place in a central European tradition.

We are now at last prepared to begin the study of the Renaissance transformation of the art of memory, taking as our first example of the momentous change, the Memory Theatre of Giulio Camillo.

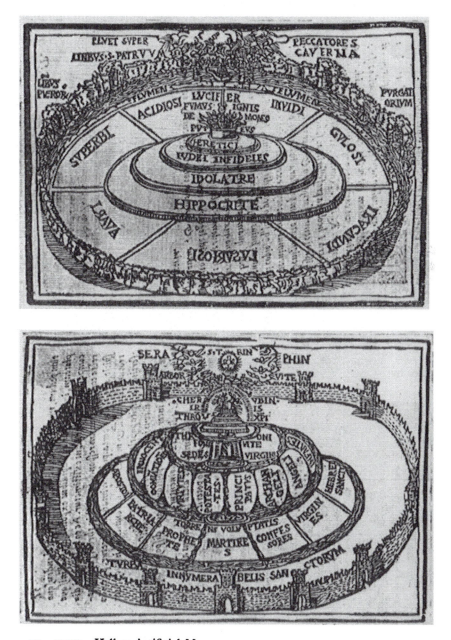

7a ABOVE Hell as Artificial Memory
7b BELOW Paradise as Artificial Memory
From Cosmas Rossellius, *Thesaurus Artificiosae Memoriae*, Venice 1579 (p. 122)

Chapter VI

❖◆❖

RENAISSANCE MEMORY[1]: THE MEMORY THEATRE OF GIULIO CAMILLO

❖◆❖

GIULIO Camillo, or Giulio Camillo Delminio to give him his full name, was one of the most famous men of the sixteenth century.[2] He was one of those people whom their contemporaries regard with awe as having vast potentialities. His Theatre was talked of in all Italy and in France; its mysterious fame seemed to grow with the years. Yet what was it exactly? A wooden Theatre, crowded with images, was shown by Camillo himself in Venice to a correspondent of Erasmus; something similar was later on view in Paris. The secret of how it really

[1] The art of memory is now entering on the phase in which Renaissance occult influences come into it. I have outlined the history of the Renaissance Hermetic-Cabalist tradition, from Marsilio Ficino and Pico della Mirandola up to the appearance of Bruno, in the first ten chapters of my book, *Giordano Bruno and the Hermetic Tradition*, London and Chicago, 1964. Though this book does not mention Camillo, it provides the background for the outlook expressed in his Memory Theatre. It will be henceforward referred to under the abbreviation *G.B. and H.T.*

A fuller treatment of Ficino's magic and of its basis in the Hermetic *Asclepius* will be found in D. P. Walker, *Spiritual and Demonic Magic from Ficino to Campanella*, Warburg Institute, London, 1958, henceforward referred to as Walker, *Magic.*

The best modern edition of the Hermetic treatises which Camillo is using is that by A. D. Nock and A. J. Festugière, *Corpus Hermeticum*, Paris, 1945 and 1954, 4 vols. (with French translation).

[2] This statement in the article 'Delminio, Giulio Camillo' in the *Enciclopedia italiana* is not an exaggeration.

129

8a   The Places of Hell
Fresco by Nardo di Cione (Detail), Santa Maria Novella, Florence (pp. 94-5)

8b   Titian, Allegory of the
Three Parts of Prudence
(p. 162)

worked was to be revealed to only one person in the world, the King of France. Camillo never produced the great book, which he was always about to produce, in which his lofty designs were to be preserved for posterity. It is thus not surprising that posterity forgot this man whom his contemporaries hailed as 'the divine Camillo'. The eighteenth century still remembered him,[3] rather patronisingly, but thereafter he disappeared, and it is only in recent years that some people[4] have begun to talk again of Giulio Camillo.

He was born about 1480. For some time he held a professorship at Bologna, but the greater part of his life was spent in the abstruse labours on the Theatre for which he was always in need of financial support. Francis I was informed of it, apparently through Lazare de Baïf,[5] the French ambassador in Venice, and in 1530 Camillo went to France. The King gave him money towards his work, with promise of more. He returned to Italy to perfect it and in 1532 Viglius Zuichemus, then in Padua, wrote to Erasmus that everyone was talking about a certain Giulio Camillo. 'They say that this man has constructed a certain Amphitheatre, a work of wonderful skill, into which whoever is admitted as spectator will be able to

---

[3] Two memoirs of Camillo were published in the eighteenth century: F. Altani di Salvarolo, 'Memorie intorno alla vita ed opere di G. Camillo Delminio', in *Nuova raccolta d'opuscoli scientifici e filologici*, ed. A. Calogiera and F. Mandelli, Venice, 1755-84, Vol. XXII; G. G. Liruti, *Notizie delle vite ed opere . . . da' letterati del Friuli*, Venice, 1760, Vol. III, pp. 69 ff.; cf. also Tiraboschi, *Storia della letteratura italiana*, VII (4), pp. 1513 ff.

[4] E. Garin in *Testi umanistici sulla retorica*, Rome-Milan, 1953, pp. 32-5; R. Bernheimer, 'Theatrum Mundi', *Art Bulletin*, XXVIII (1956), pp. 225-31; Walker, *Magic*, 1958, pp. 141-2; F. Secret, 'Les chemine-ments de la Kabbale à la Renaissance; le Théâtre du Monde de Giulio Camillo Delminio et son influence', *Rivista critica di storia della filosofia*, XIV (1959), pp. 418-36 (see also F. Secret's book *Les Kabbalistes Chré-tiens de la Renaissance*, Paris, 1964, pp. 186, 291, 302, 310, 314, 318); Paolo Rossi, 'Studi sul lullismo e sull'arte della memoria: I teatri del mondo e il lullismo di Giordano Bruno', *Rivista critica di storia della filosofia*, XIV (1959), pp. 28-59; Paolo Rossi, *Clavis universalis*, Milan, 1960, pp. 96-100.

In a lecture given at the Warburg Institute in January, 1955, I showed as a slide the plan of Camillo's Theatre here reproduced and compared it with the memory systems of Bruno, Campanella, and Fludd.

[5] Liruti, p. 120.

discourse on any subject no less fluently than Cicero. I thought at first that this was a fable until I learned of the thing more fully from Baptista Egnatio. It is said that this Architect has drawn up in certain places whatever about anything is found in Cicero . . . Certain orders or grades of figures are disposed . . . with stupendous labour and divine skill.'[6] Camillo is said to be making a copy of this splendid invention which he destines for the King of France, to whom he recently offered it and who has given five hundred ducats towards its completion.

When next Viglius writes to Erasmus he has been to Venice and has met Camillo who has allowed him to see the Theatre (it was a theatre, not an amphitheatre, as will appear later). 'Now you must know', he writes, 'that Viglius has been in the Amphitheatre and has diligently inspected everything.' The object was thus clearly more than a small model; it was a building large enough to be entered by at least two people at once; Viglius and Camillo were in it together.

The work is of wood [continues Viglius], marked with many images, and full of little boxes; there are various orders and grades in it. He gives a place to each individual figure and ornament, and he showed me such a mass of papers that, though I always heard that Cicero was the fountain of richest eloquence, scarcely would I have thought that one author could contain so much or that so many volumes could be pieced together out of his writings. I wrote to you before the name of the author who is called Julius Camillus. He stammers badly and speaks Latin with difficulty, excusing himself with the pretext that through continually using his pen he has nearly lost the use of speech. He is said however to be good in the vernacular which he has taught at some time at Bologna. When I asked him concerning the meaning of the work, its plan and results—speaking religiously and as though stupefied by the miraculousness of the thing—he threw before me some papers, and recited them so that he expressed the numbers, clauses, and all the artifices of the Italian style, yet slightly unevenly because of the impediment in his speech. The King is said to be urging that he should return to France with the magnificent work. But since the King wished that all the writing should be translated into French, for which he had tried an interpreter and scribe, he said that he thought that he would defer his journey rather than exhibit an

---

[6] Erasmus, *Epistolae*, ed. P. S. Allen and others, IX, p. 479.

131

imperfect work. He calls this theatre of his by many names, saying now that it is a built or constructed mind and soul, and now that it is a windowed one. He pretends that all things that the human mind can conceive and which we cannot see with the corporeal eye, after being collected together by diligent meditation may be expressed by certain corporeal signs in such a way that the beholder may at once perceive with his eyes everything that is otherwise hidden in the depths of the human mind. And it is because of this corporeal looking that he calls it a theatre.

When I asked him whether he had written anything in defence of his opinion, since there are many to-day who do not approve of this zeal in imitating Cicero, he replied that he had written much but had as yet published little save a few small things in Italian dedicated to the King. He has in mind to publish his views on the matter when he can have quiet, and the work is perfected to which he is giving all his energies. He says that he has already spent 1,500 ducats on it, though the King has so far only given 500. But he expects ample reward from the King when he has experienced the fruits of the work.[7]

Poor Camillo! His Theatre was never fully perfected; his great work was never written. Even under normal circumstances, this is a condition which gives rise to much anxiety. How heavy must the burden be when one is a divine man of whom divine things are expected! And when the final secret of the work is magical, mystical, belonging to the occult philosophy, impossible to explain to a rational enquirer, like this friend of Erasmus, under whose eye the Idea of the Memory Theatre dissolves into stammering incoherence.

For Erasmus, the classical art of memory was a rational mnemotechnic, possibly useful in moderation but to which more ordinary methods of memorising were to be preferred. And he was strongly against all magical short cuts to memory. What will he think of this Hermetic memory system? Viglius is well aware of what the attitude of his learned friend will be to Camillo's Theatre, and he apologises at the beginning of the letter for offending his serious ear with trifles.

Camillo returned to France at some time after the interview at Venice described by Viglius. The exact dates of his journeys to

[7] *Ibid.*, X, pp. 29–30.

France are not fixed[8] but he was certainly in Paris in 1534 when Jacques Bording, in a letter to Etienne Dolet, says that he has recently arrived there to instruct the King, adding that, 'He is constructing here an amphitheatre for the King, for the purpose of marking out divisions of memory.'[9] In a letter of 1558, Gilbert Cousin says that he has seen Camillo's Theatre, a structure made of wood, at the French court. Cousin is writing more than ten years after Camillo's death and his description of the Theatre is copied from the letters of Viglius, then unpublished but to which he could have had access as Erasmus' secretary.[10] This rather diminishes the value of Cousin's letter as a first hand account of what he saw in France, but it is probable that the Theatre constructed in France closely followed the model which Viglius saw in Venice. The French version of the Theatre seems to have disappeared early. In the seventeenth century, the great French antiquary Montfaucon made enquiries about it but could find no trace of it.[11]

Camillo and his Theatre were as much talked of at the French court as they were in Italy, and various legends about his stay in France are extant. The most intriguing of these is the lion story, one version of which is told by Betussi in his dialogues published in 1544. He says that one day in Paris Giulio Camillo went to see some wild animals, together with the Cardinal of Lorraine, Luigi Alamanni, and other gentlemen, including Betussi himself. A lion escaped and came towards the party.

> The gentlemen were much alarmed and fled hither and thither, except Messer Giulio Camillo who remained where he was, without moving. This he did, not in order to give proof of himself, but because of the weight of his body which made him slower in his movements than the others. The king of animals began to walk round him and to caress him, without otherwise molesting him, until it was chased back to its place. What will you say to this? Why was he not killed? It was thought by all that he remained safe and sound because he was under the planet of the sun.[12]

[8] A summary of what is known of Camillo's movements is given in the note to Erasmus, *Epist.*, IX, p. 479.

[9] R. C. Christie, *Etienne Dolet*, London, 1880, p. 142.

[10] See the note to Erasmus, *Epist.* IX, p. 475. Cousin's quotations from Viglius on the Theatre are in *Cognati opera*, Bâle, 1562, I, pp. 217–18, 302–4, 317–19. Cf. also Secret, *article cited*, p. 420.

[11] Liruti, p. 129

[12] G. Betussi, *Il Raverta*, Venice, 1544; ed. G. Zonta, Bari, 1912, p. 133.

The lion story is repeated with complacency by Camillo himself[13] as proof of his possession of 'solar virtue', though he does not mention the reason why, according to Betussi, he did not run away as fast as the others. The behaviour of the solar animal in the presence of the Magus whose Hermetic memory system, as we shall see later, was centred on the sun was evidently a valuable asset for his publicity.

According to Camillo's friend and disciple, Girolamo Muzio, the great man was back in Italy in 1543.[14] It would seem from a hint in a letter of Erasmus to Viglius that the ducats did not flow as liberally from the French King as he had hoped.[15] At any rate, on his return to Italy Camillo appears to have been out of a job, or rather out of a patron. The Marchese del Vasto (Alfonso Davalos, the Spanish governor of Milan who had been the patron of Ariosto) enquired of Muzio whether anything had come of Camillo's hopes of the King of France. If not, he would give him a pension in return for being taught 'the secret'.[16] This offer was accepted, and Camillo spent what remained of his life as Del Vasto's pensioner, discoursing in his presence and in various Academies. He died at Milan in 1544.

In 1559 a little guide book to the villas near Milan and the collections of their wealthy owners was published. Here we read that a most virtuous gentleman of the name of Pomponio Cotta sometimes escapes from noisome imprisonment in Milan (in other words from the pressure of city life) to the solitudes of his villa, there to flee the society of others in order to find himself. Here he employs himself now in hunting, now in reading books on agriculture, now in having *imprese* painted, with mottoes full of subtlety which give proof of his remarkable intelligence.

> And amongst the marvellous pictures ('pitture') which are there, may be seen the lofty and incomparable fabric of the marvellous Theatre of the most excellent Giulio Camillo'[17]

Unfortunately, the description of the Theatre which follows consists of verbal quotations from the printed *Idea del Theatro*,

[13] See below, p. 152.
[14] G. Muzio, *Lettere*, Florence, 1590, pp. 66 ff.; cf. Liruti, pp. 94 ff.
[15] *Epist.*, X, p. 226.
[16] Muzio, *Lettere*, pp. 67 ff.; cf. Liruti, *loc. cit.*
[17] Bartolomeo Taegio, *La Villa*, Milan, 1559, p. 71.

published in 1550, and so cannot be relied upon as a description of what was actually in the villa. Had the owner of the villa picked up the Theatre itself, or one of the versions of it, to add to his collection of rarities ? Tiraboschi thought that the 'pitture' were frescoes painted from themes in the imagery of the Theatre,[18] but Tiraboschi did not believe that the Theatre had ever really existed as an object, as we know that it did. But his interpretation of the 'pitture' may be correct, since it is stated in the preface to the *Idea del Theatro* that 'the entire machine of so superb an edifice cannot now be found',[19] which sounds as though the Theatre as an object could not be traced in Italy by 1550.

In spite of, or perhaps even because of, the fragmentary nature of his achievement, the fame of Giulio Camillo suffered no diminution at his death, but on the contrary glowed more brightly than ever. In 1552 Ludovico Dolce, a popular writer with a keen sense of what would interest the public, wrote a preface for a collected edition of Camillo's somewhat scanty works in which he lamented the early death of this genius who, like Pico della Mirandola, had not completed his work nor brought forth the full fruit of his 'more divine than human intellect'.[20] In 1588, Girolamo Muzio in an oration at Bologna extolled the philosophies of Mercurius Trismegistus, Pythagoras, Plato, Pico della Mirandola, with which he grouped the Theatre of Giulio Camillo.[21] In 1578, J. M. Toscanus published at Paris his *Peplus Italiae,* a series of Latin poems on famous Italians, amongst which is one on Camillo to whose marvellous Theatre the seven wonders of the world must do homage. In a note to the poem Camillo is described as most learned in the mystical traditions of the Hebrews which are called Cabala, and profoundly versed in the philosophies of the Egyptians, the Pythagoreans, and the Platonists.[22]

In the Renaissance the 'philosophies of the Egyptians' mean

[18] Tiraboschi, VII (4), p. 1523.

[19] The author of this preface, L. Dominichi, says that he is publishing this description of the Theatre 'non potendosi anchora scoprire la macchina intera di si superbo edificio'.

[20] G. Camillo, *Tutte le opere,* Venice, 1552; preface by Ludovico Dolce. There were at least nine other editions of *Tutte le opera* between 1554 and 1584, all at Venice. See C. W. E. Leigh, *Catalogue of the Christie Collection,* Manchester University Press, 1915, pp. 97–80.

[21] Liruti, p. 126.

[22] J. M. Toscanus, *Peplus italiae,* Paris, 1578, p. 85.

chiefly the supposed writings of Hermes, or Mercurius, Trismegistus, otherwise the *Corpus Hermeticum* and the *Asclepius,* so deeply meditated upon by Ficino. To these Pico della Mirandola had added the mysteries of the Jewish Cabala. It is no accident that Camillo's name is so frequently linked by his admirers with that of Pico della Mirandola, for he belonged fully and enthusiastically to the Hermetic-Cabalist tradition which Pico founded.[23] His great work in life was to adapt that tradition to the classical art of memory.

When towards the end of his life Camillo was at Milan in the service of Del Vasto, he dictated to Girolamo Muzio, on seven mornings, an outline of his Theatre.[24] After his death the manuscript passed into other hands and was published at Florence and Venice in 1550 with the title *L'Idea del Theatro dell'eccellen. M. Giulio Camillo.*[25] It is this work which enables one to reconstruct the Theatre to some extent, and on it our plan (*see Folder*) is based.

The Theatre rises in seven grades or steps, which are divided by seven gangways representing the seven planets. The student of it is to be as it were a spectator before whom are placed the seven measures of the world 'in spettaculo', or in a theatre. And since in ancient theatres the most distinguished persons sat in the lowest seats, so in this Theatre the greatest and most important things will be in the lowest place.[26]

We have heard some of Camillo's contemporaries describe his work as an amphitheatre, but these indications make it quite certain that he was thinking of the Roman theatre as described by Vitruvius. Vitruvius says that in the auditorium of the theatre the seats are divided by seven gangways, and he also mentions that the upper classes sat in the lowest seats.[27]

Camillo's Memory Theatre is however a distortion of the plan of the real Vitruvian theatre. On each of its seven gangways are seven

[23] See *G.B. and H.T.,* pp. 84 ff.

[24] Muzio, *Lettere,* p. 73; Liruti, p. 104; Tiraboschi, *vol. cit.,* p. 1522.

[25] Page references to *L'Idea del Theatro* in this chapter are to the Florentine edition. *L'Idea del Theatro* is also printed in all the editions of *Tutte le opere.*

[26] *L'Idea del Theatro,* p. 14.

[27] Vitruvius, *De architectura,* Lib. V, cap. 6. On the plan of Camillo's Theatre, the central gangway has been made wider than the others. Camillo does not state that this is to be so but there is a warrant in ancient theatre design for it. L. B. Alberti in his *De re aedificatoria* (Lib. VIII, cap. 7) calls the wider central gangway the 'via regia'.

gates or doors. These gates are decorated with many images. On our plan, the gates are schematically represented and on them are written English translations of the descriptions of the images. That there would be no room for an audience to sit between these enormous and lavishly decorated gangway gates does not matter. For in Camillo's Theatre the normal function of the theatre is reversed. There is no audience sitting in the seats watching a play on the stage. The solitary 'spectator' of the Theatre stands where the stage would be and looks towards the auditorium, gazing at the images on the seven times seven gates on the seven rising grades.

Camillo never mentions the stage and I have therefore omitted it on the plan. In a normal Vitruvian theatre the back of the stage, the *frons scaenae*, has five decorated doors[28] through which the actors make their exits and their entrances. Camillo is transferring the idea of the decorated door from those in the *frons scaenae* to these imaginary decorated doors over the gangways in the auditorium which would make it impossible to seat an audience. He is using the plan of a real theatre, the Vitruvian classical theatre, but adapting it to his mnemonic purposes. The imaginary gates are his memory places, stocked with images.

Looking at our plan, we can see that the whole system of the Theatre rests basically upon seven pillars, the seven pillars of Solomon's House of Wisdom. 'Solomon in the ninth chapter of *Proverbs* says that wisdom has built herself a house and has founded it on seven pillars. By these columns, signifying most stable eternity, we are to understand the seven Sephiroth of the super-celestial world, which are the seven measures of the fabric of the celestial and inferior worlds, in which are contained the Ideas of all things both in the celestial and in the inferior worlds.'[29] Camillo is speaking of the three worlds of the Cabalists, as Pico della Miran-dola had expounded them; the supercelestial world of the Sephi-roth or divine emanations; the middle celestial world of the stars; the subcelestial or elemental world. The same 'measures' run through all three worlds though their manifestations are different in each. As Sephiroth in the supercelestial world they are here equated with the Platonic ideas. Camillo is basing his memory system on first causes, on the Sephiroth, on the Ideas; these are to be the 'eternal places' of his memory.

[28] See further below, p. 171.   [29] *L'Idea dela Theatro*, p. 9.

Now if the ancient orators, wishing to place from day to day the parts of the speeches which they had to recite, confided them to frail places as frail things, it is right that we, wishing to store up eternally the eternal nature of all things which can be expressed in speech . . . should assign them to eternal places. Our high labour, therefore, has been to find an order in these seven measures, capacious and distinct from one another, and which will keep the mind awake and move the memory.[30]

As these words show, Camillo never loses sight of the fact that his Theatre is based on the principles of the classical art of memory. But his memory building is to represent the order of eternal truth; in it the universe will be remembered through organic association of all its parts with their underlying eternal order.

Since, as Camillo explains, the highest of the universal measures, the Sephiroth, are remote from our knowledge and only mysteriously touched upon by the prophets, he places, not these, but the seven planets on the first grade of the Theatre, for the planets are nearer to us and their images are better grasped as memory images, being strikingly differentiated from one another. But the planet images, and the characters of the planets, which are placed on the first grade are to be understood, not as termini beyond which we cannot rise, but as also representing, as they do in the minds of the wise, the seven celestial measures above them.[31] We have indicated this idea on the plan by showing on the gates of the first or lowest grade, the characters of the planets, their names (standing for their images) and then the names of the Sephiroth and angels with which Camillo associates each planet. To bring out the importance of Sol, he varies the arrangement in this case by representing the Sun on the first grade by the image of a pyramid, placing the image of the planet, an Apollo, above this on the second grade.

Thus, following the custom in ancient theatres in which the most important people sat in the lowest seats, Camillo has placed in his lowest grade the seven essential measures on which, according to magico-mystical theory, all things here below depend, the seven planets. Once these have been organically grasped, imprinted on memory with their images and characters, the mind can move from this middle celestial world in either direction; up into the supercelestial world of the Ideas, the Sephiroth and the angels, entering

[30] *Ibid.*, pp. 10–11   [31] *Ibid.*, p. 11.

Solomon's Temple of Wisdom, or down into the subcelestial and elemental world which will range itself in order on the upper grades of the Theatre (really the lower seats) in accordance with the astral influences.

Each of the six upper grades has a general symbolic meaning represented by the same image on each of its seven gates. We have shown this on the plan by giving the name of the general image for a grade at the top of all its gates, together with the characters of the planets, indicating to which planetary series each gate belongs.

Thus, on the second grade, the reader will see 'The Banquet' written at the top of all the gates (except in the case of Sol where 'The Banquet' is placed on the first grade, an inversion to differentiate the series of the Sun from the others), for this is the image expressive of the general meaning of this grade. 'The second grade of the Theatre will have depicted on all its gates the same image, and this will be a banquet. Homer feigns that Ocean made a banquet for all the gods, nor was it without lofty mysterious meanings that this lofty poet invented this fiction.'[32] The Ocean, explains Camillo, is the waters of wisdom which were in existence before the *materia prima*, and the invited gods are the Ideas existing in the divine exemplar. Or the Homeric banquet suggests to him St. John's Gospel, 'In the beginning was the Word'; or the opening words of *Genesis*, 'In the beginning'. In short, the second grade of the Theatre is really the first day of creation, imaged as the banquet given by Ocean to the gods, the emerging elements of creation, here in their simple unmixed form.

'The third grade will have depicted on each of its gates a Cave, which we call the Homeric Cave to differentiate it from that which Plato describes in his Republic.' In the cave of the Nymphs described in the *Odyssey*, nymphs were weaving and bees were going in and out, which activities signify, says Camillo, the mixtures of the elements to form the *elementata* 'and we wish that each of the seven caves may conserve the mixtures and *elementata*

---

[32] *Ibid.*, p. 17. Cf. Homer, *Iliad*, I, 423-5. Camillo may have in mind Macrobius's interpretation of the myth, that the gods who go with Jupiter to feast with Ocean are the planets. See Macrobius, *Commentary on the Dream of Scipio*, trans. W. H. Stahl, Columbia, 1952, p. 218.

belonging to it in accordance with the nature of its planet.'[33] The Cave grade thus represents a further stage in creation, when the elements are mixed to form created things or *elementata*. This stage is illustrated with quotation from Cabalistic commentary on *Genesis*.

With the fourth grade we reach the creation of man, or rather the interior man, his mind and soul. 'Let us now rise to the fourth grade belonging to the interior man, the most noble of God's creatures which He made in his own image and similitude.'[34] Why then does this grade have as the leading image to be depicted on all its gates the Gorgon Sisters, the three sisters described by Hesiod[35] who had only one eye between them ? Because Camillo adopts from Cabalist sources the view that man has three souls. Therefore the image of the three sisters with one eye may be used for the fourth grade which contains 'things belonging to the interior man in accordance with the nature of each planet'.[36]

On the fifth grade, the soul of man joins his body. This is signified under the image of Pasiphe and the Bull which is the leading image on the gates of this grade. 'For she (Pasiphe) being enamoured of the Bull signifies the soul which, according to the Platonists, falls into a state of desiring the body.'[37] The soul in its downward journey from on high, passing through all the spheres, changes its pure igneous vehicle into an aerial vehicle through which it is enabled to become joined to the gross corporeal form. This junction is symbolised by the union of Pasiphe with the Bull. Hence the image of Pasiphe on the gates of the fifth grade of the Theatre 'will cover all the other images (on these gates) to which will be attached volumes containing things and words belonging, not only to the interior man, but also to the exterior man and concerning the parts of his body in accordance with the nature of each planet . . .'[38] The last image on each of the gates of this grade is to be that of a Bull alone, and these Bulls represent the different parts of the human body and their association with the twelve signs of the zodiac. On the plan, these Bulls, the parts of the body

---

[33] *L'Idea del Theatro*, p. 29. Cf. Homer, *Odyssey*, XIII, 102 ff. The interpretation of the Cave of the Nymphs as the mixture of the elements derives from Porphyry, *De antro nympharum*.
[34] *L'Idea del Theatro*, p. 53.   [35] Hesiod, *Shield of Hercules*, 230.
[36] *L'Idea del Theatro*, p. 62.   [37] *Ibid.*, p. 67.
[38] *Ibid.*, p. 68.

they represent and the relevant signs of the zodiac, are indicated at the bottom of all the gates on the fifth grade.

'The sixth grade of the Theatre has on each of the gates of the planets, the Sandals, and other ornaments, which Mercury puts on when he goes to execute the will of the gods, as the poets feign. Thereby the memory will be awakened to find beneath them all the operations which man can perform naturally . . . and without any art.'[39] We have thus to imagine the Sandals and other attributes of Mercury placed on the top of all the gates on this grade.

'The seventh grade is assigned to all the arts, both noble and vile, and above each gate is Prometheus with a lighted torch.'[40] The image of Prometheus who stole the sacred fire and taught men knowledge of the gods and of all the arts and sciences thus becomes the topmost image, at the head of the gates on the highest grade of the Theatre. The Prometheus grade includes not only all the arts and sciences, but also religion, and law.[41]

Thus Camillo's Theatre represents the universe expanding from First Causes through the stages of creation. First is the appearance of the simple elements from the waters on the Banquet grade; then the mixture of the elements in the Cave; then the creation of man's *mens* in the image of God on the grade of the Gorgon Sisters; then the union of man's soul and body on the grade of Pasiphe and the Bull; then the whole world of man's activities; his natural activities on the grade of the Sandals of Mercury; his arts and sciences, religion and laws on the Prometheus grade. Though there are unorthodox elements (to be discussed later) in Camillo's system, his grades contain obvious reminiscences of the orthodox days of creation.

And if we go up the Theatre, by the gangways of the seven planets, the whole creation falls into order as the development of the seven fundamental measures. Look, for example, at the Jupiter series. Jupiter as a planet is associated with the element of air. On the Banquet grade in the jupiter series, the image of Juno suspended[42]

---

[39] *Ibid.*, p. 76.

[40] *Ibid.*, p. 79 (wrongly numbered 71 in the text).

[41] *Ibid.*, p. 81.

[42] Homer, *Iliad*, 18 ff. This image was anciently interpreted as an allegory of the four elements; the two weights attached to Juno's feet being the two heavy elements, earth and water; Juno herself, air; Jupiter the highest fiery air or ether. See F. Buffière, *Les mythes d'Homère et la pensée grecque*, Paris, 1956, p. 43.

means air as a simple element; under the Cave, the same image means air as a mixed element; with the Sandals of Mercury, it stands for the natural operations of breathing, sighing; on the Prometheus grade it means arts using air, such as windmills. Jupiter is a useful, benevolent planet whose influences are pacificatory. In the Jupiter series the image of the Three Graces means under the Cave, useful things; with Pasiphe and the Bull, a beneficent nature; with the Sandals of Mercury, exercising benevolence. The changing meaning of an image on different grades, without losing its basic theme, is a carefully thought out characteristic of the imagery of the Theatre. On the Gorgon Sisters grade, the elaborate image of the Stork and Caduceus represents Jovial characteristics in their purely spiritual or mental form, the heavenward flight of the tranquil soul . . . choice, judgment, counsel. Joined to the body under Pasiphe and the Bull, the Jovial personality is represented by images suggestive of goodness, friendliness, good fortune and wealth. The natural Jovial operations appear on the grade of the Sandals of Mercury with images representing exercising virtue, exercising friendship. On the Prometheus level, the Jovial character is represented by images standing for religion and the law.

Or take, as a contrast, the Saturn series.[43] Saturn's association with the element of earth appears under the Banquet as the image of Cybele, meaning earth as a simple element; Cybele under the Cave is earth as a mixed element; Cybele with the Sandals of Mercury is natural operations concerned with earth; Cybele with Prometheus is arts concerned with earth, as geometry, geography, agriculture. The sadness and solitariness of the Saturnian temperament is expressed by the image of the Solitary Sparrow which recurs under the Cave, Pasiphe, and Sandals of Mercury. The mental characteristics of the Saturnian temperament appear under the Gorgon Sisters in the image of Hercules and Antaeus with its sense of struggle with earth to rise to heights of contemplation (compare the easy, aerial ascent of the Jovial mind on this same grade). Saturn's association with time is expressed under the Cave in the image of the heads of a wolf, lion, and dog, signifying past,

---

[43] On Saturnian associations and characteristics, see *Saturn and Melancholy*, by R. Klibansky, E. Panofsky, F. Saxl, London, 1964.

present, and future.[44] The association of this planet with ill fortune and poverty is expressed by the images of Pandora, in the Cave, Pasiphe, and Sandals of Mercury grades. One of the humblest of the 'occupations of Saturn', carrying and porterage, appears under Prometheus, symbolised by the Ass.

Once the method is understood, it can be followed in all the other planetary series. The watery Luna has Neptune for water as simple element under the Banquet, with the usual variations of the same image on other grades, and the usual type of allusions to the Lunar temperament and occupations. The Mercury series works out very interestingly the Mercurial gifts and aptitudes. The Venus series does the same for the Venereal side of life. Similarly the Mars series, which uses Vulcan as the image of fire on the various grades, alludes to the Martial temperament and occupations.

Most important of all is the great central series on Sol, Apollo, the Sun, but we reserve discussion of this until later.

So we begin to perceive the vast scope of the Memory Theatre of the divine Camillo. But let us quote his own words:

This high and incomparable placing not only performs the office of conserving for us the things, words, and arts which we confide to it, so that we may find them at once whenever we need them, but also gives us true wisdom from whose founts we come to the knowledge of things from their causes and not from their effects. This may be more clearly expressed from the following illustration. If we were to find ourselves in a vast forest and desired to see its whole extent we should not be able to do this from our position within it for our view would be limited to only a small part of it by the immediately surrounding trees which would prevent us from seeing the distant view. But if, near to this forest, there were a slope leading up to a high hill, on coming out of the forest and ascending the slope we should begin to see a large part of the form of the forest, and from the top of the hill we should see the whole of it. The wood is our inferior world; the slope is the heavens; the hill is the supercelestial world. And in order to understand the things of the lower world it is necessary to ascend to superior things, from whence, looking down from on high, we may have a more certain knowledge of the inferior things.[45]

[44] This is the time symbol associated with Serapis and described by Macrobius; cf. E. Panofsky, 'Signum Triciput: Ein Hellenistisches Kultsymbol in der Kunst der Renaissance', in *Hercules am Scheidewege*, Berlin, 1930, pp. 1–35.

[45] *L'Idea del Theatro*, pp. 11–12.

The Theatre is thus a vision of the world and of the nature of things seen from a height, from the stars themselves and even from the supercelestial founts of wisdom beyond them.

Yet this vision is very deliberately cast within the framework of the classical art of memory, using the traditional mnemonic terminology. The Theatre is a system of memory places, though a 'high and incomparable' placing; it performs the office of a classical memory system for orators by 'conserving for us the things, words, and arts which we confide to it.' Ancient orators confided the parts of the speeches they wished to remember to 'frail places', whereas Camillo 'wishing to store up eternally the eternal nature of all things which can be expressed in speech' assigns to them 'eternal places'.

The basic images in the Theatre are those of the planetary gods. The affective or emotional appeal of a good memory image—according to the rules—is present in such images, expressive of the tranquillity of Jupiter, the anger of Mars, the melancholy of Saturn, the love of Venus. Here again the Theatre starts with causes, the planetary causes of the various affects, and the differing emotional currents running through the seven-fold divisions of the Theatre from their planetary sources perform that office of stirring the memory emotionally which was recommended in the classical art, but perform this organically in relation to causes.

It appears from Viglius's description of the Theatre that under the images there were drawers, or boxes, or coffers of some kind containing masses of papers, and on these papers were speeches, based on the works of Cicero, relating to the subjects recalled by the images. This system is frequently alluded to in *L'Idea del Theatro*, for example in the statement quoted above that the images on the gates on the fifth grade will have attached to them 'volumes containing things and words belonging not only to the interior man but also to the exterior man.' Viglius saw Camillo excitedly manipulating 'papers' in the Theatre; he was doubtless drawing out the many 'volumes' from the receptacles for them under the images. He had hit upon a new interpretation of memory for 'things' and 'words' by storing written speeches under the images (all this written material from the Theatre appears to have been lost, though Alessandro Citolini was suspected of having stolen it and published it under his own name).[46] When one thinks of all

[46] See below, p. 239.

THE MEMORY THEATRE
of GIULIO CAMILLO

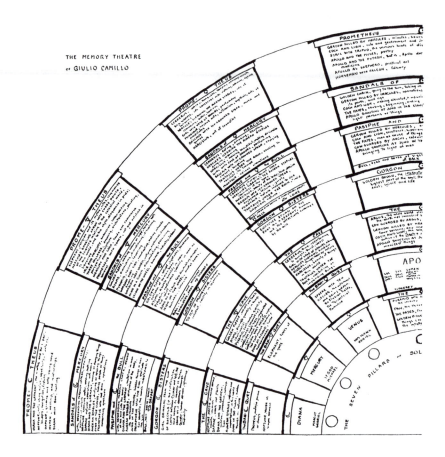

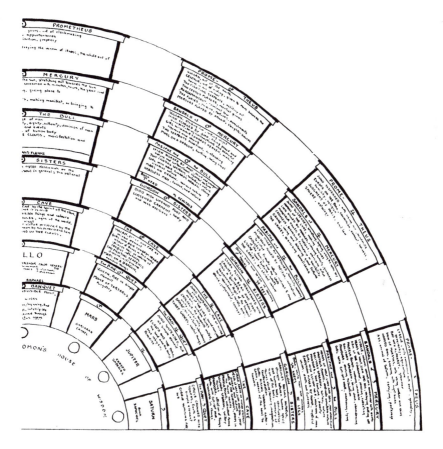

these drawers or coffers in the Theatre it begins to look like a highly ornamental filing cabinet. But this is to lose sight of the grandeur of the Idea—the Idea of a memory organically geared to the universe.

Though the art of memory is still using places and images according to the rules, a radical change had come over the philosophy and psychology behind it, which is now no longer scholastic but Neoplatonic. And Camillo's Neoplatonism is most strongly infused with those Hermetic influences at the core of the movement inaugurated by Marsilio Ficino. The body of writings known as the *Corpus Hermeticum* was rediscovered in the fifteenth century and translated into Latin by Ficino, who believed—and the belief was universal—that they were the work of the ancient Egyptian sage, Hermes (or Mercurius) Trismegistus.[47] They represented a tradition of ancient wisdom earlier than Plato, and which had inspired Plato and the Neoplatonists. Encouraged by some of the Fathers of the Church, Ficino attached a peculiarly sacred character to the Hermetic writings as Gentile prophecies of the coming of Christianity. The *Corpus Hermeticum* as a sacred book of most ancient wisdom was almost more important to the Renaissance Neoplatonist than Plato himself. And the *Asclepius*, which had been known in the Middle Ages, was associated with it as another inspired writing by Trismegistus. The enormous importance of these Hermetic influences in the Renaissance is coming to be more and more realised. Camillo's Theatre is impregnated with them, through and through.

Into the old bottles of the art of memory there has been poured the heady wine of the currents of Renaissance 'occult philosophy', running fresh and strong into sixteenth-century Venice from its springs in the movement inaugurated by Ficino in Florence in the late fifteenth century. The body of Hermetic doctrine available to Camillo consisted of the first fourteen treatises of the *Corpus Hermeticum*, in Ficino's Latin translation, and the *Asclepius* in the Latin translation known in the Middle Ages. He makes numerous verbal quotations from these works of 'Mercurius Trismegistus'.

In the Hermetic account of creation in the first treatise of the *Corpus*, called the *Pimander*, Camillo had read of how the demiurge fashioned 'the Seven Governors who envelop with their circles the

[47] See *G.B. and H.T.*, pp. 6 ff.

sensible world'. He quotes this passage, in Ficino's Latin, stating that he is quoting 'Mercurio Trismegisto nel Pimandro', and adding this remark:

> And in truth since the divinity produced out of itself these seven measures, it is a sign that they were always implicitly contained within the abyss of the divinity.[48]

The Seven Governors of the Hermetic *Pimander* are thus behind those seven measures upon which Camillo founds his Theatre and which have their continuation into the Sephiroth, into the abyss of the divinity. The seven are more than planets in the astrological sense; they are divine astral beings.

After the Seven Governors have been created and set in motion there comes in the *Pimander* the account of the creation of man, which differs radically from the account in *Genesis*. For the Hermetic man is created in the image of God in the sense that he is given the divine creative power. When he saw the newly created Seven Governors, the Man wished also to produce a work and 'permission to do this was given him by the Father'.

> Having thus entered into the demiurgic sphere in which he had full power ... the Governors fell in love with him, and each gave to him a part in their own rule.[49]

Man's mind is a direct reflection of the divine *mens* and has within it all the powers of the Seven Governors. When he falls into the body he does not lose this divinity of his mind and he can recover his full divine nature, as the rest of the *Pimander* recounts, through the Hermetic religious experience in which the divine light and life within his own *mens* is revealed to him.

In the Theatre, the creation of man is in two stages. He is not created body and soul together as in *Genesis*. First there is the appearance of the 'interior man' on the grade of the Gorgon Sisters, the most noble of God's creatures, made in his image and similitude. Then on the grade of Pasiphe and the Bull man takes on a body the parts of which are under the domination of the zodiac. This is what happens to man in the *Pimander*; the interior man, his *mens*, created divine and having the powers of the star-rulers,

---

[48] *L'Idea del Theatro*, p. 10, The passage is quoted in Ficino's Latin (Ficino, *Opera*, ed. Bâle, 1576, p. 1837).
[49] Quoted as translated in *G.B. and H.T.*, p. 23.

on falling into the body comes under the domination of the stars, whence he escapes in the Hermetic religious experience of ascent through the spheres to regain his divinity.

On the grade of the Gorgon Sisters, Camillo discusses what the creation of man in God's image and similitudes can mean. He quotes a passage from the *Zohar* on these words in which they are interpreted to mean that, though like God, the interior man is not actually divine. Camillo contrasts this with the Hermetic account:

> But Mercurius Trismegistus in his Pimander takes the image and similitude for the same thing, and the whole for the divine grade.[50]

He then quotes the opening of the passage in the *Pimander* on the creation of man. He is agreeing with Trismegistus, that the interior man was created 'on the divine grade'. And he follows this up by quotation of the famous passage in the *Asclepius* on man, the great miracle:

> Oh Asclepius, what a great miracle is man, a being worthy of reverence and honour. For he goes into the nature of a god, as though he were himself a god; he is familiar with the race of demons, knowing that he is issued from the same origin; he despises that part of his nature which is only human, for he has put his hope in the divinity of the other part.[51]

This again affirms the divinity of man, and that he belongs to the same race as the creative star-demons.

The divinity of man's intellect is again affirmed in the twelfth treatise of the *Corpus Hermeticum*, and this was a favourite treatise of Camillo's from which he frequently quotes. The intellect is drawn from the very substance of God. In men this intellect is God; and so some men are gods and their humanity is near to the divinity. The world too is divine; it is a great god, image of a greater God.[52]

These Hermetic teachings on the divinity of man's *mens* in which Camillo was saturated, are reflected in his memory system. It is because he believes in the divinity of man that the divine Camillo makes his stupendous claim of being able to remember the universe by looking down upon it from above, from first causes, as

[50] *L'Idea del Theatro*, p. 53.

[51] *Ibid., loc. cit.*

[52] Quotation from *Corpus Hermeticum* XII, 'On the common intellect', in *L'Idea del Theatro*, p. 51.

though he were God.[53] In this atmosphere, the relationship between man, the microcosm, and the world, the macrocosm, takes on a new significance. The microcosm can fully understand and fully remember the macrocosm, can hold it within his divine *mens* or memory.

A memory system based on such teachings as this, though it uses the old places and images, must clearly have very different implications for its user from these of the old times, when man was allowed to use images in memory as a concession to his weakness.

To the strong Hermetic influences stemming from Ficino's philosophy, Pico della Mirandola had joined influences from his popularisation of the Jewish Cabala, in a Christianised form. The two types of cosmic mysticism have affinities with one another, and they amalgamated to form the Hermetic-Cabalist tradition, so powerful a force in the Renaissance after Pico.

That there is a strong Cabalist influence on the Theatre is obvious. The ten Sephiroth as divine measures in the super-celestial world corresponding to the ten spheres of the universe had been adopted by Pico from Cabalism. For Camillo, it is the correspondence of the seven planetary measures of the celestial world with the supercelestial Sephiroth which gives the Theatre its prolongation up into the supercelestial world, into the abyss of the divine wisdom and the mysteries of the Temple of Solomon. Camillo has, however, juggled with the normal arrangements. The correlations between planetary spheres and Jewish Sephiroth and angels, as he gives them, run thus:

Planets	Sephiroth	Angels
Luna (Diana)	Marcut	Gabriel
Mercury	Iesod	Michael
Venus	Hod and Nisach	Honiel
Sol	Tipheret	Raphael
Mars	Gabiarah	Camael
Jupiter	Chased	Zadchiel
Saturn	Bina	Zaphkiel

[53] Presumably he has made the gnostic ascent through the spheres to his divine origin. According to Macrobius, souls descend through Cancer where they drink the cup of forgetfulness of the higher world, and ascend back to the higher world through Capricorn. See the plan of the Theatre, Saturn series, Gorgon Sisters grade, 'Girl rising through Capricorn'; and Luna series, Gorgon Sisters grade, 'Girl drinking from the cup of Bacchus'.

He has left out the two highest Sephiroth, Kether and Hokmah. This was done intentionally, for he explains that he is not going above Bina, to which Moses ascended, and he therefore stops his series at Bina-Saturn.[54] There is also some confusion or anomaly in his giving two Sephiroth to Venus. Otherwise his Sephiroth-planet correlations are not unusual ones, though F. Secret points out that he has slightly deformed the names of the Sephiroth and suggests Egidius of Viterbo as a probable intermediary.[55] With the Sephiroth-planets, Camillo puts seven angels; his angel correlations are also fairly normal.

As well as the adoption of the Jewish Sephiroth and angels and their connections with the planetary spheres, there are numerous other Cabalist influences in the Theatre, the most noteworthy of which is the quotation from the *Zohar* on man having three souls; Nessamah, the highest soul; the middle soul, Ruach; and a lower soul, Nephes.[56] This Cabalistic concept he invests with the image of the three Gorgon Sisters, with one eye between them, as the leading image on the grade of the Theatre dealing with the 'interior man'. In his anxiety to make the interior man wholly divine, with Trismegistus, he emphasises Nessamah. The extra-ordinary medley of Cabalistic, Christian, and philosophical sources with which Camillo supports his notions is well exemplified in the explanation which he gives, in his *Lettera del rivolgimento dell'huomo a Dio*, of the meaning of the Gorgon Sisters grade in the Theatre. This letter about the return of man to God is, at bottom, a commentary on the Theatre, as are other of Camillo's minor writings. After mentioning Nessamah, Ruach, and Nephes as the three souls in man symbolised by the Gorgon Sisters in the Theatre, he expands the meaning of the highest soul thus:

... We have three souls, of which the one nearest to God is called by Mercurius Trismegistus and Plato *mens*, by Moses the spirit of

[54] *L'Idea del Theatro*, p. 13.
[55] Secret, *article cited*, p. 422; and Egidio da Viterbo, *Scechina e Libellus de litteris hebraicis*, ed. F. Secret, Rome, 1959, I, Introduction, p. 13. Other members of the circle of Cardinal Egidius of Viterbo, who was deeply interested in Cabalistic studies, were Francesco Giorgi, the author of the *De harmonia mundi*, and Annius of Viterbo.
[56] *L'Idea del Theatro*, pp. 56–7; cf. *Zohar*, I, 206a; II, 141b; III, 70b, and G. G. Scholem, *Major Trends in Jewish Mysticism*, Jerusalem, 1941, pp. 236–7.

life, by St. Augustine the higher part, by David light, when he says 'In thy light shall we see light', and Pythagoras agrees with David in that celebrated precept, 'No man may speak of God without light.' Which light is called by Aristotle the *intellectus agens*, and it is that one eye by which all the three Gorgon Sisters see, according to the symbolic theologians. And Mercurius says that if we join ourselves to this *mens* we may understand, through the ray from God which is in it, all things, present, past, and future, all things, I say, which are in heaven and earth.[57]

Looking now at the image of the Golden Bough on the Gorgon Sisters grade of the Theatre, we may understand its meanings: the *intellectus agens*, Nessamah or the highest part of the soul, the soul in general, the rational soul, spirit and life.

Camillo erects his Theatre in the spiritual world of Pico della Mirandola, the world of Pico's Conclusions and Oration on the Dignity of Man and *Heptalus*, with its angelic spheres, Sephiroth, days of creation, mingled with Mercurius Trismegistus, Plato, Plotinus, St. John's Gospel, St. Paul's epistles—all that heterogeneous array of references, pagan, Hebraic, or Christian, through which Pico moves with such assurance as though he had found the master-key. Pico's key is the same as that of Camillo. In this world, man with his mind made in the image of God has the middle place (compare the Gorgon Sisters grade in the middle of the Theatre). He can move amidst it with understanding and draw it into himself with subtle religious magics, Hermetic and Cabalist, which bring him back on to that divine grade which is his by right. Being organically related in his origin to the Seven Governors ('Oh what a miracle is man', cries Pico at the beginning of the Oration, quoting Mercurius Trismegistus) he can communicate with the seven planetary rulers of the world. And he can rise beyond these and hold communion, through Cabalist secrets, with the angels— moving with his divine mind through all the three worlds, super-celestial, celestial, terrestrial.[58] Even so, in the Theatre, does Camillo's mind range through all the worlds. These things must be hidden under a veil explains Pico. The Egyptians sculptured a sphinx on their temples, signifying that the mysteries must be kept inviolate. The highest revelations made to Moses are kept secret

[57] Camillo, *Tutte le opere*, ed. of Venice, 1552, pp. 42–3.
[58] Pico della Mirandola, *De hominis dignitate*, ed. E. Garin, Florence, 1942, pp. 157, 159.

in the Cabala. In exactly the same vein, Camillo, in the opening pages of the *Idea del Theatro* speaks of its hidden mysteries. 'Mercurius Trismegistus says that religious speech, full of God, is violated by the intrusion of the vulgar. For this reason the ancients ... sculptured a sphinx on their temples ... Ezechiel was rebuked by the Cabalists ... for having revealed what he had seen ... let us now pass in the name of the Lord to speak of our Theatre.'[59]

Camillo brings the art of memory into line with the new currents now running through the Renaissance. His Memory Theatre houses Ficino and Pico, Magia and Cabala, the Hermetism and Cabalism implicit in Renaissance so-called Neoplatonism. He turns the classical art of memory into an occult art.

Where is the magic in such an occult memory system as this, and how does it work, or how is it supposed to work? It was Ficino's-astral magic[60] which influenced Camillo and which he was attempting to use.

Ficino's 'spiritus' magic was based on the magical rites described in the Hermetic *Asclepius* through which the Egyptians, or rather the Hermetic pseudo-Egyptians, were said to animate their statues by drawing into them the divine, or demonic, powers of the cosmos. Ficino describes in his *De vita coelitus comparanda* ways of drawing down the life of the stars, of capturing the astral currents pouring down from above and using them for life and health. The celestial life, according to the Hermetic sources, is born on air, or spiritus, and it is strongest in the sun which is its chief transmitter. Ficino therefore seeks to cultivate the sun and his therapeutic astral cult is a revival of sun worship.

Though the Ficinian influence is everywhere present in Camillo's Theatre, it is in the great central series of the Sun that it is most apparent. Most of Ficino's ideas on the sun are set out in his *De sole*,[61] though they also appear in his other works. In the *De sole*, the Sun is called the *statua Dei* and is compared to the Trinity. On the Banquet grade of the Sun series, Camillo places the image of a pyramid, representing the Trinity. On the gate above this,

---

[59] *L'Idea del Theatro*, pp. 8–9.

[60] On Ficino's magic, see Walker, *Magic*, pp. 30 ff.; Yates, *G.B. and H.T.*, pp. 62 ff.

[61] Ficino, *Opera, ed. cit.*, pp. 965–75; see also *De lumine, ibid.*, pp. 976–86; and cf. *G.B. and H.T.*, pp. 120, 153.

where is the main image of Apollo, Camillo sets out a 'light' series: *Sol, Lux, Lumen, Splendor, Calor, Generatio*. Ficino has a similar hierarchical light series in the *De sole*. The Sun is first of all God; then Light in the heavens; then *Lumen* which is a form of spiritus; then Heat which is lower than *Lumen*; then Generation, the lowest of the series. Camillo's series is not quite the same; and Ficino is not quite consistent in the way he sets out the hierarchy of light in different works. But Camillo's arrangement is completely Ficinian in spirit, in its suggestion of a hierarchy descending from the Sun as God to other forms of light and heat in lower spheres, transmitting the spiritus in his rays.

Going further up the gates in the Sun series we find on the Cave grade, the image of Argus with, as one of its meanings, the whole world vivified by the spirit of the stars, suggestive of one of the basic principles of Ficinian magic, that the astral spiritus is transmitted mainly by the sun. And on the Sandals of Mercury grade, the image of the Golden Chain expresses the operations of going to the sun, taking in the sun, stretching out towards the sun, suggestive of the operations of Ficinian solar magic. Camillo's suns series shows a typically Ficinian combination of sun mysticism with magical solarianism.

And it is significant that with the image of the Cock and Lion on the Cave grade, Camillo recounts the lion story, which we have already heard in a slightly less flattering form from another source:

> When the author of this Theatre was in Paris in the place called the Tornello, being with many other gentlemen in a room the windows of which overlooked a garden, a Lion escaped from imprisonment came into this room, and coming up to him from behind, took hold of him by the thighs with his claws but without harming him, and began to lick him. And when he turned round, having felt the touch and breath of the animal—all the others having fled hither and thither—the Lion humbled itself before him, as though to ask his forgiveness. This can only mean that this animal recognised that there was much of Solar Virtue in him.[62]

[62] *L'Idea del Theatro*, p. 39. The 'Cock and Lion' might have been suggested by Proclus's *De sacra et magia* in which it is stated that of these two solarian creatures, the cock is the more solarian since it sings hymns to the rising sun. Cf. Walker, *Magic*, p. 37, note 2.

There is possibly an allusion to the French King in the cock. Cf. Bruno on the solar French cock, quoted in *G.B. and H.T.*, p. 202.

The behaviour of this unfortunate lion evidently proved, not only to the bystanders but to Camillo himself, that the author of the Theatre was a Solar Magus!

The reader may smile at Camillo's lion, but he should not look too patronisingly at the great central Sun series in the Theatre. He should remember that Copernicus, when introducing the heliocentric hypothesis, quoted the words of Hermes Trismegistus in the *Asclepius* on the sun;[63] that Giordano Bruno when expounding Copernicanism at Oxford associated it with Ficino's *De vita coelitus comparanda*;[64] that the Hermetic view that the earth is not immobile because it is alive, quoted by Camillo with the Argus image on the Cave grade of the Sun series,[65] was adapted by Bruno for his defence of the movement of the earth.[66] The Sun series of the Theatre shows within the mind and memory of a man of the Renaissance the Sun looming with a new importance, mystical, emotional, magical, the Sun becoming of central significance. It shows an inner movement of the imagination towards the Sun which must be taken into account as one of the factors in the heliocentric revolution.

Camillo, like Ficino, is a Christian Hermetist, who endeavours to correlate Hermetic teachings with Christianity. Hermes Trismegistus in these circles was a sacred figure, who was believed to have prophesied the coming of Christianity through his allusions to a 'Son of God'.[67] The sanctity of Hermes as a Gentile prophet helped to make easy the path of a Magus who wished to remain a Christian. We have already seen that the sun as the most powerful of the astral gods and the chief transmitter of spiritus is, in his highest manifestation an image of the Trinity, for Camillo as for Ficino. Camillo is, however, rather unusual in identifying the spiritus proceeding from the Sun, not with the Holy Spirit, as was usually done, but with the 'spirit of Christ'. Quoting from *Corpus Hermeticum*, V, 'That god is both apparent and inapparent', Camillo identifies the divine spirit latent in the creation, which is

[63] Cf. *G.B. and H.T.*, p. 154.

[64] *Ibid.*, pp. 155, 208–11.

[65] *L'Idea del Theatro*, p. 38, quoting *Corpus Hermeticum*, XII.

[66] Cf. *G.B. and H.T.*, pp. 241–3. Bruno quotes the same passage from *Corpus Hermeticum* XII when arguing in favour of earth movement in the *Cena de le ceneri*.

[67] Cf. *G.B. and H.T.*, pp. 7 ff.

the theme of this treatise, with the Spirit of Christ. He quotes St. Paul on 'Spiritus Christi, Spiritus vivificans' adding that 'about this Mercurius made a book, *Quod Deus latens simul, ac patens sit*' (that is *Corpus Hermeticum*, V).[68] That Camillo was able to think of the *spiritus mundi* as the spirit of Christ enabled him to impart Christian overtones to his ardent adoption of Ficino's spiritus magic with which his Theatre is redolent.

How would the Ficinian magic be supposed to work within a memory system using places and images in the classical manner? The secret of this is, I believe, that the memory images were regarded as, so to speak, inner talismans.

The talisman is an object imprinted with an image which has been supposed to have been rendered magical, or to have magical efficacy, through having been made in accordance with certain magical rules. The images of talismans are usually, though not always, images of the stars, for example, an image of Venus as the goddess of the planet Venus, or an image of Apollo as the god of the planet Sol. The handbook of talismanic magic called the *Picatrix*, which was well known in the Renaissance, describes the processes through which talismanic images were supposed to be made magical by becoming infused with the astral spiritus.[69] The Hermetic book which was the theoretical basis of talismanic magic was the *Asclepius* in which the magical religion of the Egyptians is described. According to the author of the *Asclepius* the Egyptians knew how to infuse the statues of their gods with cosmic and magical powers; by prayers, incantations, and other processes they gave life to these statues; in other words, the Egyptians knew how to 'make gods'. The processes by which the Egyptians are said in the *Asclepius* to make their statues into gods are similar to the processes by which a talisman is made.

Ficino made some use of talismans in his magic, as described in his *De vita coelitus comparanda*, where he quotes descriptions of talismanic images, probably derived, some of them, from *Picatrix*. It has been shown that the passages in Ficino's book on talismans are derived with some modifications, from the passages in the *Asclepius* on how the Egyptians infused magical and divine powers into the statues of their gods.[70] Ficino was using this magic with

---

[68] *L'Idea del Theatro*, pp. 20–1.
[69] Cf. *G.B. and H.T.*, pp. 49 ff.
[70] Cf. Walker, *Magic*, pp. 1–24 and *passim*.

caution, and somewhat disguising its basis in the magical passages in the *Asclepius*. Nevertheless there can be no doubt that this was his source, and that he was encouraged to take up talismanic magic through his respect and reverence for the divine teacher, Mercurius Trismegistus.

Like all his magic, Ficino's use of talismans was a highly subjective and imaginative one. His magical practices, whether poetic and musical incantations, or the use of magicised images, were really directed towards a conditioning of the imagination to receive celestial influences. His talismanic images, evolved into beautiful Renaissance forms, were intended to be held within, in the imagination of their user. He describes how an image drawn from astralised mythology could be imprinted inwardly on the mind with such force that when a person, with this imprint in his imagination came out into the world of external appearances, these became unified through the power of the inner image, drawn from the higher world.[71]

Such inner, or imaginative, use of talismanic imagery, would surely find a most suitable vehicle for its use in the occultised version of the art of memory. If the basic memory images used in such a memory system had, or were supposed to have, talismanic power, power to draw down the celestial influences and spiritus within the memory, such a memory would become that of the 'divine' man in intimate association with the divine powers of the cosmos. And such a memory would also have, or be supposed to have, the power of unifying the contents of memory by basing it upon these images drawn from the celestial world. The images of Camillo's Theatre seem to be supposed to have in them something of this power, enabling the 'spectator' to read off at one glance, through 'inspecting the images' the whole contents of the universe. The 'secret', or one of the secrets, of the Theatre is, I believe, that the basic planetary images are supposed to be talismans, or to have talismanic virtue, and that the astral power from them is supposed to run through the subsidiary images—a Jupiter power, for example, running through all the images in the Jupiter series, or a Sun power through the Sun series. In this way, the cosmically based memory would be supposed, not only to draw power from the cosmos into the memory, but to unify memory. All the details

[71] Cf. *G.B. and H.T.*, pp. 75–6.

of the world of sense, reflected in memory, would be unified organically within the memory, because subsumed and unified under the higher celestial images, the images of their 'causes'.

If this was the theory of underlying the images of Camillo's occult memory system, it would have been based on the magical passages in the *Asclepius*. The 'god making' passages in that work are not quoted or referred to in *L'Idea del Theatro*, but in a speech about his Theatre, which he probably delivered in some Venetian academy, Camillo does refer to the magic statues of the *Asclepius*, and gives a very subtle interpretation of their magic.

> I have read, I believe in Mercurius Trismegistus, that in Egypt there were such excellent makers of statues that when they had brought some statue to the perfect proportions it was found to be animated with an angelic spirit: for such perfection could not be without a soul. Similar to such statues, I find a composition of words, the office of which is to hold all the words in a proportion grateful to the ear . . . Which words as soon as they are put into their proportion are found when pronounced to be as it were animated by a harmony.[72]

Camillo has interpreted the magic of the Egyptian statues in an artistic sense; a perfectly proportioned statue becomes animated with a spirit, becomes a magic statue.

This seems to me to be a pearl of great price with which Giulio Camillo has presented us, an interpretation of the magic statues of the *Asclepius* in terms of the magical effect of perfect proportions. Such a development could have been suggested by the statement in the *Asclepius* that the Egyptian magicians maintained the celestial spirit in their magic statues with celestial rites, reflecting the harmony of heaven.[73] Renaissance theory of proportion was based on the 'universal harmony', the harmonious proportions of the world, the macrocosm, reflected in the body of man, the microcosm. To make a statue in accordance with the rules of proportion could thus be a way of introducing into it the celestial harmony, thereby imparting to it a magical animation.

Applied to the inner talismanic images of an occult memory system, this would mean that the magical power of such images would consist in their perfect proportions. Camillo's memory

[72] Giulio Camillo, *Discorso in materia del suo Teatro*, in *Tutte le opere, ed. cit.*, p. 33.
[73] Quoted in *G.B. and H.T.*, p. 37.

system would reflect the perfectly proportioned images of Renaissance art, and in this their magic would consist. One becomes seized with an intense desire to have that opportunity of inspecting the images in the Theatre which was rather wasted on the friend of Erasmus.

These subtleties did not save Camillo from the charge of having dabbled in dangerous magic. One Pietro Passi, who published a book on natural magic at Venice in 1614, warns against the statues of the *Asclepius*, 'of which Cornelius Agrippa has dared to affirm in his book on Occult Philosophy that they were animated by celestial influences.'

> And Giulio Camillo, otherwise a judicious and polite writer, is not far off from this error in the *Discorso in materia del suo Theatro*, where, in speaking of the Egyptian statues, he says that the celestial influences descend into statues which are constructed with rare proportions. In which both he and others are in error . . .[74]

Camillo thus did not escape the accusation of being a magician which any dabbling in the magical passages of the *Asclepius* always brought with it. And Passi's accusation shows that the 'secret' of the Theatre was indeed supposed to be a magical secret.

The Theatre presents a remarkable transformation of the art of memory. The rules of the art are clearly discernible in it. Here is a building divided into memory places on which are memory images. Renaissance in its form, for the memory building is no longer a Gothic church or cathedral, the system is also Renaissance in its theory. The emotionally striking images of classical memory, transformed by the devout Middle Ages into corporeal similitudes, are transformed again into magically powerful images. The religious intensity associated with mediaeval memory has turned in a new and bold direction. The mind and memory of man is now 'divine', having powers of grasping the highest reality through a magically activated imagination. The Hermetic art of memory has

---

[74] Pietro Passi, *Della magic'arte, ouero della Magia Naturale*, Venice, 1614, p. 21. Cf. Secret, *article cited*, pp. 429–30. One wonders whether the eccentric eighteenth-century German sculptor, F. X. Messerschmidt, who combined an intense religious cult of Hermes Trismegistus with intense study of an 'old Italian book' on proportion (see R. and M. Wittkower, *Born under Saturn*, London, 1963, pp. 126 ff.) had picked up some tradition descending from the Venetian academies.

become the instrument in the formation of a Magus, the imaginative means through which the divine microcosm can reflect the divine macrocosm, can grasp its meaning from above, from that divine grade to which his *mens* belongs. The art of memory has become an occult art, a Hermetic secret.

When Viglius asked Camillo concerning the meaning of the work as they both stood in the Theatre, Camillo spoke of it as representing all that the mind can conceive and all that is hidden in the soul—all of which could be perceived at one glance by the inspection of the images. Camillo is trying to tell Viglius the 'secret' of the Theatre, but an immense and unbridgeable gulf of mutual incomprehension lies between the two men.

Yet both were products of the Renaissance. Viglius represents Erasmus, the humanist scholar, opposed by temperament and training to all that mysterious occult side of the Renaissance to which Camillo belongs. The meeting of Viglius and Camillo in the Theatre does not represent a conflict between north and south. At the time of this meeting Cornelius Agrippa had already written his *De occulta philosophia* which was to carry the occult philosophy all through the north. The meeting in the Theatre represents a conflict between two different types of mind which take up different sides of the Renaissance. The rational humanist is Erasmus-Viglius. The irrationalist, Camillo, descends from the Renaissance on its occult side.

For the Erasmian type of humanist the art of memory was dying out, killed by the printed book, unfashionable because of its mediaeval associations, a cumbrous art which modern educators are dropping. It was in the occult tradition that the art of memory was taken up again, expanded into new forms, infused with a new life.

The rational reader, if he is interested in the history of ideas, must be willing to hear about all ideas which in their time have been potent to move men. The basic changes of orientation within the psyche which are shown to us by Camillo's memory system have vital connections with changes of outlook out of which new movements were to come. The Hermetic impulse towards the world and its workings is a factor in turning men's minds towards science. Camillo is nearer than Erasmus to the scientific movements, still veiled in magic, which are stirring obscurely in the Venetian academies.

And for the understanding of the creative impulses behind the artistic achievements of the Renaissance, of those celestial harmonies of perfect proportion which the divine artists and poets knew how to infuse into their works, the divine Camillo with his subtle artistic magics has something to tell us.

Chapter VII

CAMILLO'S THEATRE AND THE
VENETIAN RENAISSANCE

T HE phenomenon of the Theatre, once so famous and so long forgotten, suggests many problems, a few of which will be briefly raised in this chapter, though a whole book might be written on this subject. Did Camillo invent his momentous transformation of the art of memory, or was it already adumbrated in the Florentine movement whence he drew his inspiration? Was such a view of memory seen as a total break with the older memory tradition, or was there any continuity between the old and the new? And, finally, what are the links between the memory monument which Camillo raised in the midst of the Venetian Renaissance of the early sixteenth century and other Renaissance manifestations in that time and place?

Ficino certainly knew of the art of memory. In one of his letters he gives some precepts for improving the memory in the course of which he lets fall the following remark:

> Aristotle and Simonides think it useful to observe a certain order in memorising. And indeed an order contains proportion, harmony and connection. And if matters are digested into a series, if you think of one, others follow as by natural necessity.[1]

Simonides in connection with memory must mean the classical art; and his association with Aristotle may mean the classical art as transmitted by the scholastics. Proportion and harmony are, so far

---

[1] Ficino, *Opera, ed. cit.,* p. 616; P. O. Kristeller, *Supplementum Ficinianum,* Florence, 1937, I, p. 39.

as I know, new and significant Ficinian additions to the memory tradition. Ficino therefore had the materials for doing what Camillo did, for housing a Hermetised art of memory in a memory building stored with the talismanic, astralised mythological imagery which he was such an adept at inventing. In the *De vita coelitus comparanda* he speaks of constructing an 'image of the world'.[2] To form such an image within an artistic architectural framework within which astral memory imagery was skilfully arranged might have been very congenial to Ficino. One wonders whether some of the peculiarities of Ficino's imagery, the fluctuating meanings which he attaches to the same image—the image of the Three Graces for example[3]—might be explained if the same image were to be thought of as on different grades, as in Camillo's Theatre.

I do not know of any actual mention of the art of memory in Pico della Mirandola's works, though the opening words of his Oration on the Dignity of Man might have suggested the form of Camillo's memory building:

> I have read in the writings of the Arabs that Abdullah the Saracen, when asked what seemed to him most marvellous in this theatre of the world (*mundana scaena*) replied that nothing seemed to him more splendid than man. And this accords with the famous saying of Mercurius Trismegistus, 'What a miracle is man, O Asclepius.'[4]

Pico is of course here speaking of the world as a theatre only in a general sense, as a well known topos.[5] Yet the description of Camillo's Theatre is so full of echoes of the Oration, that it is possible that its opening allusion to Hermetic man as dominating the theatre of the world might have suggested the theatre form for the Hermetic memory system.[6] But it remains unknown whether Pico had himself thought of constructing a 'theatre of the world'

---

[2] See *G.B. and H.T.*, pp. 73 ff.

[3] On varying interpretations of the Three Graces by Ficino, see E. H. Gombrich, 'Botticelli's Mythologies: A Study in the Neoplatonic Symbolism of his Circle', *Journal of the Warburg and Courtauld Institutes*, VIII (1945), pp. 32 ff.

[4] Pico della Mirandola, *De hominis dignitate, ed. cit.*, p. 102.

[5] On the theatre topos, see E. R. Curtius, *European Literature in the Latin Middle Ages*, London, 1953, pp. 138 ff.

[6] As suggested by Secret, *art. cit.*, p. 427.

illustrating the lay-out of his mind as expressed in the *Heptaplus*, as Camillo's Theatre does.

Though these are but fragmentary suggestions, it is, I think, unlikely that the occult memory system was invented by Camillo. More probably he was developing in a Venetian setting an inward use of Hermetic and Cabalist influences in the framework of the classical art of memory which had been earlier adumbrated by Ficino and Pico. Nevertheless the fact that his Theatre was so universally acclaimed as a novel and striking achievement shows that it was he who first put Renaissance occult memory on a firm basis. And, so far as the historian of the art of memory is concerned, his Theatre is the first great landmark in the story of the transformation of the art of memory through the Hermetic and Cabalist influences implicit in Renaissance Neoplatonism.

There can be no possible connection, one would suppose, between the occult transformation of artificial memory and the earlier memory tradition. But let us look once again at the plan of the Theatre.

Saturn was the planet of melancholy, good memory belonged to the melancholic temperament, and memory was a part of Prudence. All this is indicated in the Saturn series of the Theatre where, on the Cave grade, we see the famous time symbol of the heads of a wolf, a lion, and a dog, signifying past present and future. This could be used as a symbol of Prudence and her three parts of *memoria, intelligentia, providentia*, as shown in the famous picture by Titian, labelled 'Prudence' (Pl. 8a), of a man's face with the three animal heads below it. Camillo, who moved in the main Venetian artistic and literary circles is rumoured to have known Titian,[7] but in any case would know of the three animal heads as a symbol of Prudence in her time aspect. And now, continuing to look at the Saturn series of the Theatre, we perceive that the image of Cybele vomiting fire on the Banquet grade of this series means Hell. Remembering Hell as a part of Prudence is thus represented in the Theatre. Moreover, the image of Europa and the Bull on the Banquet grade of Jupiter means true religion or Paradise. The image of the Mouth of Tartarus on the Banquet grade of Mars means Purgatory. The image of a sphere with

---

[7] Altani di Salvarolo, p. 266.

Ten Circles on the Banquet grade of Venus means the Earthly Paradise.

Thus beneath the splendid Renaissance surface of the Theatre there still survives artificial memory of the Dantesque type. What did the coffers or boxes under the images of Hell, Purgatory, the Earthly Paradise, and Paradise in the Theatre contain? Hardly Ciceronian speeches surely. They must have been full of sermons. Or of cantos of the *Divine Comedy*. In any case, we certainly have in these images vestiges of older uses and interpretations of artificial memory.

Moreover, there is probably some connection between the stir caused by Camillo's Theatre and the revival of interest in Venice in the Dominican memory tradition. As already mentioned, Lodovico Dolce, the ready purveyor of literature likely to be popular, wrote the preface for the collected edition of Camillo's works (1552), which included *L'Idea del Theatro*, in which he spoke of Camillo's 'more divine than human intellect'. Ten years later, Dolce came out with a work on memory in Italian,[8] very elegantly expressed in the fashionable dialogue form, modelled on Cicero's *De oratore*; one of the speakers is Hortensio, recalling the Hortensius in Cicero's work. This little book has a surface of Venetian Ciceronianism in the *volgare*, classical rhetoric in Italian, which is exactly the style of the Bembist school to which Camillo had belonged (as will appear later). But what is this modern-looking dialogue on memory by Dolce, the admirer of Camillo? It is a translation, or rather adaptation, of Romberch's 'Congestion'. The crabbed Latin of the German Dominican is transformed into elegant Italian dialogues, some of his examples are modernised, but the substance of the book is Romberch. We hear in the dulcet tones of Dolce's 'Ciceronian' Italian the scholastic reason why images may be used in memory. And Romberch's diagrams are exactly reproduced; we see once again his cosmic diagram for Dantesque artificial memory, and the antiquated figure of Grammar, stuck over with visual alphabets.

Amongst Dolce's expansions of Romberch's text, is the one, mentioned earlier, in which he brings in the allusion to Dante as a guide to remembering Hell.[9] Other expansions by Dolce are

---

[8] L. Dolce, *Dialogo nel quale si ragiona del modo di accrescere et conservar la memoria*, Venice, 1562 (also 1575, 1586).

[9] See above, p. 95.

modernisations of Romberch's memory instructions through bringing in modern artists whose pictures are useful as memory images. For example:

> If we have some familiarity with the art of painters we shall be more skilful in forming our memory images. If you wish to remember the fable of Europa you may use as your memory image Titian's painting: also for Adonis, or any other fabulous history, profane or sacred, choosing figures which delight and thereby excite the memory.[10]

Thus, whilst recommending Dantesque imagery for remembering Hell, Dolce also brings the memory image up to date by recommending mythological forms as painted by Titian.

The publication of Rossellius's book at Venice in 1579 is another indication of the popularity of the older memory tradition. As well as its powerful exposition of Dantesque artificial memory, this book also reflects some more modern trends. An example of this is Rossellius's choice of notable practitioners of arts and sciences to 'place' in memory as memory images of them. This most ancient tradition, going right back to remote Greek antiquity, when they placed Vulcan for Metallurgy,[10a] and of which we have seen one mediaeval example in the row of figures placed in front of the arts and sciences in the Chapter House fresco glorifying Thomas Aquinas, is being carried on by Rossellius:

> Thus for Grammar, I place Lorenzo Valla or Priscian; for Rhetoric I place Marcus Tullius; for Dialectic Aristotle, and also for philosophy; for Theology Plato . . . for Painting, Phidias or Zeuxis . . . for Astrology, Atlas, Zoroaster, or Ptolomey; for Geometry, Archimedes; for Music, Apollo, Orpheus . . .[11]

Are we now looking at Raphael's 'School of Athens' as useful for memory and 'placing' his Plato as Theology, his Aristotle as Philosophy? In the same passage, Rossellius 'places' Pythagoras and Zoroaster as representing 'Magia, and this in a list of figures which he is placing for remembering virtues. It is interesting to find that 'Magia' has moved up into the virtues, and there are other indications in Rossellius's book that the Dominican memory tradition is moving in modern directions.

[10] Dolce, *Dialogo*, p. 86 *recto*.
[10a] See above, p. 30.
[11] Rossellius, *Thesaurus*, p. 113 *recto*.

Infiltration of Neoplatonism into the older memory tradition is also present in the *Plutosofia* by the Franciscan, Gesualdo, published at Padua in 1592.[12] Gesualdo opens his chapter on the art of memory with quotations from Ficino in the *Libri de vita* (Gesualdo might be used in future efforts to solve the problem of Ficino and memory). He sees memory on three levels; it is like the Ocean, father of waters, for from memory flow all words and thoughts; it is like the heaven, with its lights and operations; it is the divine in man, the image of God in the soul. In another passage he compares memory to the highest celestial sphere (the zodiac) and to the highest supercelestial sphere (the sphere of the Seraphim). Clearly Gesualdo's memory moves amongst the three worlds, in a manner similar to that shown in the lay-out of the Theatre. Yet after his Ficinian and Camillan introduction, Gesualdo devotes the bulk of his treatise to the old type of memory material.

Thus it would appear that the older memory tradition mingled with the new type of occult memory, that the thunders of a friar's sermon on rewards and punishments, or the warnings of the *Divine Comedy*, might still be heard echoing somehow together with, or below the surface of, the new style of oratory with its new style arrangement of memory, and that our discovery of Hell, Purgatory, and Paradise in Camillo's Theatre belongs into a general atmosphere in which old style memory merges with the new. The Renaissance occult philosopher had a great gift for ignoring differences and seeing only resemblances. Ficino was able happily to combine the *Summa* of Thomas Aquinas with his own brand of Platonic theology, and it would be quite in keeping with the general confusion if he and his followers failed to notice any essential difference between Thomas Aquinas's recommendation of 'corporeal similitudes' in memory and the astralised images of occult memory.

Camillo belongs, not to the Florentine Renaissance of the late fifteenth century, but to the Venetian Renaissance of the early sixteenth century, in which the Florentine influences were absorbed but took on characteristically Venetian forms, one of the most characteristic of which was Ciceronian oratory. The recommendation of the artificial memory in *De oratore*, a work devoutly

---

[12] Another edition at Vicenza in 1600.

imitated by the 'Ciceroniani', would carry weight in these fashionable circles. Camillo was himself an orator and an admirer of Cardinal Bembo, the leader of the 'Ciceroniani', to whom he dedicated a Latin poem about his Theatre.[13] The memory system of the Theatre is intended to be used for memorising every notion to be found in Cicero's works; the drawers under the images contained Ciceronian speeches. The system, with its Hermetic-Cabalist philosophy and foundation, belongs into the world of Venetian oratory, as the memory system of a 'Ciceronianus' who intends to deliver Ciceronian speeches in the *volgare*. Such was the material which Camillo drew out of the drawers and recited with such excitement to Viglius.

With the Theatre, the art of memory has returned to its classical position as a part of rhetoric, as the art used by the great Cicero. Yet it is not as a 'straight mnemotechnic' that it is being used by the Venetian Ciceronian. One of the most purely classical in appearance of Renaissance phenomena, the revival of Ciceronian oratory, is here found associated with a mystico-magical artificial memory. And this revelation of what the memory of a Venetian orator could be like is important for the investigation of Erasmus's well-known attack on the Ciceronians of Italy in his *Ciceronianus* (1528). A fierce anonymous reply to this work, which was both a defence of the Ciceronians and a personal attack on Erasmus, had been published in 1531. Its author was Julius Caesar Scaliger, but this was not known at the time, and suspicion had fallen on Giulio Camillo as possibly the author. Viglius believed this, and the erroneous conviction that Camillo had attacked his famous friend is behind Viglius's reports to Erasmus about the Theatre.[14]

No one has suspected that Erasmus's objections to the 'Ciceroniani' might have included distaste for a tendency to occultism. This may or may not be the case. But at any rate the *Ciceronianus* controversy should not be studied without reference to Camillo and his Theatre, and what was said about it in the Venetian academies.

The proliferation of academies was a notable phenomenon of the

[13] There is a Latin poem by Camillo dedicated to Bembo and mentioning the Theatre in the Paris manuscript Lat. 8139, item 20. For references about Camillo and Bembo, see Liruti, pp. 79, 81.

[14] See Erasmus, *Epistolae*, IX, 368, 391, 398, 406, 442; X, 54, 98, 125, 130 etc.; and cf. Christie, *Etienne Dolet*, pp. 194 ff.

Venetian Renaissance, and Camillo is a typical Venetian academician. He is said to have himself founded an academy;[15] several of his surviving literary remains probably originated as academic discourses; and his Theatre was still being discussed more than forty years after his death in a Venetian academy. This was the *Accademia degli Uranici*, founded in 1587 by Fabio Paolini who published a large volume, entitled *Hebdomades*, reflecting discourses made in this academy. It is divided into seven books, each containing seven chapters, and 'seven' is the mystical theme of the whole.

Paolini's thick volume has been studied by D. P. Walker,[16] who regards it as representing the occult core of Renaissance Neoplatonism as it had developed when transferred from Florence to Venice. Here are the Hermetic influences operating in the Venetian setting. Within the seven-fold arrangement, Paolini presents 'not only the whole theory of Ficino's magic, but also the whole complex of theories of which it is a part.'[17] He quotes the passage on the magic statues from the *Asclepius* and goes as far as he dares in the magical direction. It may be added that he was also interested in Cabala, and in the angel magic of Trithemius, quoting the names of the Cabalistic angels which go with the planets in the same form as they are given by Camillo.[18]

One of the chief aims of Paolini and his academy, as revealed in the *Hebdomades*, was to apply the magical theories to that leading interest of the Venetians, oratory. Ficino's theories about 'planetary music' designed to draw down planetary powers through musical correspondencies, were transferred by Paolini to oratory. 'He believed', says Walker, 'that just as a proper mixture of tones could give music a planetary power, so a proper mixture of "forms" could produce a celestial power in an oration . . . The set (of forms) has something to do with the number seven, and some of the things are the sounds of words, figures of speech, and Hermogenes' seven Ideas, that is the general qualities of good oratory.'[19]

[15] Liruti, p. 78.
[16] On Paolini's academy, the *Hebdomades*, and the mentions in the latter of Camillo's Theatre, see Walker, *Magic*, pp. 126–44, 183–5.
[17] *Ibid.*, p. 126.
[18] F. Paolini, *Hebdomades*, Venice, 1589, pp. 313–14. Paolini refers for these seven angels and their powers to Trithemius's *De septem secundadeis* which is a treatise on 'practical Cabala', or conjuring.
[19] Walker, *Magic*, pp. 139–40. Walker suggests that Paolini's interest

The close connection of Paolini's ideas on magical oratory with Camillo's memory system for orators, based on seven, is obvious, and indeed Paolini quotes long passages from *L'Idea del Theatro*, including the one describing its seven-fold construction, based on the planetary seven.[20] The *Hebdomades* might take the place of the great work explaining the background of his Theatre which Camillo himself never wrote. And we learn from it that a kind of 'planetary oratory' was envisaged which should produce effects on its hearers, like the fabled effects of ancient music, since the words of the speaker were activated by planetary influences drawn into them.

The *Hebdomades* discovers for us a 'secret' of Camillo's Theatre which otherwise we would never have guessed. As well as providing a magically activated, because based on the fundamental Seven, memory system for orators, the Theatre also magically activated the speeches which the orator remembered by it, infusing them with planetary virtue through which they would have magical effects on the hearers. It may be suggested that Camillo's interpretation of the magic of the statues of the *Asclepius* may be of importance here. The connection of the right and perfect and therefore magical forms of oratory with the magic memory image might be through the interpretation of the magic statues whereby their power is due to their reflection of celestial harmony through their perfect proportions. Thus the perfect proportions of, let us say, the magical Apollo image, would produce the perfectly proportioned, and therefore magical, speech about the sun. The Venetian magicians are presenting us with extremely subtle interpretations of the magic of the Renaissance.

---

[20] *Hebdomades*, p. 27, quoting *L'Idea del Theatro*, p. 14; cf. Walker, p. 141.

---

in the seven forms of good oratory laid down by Hermogenes (the Greek writer on rhetoric of the first century A.D.) probably connected with the 'sevens' mystique. Camillo had also been interested in Hermogenes; see the *Discorso di M. Giulio Camillo sopra Hermogene*, in *Tutte le opere, ed. cit.*, II, pp. 77 ff.

Paolini makes the remark that J. C. Scaliger believed in the seven forms of Hermogenes and showed them 'quasi in Theatrum' (*Hebdomades*, p. 24). I do not know to what work of Scaliger's this can refer, but the remark may suggest that Paolini saw Erasmus's opponent as belonging to the mystical 'Sevens' school in rhetoric and memory.

We now begin to understand the huge fame of Camillo's Theatre. To those outside the Renaissance occult tradition, it was the work of a charlatan and an imposter. To those within that tradition, it held an unbounded fascination. It proposed to show how Man, the great Miracle, who could harness the powers of the cosmos with Magia and Cabala as described in Pico's Oration on the Dignity of Man, might develop magical powers as an orator by speaking from a memory organically affiliated to the proportions of the world harmony. Francesco Patrizi, the Hermetic philosopher of Ferrara, speaks with ecstacy of how Camillo has released the precepts of the masters of rhetoric from narrow bounds, extending them to 'the most ample places of the Theatre of the whole world'.[21]

In ancient rhetorical theory, oratory is closely bound up with poetry, as Camillo, himself a Petrarchan poet, was fully aware. And it is with a certain amazement—as of stumbling upon something strange—that one finds that Camillo is mentioned with approval by the two most famous Italian poets of the sixteenth century. In Ariosto's *Orlando furioso*, Giulio Camillo appears as 'he who showed a smoother and shorter way to the heights of Helicon'.[22] And Torquato Tasso discusses at some length in one of his dialogues the secret which Camillo revealed to the King of France, stating that Camillo was the first since Dante who showed that rhetoric is a kind of poetry.[23] To find Ariosto and Tasso among the hosts of Camillo's admirers forbids us to dismiss the Theatre as historically unimportant.

Another manifestation of the Renaissance with which the tone of the Theatre is in keeping is the symbolic statement in the form of the *impresa* or device. Some of the images in the Theatre are very like *imprese*, the fashion for which was being particularly developed in Venice in Camillo's time. The *impresa* is related to the memory image, as already suggested, and in commentaries on *imprese* there

---

[21] Patrizi's preface to Camillo's *Discorso* on Hermogenes (*Tutte le opere, ed. cit.*, II, p. 74). Patrizi also praises Camillo in his own *Retorica* (1562). On Camillo and Patrizi, see E. Garin, *Testi umanistici sulla retorica*, Rome-Milan, 1953, pp. 32–5.

[22] *Orlando furioso*, XLVI, 12.

[23] Torquato Tasso, *La Cavaletta overo de la poesia toscana (Dialoghi*, ed. E. Raimondi, Florence, 1958, II, pp. 661–3).

is frequently to be found a blend of Hermetic-Cabalist mysticism like that which inspires the Theatre. An example is the device shown by Ruscelli of a heliotrope turning towards the sun, expounded in the commentary on it with many allusions to Mercurius Trismegistus and the Cabala.[24] Among the symbols of Achilles Bocchius who, like many of the writers on symbols and *imprese* of the period, belonged into the circle of the famous Camillo, we see a figure (*Frontispiece*) wearing the winged hat of Mercury, but holding, not the caduceus, but the seven-branched golden candlestick of the Apocalypse.[25] The accompanying Latin poem makes it clear that this figure is Mercurius Trismegistus; he puts his finger to his lips to enjoin silence. This figure would do very well as a symbolic statement about the Theatre, with its Hermetic mysteries and its mystical Sevens.

The Theatre thus stands in the midst of the Venetian Renaissance, organically related to some of its most characteristic products, its oratory, its imagery, and, it may be added, its architecture. The revival of Vitruvius by the Venetian architects, culminating in Palladio, is surely one of the most distinctive features of the Venetian Renaissance, and here, too, Camillo with his adaptation of the Vitruvian theatre to his mnemonic purposes is at the centre.

The classical theatre, as described by Vitruvius, reflects the proportions of the world. The positions of the seven gangways in the auditorium and of the five entrances on to the stage are determined by the points of four equilateral triangles inscribed within a circle, the centre of which is the centre of the orchestra. These triangles, says Vitruvius, correspond to the *trigona* which astrologers

---

[24] G. Ruscelli, *Imprese illustri*, ed. of Venice, 1572, pp. 209 ff. Ruscelli states that he knew Camillo (*Trattato del modo di comporre in versi nella lingua italiana*, Venice, 1594, p. 14). Another disciple of Camillo's was Alessandro Farra whose *Settenario della humana riduttione*, Venice, 1571, contains a discussion of the philosophy of the *impresa*.

[25] Achilles Bocchius, *Symbolicarum quaestionum . . . libri quinque*, Bologna, 1555, p. cxxxviii. Another of the symbols is dedicated to Camillo.

John Dee's *Monas Hieroglyphica* (Antwerp, 1564) is a composite symbol of the seven planets, based on the character for Mercury, and which moves in a similar kind of country of the mind to the Bocchius symbol of Mercurius with the seven-branched candlestick. So, later on, will Jacob Boehme meditate Hermetically on the seven forms of his spiritual alchemy.

inscribe within the circle of the zodiac.[26] The circular form of the theatre thus reflects the zodiac, and the seven entrances to the auditorium and the five entrances to the stage correspond to positions of the twelve signs and of the four triangles connecting them. This arrangement can be seen in the plan of the Roman theatre (Pl. 9a) in Daniele Barbaro's commentary on Vitruvius, first published at Venice in 1556,[27] the illustrations of which were influenced by Palladio.[28] The plan which Barbaro illustrates is thus really Palladio's reconstruction of the Roman theatre. Here we see four triangles inscribed within the circle of the theatre. The base of one of them is seen to determine the position of the *frons scaenae* or back of the stage; its apex points towards the central gangway of the auditorium. Six other triangle apices mark the positions of six other gangways; and five triangle apices mark the positions of the five doors in the *frons scaenae*.

This was the Vitruvian type of theatre which Camillo had in mind, but which he distorted by decorating with images, not the five doors of the stage, but his imaginary gates in the seven gangways of the auditorium. But though he distorts the Vitruvian theatre for his mnemonic purposes, Camillo was certainly aware of the astrological theory underlying it. He would think of his Memory Theatre of the World as magically reflecting the divine world proportions in its architecture as well as in its imagery.

Camillo erected his Memory Theatre in Venice at a time when the revival of the ancient theatre, due to the recovery of the text of Vitruvius by the humanists, was in full swing.[29] It was to culminate in the Teatro Olimpico (Pl. 9b), designed by Palladio and erected at Vicenza in the fifteen-eighties. One wonders whether the Idea of Camillo's Theatre, so famous in its time and so long the subject of discussion in academies, may have had some influence on both Barbaro and Palladio. The mythological images which

[26] Vitruvius, *De architectura*, Lib. V, cap. 6.

[27] Vitruvius, *De architectura cum commentariis Danielis Barbari*, edition of Venice, 1567, p. 188.

[28] See R. Wittkower, *Architectural Principles in the Age of Humanism*, London, Warburg Institute, 1949, p. 59.

[29] See H. Leclerc, *Les origines italiennes de l'architecture théâtrale moderne*, Paris, 1946, pp. 51 ff.; R. Klein and H. Zerner, 'Vitruve et le théâtre de la Renaissance italienne', in *Le Lieu théâtral à la Renaissance*, ed. J. Jacquot, Centre National de la Recherche Scientifique, Paris, 1964, pp. 49–60.

decorate the *frons scaenae* of the Teatro Olimpico are extraordinarily elaborate. This theatre does not, of course, reverse the arrangement of the Vitruvian theatre, as Camillo did, by transferring the decorated doors from the stage to the auditorium. Yet it has a certain unreal and imaginative quality.

We have tried in these chapters to reconstruct a vanished wooden theatre, the fame of which was great, not only in Italy but also in France, whither it was exported. Why does this vanished wooden theatre seem to connect so mysteriously with many aspects of the Renaissance? It is, I would suggest, because it represents a new Renaissance plan of the psyche, a change which has happened within memory, whence outward changes derived their impetus. Mediaeval man was allowed to use his low faculty of imagination to form corporeal similitudes to help his memory; it was a concession to his weakness. Renaissance Hermetic man believes that he has divine powers; he can form a magic memory through which he grasps the world, reflecting the divine macrocosm in the microcosm of his divine *mens*. The magic of celestial proportion flows from his world memory into the magical words of his oratory and poetry, into the perfect proportions of his art and architecture. Something has happened within the psyche, releasing new powers, and the new plan of artificial memory may help us to understand the nature of that inner event.

Chapter VIII

LULLISM AS AN ART OF MEMORY

T HOUGH we have now reached the Renaissance, with Camillo, we have to retrace our steps to the Middle Ages during this chapter. For there was another kind of art of memory which began in the Middle Ages, which continued into the Renaissance and beyond, and which it was the aim of many in the Renaissance to combine with the classical art in some new synthesis whereby memory should reach still further heights of insight and of power. This other art of memory was the Art of Ramon Lull.

Lullism and its history is a most difficult subject and one for the exploration of which the full materials have not yet been assembled. The enormous number of Lull's own writings, some of them still unpublished, the vast Lullist literature written by his followers, the extreme complexity of Lullism, make it impossible as yet to reach very definite conclusions about what is, undoubtedly, a strand of major importance in the European tradition. And what I have to do now is to write one not very long chapter giving some idea of what the Art of Ramon Lull was like, of why it was an art of memory, of how it differs from the classical art of memory, and of how Lullism became absorbed at the Renaissance into Renaissance forms of the classical art.

Obviously I am attempting the impossible, yet the impossible must be attempted because it is essential for the later part of this book that there should be some sketch at this stage of Lullism itself. The chapter is based on my own two articles on the art of Ramon Lull;[1] it is orientated towards a comparison of Lullism as

---

[1] 'The Art of Ramon Lull: An Approach to it through Lull's Theory of

an art of memory with the classical art; and it is not concerned solely with 'genuine' Lullism but also with the Renaissance interpretation of Lullism, for it is this which is important for the next stages of our history.

Ramon Lull was about ten years younger than Thomas Aquinas. He was propagating his Art at the time when the mediaeval form of the classical art of memory, as laid down and encouraged by Albertus and Thomas, was in its most flourishing state. Born about 1235 in Majorca, he passed his youth as a courtier and troubadour. (He never had any regular clerical education.) About the year 1272, he had an illuminative experience on Mount Randa, an island in Majorca, in which he saw the attributes of God, his goodness, greatness, eternity, and so on, infusing the whole creation, and realised that an Art founded on those attributes might be constructed which would be universally valid because based on reality. Shortly afterwards he produced the earliest version of his Art. The whole of the rest of his life was spent in writing books about the Art, of which he made various versions, the last being the *Ars Magna* of 1305–8, and in propagating it with the utmost zeal. He died in 1316.

In one of its aspects, the Lullian Art is an art of memory. The divine attributes which are its foundation form themselves into a Trinitarian structure through which it became, in Lull's eyes, a reflection of the Trinity, and he intended that it should be used by all those three powers of the soul which Augustine defined as the reflection of the Trinity in man. As *intellectus*, it was an art of knowing or finding out truth; as *voluntas* it was an art of training the will towards loving truth; as *memoria*, it was an art of memory for remembering truth.[2] One is reminded of the scholastic formulations concerning the three parts of Prudence, *memoria, intelligentia, providentia*, the artificial memory belonging to one of the parts. Lull was certainly aware of the Dominican art of memory,

---

[2] See 'The Art of R.L.', p. 162; and T. and J. Carreras y Artau, *Historia de la filosofia española*, Madrid, 1939, 1943, I, pp. 534 ff. Augustine's definitions of the three powers of the soul in relation to the Trinity are given in his *De trinitate*.

---

the Elements', *Journal of the Warburg and Courtauld Institutes*, XVII (1964), pp. 115–73; 'Ramon Lull and John Scotus Erigena', *ibid.*, XXIII (1960), pp. 1–44. These articles will hereafter be referred to as 'The Art of R.L.' and 'R.L. and S.E.'

looming with immense force in his age, and he was strongly attracted to the Dominicans and tried to interest the Order in his own Art, but without success.[3] The Dominicans had their own art of memory. But the other great Order of preaching friars, the Franciscans, evinced an interest in Lull, and Lullism in its later history is very often to be found associated with Franciscans.

It is a fact of some historical importance that the two great mediaeval methods, the classical art of memory in its mediaeval transformation and the art of Ramon Lull, were both rather particularly associated with the mendicant orders, the one with the Dominicans the other with the Franciscans. Owing to the mobility of the friars, this meant that these two mediaeval methods were pretty well diffused all over Europe.

Though the Art of Lull in one of its aspects can be called an art of memory, it must be strongly emphasised that there are the most radical differences between it and the classical art in almost every respect. I want to drive this home by running over, before we start on Lullism, some of these essential differences.

Take, first of all, the question of their respective origins. Lullism as an art of memory does not come out of the classical rhetoric tradition, like the other art of memory. It comes out of a philosophical tradition, that of Augustinian Platonism to which other, much more strongly Neoplatonic, influences have been added. It claims to know first causes, called by Lull the Dignities of God. All Lull's arts are based on these *Dignitates Dei*, which are Divine Names or attributes, thought of as primordial causes as in the Neoplatonic system of Scotus Erigena by which Lull was influenced.

Contrast this with scholastic memory, which comes out of the rhetoric tradition, which claims only to clothe spiritual intentions in corporeal similitudes, and not to base memory on philosophic 'reals'. This divergence indicates a basic underlying philosophical difference between Lullism and scholasticism. Though Lull's life was passed in the great age of scholasticism, he was in spirit a man of the twelfth century rather than of the thirteenth, a Platonist, and a reactionary towards the Christian Platonism of Anselm and the Victorines to which was added a strong dose of more extreme

---

[3] On at least three occasions, Lull attended the Chapter General of the Dominicans in the hope of interesting the Order in his Art; see E. A. Peers, *Ramon Lull, A Biography*, London, 1929, pp. 153, 159, 192, 203.

Neoplatonism from Scotus Erigena. Lull was not a scholastic, he was a Platonist, and in his attempt to base memory on Divine Names which verge on Platonic Ideas in his conception of them[4] he is closer to the Renaissance than to the Middle Ages.

Secondly, there is nothing corresponding to the images of the classical art in Lullism as taught by Lull himself, none of that effort to excite memory by emotional and dramatic corporeal similitudes which creates that fruitful interaction between the art of memory and the visual arts. Lull designates the concepts used in his art by a letter notation, which introduces an almost algebraic or scientifically abstract note into Lullism.

Finally, and this is probably the most significant aspect of Lullism in the history of thought, Lull introduces movement into memory. The figures of his Art, on which its concepts are set out in the letter notation, are not static but revolving. One of the figures consists of concentric circles, marked with the letter notations standing for the concepts, and when these wheels revolve, combinations of the concepts are obtained. In another revolving figure, triangles within a circle pick up related concepts. These are simple devices, but revolutionary in their attempt to represent movement in the psyche.

Think of the great mediaeval encyclopaedic schemes, with all knowledge arranged in static parts, made yet more static in the classical art by the memory buildings stocked with the images. And then think of Lullism, with its algebraic notations, breaking up the static schemata into new combinations on its revolving wheels. The first art is the more artistic, but the second is the more scientific.

For Lull himself, the great aim of the Art was a missionary aim. He believed that if he could persuade Jews and Muslims to do the Art with him, they would become converted to Christianity. For the Art was based on religious conceptions common to all the three great religions, and on the elemental structure of the world of nature universally accepted in the science of the time. Starting from premisses common to all, the Art would demonstrate the necessity of the Trinity.

The common religious conceptions were the Names of God,

---

[4] Lull himself never uses the word 'Ideas' of his Divine Names or Dignities, but the creative Names are identified with Platonic Ideas by Scotus; see 'R.L. and S.E.', p. 7.

that God is good, great, eternal, wise, and so on. Such Names of God belong very strongly into the Christian tradition; many of them are mentioned by Augustine, and in the *De divinibus nominibus* of Pseudo Dionysius they are listed at length. The names used by Scotus Erigena and by Ramon Lull are nearly all to be found in the book *On the Divine Names* of Pseudo Dionysius.[5]

The Names of God are fundamental in Judaism, and particularly to the type of Jewish mysticism known as the Cabala. Spanish Jews contemporary with Lull were meditating with particular intensity on the Names of God under the influence of Cabala, the doctrines of which were being propagated in Spain. A main text of the Cabala, the *Zohar* was written in Spain in Lull's time. The Sephiroth of the Cabala are really Divine Names as creative principles. The sacred Hebrew alphabet is, mystically speaking, supposed to contain all the Names of God. A form of Cabalist meditation particularly developed in Spain at this time consisted in meditating on the letters of the Hebrew alphabet, combining them and recombining them to form the Names of God.[6]

Mohammedanism, particularly in its mystical form, Sufism, also attaches great importance to meditating on the Names of God. This had been particularly developed by the Sufi mystic, Mohidin, the influence of whom on Lull has been suggested.[7]

All Lull's arts are based on Names or attributes of God, on concepts such as *Bonitas, Magnitudo, Eternitas, Potestas, Sapientia, Voluntas, Virtus, Veritas, Gloria* (Goodness, Greatness, Eternity,

[5] See 'R.L. and S.E.', pp. 6 ff.

[6] See G. G. Scholem, *Major Trends in Jewish Mysticism*, Jerusalem, 1941 (second edition, New York, 1942). The Spanish Cabala of Lull's time had as its basis the ten Sephiroth and the twenty-two letters of the Hebrew alphabet. The Sephiroth are 'the ten Names most common to God and in their entirety they form his one great Name' (Scholem, p. 210). They are 'the creative Names which God called into the world' (*Ibid.*, p. 212). The Hebrew alphabet, the other basis of Cabala, also contains the Names of God. The Spanish Jew, Abraham Abulafia, was contemporary with Lull and was an adept in the Cabalist science of the combination of Hebrew letters. These are combined with one another in an endless series of permutations and combinations which may seem meaningless, but not to Abulafia who accepts the Cabalist doctrine of divine language as the substance of reality (*Ibid.*, p. 131).

[7] See M. Asin Palacios, *Abenmassara y su escuela*, Madrid, 1914, and *El Islam Christianizado*, Madrid, 1931.

Power, Wisdom, Will, Virtue, Truth, Glory). Lull calls such concepts the 'Dignities of God'. Those just listed form the basis of the 'nine' forms of the Art. Other forms of the Art add other Divine Names or attributes to this list and are based on a greater number of such Names or Dignities. Lull designates these concepts by his letter notation. The nine listed above are designated by the letters BCDEFGHIK.

The basic Divine Names of the Art in all its forms rested it on religious concepts common to Christianity, Judaism, and Mohammedanism. And the cosmological structure of the Art rested it on scientific concepts universally accepted. As Thorndike pointed out,[8] the derivation from cosmological 'rotae' of the wheels of the Art is obvious, and it becomes very apparent when Lull uses the figures of the Art to do a kind of astrological medicine, as he does in his *Tractatus de astronomia*.[9] Moreover, the four elements in their various combinations enter very deeply into the structure of the Art, even into the kind of geometrical logic which it uses. The logical square of opposition is identified in Lull's mind with the square of the elements,[10] hence his belief that he has found a 'natural' logic, based on reality[11] and therefore greatly superior to scholastic logic.

How did Lull reconcile the two basic features of his Art, its religious basis in the Divine Names, and its cosmological or elemental basis? The answer to this question was found when the influence on Lull of the *De divisione naturae* of John Scotus Erigena was detected.[12] In Erigena's great Neoplatonic vision, which is also a Trinitarian and Augustinian vision, the Divine Names are primordial causes out of which issue directly the four elements in their simple form as the basic structures of the creation.

Here then, or so I believe, is the major clue to the underlying

---

[8] *History of Magic and Experimental Science*, II, p. 865. For illustrations of the types of cosmological 'rotae' suggestive of Lull's figures, see H. Bober, 'An illustrated mediaeval school-book of Bede's *De natura rerum*', *Journal of the Walters Art Gallery*, XIX–XX (1956–7), pp. 65–97.

[9] See 'The Art of R.L.', pp. 118 ff.

[10] *Ibid.*, pp. 115 ff.

[11] *Ibid.*, pp. 158–9.

[12] See 'R.L. and S.E.'. I did not succeed in this article in identifying the actual channels through which some knowledge of the Scotist system reached Lull, though I suggested Honorius Augustoduniensis as one of the intermediaries.

suppositions of the Lullian Art. The Divine Dignities form into triadic structures,[13] reflected from them down through the whole creation; as causes they inform the whole creation through its elemental structure. An Art based on them constructs a method by which ascent can be made on the ladder of creation to the Trinity at its apex.

The Art works on every level of creation, from God, to the angels, the stars, man, animals, plants, and so on—the ladder of being as envisaged in the Middle Ages—by abstracting the essential bonitas, magnitudo, and so on, on each level. The meanings of the letter notation change in accordance with the level on which the Art is being used. Let us follow how this works out in the case of B for Bonitas as it moves down the ladder of creation, or through the nine 'subjects' listed in the nine-form of the Art as those with which the Art will deal.

On the level	Deus	B = Bonitas as a Dignitas Dei
	Angelus	B = the bonitas of an angel
	Coelum	B = the bonitas of Aries and the rest of the 12 signs of the zodiac, and of Saturn and the rest of the 7 planets
	Homo	B = bonitas in man
	Imaginativa	B = bonitas in the imagination
	Sensitiva	B = bonitas in the animal creation, as the bonitas in a lion.
	Vegetativa	B = bonitas in the vegetable creation, as the bonitas in the pepper plant.
	Elementativa	B = bonitas in the four elements, as the bonitas in fire
	Instrumentativa	B = bonitas in the virtues and in the arts and sciences.

I have here set out the nine subjects on which the Art works as given in the alphabet of the *Ars brevis*. The examples of *bonitas* on the different levels of the ladder of being are taken from Lull's

[13] The triadic or correlative patterns in the Art have been studied by R. D. F. Pring-Mill, 'The Trinitarian World Picture of Ramon Lull', *Romanistisches Jahrbuch*, VII (1955–6), pp. 229–56. Correlativism is also present in Scotus' system; see 'R.L. and S.E.', pp. 23 ff.

Fig. 4 The Ladder of Ascent and Descent. From Ramon Lull's *Liber de ascensu et descensu intellectus*, ed. of Valencia, 1512

Liber de ascensu et descensu intellectus, which is illustrated with a cut (Fig. 4) in an early sixteenth-century edition of it, in which we see Intellectus, holding one of the figures of the Art, ascending the scale of creation, the various steps of which are illustrated with, for example, a tree on the plant step, a lion on the brute step, a man on the step *Homo*, stars on the step *coelum*, an angel on the angel

180

step, and on reaching the summit with *Deus*, the Intellect enters the House of Wisdom.

It is fundamental for the approach to the Lullian Art to realise that it is an *ars ascendendi et descendendi*. Bearing the geometrical figures of the Art, inscribed with their letter notations, the 'artista' ascends and descends on the ladder of being, measuring out the same proportions on each level. The geometry of the elemental structure of the world of nature combines with the divine structure of its issue out of the Divine Names to form the universal Art which can be used on all subjects because the mind works through it with a logic which is patterned on the universe. An attractive fourteenth-century miniature (Pl. 10) illustrates this aspect of the Art.

That the divine goodness and other attributes are present on all the levels of being was a notion having its origins in the Mosaic account of creation, at the end of the 'days' of which God saw that His work was good. The idea of the 'Book of Nature' as a road to God was present in the traditions of Christian mysticism, particularly the Franciscan tradition. Lull's peculiarity is the selection of a certain number of *Dignitates Dei* and to find these descending in a precisely calculable manner, almost like chemical ingredients, on the grades of creation. This notion is however the constant of Lullism. All the arts are based on such principles; they could be applied to any subject. And when Lull writes a book on any subject it begins with the enumeration of B to K in this subject. This makes for tedium, but it is the root of his claim that he had a universal Art, infallible for any subject, because based on reality.

The workings of the Art in its various forms are of a complexity impossible to suggest here, but the reader must be made familiar with the appearance of certain basic figures. The three shown are taken from the *Ars brevis*, the shortened form of the *Ars magna*.

The A figure (Fig. 5) shows B to K set out on a wheel and joined by complex triangulations. This is a mystical figure in which we meditate on the complex relations of the Names with one another as they are in the Godhead, before extension into the creation, and as aspects of the Trinity.

The T figure shows the *relata* of the Art (*differentia, concordia, contrarietas; principium, medium, finis, majoritas, equalitas, minoritas*) set out as triangles within a circle. Through the triangulations

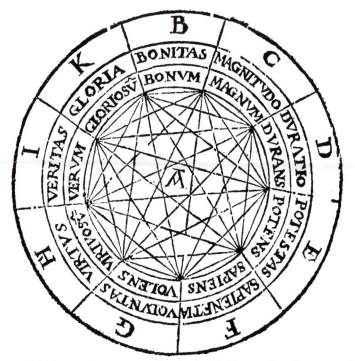

Fig. 5 'A' Figure. From R. Lull's *Ars brevis* (*Opera*, Strasburg, 1617)

of the *relata* the Trinitarian structure of the Art is maintained on every level.

The most famous of all the Lullian figures is the combinatory figure (Fig. 6). The outer circle, inscribed B to K, is stationary and within it revolve circles similarly inscribed and concentric with it. As the circles revolve, combinations of the letters B to K can be read off. Here is the renowned *ars combinatoria* in its simplest form.

The Art uses only three geometrical figures, the circle, the triangle, and the square, and these have both religious and cosmic significance. The square is the elements; the circle, the heavens; and the triangle, the divinity. I base this statement on Lull's allegory of the Circle, the Square, and the Triangle in the *Arbor scientiae*. Circle is defended by Aries and his brothers and by Saturn and his brothers as the figure most like to God, with no beginning or end. Square maintains that it is he who is most like

182

to God in the four elements. Triangle says that he is nearer to the soul of man and to God the Trinity than are his brothers Circle and Square.[14]

As already mentioned, the Art was to be used by the three powers of the soul, one of which is memory. How was the Art as *memoria* to be distinguished from the Art as *intellectus* or as *voluntas*. It is not easy to separate the operations of intellect, will,

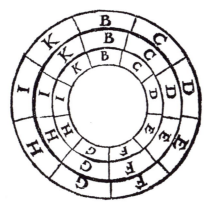

Fig. 6 Combinatory Figure. From Lull's *Ars brevis*

and memory in the Augustinian rational soul, for they are one, like the Trinity. Nor is it easy to distinguish these operations in the Lullian Art, for the same reason. In an allegory in his *Book of Contemplation*, Lull personifies the three powers of the soul as three noble and beautiful damsels standing on top of a high mountain, and describes their activities thus:

> The first remembers that which the second understands and the third wills; the second understands that which the first remembers and the third wills; the third wills that which the first remembers and the second understands.[15]

---

[14] *Arbre de ciencia*, in R. Lull, *Obres essencials*, Barcelona, 1957, I, p. 829 (the Catalan version of this work is more accessible than the Latin one since it is published in *Obres essencials*); quoted in 'The Art of R.L.', pp. 150–1.

[15] *Libri contemplationis in Deum*, in R. Lull, *Opera omnia*, Mainz, 1721–42, X, p. 530.

If the Lullian Art as memory consists in memorising the Art as intellect and will, then the Lullian Art as memory consists in memorising the Art as a whole, in all its aspects and operations. And it is fairly clear from other passages that this was, in fact, what the Lullian Art as memory did mean.

In the 'Tree of Man' in the *Arbor scientiae*, Lull analyses memory, intellect and will, ending the treatment of memory with the words:

> And this treatise of memory which we give here could be used in an *Ars memorativa* which could be made in accordance with what is said here.[16]

Though the expression *Ars memorativa* is the familiar term for the classical art, what Lull proposes to memorise by the proposed memory treatise is really the principles, terminology, and operations of his Art. This is yet more clearly stated in the trilogy, which he wrote later, *De memoria, De intellectu,* and *De voluntate.* These three treatises outline the whole paraphernalia of the Art which is to be used by all the three powers. These three treatises are set out in the tree form, so characteristic of Lull; the 'Tree of Memory' is a diagrammatic exposition of the Art, using the familiar nomenclatures. This Tree of Memory leads us once more to the assumption that the Lullian Art of Memory would consist in remembering the Lullian Art. But the Tree of Memory concludes with these words:

> We have spoken of memory and given the doctrine for artificial memory that it may attain its objects artificially.[17]

Thus Lull can call the memorising of his Art 'artificial memory', and an *Ars memorativa,* expressions undoubtedly influenced by the terminology of the classical art. The memorative side, the memo-

---

[16] *Arbre de ciencia,* in *Obres essencials,* I, p. 619.

[17] The trilogy is unpublished. The manuscript of the *De memoria* which I have read is Paris, B.N., Lat. 16116. Some other quotations from this work are made by Paolo Rossi, 'The Legacy of Ramon Lull in Sixteenth-Century Thought', *Mediaeval and Renaissance Studies,* Warburg Institute, V (1961), pp. 199–202.

Another 'Tree' work in which there is some discussion of memory is the *Arbre de filosofia desiderat* (published in the Palma edition of Lull's *Obres,* XVII (1933), ed. S. Galmes, pp. 399–507). This work is also said by Lull to be a specimen of a projected *ars memorativa*; again the art of memory here consists in memorising the procedures of the Art. Cf. Carreras y Artau, I, pp. 534–9; Rossi, *Clavis universalis,* pp. 64 ff.

rising of the principles and procedures of the Art, was strongly insisted on by Lull, and he seems to have thought of the diagrams of the Art as in some sense 'places'. And there is a classical precedent for the use of mathematical or geometrical order in memory of Aristotle's *De memoria et reminiscentia*, a work which Lull knew.

That Lullism as 'artificial memory' was the memorising of the procedures of the Art introduces something new into memory. For the Art as Intellect was an art of investigation, an art of finding out truth. It asked 'questions', based on the Aristotelian categories, of every subject. And although the questions and the answers are largely pre-determined by the presuppositions of the Art (there can be only one answer, for example, to the question 'Is God good?') yet memory in memorising such procedures is becoming a method of investigation, and a method of logical investigation. Here we have a point, and a very important one, in which Lullism as memory differs fundamentally from the classical art, which seeks only to memorise what is given.

And what is totally absent from genuine Lullism as artificial memory is the use of images in the manner of the classical artificial memory of the rhetoric tradition. The principle of stimulating memory through the emotional appeal of striking human images has no place in the Lullian Art as memory, nor do the corporeal similitudes developed out of the art in the mediaeval transformation of it ever appear in Lull's conception of artificial memory. What indeed could seem more totally remote from classical artificial memory, in its contemporary scholastic transformation, than the Lullian Art as artificial memory? To reflect in memory the letter notations moving on the geometrical figures as the apparatus of Art works up and down the ladder of being would seem an exercise of an utterly different character from the construction of vast memory buildings stored with emotionally stimulating corporeal similitudes. The Lullian Art works with abstractions, reducing even the Names of God to B to K. It is more like a mystical and cosmological geometry and algebra than it is like the *Divine Comedy* or the frescoes of Giotto. If it is to be called 'artificial memory', then it is of a kind which Cicero and the author of *Ad Herennium* could not have recognised as descended from the classical tradition. And in which Albertus Magnus and Thomas Aquinas could have seen no trace of the places and images of the artificial memory recommended by Tullius as a part of Prudence.

It cannot be said that the great principle of classical artificial

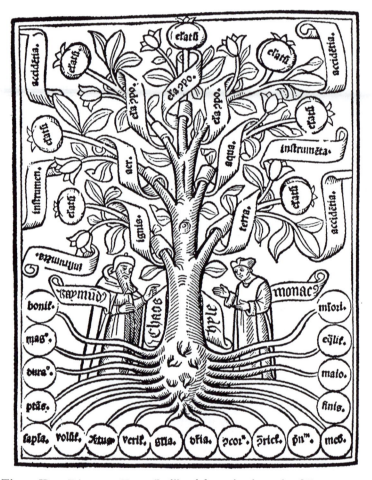

Fig. 7 Tree Diagram. From Lull's *Arbor scientiae*, ed. of Lyons, 1515

memory, the appeal to the sense of sight, is absent from Lullism, for memorisation from diagrams, figures, and schematisations is a kind of visual memory. And there is a point at which Lull's conception of places verges rather closely on classical visualisation of

186

places, namely in his fondness for diagrams in the form of trees. The tree, as he uses it, is a kind of place system. The most notable example of this is the *Arbor scientiae* in which the whole encyclopedia of knowledge is schematised as a forest of trees, the roots of which are B to K as principles and *relata* of the Art (Fig. 7). We even have in this series trees of Heaven and Hell and of virtues and vices. But there are no 'striking' images of the kind advised in 'Tullian' artificial memory on these trees. Their branches and leaves are decorated only with abstract formulae and classifications. Like everything else in the Art, virtues and vices work with the scientific precision of elemental compounds. One of the most valuable aspects of the Art was, in fact, that doing it made one virtuous, as vices were 'devicted' by virtues on the analogy of elemental processes.[18]

Lullism had a vast diffusion which has only recently begun to be systematically studied. Owing to the core of Platonism, and of Scotist Neoplatonism, within it, it formed a current which, not acceptable to many in the ages dominated by scholasticism, found itself in a much more welcoming atmosphere at the Renaissance. A symptom of the popularity which it would gain in the full Renaissance is the interest accorded to it by Nicholas of Cusa.[19] In the full Neoplatonic stream of the Renaissance, stemming from Ficino and Pico, Lullism took a place of honour. Renaissance Neoplatonists were able to recognise in it notions very congenial to them and reaching them from mediaeval sources which, unlike the humanists, they did not despise as barbarous.

There is even, at the heart of Lullism, a kind of interpretation of astral influences which would have aroused interest in the age of Ficino and Pico. When the Art is done on the level *coelum*, it becomes a manipulation of the twelve signs of the zodiac and the seven planets, in combination with B to K, to form a kind of benevolent astral science, which can be worked as astral medicine, and which, as Lull points out in the preface to his *Tractatus de astronomia*, is a very different matter from ordinary judicial astrology.[20] The Lullian medicine has not yet been adequately

[18] See 'The Art of R.L.', pp. 151–4.

[19] See 'R.L. and S.E.', pp. 39–40; E. Colomer, *Nikolaus von Kues und Raimund Lull*, Berlin, 1961.

[20] See 'The Art of R.L.', pp. 118–32.

studied. It may conceivably have influenced Ficino.[21] It was certainly taken up by Giordano Bruno, who states it as his belief that the Paracelsan medicine was largely derived from it.[22]

Lullism thus establishes itself at the Renaissance as belonging with the fashionable philosophy, and becomes assimilated to various aspects of the Hermetic-Cabalist tradition. The relationship of Lullism to Cabalism at the Renaissance is particularly important.

It is my opinion that there was a Cabalist element in Lullism from the start. So far as I know, the practice of meditating on combinations of letters was, before Lull, an exclusively Jewish phenomenon, developed particularly in Spanish Cabala as the meditation on combinations of the sacred Hebrew alphabet, which, according to mystical theory, contains symbolically within it the whole universe and all the Names of God. Lull does not combine Hebrew letters in his Art, but he combines B to K (or more letters in Arts based on more Divine Dignities than those used in the nine form). Since these letters stand for the divine attributes, or Names of God, he is therefore, it seems to me, adapting a Cabalist practice to Gentile uses. This would be, of course, a part of his appeal to the Jews to accept Trinitarian Christianity through the use of one of their own sacred methods. The question of the influence of Cabalism on Lull is, however, still undecided, and we may leave it as an open question, since all that matters here is the fact that in the Renaissance Lullism was certainly closely associated with Cabalism.

Pico della Mirandola was, so far as I know, the first to make explicitly such an association. When discussing Cabala in his Conclusions and Apology, Pico states that one type of Cabala is an

[21] Evidence of the diffusion of Lullism in the vicinity of Ficino has been published by J. Ruysschaert, 'Nouvelles recherches au sujet de la bibliothèque de Pier Leoni, médecin de Laurent le Magnifique', *Académie Royale de Belgique, Bulletin de la Classe des Lettres et des Sciences Morales et Politiques*, 5e série, XLVI (1960), pp. 37–65. It appears that Lorenzo de' Medici's doctor had a considerable number of Lull manuscripts in his library.

[22] Bruno's *Medicina Lulliana* (*Op. lat.*, III, pp. 569–633) is based on Lull's *Liber de regionibus sanitatis et infirmitatis*, the revolving figure of which Bruno is working. See 'The Art of R.L.', p. 167. In the preface to the *De lampade combinatoria lulliana* (*Op. lat.*, II, ii, p. 234) Bruno accuses Paracelsus of having borrowed his medicine from Lull.

ars combinandi, done with revolving alphabets, and he further states that this art is like 'that which is called amongst us the *ars Raymundi*',[23] that is, the Art of Ramon, or Raymond Lull. Whether rightly or wrongly, Pico therefore thought that the Cabalist art of letter combinations was like Lullism. The Renaissance followed him in this belief which gave rise to a work entitled the *De auditu kabbalistico*, the first editions of which were at Venice in 1518 and 1533.[24] This work appears to be, and indeed is, doing the Lullian Art using the normal Lullian figures. But Lullism is now called Cabalism and B to K are more or less identified with Cabalist Sephiroth and associated with Cabalist angel names. Pico's identification of Cabalist *ars combinandi* with the *ars Raymundi* has borne fruit in work, the authorship of which is attributed to Lull, in which Lullism has become inextricably associated with Cabalism. It is now known who was the real author of this work,[25] but the Renaissance firmly believed in its false attribution to Lull. Renaissance Lullists read the Pseudo-Lullian *De auditu kabbalistico* as a genuine work by Lull and it confirmed them in their belief that Lullism was a kind of Cabalism. In the eyes of Christian Cabalists it would have the advantage of being a Christian Cabala.

Other works wrongly attributed to Lull were accepted as genuine in the Renaissance and added to his reputation. These were the Pseudo-Lullian alchemical works.[26]

From the early fourteenth century onwards numbers of treatises on alchemy appear under the name of the great Raymundus Lullus. Written after his death, these works were certainly not by Lull himself. So far as is known, Lull never used the Art on the subject of alchemy, but he did use it on the cognate subject of astral medicine, and the Art, with its 'elemental' basis, did provide a method for working with elemental patterns of a similar kind to

[23] Pico della Mirandola, *Opera omnia*, Bâle, 1572, p. 180; cf. G. Scholem, 'Zur Geschichte der Anfänge der christlichen Kabbala', in *Essays presented to L. Baeck*, London, 1954, p. 164; Yates, *G.B. and H.T.*, pp. 94–6.

[24] See Carreras y Artau, II, p. 201.

[25] See P. O. Kristeller, 'Giovanni Pico della Mirandola and his Sources', *L'Opera e il Pensiero di Giovanni Pico della Mirandola*, Istituto Nazionale di Studi sul Rinascimento, Florence, 1965, I, p. 75; M. Batllori, 'Pico e il lullismo italiano', *ibid.*, II, p. 9.

[26] On Pseudo Lullian alchemy, see F. Sherwood Taylor, *The Alchemists*, London, 1951, pp. 110 ff.

those which alchemy uses. The figures of Pseudo-Lullian alchemical works bear some resemblance to genuine Lullian figures. For example, in the diagram from a fifteenth-century Pseudo-Lullian alchemical treatise, illustrated in Sherwood Taylor's book, we see what look like combinatory wheels marked with letters at the root of a Lullian type of tree diagram; at the top of the tree are wheels marked with the twelve signs and the seven planets. An alchemist might possibly have developed this figure out of what is said about elemental and celestial correspondences in the matter accompanying the 'Tree of the Elements' and the 'Tree of Heaven' in Lull's *Arbor scientiae*. Nevertheless, no genuine Lullian Art uses so many letters as there are on the wheels here. But disciples of Lull may well have believed that they were developing Lullism in paths indicated by the Master with their Pseudo-Lullian alchemy.[27] At any rate, the Renaissance certainly associated Lull with alchemy and accepted the alchemical works bearing his name as genuinely by him.

So we see the Renaissance Lull building up as a kind of Magus, versed in the Cabalist and Hermetic sciences cultivated in the occult tradition. And we find the mysterious language of Renaissance occultism and magic, speaking of a new light emerging from darkness and urging a Pythagorean silence, in yet another Pseudo-Lullian work in which Lullism is associated with yet another Renaissance interest, rhetoric.[28]

What then will be the position in regard to Lullism and the classical art of memory of the rhetoric tradition which we have seen in the last chapter developing into a Renaissance occult form? Is Lullism as an art of memory so radically different from the classical art that any amalgamation of the two is out of the question? Or will ways be sought in the Renaissance atmosphere of fusing two arts both so attractive to those in the Renaissance

---

[27] See 'The Art of R.L.', pp. 131–2; 'R.L. and S.E.', pp. 40–1.

[28] The *In Rhetoricen Isagoge*, of which the first edition was at Paris in 1515, is attributed on its title page to 'the divine and illuminated hermit Raymundus Lullus'. Its real author was Remigius Rufus, a disciple of Bernardus de Lavinheta who taught Lullism at the Sorbonne. See Carreras y Artau, II, pp. 214 ff.; Rossi, 'The Legacy of Ramon Lull in Sixteenth-Century Thought', pp. 192–4. The work contains at the end a specimen oration mystically covering the whole universe and the encyclopaedia of all the sciences.

Hermetic-Cabalist tradition as Lullism and the classical art of memory?

There is a short treatise by Lull on memory, not so far mentioned in this chapter, which is of basic importance in this connection. This is the *Liber ad memoriam confirmandam*.[29] This very short work is the nearest thing to an actual 'memory treatise' by Lull that we have, a treatise giving directions on how to strengthen and confirm memory. Its concluding words state that it was written 'in the city of Pisa in the monastery of San Donnino[30] by Raymundus Lullus'. This serves to date it as having been written in about 1308 when Lull was in Pisa. He was now an old man. He had been ship-wrecked off Pisa when returning from his second missionary journey to North Africa, and in Pisa he completed the last version of the Art, the *Ars generalis ultima*, or *Ars Magna*, and also wrote the *Ars brevis*, the abbreviated form of the Art. The *Liber ad memoriam confirmandam*, also written in Pisa at this time, therefore belongs to the period of Lull's life when he was drawing up the Art in its final forms. It is a perfectly authentic and genuine work by Lull—we are not dealing here with a Pseudo-Lullian product—though it is very obscure and the manuscripts may be corrupt in places.

[29] Five manuscripts of the *Liber ad memoriam confirmandam* are known; two in Munich (Clm. 10593, f. 1–4; and *ibid.*, f. 218–221); one in Rome (Vat. lat. 5347, f. 68–74); one in Milan (Ambrosiana, I, 153 inf. f. 35–40); and one in Paris (B. N. Lat. 17820, f. 437–44). I wish here to express my gratitude to Dr. F. Stegmuller for supplying me with photostats of the Munich and Vatican manuscripts.

The *Liber ad memoriam confirmandam* was published by Paolo Rossi in 1960 as an appendix to his *Clavis universalis*, pp. 261–70. Rossi's text is not quite satisfactory since he used only three of the manuscripts. However it is very useful that he has made a provisional text available. Rossi discusses the work in *Clavis universalis*, pp. 70–4; and in 'The Legacy of R.L.', pp. 203–6.

On possible echoes of John of Salisbury's *Metalogicon* in the *Liber ad memoriam confirmandam*, see above, p. 56, note 16.

[30] All five manuscripts read 'in monasterio sancti Dominici' which is accepted by Rossi (*Clavis*, p. 267). It is known however that Lull did not stay in the Dominican convent at Pisa but in the Cistercian convent of San Donnino. The oldest manuscripts of works written by Lull at Pisa have 'S. Donnini' as the house in which they were written, which later copyists corrupted to 'Dominici'. See J. Tarré, 'Los códices lulianos de la Biblioteca Nacional de Paris', *Analecta Sacra Tarraconensia*, XIV (1941), p. 162. (I am indebted to J. Hillgarth for this reference.)

Memory, says Lull, has been defined by the ancients as of two kinds, one natural, the other artificial. He gives a reference as to where the ancients have made this statement, namely in 'the chapter on memory'.[31] This must be a reference to the memory section of *Ad Herennium*. 'Natural memory', he continues, 'is that which a man receives in creation or generation, and according to what influence he receives from the reigning planet, according to which we see that some men have better memories than others.'[32] This is an echo of *Ad Herennium* on natural memory, with the addition of planetary influences as a factor in natural memory.

'The other kind of memory', he continues, 'is artificial memory and this is of two kinds.' One consists in the use of medicines and plasters for the improvement of memory, and these he does not recommend. The other kind consists in frequently going over in memory what one wishes to retain, like an ox chewing the cud. For 'as it is said in the book of memory and reminiscence by frequent repetition (memory) is firmly confirmed'.[33]

We have to think this over. This is a memory treatise by Lull which looks as though it is going to be on classical lines. He must know what the ancients have said about artificial memory consisting in places and images, since he refers to the memory section of *Ad Herennium*. But he deliberately leaves out the 'Tullian' rules. The only rule which he gives is taken from Aristotle's *De memoria et reminiscentia* on frequent meditation and repetition. This shows that he knows the scholastic conflation of the rules of *Ad Herennium* with Aristotle on memory, for Lull's one and only rule for 'artificial memory' is Thomas Aquinas' fourth rule, that we should meditate frequently on what we wish to remember, as Aristotle advises.[34] Lull omits (and one must suppose that by this deliberate

---

[31] 'Venio igitur . . . ad memoriam quae quidem secundum Antiquos in capite de memoria alia est naturalis alia est artificialis.' Four of the five manuscripts give the reference 'in capite de memoria' so this should not be relegated to a footnote as a variant found only in the Paris manuscript (Rossi, *Clavis*, pp. 264 and 268, note 126).

[32] Rossi, *Clavis*, p. 265.

[33] . . . ut habetur in libro de memoria et reminiscentia per saepissimam reiterationem firmiter confirmatur' (Rossi, *ibid., loc. cit.*) The specific reference to the *De memoria et reminiscentia* is given in four of the manuscripts; only one of them (the Ambrosiana manuscript) omits it. Rossi's statements about this in 'The Legacy of R.L.', p. 205 are confused.

[34] See above, pp. 75–6.

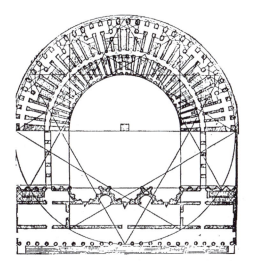

9a Palladio's Reconstruction of the Roman Theatre. From Vitruvius, *De architectura cum commentariis Danielis Barbari,* ed. of Venice, 1567 (pp. 171, 356, 359)

9b   The Teatro Olimpico, Vicenza (pp. 171-2)

omission, he rejects) the three other rules of Thomas with their adoption of the rules of *Ad Herennium* as 'corporeal similitudes' ranged in order.

It is worth reminding ourselves here that the Dominican monastery at Pisa (in which Lull was not actually staying, but at another monastery in Pisa) was to be an active centre in propagating the Thomist artificial memory, now beginning to be diffused in great strength. Bartolomeo da San Concordio was a Dominican of Pisa and we have studied in an earlier chapter his propagation of the 'Ad Herennian' rules conflated with Aristotle in the Thomist manner.[35] It would thus be likely that Lull, whilst in Pisa might have been confronted with the growing Dominican activity in propagating the mediaeval transformation of artificial memory. This makes it all the more significant that he so pointedly leaves out of his definition of artificial memory the use of the striking corporeal similitudes, so advantageous for remembering virtues and vices and the roads to Heaven and Hell.

The almost definite opposition to Dominican artificial memory which one senses in this treatise reminds one of the story told in the contemporary life of Lull of the alarming vision that he had in a Dominican church in which a voice told him that only in the Order of Preachers would he find salvation. But to enter the Order of Preachers he must abandon his Art. He made the bold decision to save his Art at the possible expense of his soul 'choosing rather that he himself should be damned than that his art, whereby many might be saved, should be lost.'[36] Was Lull threatened with insufficient emphasis on Remembering Hell in his Art which made no use of striking corporeal similitudes?

What does Lull teach us to remember in the *Liber ad memoriam confirmandam* by his artificial memory which has only one rule, the Aristotelian rule of constant repetition? It is the Lullian Art and all its procedures. The treatise opens with prayers to the divine Bonitas and other attributes, prayed to in association with the Virgin Mary and with the Holy Spirit. This is the Art as *voluntas*, its direction of the will. And in the rest of the treatise, the procedures of the Art as *intellectus* are alluded to, its mode of

[35] See above, pp. 86 ff.

[36] *Vida coetània*, in R. Lull, *Obres essencials*, I, p. 43. The story is quoted in English translation by Peers, *Ramon Lull*, pp. 236–8. It belongs to an earlier period in Lull's life than the stay at Pisa.

10 Ramon Lull with the Ladders of his Art.
Fourteenth-Century Miniature, Karlsruhe Library (Cod. St. Peter 92)
(p. 181)

ascending and descending through the hierarchy of being, its power of making logical judgments through that part of memory which Lull calls *discretio*, through which the contents of memory are examined to reply to enquiries as to whether things are true or certain. Once again, we are led to the conviction that Lullian artificial memory consists in memorising the Lullian Art as *voluntas* and as *intellectus*. And we are further again led to the conviction that the images or 'corporeal similitudes' of classical memory of the rhetorical tradition are incompatible with that Lull calls 'artificial memory'.

In the early sixteenth century, Bernardus de Lavinheta, the holder of the newly established chair of Lullism at the Sorbonne, quoted and commented on the *Liber ad memoriam confirmandam* in an appendix on memory at the end of his large and influential compendium on Lullism. He groups things to be remembered into 'sensibilia' and 'intelligibilia'. For remembering the 'sensibilia' he recommends the classical art, and gives a short account of its places and images. But for remembering the 'intelligibilia', or 'speculative matters which are far remote not only from the senses but even from the imagination one must proceed by another method of remembering. And for this is necessary the *Ars generalis* of our Doctor Illuminatus, who collects all things in his places, comprehending much in little.' This is followed by a brief mention of the figures, rules, and letters of the Lullian Art.[37] By a curious misuse of the scholastic terminology (in which, of course, 'sensible' images are used to remember 'intelligible' things), Lavinheta makes the classical art an inferior discipline used only for remembering 'sensibilia', whilst the higher 'intelligibilia' are to be remembered by a different Art, that of Lullism. Lavinheta leads us back once again to the same point. Images and 'corporeal similitudes' are incompatible with genuine Lullism.

There would seem, therefore, to be no possible point of contact between Renaissance Lullism, which we have seen to be congenial

---

[37] Bernardus de Lavinheta, *Explanatio compendiosaque applicatio artis Raymundi Lulli*, Lyons, 1523; quoted from the second edition in B. de Lavinheta, *Opera omnia quibus tradidit Artis Raymundi Lullii compendiosam explicationem*, ed. H. Alsted, Cologne, 1612, pp. 653–6. See Carreras y Artau, II, pp. 210 ff.; C. Vasoli, 'Umanesimo e Simbologia nei primi scritti Lulliani e mnemotecnici del Bruno', in *Umanesimo e simbolismo*, ed. E. Castelli, Padua, 1958, pp. 258–60; Rossi, 'The Legacy of R.L.', pp. 207–10.

to the Renaissance Neoplatonic and occult tradition in many ways, and the interest of that tradition in the classical art of memory, developed into occult memory.

There may, however, be a point of contact.

There is a curious feature of Lull's *Liber ad memoriam confirmandam* which has not yet been mentioned. In that work it is stated that the person who wants to strengthen his memory must use another book by the writer which will give him the real clue. This book is three times referred to as absolutely essential for memory; it is called 'The Book of the Seven Planets'.[38] There is no work by Lull with this title. The zealous eighteenth-century editor of Lull's Latin works, Ivo Salzinger, was convinced that he knew how to explain this mystery. In the first volume of his edition of Lull's Latin works, the famous Mainz edition, there is a long work by Salzinger himself entitled 'The Revelation of the Secret of the Art of Ramon Lull'. In this he quotes at great length from Lull's *Tractatus de Astronomia*, giving in full the astral-elemental theory of that work, and also quotes in full the long passage in it on why the number of the planets is seven. He then states that this work of Lull's on 'astronomy' contains, amongst other arcane arts:

[38] Near the beginning of the treatise, the reader is told to 'go to the fifth subject designated by B C D in the book of the seven planets (*in libro septem planetarum*) where we treat of miraculous things and you may gain knowledge of every natural entity'. And in the last paragraph the reader is twice referred again to the book of the seven planets as containing the whole key to memory (Rossi, *Clavis*, pp. 262, 266, 267). The three references to the *Liber septem planetarum* are in all five of the manuscripts.

Rossi has suggested ('The Legacy of R. Lull', pp. 205–6) that, though the *Liber ad memoriam confirmandam* is authentically by Lull, the manuscripts of it, none of which is earlier than the sixteenth century, may have been tampered with. If such a possibility is to be considered the tampering would not consist, in my opinion, in the insertion of references to the book of the seven planets. References to other books by himself are a constant feature of Lull's works. It is the specific references to *Ad Herennium* and to *De memoria et reminiscentia* which are a little surprising; it is very unusual for Lull to give references to works other than his own. It is therefore not out of the question that these specific references might have been added in a sixteenth-century revision, made possibly in the circle of Lavinheta. If the specific references are in fact a late addition, this would not alter the tenor of the work with its obvious quotations from *Ad Herennium* and from Aristotle.

195

An *ars memorandi,* 'through which you will retain all the secrets of this Art disclosed in these seven instruments (the seven planets)'.

He next quotes from the *Liber ad memoriam confirmandam* (giving this work explicitly as his source) that for further light on confirming memory we must consult 'The Book of the Seven Planets'. Salzinger unhesitatingly identifies this book as the *Tractatus de Astronomia.*[39]

If the sixteenth century interpreted the 'Secret of the Art of Ramon Lull' in a similar manner to Salzinger in the eighteenth century, it might therefore have found in Lullism the basing of memory on the celestial 'seven'[40] which is the outstanding feature of Camillo's Theatre.

The Renaissance had other authorities for a celestial basing of memory (Metrodorus of Scepsis, for example) but if, like Salzinger, it believed that it could find in Lullism a confirmation of that practice, it would *not* have found in Lullism the use of magic or talismanic images of the stars in memory. For Lull's avoidance of images and similitudes is as notable in his astrology, or rather his astral science, as it is in his attitude to artificial memory. Lull never uses the images of planets or of the signs, nor refers to all that array of animal and human images in the constellations of the astrological world picture. He does his astral science in a completely abstract and imageless way, with geometrical figures and letter notations. Where there might be, however, an element of abstract or geometrical magic in Lullism would be in the figures themselves;

[39] Ivo Salzinger, 'Revelatio Secretorum Artis', in R. Lull, *Opera omnia,* Mainz, 1721–42, I, p. 154. Salzinger interprets the 'fifth subject' to mean the heaven (*coelum*). Neither the *Tractatus de astronomia* nor the *Liber ad memoriam confirmandam* were published in the Mainz edition (which was never completed) but Salzinger quotes long extracts from them in his 'Revelation' and seems to regard them as fundamental for the Secret.

[40] Neither of the two relevant works was available in printed form in the Renaissance. But Lull manuscripts were circulating. The *Liber ad memoriam confirmandam* is quoted by Lavinheta. And practically the whole of the *Tractatus de astronomia,* including the passage on why there are seven planets, is quoted in G. Pirovanus, *Defensio astronomiae,* Milan, 1507 (see 'R.L. and S.E.', p. 30, note). The *Tractatus de astronomia* may thus have helped to swell the chorus of the 'Seven' mystique (see above, p. 168).

in the square on which the elements move 'quadrangulariter, circulariter, et triangulariter';[41] in the revolving circles reflecting the spheres of Aries and his brothers, and of Saturn and his brothers; in the divine triangular patterns.[42] Or in the letter notations themselves which (as in Cabalist use of the Hebrew alphabet) would have a hieroglyphic as well as a purely notatory value.

But the proliferation of imagery such as we see in Camillo's Theatre belongs into a different line of country from Lullism. It belongs to artificial memory of the rhetoric tradition, with its images; developed into corporeal similitudes in the Middle Ages; and developed in the Renaissance Hermetic atmosphere into astralised and talismanic images. It belongs, in fact, to just that side of 'artificial memory' which Lull himself excluded.

Nevertheless, it was to be a grand Renaissance aim to bring together Lullism and the classical art of memory by using magic images of the stars on the Lullian figures.

Let us enter once more Camillo's Theatre, looking this time for traces of the Renaissance Lull. Camillo is known to have been interested in Lullism, and 'Raimundo Lulio' is mentioned in *L'Idea del Theatro*, with a quotation from his *Testament*.[43] This is a Pseudo-Lullian alchemical work. Camillo thus thought of Lull as an alchemist. When we see the seven planets of the Theatre extending into the supercelestial world as Sephiroth, we may wonder whether Camillo also knew the Cabalist Lull of the *De auditu kabbalistico*. One feature of the Theatre, the changes in meaning of the same images on different grades, may remind us of how B to K takes on different meanings as they move up and down the ladder of being.

Nevertheless, though the conflation of Lullism with Renaissance occultised classical memory may be casting the shadow of its approach on the Theatre, Giulio Camillo still belongs almost

[41] I have studied these ingenious patterns in the Elemental Figures of the *Ars demonstrativa* in my article 'La teoría luliana de los elementos' in *Estudios Lulianos*, IV (1960), pp. 56–62.

[42] The significant 'Figure of Solomon' is mentioned by Lull in his *Nova geometria*, ed. J. Millas Vallicrosa, Barcelona, 1953, pp. 65–6.

[43] *L.Idea del Theatro*, p. 18. On the Pseudo-Lullian *Testament*, see Thorndike, *History of Magic and Experimental Science*, IV, pp. 25–7.

entirely to an earlier phase. The Theatre can be fully explained as the classical art of memory galvanised into a new and strange life by Hermetic-Cabalist influences deriving from Ficino's and Pico's movements. And from the formal point of view the Theatre is fully classical. Occult memory is still firmly anchored to a building. Before we can be really convinced that we are seeing Lullism married to the classical art, we must see the images placed on the revolving wheels of Lullist figures. Memory may be already dynamised by magic images in the Theatre; but it is still static in a building.

We are about to meet the master mind who will place magic images of the stars on the revolving combinatory wheels of Lullism, thus achieving the fusion of occultised classical memory with Lullism for which the world is waiting.

Chapter IX

GIORDANO BRUNO: THE SECRET OF *SHADOWS*

GIORDANO Bruno[1] was born four years after the death of Camillo, in 1548. He entered the Dominican Order in 1563. Trained as a Dominican in the convent in Naples, that training must have included an intense concentration on the Dominican art of memory, for the congestions, confusions, complications which had grown up around the 'Ad Herennian' precepts in that tradition as we find it in the treatises of Romberch and Rossellius crowd into Bruno's books on memory.[2] According to words taken down from Bruno's own lips by the librarian of the Abbey of St. Victor in Paris, he was already noted as a memory expert before he left the Dominican Order:

> Jordanus told me that he was called from Naples to Rome by Pope Pius V and Cardinal Rebiba, being brought thither in a coach to show his artificial memory. He recited the psalm *Fundamenta* in Hebrew, and taught something of this art to Rebiba.[3]

There is no means of testing the truth of this vision of Frater

---

[1] This chapter and later chapters on Bruno assume knowledge of my book *Giordano Bruno and the Hermetic Tradition* in which I analyse the Hermetic influences on Bruno and show that he belongs into the Renaissance occult tradition. The book is referred to throughout as *G.B. and H.T.*

[2] The pioneer in pointing out the influence of the memory treatises on Bruno was Felice Tocco, whose pages on this in his *Le opere latine di Giordano Bruno*, Florence, 1889, are still valuable.

[3] *Documenti della vita di G.B.*, ed. V. Spampanato, Florence, 1933, pp. 42–3.

Jordanus, not yet expelled as a heretic, gloriously transported in a coach to Rome to display to a pope and a cardinal that speciality of the Dominicans, the artificial memory.

When Bruno fled from his convent in Naples and began his life of wanderings through France, England, Germany, he had in his possession an asset. An ex-friar who was willing to impart the artificial memory of the friars would arouse interest, and particularly if it was the art in its Renaissance or occult form of which he knew the secret. The first book on memory which Bruno published, the *De umbris idearum* (1582) was dedicated to a French king, Henri III; its opening words promise to reveal a Hermetic secret. This book is the successor to Camillo's Theatre and Bruno is another Italian bringing a memory 'secret' to another King of France.

> I gained such a name that the King Henri III summoned me one day and asked me whether the memory which I had and which I taught was a natural memory or obtained by magic art; I proved to him that it was not obtained by magic art but by science. After that I printed a book on memory entitled *De umbris idearum* which I dedicated to His Majesty, whereupon he made me an endowed reader.[4]

This is Bruno's own account of his relations with Henri III in his statement to the Venetian Inquisitors, who had only to look into the *De umbris idearum* to recognise at once (being better versed in these matters than Bruno's nineteenth-century admirers) that it contained allusions to the magic statues of the *Asclepius* and a list of one hundred and fifty magic images of the stars. Clearly there *was* magic in Bruno's art of memory, and a magic of much deeper dye than Camillo had ventured upon.

When Bruno came over to England, he had fully evolved his technique of conveying his Hermetic religious message within the framework of the art of memory, and this was the purport of the book on memory which he published in England. He continued these methods in Germany, and the last book which he published at Frankfort in 1591 immediately before his return to Italy, was on the magic memory. Ciotto who gave evidence at the Venetian trial about Bruno's reputation in Frankfort, said that people who had attended his lessons in the city had told him that 'the said

---

[4] *Ibid.*, pp. 84–5.

Giordano made profession of memory and of having other similar secrets'.[5]

Finally, when Mocenigo invited Bruno to Venice—the invitation which was the occasion of his return to Italy and which led to his imprisonment and eventual death at the stake—the reason given for the invitation was the wish to learn the art of memory.

When I was in Frankfort last year, [stated Bruno to the Venetian Inquisitors], I had two letters from signor Giovanni Mocenigo, a Venetian gentleman, who wished, so he wrote, that I should teach him the art of memory . . . promising to treat me well.[6]

It was Mocenigo who delated Bruno to the Inquisition in Venice, presumably when he had learned the full 'secrets' of his art of memory. They knew a great deal about occult memory in Venice, owing to the fame of Camillo and his influence in the Venetian academies.

The art of memory is thus at the very centre of the life and death of Bruno.

Since I shall often be referring to Bruno's main works on memory, the titles of some of which are rather cumbrous, I propose to use abbreviated translations of them, as follows:

Shadows = *De umbris idearum . . . Ad internam scripturam, & non vulgares per memoriam operationes explicatis*, Paris, 1582.[7]

Circe = *Cantus Circaeus ad eam memoriae praxim ordinatus quam ipse Iudiciarum appellat*, Paris, 1582.[8]

Seals = *Ars reminiscendi et in phantastico campo exarandi; Explicatio triginta sigillorum ad omnium scientiarum et artium inventionem dispositionem et memoriam; Sigillus Sigillorum ad omnes animi operationes comparandas et earundem rationes habendas maxime conducens; hic enim facile invenies quidquid per logicam, metaphysicam, cabalam, naturalem magiam, artes magnas atque breves theorice inquiruntur*, no place or date of publication. Printed by John Charlewood in England 1583.[9]

Statues = *Lampas triginta statuarum*, probably written at Wittenberg in 1587; first published from the manuscripts in 1891.[10]

[5] *Ibid.*, p. 72.   [6] *Ibid.*, p. 77.

[7] G. Bruno, *Opere latine*, ed. F. Fiorentino and others, Naples and Florence, 1879–91, II (i), pp. 1–77.

[8] *Ibid., vol. cit.*, pp. 179–257.   [9] *Ibid.*, II (ii), pp. 73–217.

[10] *Ibid.*, III, pp. 1–258.

Images = *De imaginum, signorum et idearum compositione, ad omnia inventionum, dispositionum et memoriae genera*, Frankfort, 1591.[11]

Of these five works, the first two, *Shadows* and *Circe*, belong to Bruno's first visit to Paris (1581–3); the immensely long *Seals* belongs to his period in England (1583–5); *Statues* and *Images* were written during his German period (1586–91).

Three of these works, *Shadows*, *Circe*, and *Seals*, contain 'arts of memory' which are based on the time worn division of the memory treatise into 'rules for places' and 'rules for images'. The treatise in *Shadows* alters the old terminology calling the *locus*, the *subjectus*, and the image, the *adjectus*, but the ancient division of the two aspects of memory training is perfectly perceptible beneath this new guise, and all the ancient precepts for places and images, together with many of the elaborations which had accrued to them in the memory tradition, are present in Bruno's treatise. The memory treatise in *Circe* is again on the ancient pattern, though with changed terminology, and this treatise is reprinted in *Seals*. Though the philosophy of the magically animated imagination which Bruno presents in these treatises is totally different from the careful Aristotelian rationalisation of the memory precepts by the scholastics, yet the idea itself of philosophising the precepts had come down to him in the Dominican tradition.

Giordano Bruno always professed the greatest admiration for Thomas Aquinas, and he was proud of the famous art of memory of his Order. At the beginning of *Shadows*, there is an argument between Hermes, Philotheus, and Logifer about the book which Hermes is presenting, the book about the Shadows of Ideas containing the Hermetic art of memory. Logifer, the pedant, protests that works like this have been stated to be useless by many learned doctors.

> The most learned theologian and most subtle patriarch of letters, Magister Psicoteus, has stated that nothing of value can be drawn from the arts of Tullius, Thomas, Albertus, Lullus, and other obscure authors.[12]

---

[11] *Ibid.*, II (iii), pp. 87–322.
[12] *Ibid.*, II (i), p. 14. The text has 'Alulidus' which is presumably a misprint for Lullus.

Logifer's protests are ignored and the mysterious book offered by Hermes is opened.

The pedant doctor, 'Magister Psicoteus', has stated the case against the art of memory, now obsolescent among advanced humanist scholars and educators.[13] The dialogue introducing *Shadows* fits historically into place as belonging to the times when the old art of memory is on the wane. Bruno passionately defends the mediaeval art of Tullius, Thomas, and Albertus against modern detractors, but the version of the mediaeval art which he presents has been through a Renaissance transformation. It has become an occult art, presented by Hermes Trismegistus.

We may compare this dramatic scene between Hermes, Philotheus (who stands for Bruno himself) and Logifer, the Pedant, in which the two former defend a Hermetic art of memory, with the scene in Camillo's Theatre between Viglius-Erasmus and the inventor of the Hermetic Memory Theatre. The issue is the same; a Magus is at loggerheads with a rationalist. And just as Camillo spoke to Viglius of his Theatre as some religious miracle, so Bruno's Hermetic book on memory is presented as a religious revelation. The knowledge or art about to be revealed is like a rising sun before which the creatures of night will vanish. It is based on the 'unerring intellect' and not on 'fallacious sense'. It is akin to the insights of 'Egyptian priests'.[14]

Though the fundamental issue is the same, there are profound differences in style between the interview in Camillo's Theatre and Bruno's extraordinary dialogue. Camillo is the polished Venetian orator presenting a memory system which, though occult in essence, is ordered and neoclassical in form. Bruno is an ex-friar, infinitely wild, passionate, and unrestrained as he rushes out of the mediaevalism of the convent with his art of memory magically transformed into an inner mystery cult. Bruno comes half a century later than Camillo and out of a very different environment, not from civilised Venice but from Naples in the deep south. I do not think that he was influenced by Camillo, unless in the sense that the fame of the Theatre in France would have indicated that Kings of France were open to the reception of memory 'secrets'. Bruno's version of the Hermetically transformed art of memory was

---

[13] His name suggestive of 'Master Parrot' is perhaps an allusion to the learning by repetition now preferred to the classical art.

[14] *Op. lat.*, II (i), pp. 7–9; cf. *G.B. and H.T.*, pp. 192 ff.

generated independently from that of Camillo and in quite different surroundings.

What were those surroundings ? First of all there is the question, which I shall have to leave unsolved, as to what may, or may not, have been going on in regard to the art of memory in the Dominican convent in Naples. The convent was in a state of disorder and commotion in the late sixteenth century[15] and it is not impossible that some of the excitement might have been due to Renaissance transformations of the Dominican art of memory.

Thomas Aquinas's memory rules are very carefully framed to exclude magic, very carefully Aristotelianised and rationalised. No one who followed Thomas's rules in the spirit in which they were given could have turned the art of memory into a magical art. It had become a devotional and an ethical art, a side of it which he stressed, but the art as he recommended it was certainly not a magical art. Thomas firmly condemned the *Ars notoria*,[16] the mediaeval magical art of memory, and his adoption of the memory rules of 'Tullius' is very cautiously expounded. The subtle difference between his attitude and that of Albertus Magnus to the art as reminiscence may be due to care in avoiding pitfalls into which Albertus may have been falling.[17]

For with Albertus, the position is not so clear. We found some rather curious things in Albertus on memory, particularly the transformation of the classical memory image into a huge ram in the night skies.[18] Is it possible that in that Neapolitan convent, under the impulse of the widespread Renaissance revival of magic, the art of memory was developing in some Albertist direction, and may have been using talismanic images of the stars, in which Albertus was certainly interested ? I can only raise this as a question, for the whole problem of Albertus Magnus both in the Middle Ages and in the Renaissance—in which he was widely studied—is a more or less untrodden field from these points of view.

We have to remember, too, that ·Bruno, though he intensely

[15] See *G.B. and H.T.*, p. 365.
[16] In the *Summa Theologiae*, II, II, *quaestio* 96, *articulus* I. The question is raised whether the *Ars Notoria* is illicit, and the reply is that it is totally illicit as a false and superstitious art.
[17] See above, pp. 72–3.
[18] See above, p. 68.

admired Thomas Aquinas, admired him as a Magus, possibly reflecting a trend in Renaissance Thomism, later developed by Campanella, which again is a more or less untrodden field of study.[19] There were better grounds for an intense admiration of Albertus Magnus as a Magus, for Albertus does tend in that direction. When Bruno was arrested, he defended himself for possessing an incriminating work on magic images on the ground that it was recommended by Albertus Magnus.[20]

Leaving the, at present, insoluble problem of what the art of memory may have been like in the Dominican convent in Naples when Bruno was an inmate there, let us consider what influences outside the convent might have been brought to bear on him before he fled from Naples in 1576, never to return.

In 1560, Giovanni Battista Porta, the famous magician and early scientist, established in Naples his *Academia Secretorum Naturae*, the members of which met at his house to discuss 'secrets', some magical, some genuinely scientific. In 1558, Porta published the first version of his great work on *Magia naturalis* which was to influence profoundly Francis Bacon and Campanella.[21] In this book, Porta studies the secret virtues of plants and stones and sets out very fully the system of correspondencies between the stars and the lower world. Amongst Porta's 'secrets' was his interest in physiognomics[22] concerning which he makes a curious study of resemblances to animals in human faces. Bruno certainly knew something of Porta's animal physiognomics which he uses in his treatment of Circe's magic in *Circe*, and which can also be discerned in some of his other works. Porta was also interested in ciphers, or secret writing,[23] which he associates with Egyptian mysteries, and this again was an interest which Bruno shared.

But what chiefly concerns us here is Porta's *Ars reminiscendi*, a

---

[19] See *G.B. and H.T.*, pp. 251, 272, 379 ff. In his edition of the works of Thomas Aquinas, published in 1570, Cardinal Caiëtano defended the use of talismans; see Walker, *Magic*, pp. 214-15, 218-19.

[20] See *G.B. and H.T.*, p. 347.

[21] Thorndike has shown (*History of Magic and Experimental Science*, VI, pp. 418 ff.) that Porta's natural magic was largely influenced by a mediaeval work, the *Secreta Alberti*, attributed to Albertus Magnus though probably not really by him.

[22] G. B. Porta, *Physiognomiae coelestis libri sex*, Naples, 1603.

[23] G. B. Porta, *De furtivis litterarum notis*, Naples, 1563.

treatise on the art of memory published at Naples in 1602.[24] Imagination, says Porta, draws images as with a pencil in memory. There is both natural and artificial memory, the latter invented by Simonides. Porta regards Virgil's description of the rooms painted with pictures which Dido showed to Aeneas as really Dido's memory system, by which she remembered the history of her ancestors. Architectural places are palaces or theatres. Mathematical precepts and geometrical figures can also be used as places on account of their order, as described by Aristotle. Human figures should be used as memory images, chosen for being striking in some way, very beautiful or very ridiculous. It is useful to take pictures by good artists as memory images for these are more striking and move more than pictures by ordinary painters. For example, pictures by Michelangelo, Raphael, Titian, stay in memory. Hieroglyphs of the Egyptians may be used as memory images. There are also images for letters and numbers (referring to the visual alphabets).

Porta's memory is remarkable for its high aesthetic quality, but his is a normal type of memory treatise, in the scholastic tradition based on Tullius and Aristotle, with the usual repetitions of the rules and the usual complications such as visual alphabets. We might be reading Romberch or Rossellius, except that there is nothing about remembering Hell and Heaven. There is no overt magic in the book, so far as I can see, and he condemns Metrodorus of Scepsis for using the stars in memory. The little work shows, however, that the occult philosopher of Naples was interested in the artificial memory.

One of the main sources of Bruno's magic was Cornelius Agrippa's *De philosophia occulta* (1533). Agrippa does not mention the art of memory in this work, but in his *De vanitate scientiarum* (1530) he has a chapter on it in which he condemns it as a vain art.[25] But Agrippa in that work condemns all the occult arts which three years later he was to expound in his *De occulta philosophia*, the most important Renaissance text book on Hermetic and Cabalist magic. Various attempts have been made to explain Agrippa's

---

[24] This was the Latin version of *L'arte del ricordare* which Porta had published at Naples in 1566. It has been suggested (by Louise G. Clubb, *Giambattista Della Porta Dramatist*, Princeton, 1965, p. 14) that Porta aims at providing mnemonics for actors.

[25] See above, p. 124.

contradictory attitudes in these two books, one of the most convincing being that the *De vanitate scientiarum* was a safety device of a kind frequently employed by writers on dangerous subjects. To be able to point to a book against magic would be a protection if the *De occulta philosophia* got him into trouble. This may not be the whole explanation but it makes possible the view that the sciences which Agrippa calls 'vain' in his attack on the vanity of sciences may be those in which he was really interested. Most occult philosophers of the Renaissance were interested in the art of memory and it would be surprising if Agrippa were an exception. At any rate, it was from Agrippa's manual of magic that Bruno took the magic images of the stars which he used in the memory system in *Shadows*.

When Bruno's *Shadows* was published in Paris in 1582, the work would not have appeared so utterly strange to the contemporary French reader as it does to us. He would have been able to place it at once as belonging into certain contemporary trends. Here was a book on memory presented as a Hermetic secret and obviously full of magic. Seized with dread or disapproval, some readers would have discarded the book. Others, steeped in the prevalent Neoplatonism with its magical fringe, would have sought to discover whether this new memory expert had carried further the effort to bring the art of memory into line with the occult philosophy to which Giulio Camillo had devoted his life. Dedicated to Henri III, *Shadows* was clearly in line of descent from the Hermetic Memory Theatre which Camillo had presented to the present King's grandfather, Francis I.

The Theatre was not yet forgotten in France. A centre of occultist influence in Paris was formed by Jacques Gohorry who started a kind of medico-magical academy not far from the site of Baïf's Academy of Poetry and Music.[26] Gohorry, who was saturated with Ficinian and Paracelsist influences wrote, under the name of 'Leo Suavius', a number of extremely obscure works; in one of these, published in 1550, Gohorry gives a brief description of the 'wooden amphitheatre' which Camillo had constructed for Francis I.[27] Though Gohorry's academy or group seems to disappear about 1576, its influences probably continued, and these

[26] See Walker, *Magic*, pp. 96–106.
[27] Jacques Gohorry, *De Usu & Mysteriis Notarum Liber*, Paris, 1550, sigs. Ciii *verso*–Civ *recto*. Cf. Walker, p. 98.

would have included some knowledge of occult memory and of Camillo's Theatre about which Gohorry had written in admiring terms. Moreover, only four years before the publication of Bruno's book, Camillo's name had appeared in the *Peplus Italiae*, published in Paris, as a famous Italian, along with Pico della Mirandola and other great Renaissance names.[28]

In the later sixteenth century, the occult tradition had been growing in daring. Jacques Gohorry was one of those who thought that Ficino and Pico had been too timid in putting into practice mysteries in the writings of Zoroaster, Trismegistus, and other ancient sages which they knew, and had not made sufficient use of 'images and seals'. Their failure to make full use of their knowledge of such matters meant, thinks Gohorry, that they failed to become wonder-working Magi. Bruno's memory systems show marked progress in these directions. As compared with Camillo, he was infinitely more daring in the use of notoriously magical images and signs in the occult memory. In *Shadows* he does not hesitate to use the (supposedly) very powerful images of the decans of the zodiac; in *Circe* he introduces the art of memory with fiercely magical incantations uttered by the sorceress.[29] Bruno aimed at very much greater powers than the mild lion-taming or the planetary oratory of Camillo.

The reader of *Shadows* immediately notices the several times repeated figure of a circle marked with thirty letters. In some of these figures, concentric circles, marked with the thirty letters, are shown (Fig. 8). Paris in the sixteenth century was the foremost European centre of Lullism, and no Parisian could have failed to recognise these circles as the famous combinatory wheels of the Lullian Art.

The efforts towards finding a way of conciliating the classical art of memory, with its places and images, and Lullism with its moving figures and letters, had continued to grow in strength in the later sixteenth century. The problem must have excited a good deal of general interest, comparable to the popular interest in the mind machines of today. Garzoni in his popular work the *Piazza universale* (1578), to which I have already more than once referred,

[28] See above, p. 135.
[29] On the incantations in *Circe*, see *G.B. and H.T.*, pp. 200–2.

208

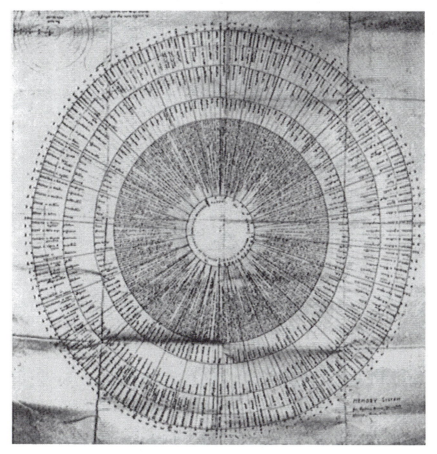

11   Memory System from Giordano Bruno's *De umbris idearum*
(*Shadows*), Paris, 1582 (pp. 212 ff.)

states that it is his ambition to produce a universal memory system combining Rossellius and Lull.[30] If an outsider and a layman, like Garzoni, hoped to do such a thing, using the published text-book on memory by Rossellius, the Dominican, how much more might an insider like Giordano Bruno be expected to produce the uni-

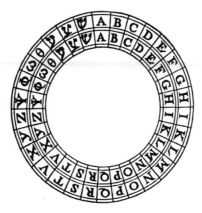

Fig. 8 Memory Wheels. From G. Bruno, *De Umbris idearum*, 1582

versal memory machine. Trained as a Dominican, expert as a Lullist, surely here was the great specialist who might finally solve the problem.

We should expect to find that Bruno's Lull would be the Renaissance Lull, not the mediaeval Lull. His Lullian circle has more letters on it than in any genuine Lullian art, and a few Greek and Hebrew letters, which are never used in genuine Lullism. His wheel is closer to those to be seen in Pseudo-Lullian al-chemical diagrams which also use some letters other than those of the Latin alphabet. And when listing Lull's works, Bruno includes the *De auditu kabbalistico* as one of them.[31] These indications suggest that Lull, the alchemist, and Lull, the Cabalist, would come into Bruno's idea of Lullism. But Bruno's Lull is even more peculiar, and more remote from the mediaeval Lull, than in normal Renaissance Lullism. He told the librarian of

[30] T. Garzoni, *Piazza universale*, Venice, 1578, chapter on 'Professori di memoria'.
[31] *Op lat.*, II (ii), pp. 62, 333.

Ao

Iu prima Tauri facie Nudus arans, de palea pileum intextum gestans, fusco colore, quem sequitur rusticus alter femina jaciens.

Av In Secunda Clauiger nudus, & coronatus aureum baltheum in humeris gestans & in sinistra sceptrum.

Ba In tertia vir sinistra serpentem gestans & dextra hastam siue Sagittam, ante quem testa ignis, & aquæ lagena.

Gemini.

Be

In prima geminorum facie, vir paratus ad seruiendum, virgam habens in dextera. Vultu hilari atque iocundo.

Bi In secunda, homo terram fondiens & laborans: iuxta quem tibicen nudis saltans pedibus & capite.
Bo In tertia Morio tibiam dextera gestans, in sinistra passerem & iuxta illum vir iratus apprehendens baculum.

IMAGINES FACIERVM

signorum ex Teucro Babilonico quæ ad vsum presentis artis quam commode trahi possunt.

Aries.

AA

Ascendit in prima facie arietis homo niger immodicæ staturæ, ardentibus oculis, seuero vultu, stans candida precinctus palla.

Ae In secunda mulier non inuenusta, alba induta thunica, pallio verò tyrio colore intincto superinduta, soluta coma, & lauro coronata.

Ai In tertia homo pallidus ruffi capilli rubris indutus vestibus, in sinistra auream gestans armillam, & ex robore baculum in dextra, inquieti & irascentis præ se ferens vultum cum cupita bona nequeat adipisci nec præstare.

12a Images of the Decans of Aries   12b Images of the Decans of Taurus and Gemini
From Giordano Bruno, *De umbris idearum* (*Shadows*), ed. of Naples, 1886 (p. 213)

the Abbey of St. Victor that he understood Lullism better than Lull himself had done,[32] and there is certainly very much to appal the genuine Lullist in Bruno's use of the art.

Why does Bruno divide his Lullian wheels into thirty segments? He was certainly thinking along lines of Names or attributes, for he lectured in Paris (these lectures are not extant) on 'thirty divine attributes.'[33] Bruno was obsessed with the number thirty. Not only is this the basic number in *Shadows*, but there are thirty seals in *Seals*, thirty statues in *Statues*, and thirty 'links' in his work on how to establish links with demons.[34] The only passage in his books, so far as I know, in which he discusses his use of 'thirty' is in the *De compendiosa architectura artis Lullii*, published in Paris in the same year as *Shadows* and *Circe*. Here after listing some of the Lullian Dignities, Bonitas, Magnitudo, Veritas, and so on, Bruno assimilates these to the Sephiroth of the Cabala:

> All these (i.e. the Lullian Dignities), the Jewish Cabalists reduce to ten sephiroth and we to thirty . . .[35]

He thus thought of the 'thirty' on which he based his arts as Lullian Dignities but Cabalised as Sephiroth. In this passage he rejects Lull's Christian and Trinitarian use of his Art. The divine Dignities, he says, really represent the four-lettered Name of God (the Tetragrammaton) which the Cabalists assimilate to the four cardinal points of the world and thence by successive multiplication to the whole universe.

It is not quite clear how he arrives at thirty out of this,[36] though this number seems to have been particularly associated with magic. A Greek magical papyrus of the fourth century gives a thirty-

[32] *Documenti*, p. 43.

[33] *Ibid.*, p. 84.

[34] *De vinculis in genere* (*Op. lat.*, III, pp. 669–70). Cf. *G.B. and H.T.*, p. 266.

[35] *Op. lat.* II (ii), p. 42. There is nothing specifically about architecture in this book 'on the architecture of the art of Lull'. It is on Lullism, but some figures are not the normal Lullian ones. The use of the word 'architecture' in the title may mean that Bruno is thinking of the Lullian figures as memory 'places' to be used instead of the architecture of a memory building. The work connects with *Shadows* and with *Circe*.

[36] The multiplication of the four-lettered Name should proceed by multiples of four and twelve, which series nowhere gives a thirty. There is a passage in Bruno's *Spaccio della bestia trionfante* on this (*Dialoghi italiani*, ed. G. Aquilecchia, 1957, pp. 782–3). Cf. *G.B. and H.T.*, p. 269.

lettered Name of God.[37] Irenaeus when thundering against gnostic heresies mentions that John the Baptist was supposed to have thirty disciples, a number suggestive of the thirty aeons of the gnostics. Still more suggestive of deep magic, the number thirty was associated with Simon Magus.[38] I am inclined to think that Bruno's actual source was probably the *Steganographia* of Trithemius in which thirty-one spirits are listed, with recipes for conjuring them. In an abstract of this work later made for Bruno, the list becomes a thirty. Amongst Bruno's contemporaries, John Dee was interested in the magical value of thirty. Dee's *Clavis angelicae* was published at Cracow in 1584[39] (two years after Bruno's *Shadows* by which, therefore, it could have been influenced). The Angelic Key describes how to conjure 'thirty good orders of the princes of the air' who rule over all the parts of the world. Dee sets out thirty magical names on thirty concentric circles and is engaged in magic for conjuring angels or demons.

Bruno several times mentions in *Shadows* a work of his called *Clavis magna*, which either never existed or has not survived. The Great Key might have explained how to use Lullian wheels as conjuring for summoning the spirits of the air. For that is, I believe, a secret of the use of the Lullian wheels in *Shadows*. Just as he converts the images of the classical art of memory into magical images of the stars to be used for reaching the celestial world, so the Lullian wheels are turned into 'practical Cabala', or conjuring for reaching the demons, or angels, beyond the stars.

Bruno's brilliant achievement in finding a way of combining the classical art of memory with Lullism thus rested on an extreme 'occultising' of both the classical art and of Lullism. He put the images of the classical art on the Lullian combinatory wheels, but the images were magic images and the wheels were conjuring wheels.

In the world in which it was first published, *Shadows* would have

[37] K. Preisendanz, *Papyri Graeci Magicae*, Berlin, 1931, p. 32. (I am indebted to E. Jaffé for this reference.)

[38] These 'thirties' are mentioned by Thorndike, *History of Magic and Experimental Science*, I, pp. 364–5.

[39] The original in Dee's handwriting is in MS. Sloane 3191, ff. 1–13; a copy by Ashmole is in MS. Sloane 3678, ff. 1–13.

The *Steganographia* was not printed until 1606 but was widely known in manuscript; see Walker, *Magic*, p. 86. For the abstract of it made for Bruno, see *Op. lat.*, III, pp. 496 ff.

fitted into certain well-known patterns. But it does not follow from this that it would have excited no surprise. On the contrary, just because the contemporary reader would recognise the kind of thing that Bruno was attempting, he would also recognise his wild abandonment of all safeguards and restraints. Here was a man who would stop at nothing, who would use every magical procedure however dangerous and forbidden, to achieve that organisation of the psyche from above, through contact with the cosmic powers, which had been the dream of the decorous and orderly Camillo, but which Giordano Bruno pursues with a much more alarming boldness and with methods infinitely more complex.

What is this curious looking object (Pl. 11) upon which the reader is now invited to direct his gaze ? Is it some disc or papyrus of incredible antiquity dug up in the sands of Egypt ? No. It is my attempt to excavate the 'secret' of *Shadows*.

Here are concentric wheels divided into thirty main segments, each of which is again subdivided into five, giving 150 divisions in all. On all these divisions there are inscriptions which will, I am afraid, hardly be legible. This does not matter for we shall never understand this thing in detail. The plan is only intended to give some idea of the general lay-out of the system, and also some idea of its appalling complexity.

How have I arrived at this, and why has this object never been seen before ? It is quite simple. No one has realised that the lists of images given in the book, each list consisting of 150 images in sets of thirty are intended to be set out on concentric wheels, like those which are several times illustrated (see Fig. 8). These wheels, intended to revolve in the Lullian manner to give the combinations, are marked with the letters A to Z, followed by some Greek and Hebrew letters, making thirty letter markings in all. The lists of images given in the book are marked off in thirty divisions marked with these letters, each division having five subdivisions marked with the five vowels. These lists, each of 150 images, are therefore intended to be set out on the concentric revolving wheels. Which is what I have done on the plan, by writing out the lists of images on concentric wheels divided into thirty segments with five subdivisions in each. The result is the ancient Egyptian looking object, evidently highly magical, for the images on the central wheel are the images of the decans of the zodiac, images of the planets, images of the mansions of the moon, and images of the houses of the horoscope.

The descriptions of these images are written out from Bruno's text on the central wheel of the plan. This heavily inscribed central wheel is the astral power station, as it were, which works the whole system.

I reproduce here (from the 1886 edition of *Shadows*) the first two pages of Bruno's list of astral images to be placed on the central wheel of the system. The first page (Pl. 12a) is headed 'The images of the faces of the signs from Teucer the Babylonian which can be used in the present art.' It shows a cut of the sign Aries, and gives descriptions of images of the first, second, and third 'faces' of Aries, that is images of the three decans of this sign. On the next page (Pl. 12b) are Taurus and Gemini, each with their three decan images. It will be noticed that the images have beside them the letter A followed by five vowels (Aa, Ae, Ai, Ao, Au); then B with five vowels. The whole of the rest of the list is similarly marked with the thirty letters of the wheel, each with the five vowel subdivisions. And all the other lists are marked in a similar way. It is these markings which give the clue that the lists of images are to be set out on concentric wheels.

Confining ourselves to the three signs on the pages of the text here reproduced, the images described for the decans of Aries are (1) a huge dark man with burning eyes, dressed in white; (2) a woman; (3) a man holding a sphere and a staff. Those for Taurus are (1) a man ploughing (2) a man bearing a key (3) a man holding a serpent and a spear. Those for Gemini are (1) a serving man holding a rod; (2) a man digging, and a flute-player, (3) a man with a flute.

These images derive from ancient Egyptian star-lore and star-magic.[40] The three hundred and sixty degrees of the zodiacal circle are divided amongst the twelve signs of the zodiac, each of which is subdivided into three 'faces' of ten degrees each. These latter are the 'decans' each of which has an image associated with it. The images of the decans go back to ancient Egyptian sidereal gods of time; the lists of them were preserved in the archives of Egyptian temples whence they passed into the lore of late antique astral

[40] On the decan images, see *G.B. and H.T.*, pp. 45–8. The representations of the decans of Aries in the Palazzo Schifanoja are reproduced on Pl. 1 in that book.

magic, handed down in texts the authorship of which is often assigned to 'Hermes Trismegistus' who is particularly associated with the decan images and their magic. These images vary in different sources, but we do not have to search remote and difficult texts to find the source of the decan images which Bruno is using. Bruno used easily accessible printed sources for most of his magic, relying chiefly on the *De occulta philosophia* of Henry Cornelius Agrippa. Agrippa introduces his list of the images of the decans with the words, 'There are in the zodiac thirty-six images . . . of which Teucer the Babylonian wrote.' Bruno copied this heading for the beginning of his list of decan images, which he took, with sometimes some very slight variations, from the list given by Agrippa.[41]

After the thirty-six images of the decans there follow, in the list of star-images in *Shadows*, forty-nine images of the planets, seven for each planet. Each group of seven images is headed by a conventional cut of the planet concerned. Examples of these planet images are:

> First image of Saturn: A man with a stag's head on a dragon, with an owl which is eating a snake in his right hand.
> Third image of Sol: A young man, diademed, from whose head spring rays of light, holding a bow and quiver.
> First image of Mercury: A beautiful young man with a sceptre, on which two serpents opposed to one another are entwined with their heads facing one another.
> First image of Luna: A horned woman riding on a dolphin; in her right hand a chameleon, in her left a lily.

As can be seen, such images express the planetary gods and their influences, after the manner of planetary talismans. Bruno derived most of the forty-nine from the list of planet images in Agrippa's *De occulta philosophia*.[42]

Next follow, in Bruno's list, the image of the *Draco lunae* together with images of the twenty-eight mansions of the moon, that is of the stations of the moon on each day of the month. These images express the rôle of the moon and her movements in passing on the zodiacal and planetary influences. These images, again, Bruno drew with only slight variations from Agrippa's *De occulta philosophia*.[43]

[41] H. C. Agrippa, *De occulta philosophia*, II, 37. On the variations, see *G.B. and H.T.*, p. 196, note 3.
[42] *De occulta philosophia*, II, 37–44. Cf. *G.B. and H.T.*, p. 196.
[43] *De occult. phil.*, II, 46; Cf. *G.B. and H.T.*, loc. cit.

We have to see all these astral images in the context of the *De occulta philosophia* to realise what Bruno is trying to do. In Agrippa's text-book of magic, such image-lists occur in the second book, the one on celestial magic which is concerned with operating on the middle world of the stars—middle as compared with the lower elemental world dealt with in the first book, and the super-celestial world to which the third book is devoted. One of the chief ways of operating (according to this kind of magical thought) with the celestial world is through the magic or talismanic images of the stars. Bruno is transferring such operations within, applying them to memory by using the celestial images as memory images, as it were harnessing the inner world of the imagination to the stars, or reproducing the celestial world within.

Finally, following a cut representing the twelve houses into which a horoscope is divided, Bruno gives a list of thirty-six images, three for each of the twelve houses. These images are expressive of the aspects of life with which the houses of a horoscope are supposed to be connected—birth, wealth, brothers, parents, children, sickness, marriage, death, religion, reign, benefactions, imprisonment. They are faintly connected with traditional images of the houses, such as can be seen, for example, in a calendar of 1515,[44] but Bruno has strangely varied and added to these to produce a very eccentric list of images which are probably largely of his own invention. We see him here at the work of 'composing' magic images on which he was later to write a whole book.

Such then, are the 150 images imprinted on the central wheel of the magic memory. The whole sky with all its complex astrological influences was on this wheel. The images of the stars formed combinations and convolutions as the wheels revolved. And the master mind who had the sky and all its movements and influences magically imprinted on memory through magic images was indeed in possession of a 'secret' worth knowing!

In the introductory pages of *Shadows*, the art of memory about to be revealed is presented as a Hermetic secret; it is said to be actually by Hermes who hands a book containing it to the philosopher.[45] Moreover the title, *De umbris idearum*, is taken from a magical work, Cecco d'Ascoli's necromantic commentary on the

[44] L. Reymann, *Nativität-Kalender*, Nüremberg, 1515; reproduced in A. Warburg, *Gesammelte Schriften*, Leipzig, 1932, II, Pl. LXXV.
[45] Bruno, *Op. lat.*, II (i), p. 9; cf. *G.B. and H.T.*, p. 193.

Sphere of Sacrobosco in which a *Liber de umbris idearum* is mentioned.[46] What then are the magical 'shadows of ideas' which are to be the basis of the Hermetic memory system?

Bruno's mind is working on lines which are extremely difficult for a modern to recapture—the lines which Ficino's mind is also following in his *De vita coelitus comparanda*—that the images of the stars are intermediaries between the ideas in the supercelestial world and the sub-celestial elemental world. By arranging or manipulating or using the star-images one is manipulating forms which are a stage nearer to reality than the objects in the inferior world, all of which depend on the stellar influences. One can act on the inferior world, change the stellar influences on it, if one knows how to arrange and manipulate the star-images. In fact the star-images *are* the 'shadows of ideas', shadows of reality which are nearer to reality than the physical shadows in the lower world. Once one grasps this (to the modern, fundamentally ungraspable) point of view, many mysteries in *Shadows* are cleared up. The book which Hermes hands to the philosopher is the book 'on the shadows of ideas contracted for inner writing',[47] that is to say it contains a list of magic images of the stars to be imprinted on memory. They are to be used on revolving wheels:

> As the ideas are the principal forms of things, according to which all is formed ... so we should form in us the shadows of ideas ... so that they may be adaptable to all possible formations. We form them in us, as in the revolution of wheels. If you know any other way, try it.[48]

By imprinting on memory the images of the 'superior agents', we shall know the things below from above; the lower things will arrange themselves in memory once we have arranged there the images of the higher things, which contain the reality of the lower things in a higher form, a form nearer to ultimate reality.

> The forms of deformed animals are beautiful in heaven. Non-luminous metals shine in their planets. Neither man, nor animals, nor metals are here as they are there ... illuminating, vivifying, uniting, conforming yourself to the superior agents, you will advance in the conception and retention of the species.[49]

---

[46] See *G.B. and H.T.*, p. 197.   [47] *Op. lat.*, II (i), p. 9.
[48] *Ibid.*, pp. 51–2.   [49] *Ibid.*, p. 46.

How is the adept to conform to the superior agents ? By inwardly conforming himself to the astral images, through which the individual species in the lower world will be united. Such an astral memory will give not only knowledge, but powers:

> There is in your primordial nature a chaos of elements and numbers, yet not without order and series . . . There are, as you may see, certain distinct intervals . . . On one the figure of Aries is imprinted; on another, Taurus, and so on for the rest (of the signs of the zodiac) . . . This is to form the inform chaos . . . It is necessary for the control of memory that the numbers and elements should be disposed in order . . . through certain memorable forms (the images of the zodiac) . . . I tell you that if you contemplate this attentively you will be able to reach such a figurative art that it will help not only the memory but also all the powers of the soul in a wonderful manner.[50]

What does this remind us of? Surely of the memory system of Metrodorus of Scepsis who used the zodiac, and probably the images of the decans, as his memory place system. The Metrodorian system has turned into a magical system. In relation to the fundamental zodiacal images, the planet images, moon station images, houses of the horoscope images of Bruno's list of magic images, move on the wheels of memory, forming and reforming the patterns of the universe from a celestial level. And the power to do this depends on the Hermetic philosophy, that man is in his origin divine, and organically related to the star-governors of the world. In 'your primordial nature' the archetypal images exist in a confused chaos; the magic memory draws them out of chaos and restores their order, gives back to man his divine powers.

Surrounding the innermost circle or wheel of the star images—the central power station of the magically animated memory—the reader will perceive on the plan other circles or wheels all inscribed with 150 items divided into groups of thirty. Again, I am carefully carrying out Bruno's instructions, for, as well as the list of 150 star images, he gives three other lists of 150 items each, all marked with the lettering of the thirty divisions of the wheels and subdivided into fives, marked with the vowels. Clearly these other three lists are also to be set out on wheels, concentric with the star-images wheel.

[50] *Ibid.*, pp. 77–8.

On the wheel immediately surrounding the star-images wheel on the plan are inscribed the items in the list which begins as follows:

Aa Oliua; Ae Laurus; Ai Myrthus; Ao Rosmarinum; Au Cypressus[51] As can be seen, these all belong to the vegetable world. There are also birds in this list; animals; stones and metals; artefacts and other objects, strangely jumbled and including even sacred objects (*ara, septem candelabra*). Roughly speaking it seems to represent the vegetable, animal, and mineral worlds, but also includes fabricated objects, though this classification perhaps makes rather too much sense of the extraordinary medley. The idea is, I believe, to represent on this wheel the inferior levels of creation, vegetable, animal, mineral, moving in dependence on the celestial wheel.

On the next wheel on the plan (the third from the centre) is inscribed the list which begins:

Aa nodosum; Ae mentitum; Ai inuolutum; Ao informe; Au famosum.[52] These are all adjectives (knotty, counterfeited, involved, formless, famous). Why given in the accusative case I cannot explain, still less explain the extraordinary selection of the 150 adjectives in this list.

Finally, on the outermost wheels of the plan, are inscribed the 150 items of the list which begins:

Aa	Rhegima	panem castanearum
Ae	Osiris	in agriculturam
Ai	Ceres	in iuga bouum
Ao	Triptolemus	serit
Au	Pitumnus	stercorat[53]

Translated, this means: 'Rhegima (the inventor of) bread from chestnuts; Osiris (the inventor of) agriculture; Ceres (the inventor of) yokes for oxen; Triptolemus (the inventor of) sowing; Pitumnus (the inventor of) manuring.'

On the plan, I show the name of the inventor on the outermost wheel, and the description of the invention on the wheel immediately adjoining it. The reader may be able to follow this series on the plan. The five quoted above will be found starting at the middle of the lower half of the outermost wheel.

No student of Giordano Bruno has ever investigated this list; still less has anyone realised that these images of human figures are

[51] *Ibid.*, p. 132.   [52] *Ibid.*, p. 129.   [53] *Ibid.*, p. 124.

218

to be placed on the outer wheel of a memory system organised and magically animated by the star images on the central wheel. In my opinion, this list is worthy of close attention. In what follows I shall try to give an impression, without full quotation of every name and the invention associated with it, of the extraordinary procession which revolves before us on this wheel.

Following the agricultural group, quoted above, come inventors of primitive instruments and procedures. Erichtonius invented the chariot; Pyrodes, drawing fire from flint. Inventors of viticulture include Noah; Isis first ordered gardens; Minerva showed the use of oil; Aristeus discovered honey. Next appear inventors of trapping, hunting, fishing. Then a group containing such little-known characters as Sargum, inventor of the basket, Doxius, of building with clay. Among inventors of tools are Talus, of the saw, Parug, of the hammer. Next come pottery, spinning, weaving, cobbling, with Choraebus as the potter. Various strangely named inventors of—to select a few examples—carding, shoes, glass, pincers, shaving, combs, carpets, and boats now pass before us.[54]

Now that the inventors of the fundamental technologies of advancing civilisation have been represented, the revolution of the wheel begins to show us other kinds of human activities. I quote in full the M and N groups:

Ma	Chiron	surgery
Me	Circe	fascination
Mi	Pharphacon	necromancy
Mo	Aiguam	circles
Mu	Hostanes	linking with demons
Na	Zoroaster	magic
Ne	Suah	chiromancy
Ni	Chaldaeus	pyromancy
No	Attalus	hydromancy
Nu	Prometheus	sacrificing bulls[55]

What a glittering vision of the inventors of the magical and demonic arts! Here is Circe, the sorceress—always to be a dominating figure in Bruno's imagination—making her first appearance in his works. Here is the inventor of 'linking with demons', a subject later to be treated by Bruno under thirty headings. Here is Zoroaster, supreme in magic.

[54] *Ibid.*, pp. 124–5.
[55] *Ibid.*, p. 126.

But why does this group end with 'sacrificing bulls'? It seems to
be a principle of the groups of five that the first figure in them
links with the preceding group, whilst the last figure links with
subjects which are to follow. The hint of religious sacrifice in
Prometheus prepares us for the religious leaders and inventors in
the O, P, and Q groups now about to rise before us in the revolution of the wheel. These include Abel, who sacrificed the flocks;
Abraham who invented circumcision; John the Baptist who
baptised; Orpheus who invented the orgies; Belus who invented
idols; Chemis who invented burial in pyramids. Thus Old Testament figures, and one New Testament figure, appear in the weird
procession.[56]

After magic and religion—indissolubly linked together and seen
as one—we reach the magician inventors of the visual and musical
arts.

Ra	Mirchanes	wax figures
Re	Giges	pictures
Ri	Marsias	the flute
Ro	Tubal	the lyre
Ru	Amphion	musical notes[57]

Other inventors of musical instruments follow in the next group
and then we are led on, through Neptune, tamer of horses, to
equestrian exercises and inventors connected with military art.

Then comes a basic invention:

Xe	Theut	inventor of writing with letters[58]

Here is Thoth-Hermes as the inventor of writing. After the
Egyptian sage we pass on to astronomy, astrology, and philosophy, to Thales and Pythagoras, to a strange mixture of names
and notions:

Ya	Nauphides	on the course of the sun
Ye	Endimion	on the moon
Yi	Hipparcus	on the leftward movement of the sphere of fixed stars
Yo	Atlas	on the sphere
Yu	Archimedes	on the heaven of brass
Za	Cleostratus	on the twelve signs
Ze	Archita	on the geometrical cube

[56] *Ibid., loc. cit.*   [57] *Ibid.*, p. 127.   [58] *Ibid., loc. cit.*

Zi	Xenophanes	on the innumerable worlds
Zo	Plato	on the ideas and from the ideas (*in ideas et ab ideis*)
Zu	Raymundus	on the nine elements[59]

In this collection we have one of the greatest astronomers of antiquity, Hipparchus; we have the model of the heavens made by Archimedes; we have 'innumerable worlds', here said to have been invented by Xenophanes; we have Plato on the ideas. And finally we have Raymundus Lullus and his Art, based on nine letters or elements.

This revolution of the wheel of memory is perhaps the most revealing of them all. The innumerable worlds, which were to be so prominent a feature of Bruno's philosophy, are here mentioned by him for the first time. And that the procession of the inventors through magic and magical religion to philosophy and Lullism has brought us into the range of Bruno's own interests, and the weird contexts in which he saw those interests, is emphasised by the first figure in the group (marked with a Greek letter) which immediately follows the Z group:

Ior.   in clauim & umbras[60]

This may seem inexplicable at first sight but it is easily explained. Bruno constantly refers in *Shadows* to a book by himself, the *Clavis magna*, which is not extant. The inventor of the 'key' and of the 'shadows' is Iordanus Brunus, abbreviated as 'Ior.', author of the *Clavis magna* and of the *De umbris idearum*. He puts the image of himself on the wheel, for has he not himself produced a very great invention? He has found out the way to use the 'shadows of ideas' on the Lullian wheels!

After this climax, the reader may feel inclined to sit back and rest. But we must follow the wheel to the end, though with only a very few selections from the last names.[61] Here is Euclid; also Epicurus characterised by 'liberty of soul'; also Philolaus who explained 'the harmony implicit in things (and is constantly referred to in Bruno's works as a precursor of Copernicus); also Anaxagoras, another of Bruno's favourite philosophers. And at last we reach the last name, the last of the 150 inventors and great

---

[59] *Ibid.*, pp. 127–8.   [60] *Ibid.*, p. 128.
[61] *Ibid.*, *loc. cit.*

men whose images revolve on the wheel of memory. It is this:

Melicus   in memoriam[62]

(The reader may pick out the name on the plan, to the left of 'Rhegima' with which we started.) Melicus is Simonides, the inventor of the classical art of memory. How fitting that Simonides should end the procession, that the revolving wheel should come back to its beginning with this name! For in all the long history of the art of memory surely no more extraordinary manifestation of the tradition can have existed than the memory system which we have excavated from *Shadows*.[63]

Bruno was drawing heavily on Polydore Vergil's *De inventoribus rerum* (1499) for his inventors and many of his names are traditional ones. On the other hand, many of them are very strange and I have not been able to trace them all. The predominance of barbaric and magical names gives a curiously archaic character to the list. The inventors' wheel shows us—through the presentation of the whole history of human civilisation—the interests, the attitudes, the inner mind of Bruno himself. The stress on magic of all kinds, the inclusion of the names of 'demonic' magicians, shows that this is the memory of an extreme magician. The daring blend of magic with religion as the religious rites and sacrifices appear on the wheel shows us the magician who believed in magical religion, who will advocate the revival of the magical religion of the Egyptians.[64] And as the wheel turns to philosophy, astronomy, to 'innumerable worlds' we realise how all these major interests of Bruno's blend in the magician's mind. There is a kind of rationalism in extremes of magic, and the procession of the inventors, ranging from technology through magic and religion to philosophy, presents a curiously modern history of civilisation.

[62] *Ibid., loc. cit.*

[63] There is yet another images list in *Shadows*, of thirty mythological images beginning with Lycaon and ending with Glaucus (pp. 107–8). These figures are lettered with the thirty divisions of the wheels, and are to be revolved on wheels, but there are only thirty of them, not 150 as in the lists in the main system. I therefore suppose that they constitute a separate system, resembling the Thirty Statues of *Statues* (see below, pp. 292–3).

[64] See *G.B. and H.T.* for Bruno's belief in 'Egyptian' or Hermetic religion.

From the memory point of view, these images belong into the same ancient tradition as that which places notable practitioners of the arts and sciences on the fresco of the Chapter House of Santa Maria Novella (Pl. 1), and which causes Rossellius to 'place' Plato and Aristotle for Theology and Philosophy.[65] Bruno's list of images of inventors to be used as memory images is in itself—however strange his use of the tradition—absolutely within the orthodox tradition of the classical art. In placing all these striking and active images of notable personages on the wheel, Bruno is pursuing his aim of combining the classical art of memory with Lullism. The revolving wheels of the Lullian Art have become the places for the reception of the images.

The most potent of the images in the system are the magic images on the central wheel. In the *Ars memoriae* which is included in the book, and which follows the traditional 'Ad Herennian' pattern in its discussion of places and images, Bruno discusses various kinds of memory images, which he regards as having different degrees of potency, some being nearer to reality than others. Those with the highest degree of potency, which are least opaque to reality, he calls 'sigilli'.[66] In such passages, he is, I believe, explaining his use of 150 such 'sigilli', or magic seals, or astral images, in the memory system.

How did the system work? By magic, of course, by being based on the central power station of the 'sigilli', the images of the stars, closer to reality than the images of things in the sublunar world, transmitters of the astral forces, the 'shadows' intermediary between the ideal world above the stars,[67] and the objects and events in the lower world.

But it is not enough to say vaguely that the memory wheels worked by magic. It was a highly systematised magic. Systematisation is one of the key-notes of Bruno's mind; there is a compulsion towards systems and systematisation in the magic mnemonics

[65] See above, p. 164.

[66] 'Signs, Notae, Characters, and Seals' all have this high degree of potency; Bruno refers for further information to the missing *Clavis Magna* (*Op. lat.*, II (i), p. 62).

[67] Near the beginning of the *Ars memoriae*, he says that the eternal ideas are received 'as an influx through the medium of the stars' (*Ibid.*, p. 58). The passage is redolent of Ficino in the *De vita coelitus comparanda*.

which drives their designer throughout his life to a perpetual search for the right system. My plan does not represent the full complexity of this system, in which the five subdivisions revolve independently within the thirty compartments of the wheels.[68] Thus the images of decans of the zodiac, the images of the planets, the images of the moon-stations would form and reform in ever changing combinations, in connection with the images of the houses. Did he intend that there would be formed in the memory using these ever-changing combinations of astral images some kind of alchemy of the imagination, a philosopher's stone in the psyche through which every possible arrangement and combination of objects in the lower world—plants, animals, stones— would be perceived and remembered? And that, in the forming and reforming of the inventor's images in accordance with the forming and reforming of the astral images on the central wheel, the whole history of man would be remembered from above, as it were, all his discoveries, thoughts, philosophies, productions?

Such a memory would be the memory of a divine man, of a Magus with divine powers through his imagination harnessed to the workings of the cosmic powers. And such an attempt would rest on the Hermetic assumption that man's *mens* is divine, related in its origin to the star-governors of the world, able both to reflect and to control the universe.

Magic assumes laws and forces running through the universe which the operator can use, once he knows the way to capture them. As I have emphasised in my other book, the Renaissance conception of an animistic universe, operated by magic, prepared the way for the conception of a mechanical universe, operated by mathematics.[69] In this sense, Bruno's vision of an animistic universe of innumerable worlds through which run the same magico-mechanical laws, is a prefiguration, in magical terms, of the seventeenth-century vision. But Bruno's main interest was not in the outer world but in the inner world. And in his memory systems we see the effort to operate the magico-mechanical laws, not externally, but within, by reproducing in the psyche the magical mechanisms. The translation of this magical conception into mathematical terms has only been achieved in our own day.

[68] As shown in the diagram, *Op. lat.*, II (i), p. 123. I do not attempt to represent this refinement on my plan.
[69] *G.B. and H.T.*, pp. 450 ff.

Bruno's assumption that the astral forces which govern the outer
world also operate within, and can be reproduced or captured there
to operate a magical-mechanical memory seems to bring one
curiously close to the mind machine which is able to do so much
of the work of the human brain by mechanical means.

Nevertheless, the approach from a mind machine angle does not
really begin to explain Bruno's effort. From the Hermetic universe
in which he lived the divine had not been banished. The astral
forces were instruments of the divine; beyond the operative stars
there were yet higher divine forms. And the highest form was, for
Bruno, the One, the divine unity. The memory system aims at
unification on the star level as a preparation for reaching the
higher Unity. For Bruno, magic was not an end in itself but a
means of reaching the One behind appearances.

This side of Bruno is not absent from *Shadows*. On the contrary,
the book starts on this level, and readers beginning at the beginning
with the 'thirty intentions of the shadows' and the 'thirty concepts
of ideas', and who either do not reach or entirely fail to recognise
the magical memory system based on thirty to which these
preliminary thirties are the introduction, have been able to accept
the book as some kind of Neoplatonic mysticism. My view, on the
contrary, is that it is only after wrestling with the memory system
that one should approach the preliminary mystical and philosophical thirties. I cannot pretend that I fully understand these,
but at least one begins to perceive something of their drift.

The first of the 'thirty intentions of the shadows' begins with
'the one God' and with quotation from the *Canticle*, 'I sat down
under the shadow of him whom I desired.'[70] One must sit under
the shadow of the good and the true. To feel towards this through
the interior senses, through the images in the human mind, is to
sit under the shadow. There follow 'intentions' on light and darkness, and on the shadows which, descending from the supersubstantial unity proceed into an infinite multitude; they descend
from the supersubstantial to its vestiges, images, and simulachra.[71] Lower things are connected with higher and higher with
lower; to the lyre of the universal Apollo there is a continual rising

---

[70] *Op. lat.*, II (i), p. 20. The quotation is from the *Canticle*, II, 3.
[71] *Op. lat.*, II (i), pp. 22–3.

and falling through the chain of the elements.[72] If the ancients knew a way by which memory, from the multitude of memorised species might reach unity, they did not teach it[73] (but Giordano Bruno will teach this). All is in all in nature. So in the intellect all is in all. And memory can memorise all from all.[74] The chaos of Anaxagoras is variety without order; we must put order into variety. By making the connections of the higher with the lower you have one beautiful animal, the world.[75] The concord between higher and lower things is the golden chain from earth to heaven; as descent can be made from heaven to earth, so ascent may be made through this order from earth to heaven.[76] These connections are an aid to memory as is shown in the following poem where Aries acts on Taurus, Taurus on Gemini, Gemini on Cancer, and so on.[77] (There follows a poem on the signs of the zodiac.) Later 'intentions' are about some kind of mystical or magical optics, and on the sun and the shadows which it casts.

The 'thirty concepts of ideas' are equally gnomic in character. (Some of them have already been quoted.) The first intellect is the light of Amphitrite. This is diffused through all; it is the fountain of unity in which the innumerable is made one.[78] The forms of deformed animals are beautiful in heaven; non-luminous metals shine in their planets; neither man, nor animals, nor metals are here as they are there. Illuminating, vivifying, uniting, conforming yourself to the superior agents you will advance in the conception and retention of the species.[79] The light contains the first life, intelligence, unity, all species, perfect truths, numbers, grades of things. Thus what in nature is different, contrary diverse, is there the same, congruent, One. Try therefore with all your might to identify, co-ordinate, and unite the received species. Do not disturb your mind nor confuse your memory.[80] Of all the forms of the world, the pre-eminent are the celestial forms.[81] Through them you will arrive from the confused plurality of things at the unity. Parts of the body are better understood together than when taken separately. Thus when the parts of the universal species are not considered separately but in relation to their underlying order, what is there that we may not memorise, understand, and do?[82] One

[72] *Ibid.*, pp. 23-4. [73] *Ibid.*, p. 25. [74] *Ibid.*, pp. 25-6.
[75] *Ibid.*, p. 27. [76] *Ibid.*, pp. 27-8. [77] *Ibid.*, pp. 28-9.
[78] *Ibid.*, p. 45. [79] *Ibid.*, p. 46. [80] *Ibid.*, loc. cit.
[81] *Ibid.*, p. 47. [82] *Ibid.*, loc. cit.

is the splendour of beauty in all. One is the brightness emitted from the multitude of species.[83] The formation of things in the lower world is inferior to true form, a degradation and vestige of it. Ascend, then, to where the species are pure, and formed with true form.[84] Everything that is, after the One, is necessarily multiplex and numerous. Thus on the lowest grade of the scale of nature is infinite number, on the highest is infinite unity.[85] As the ideas are the principal forms of things, according to which all is formed, so we should form in us the shadows of ideas. We form them in us, as in the revolution of wheels.[86]

I have strung together in the two preceding paragraphs quotations from the 'thirty intentions of the shadows' and the 'thirty concepts of ideas'. These two sets of thirty statements are headed by thirty letters, which are the same as the letters of the wheel, and they are illustrated in the text with wheels marked with the thirty letters. This proves, I think, that the two groups of thirty mysterious sayings are really *about* the memory system with its wheels based on thirty, about a way of grouping, co-ordinating, unifying, the multiplicity of phenomena in memory, by basing memory on the higher forms of things, on the star images which are the 'shadows of ideas'.

The thirty 'intentions' contain within them, I think, the element of *voluntas* of the direction of the will in love towards truth which was one aspect of Lullian artificial memory. Hence they can begin with love poetry from the *Canticle*. And it is significant that the wheel which is said to be the 'type of the ideal intentions' has a sun at the centre of it, emblem of Bruno's inner strivings to arrive at the One Light which is to appear in memory when all the multiplicity of appearances have been co-ordinated in memory through the complex techniques of the magic memory system.

This extraordinary work, which was Bruno's first work, is, I believe, a Great Key to his whole philosophy and outlook, as he was soon to express it in the Italian dialogues which he published in England. I have elsewhere pointed out[87] that the dialogue with which *Shadows* opens in which Hermes presents the book on memory is couched in terms of a rising sun of Egyptian revelation,

---

[83] *Ibid.*, pp. 47–8.   [84] *Ibid.*, p. 48.   [85] *Ibid.*, p. 49.
[86] *Ibid.*, pp. 51–2.
[87] *G.B. and H.T.*, pp. 193–4.

opposed by pedants, which is very similar to those used in the *Cena de le ceneri* when Bruno is defending Copernican heliocentricity from pedants. The inner Sun reached in *Shadows* is the inner expression of what was to be Bruno's 'Copernicanism', his use of heliocentricity as a kind of portent of the return of 'Egyptian' vision and of Hermetic religion.

The philosophy of the two groups of thirty sayings in *Shadows* is Bruno's philosophy as we find it in the Italian dialogues. In the *De la causa* he cries that the unity of the All in the One is

> a most solid foundation for the truths and secrets of nature. For you must know that it is by one and the same ladder that nature descends to the production of things and the intellect ascends to the knowledge of them; and that the one and the other proceeds from unity and returns to unity, passing through the multitude of things in the middle.[88]

The aim of the memory system is to establish within, in the psyche, the return of the intellect to unity through the organisation of significant images.

In the *Spaccio*, he says of the magical religion of the pseudo-Egyptians of the *Asclepius*, which was his own religion, that

> with magic and divine rites (they) . . . ascended to the height of the divinity by that same scale of nature by which the divinity descends to the smallest things by the communication of itself.[89]

The aim of the memory system is to establish this magical ascent within, through the memory based on the magical star-images.

And in the *Eroici furori* the enthusiast hunting after the vestiges of the divine obtains the power of contemplating the beautiful disposition of the body of nature. He sees Amphitrite, who is the source of all numbers, the monad, and if he does not see it in its essence, the absolute light, he sees it in its image, for from the monad which is the divinity proceeds this monad which is the world.[90] The aim of the memory system is to achieve this unifying vision within where alone it can be done, for the inner images of things are nearer to reality, less opaque to the light, than are the things themselves in the outer world.

---

[88] *Dialoghi italiani, ed. cit.,* p. 329; cf. *G.B. and H.T.,* p. 248.
[89] *Dialoghi italiani, ed. cit.,* p. 778; cf. *G.B. and H.T.,* p. 249.
[90] *Dialoghi italiani, ed. cit.,* pp. 1123–6; cf. *G.B. and H.T.,* p. 278

Thus the classical art of memory, in the truly extraordinary Renaissance and Hermetic transformation of it which we see in the memory system of *Shadows* has become the vehicle for the formation of the psyche of a Hermetic mystic and Magus. The Hermetic principle of reflection of the universe in the mind as a religious experience is organised through the art of memory into a magico-religious technique for grasping and unifying the world of appearances through arrangements of significant images. We saw this Hermetic transformation of the art of memory taking place in a much simpler way in Camillo's Theatre. In Bruno, the transformation is both infinitely more complex and also very much more intense, both more extremely magical and also more extremely religious. The amiable Camillo with his magical memory and his magical Ciceronian oratory is a very different figure from the passionate ex-Dominican with his 'Egyptian' religious message.

Nevertheless, comparison of Bruno's system with Camillo's is helpful for the understanding of both.

If we think of the seven-fold planetary foundation of Camillo's Theatre, and of the different grades of being represented on the upper grades until on the top or 'Prometheus' grade all arts and sciences were remembered, it is clear that a similar process is going on in Bruno's system, based on the stars, including animal, vegetable and mineral worlds on the next wheel and comprising, with the inventors' wheel, all arts and sciences.

In Camillo's seven-fold system, the seven planetary images, through which he unifies on the celestial level, connect with and pass on into a supercelestial world of angelic and Sephirothic principles. Bruno uses his peculiar transformation of Lullism as the substitute for Cabalism. His 'Thirty', like Dignities of a Lullian Art, pass up and down through the lower world, the celestial world, the divine world, strengthening the ladder between all levels.

Camillo is much nearer to Pico's original Christian synthesis of the occult tradition than Bruno. He is able to think of himself as a Christian Magus in contact with angelic and divine powers which can ultimately be interpreted as representing the Trinity. Bruno by his abandonment of the Christian and Trinitarian interpretation of the *Hermetica* and by his fervent acceptance of the magical pseudo-Egyptian religion of the *Asclepius* as better than

Christianity,[91] moves back towards a darker magic a more purely pagan theurgy. He seeks to reach, not a Trinity, but a One. And this One he thinks of as, not above, but within the world. But his method of reaching it by first unifying memory on the star level as the preliminary to arriving at the vision within of the One light diffused through all, is similar to Camillo's aim, who plans memory like the ascent of a mountain from the summit of which all below is unified. In a similar way, Bruno adapts the methods of the fervently Christian and Trinitarian Lull to his aim of reaching the One through the All.

These most singular phenomena, the memory systems of Camillo and of Bruno—both of which were 'secrets' brought to Kings of France—belong into the Renaissance. No student of the Renaissance can ignore the glimpses into the Renaissance mind which they reveal. They belong into that particular strand of the Renaissance which is the occult tradition. They exhibit a profound conviction that man, the image of the greater world, can grasp, hold, and understand the greater world through the power of his imagination. We come back here to that basic difference between Middle Ages and Renaissance, the change in the attitude to the imagination. From a lower power which may be used in memory as a concession to weak man who may use corporeal similitudes because only so he can retain his spiritual intentions towards the intelligible world, it has become man's highest power, by means of which he can grasp the intelligible world beyond appearances through laying hold of significant images. The difference is profound, and, one would have thought, presents an insuperable obstacle to any sort of continuity between the art of memory as understood in the Middle Ages and the Renaissance transformation of the art. Yet Camillo includes remembering Heaven and Hell in his Theatre. Bruno in the opening dialogue of *Shadows* defends the art of Tullius, Thomas, and Albertus from the attacks of modern 'pedants'. The Middle Ages had transformed the classical art into a solemn and religious art; and Renaissance occult memory artists like Camillo and Bruno see themselves as in continuity with the mediaeval past.

[91] See *G.B. and H.T.*, pp. 195, 197 etc.

Chapter X

RAMISM AS AN ART OF
MEMORY

URING the period in which occult memory was thus gathering momentum and becoming increasingly daring in its aims, the movement against the artificial memory—and I speak of it now as the rational mnemo-technic as a part of classical rhetoric—had also been growing much stronger. As mentioned in an earlier chapter, the influence of Quintilian on the humanists was not favourable to the art, and we have heard Erasmus echoing Quintilian's lukewarm attitude to places and images and his emphasis on order in memory.

As the sixteenth century advanced, much thought was given by humanist educators to rhetoric and its parts. For the traditional five parts as defined by Cicero different arrangements were suggested in which memory dropped out.[1] In these trends the influence of Quintilian was again important, for Quintilian mentions that some rhetoricians of his time were not including memory as a part of rhetoric. Amongst the new style sixteenth-century educators who were omitting memory from the parts of rhetoric was Melanchthon. Naturally, the omission of memory from rhetoric means that the artificial memory is discarded, and repetition or learning by heart becomes the only art of memory advised.

Of all the reformers of educational methods in the sixteenth century the most prominent, or the most self-advertised, was Pierre de la Ramée, more generally known as Peter Ramus. Ramus

[1] See W. S. Howell, *Logic and Rhetoric in England, 1500–1700*, Princeton, 1956, pp. 64 ff.

and Ramism have been extensively studied in recent years.[2] In what follows I shall abbreviate as much as possible the complexities of Ramism, referring the reader for further information to the works of others, my aim being solely to place Ramism within the context of the argument of this book, where it may come out in a somewhat new light.

The French dialectician whose simplification of teaching methods made such a stir was born in 1515 and died in 1572, massacred as a Huguenot in the Massacre of St. Bartholomew. This end recommended him to Protestants, to whom his pedagogical reforms were also welcome as a means of sweeping out the complexities of scholasticism. Amongst the complexities of which Ramus made a clean sweep were those of the old art of memory. Ramus abolished memory as a part of rhetoric, and with it he abolished the artificial memory. This was not because Ramus was not interested in memorising. On the contrary, one of the chief aims of the Ramist movement for the reform and simplification of education was to provide a new and better way of memorising all subjects. This was to be done by a new method whereby every subject was to be arranged in 'dialectical order'. This order was set out in schematic form in which the 'general' or inclusive aspects of the subject came first, descending thence through a series of dichotomised classifications to the 'specials' or individual aspects. Once a subject was set out in its dialectical order it was memorised in this order from the schematic presentation—the famous Ramist epitome.

As Ong has said, the real reason why Ramus could dispense with memory as a part of rhetoric 'is that his whole scheme of the arts based on a topically conceived logic, is a system of local memory'.[3] And Paolo Rossi has seen that by absorbing memory into logic, Ramus identified the problem of method with that of memory.[4]

Ramus knew very well the precepts of the old artificial memory

---

[2] Particularly by W. J. Ong, *Ramus: Method and the Decay of Dialogue*, Harvard University Press, 1958; Howell, *Logic and Rhetoric*, pp. 146 ff.; R. Tuve, *Elizabethan and Metaphysical Imagery*, Chicago, 1947, pp. 331 ff.; Paolo Rossi, *Clavis universalis*, Milan, 1960, pp. 135 ff.; Neal W. Gilbert, *Renaissance Concepts of Method*, Columbia University Press, 1960, pp. 129 ff.

[3] Ong, *Ramus*, p. 280.

[4] Rossi, *Clavis*, p. 140.

which he was consciously supplanting, and he had been influenced by Quintilian's criticism of it. In an important and, I believe, unnoticed passage in the *Scholae in liberales artes*, Ramus quotes Quintilian's remarks on the ineptitude of places and images for confirming memory, his rejection of the methods of Carneades, Metrodorus, and Simonides, and his recommendation of a simpler way of memorising through dividing and composing the material. He approves and praises Quintilian for these views and asks where can such an art of memory be found which will teach to memorise, not with places and images, but through 'dividing and composing' as Quintilian advises.

> The art of memory (says Quintilian) consists entirely in division and composition. If we seek then an art which will divide and compose things, we shall find the art of memory. Such a doctrine is expounded in our dialectical precepts . . . and method . . . For the true art of memory is one and the same as dialectics.[5]

Thus Ramus thinks of his dialectical method for memorising as the true classical art of memory, the way which Quintilian preferred to the places and images of Cicero and of the author of *Ad Herennium*.

Though Ramus rejects the *loci* and *imagines* his method yet includes some of the old precepts. Arrangement in order had been one of these, strongly insisted on by Aristotle and by Thomas Aquinas. In the memory text-books of Romberch and Rossellius a way is taught of arranging material in inclusive 'common places' within which are individual places; this has something in common with Ramus's insistence on descending from 'generals' to 'specials'. Ramus classifies memory into 'natural' and 'prudential'; in the latter term he may be influenced by the old insistence on memory as a part of Prudence. And, as Ong has pointed out,[6] the memorising from the epitomes set out in order on the printed page has in it an element of spatial visualisation. It should be added that here again the influence of Quintilian is to be perceived, who advised memorising from visualisation of the actual page or tablet on which the speech was written. Where I would differ from Ong is in his

---

[5] P. Ramus, *Scholae in liberales artes, Scholae rhetoricae*, Lib. XIX (ed. of Bâle, 1578, col. 309). Cf. Quintilian, *Institutio oratoria*, XI, ii, 36.

[6] *Ramus*, pp. 307 ff.

233

insistence that this spatial visualisation for memorisation was a new development introduced by the printed book.[7] Rather, it would seem to me, the printed Ramist epitomes are a transfer to the printed book of the visually ordered and schematised lay-outs of manuscripts. The late F. Saxl made a study of the transition of manuscript illustrations to early printed books;[8] the transition of schematic lay-outs of material from manuscripts to the printed Ramist epitomes would be a parallel phenomenon.

Though many surviving influences of the old art of memory may be detected in the Ramist 'method' of memorising through dialectical order, yet he deliberately gets rid of its most characteristic feature, the use of the imagination. No more will places in churches or other buildings be vividly impressed on the imagination. And, above all, gone in the Ramist system are the images, the emotionally striking and stimulating images the use of which had come down through the centuries from the art of the classical rhetor. The 'natural' stimulus for memory is now not the emotionally exciting memory image; it is the abstract order of dialectical analysis which is yet, for Ramus, 'natural', since dialectical order is natural to the mind.

An example may bring out the abandonment of a most ancient mental habit brought about by the Ramist reform. We want to remember, or to teach to the young, the liberal art of Grammar and its parts. Romberch gives in a column on his printed page the parts of Grammar set out in order—an arrangement analogous to the Ramist epitome. But Romberch teaches that we are to remember Grammar with an image—the ugly old woman Grammatica— and on her stimulating-to-memory form we visualise the arguments about her parts through subsidiary images, inscriptions and the like.[9] Under Ramism, we smash the inner image of old Grammatica, and teach little boys to do so, substituting for her the imageless Ramist epitome of Grammar memorised from the printed page.

The extraordinary success of Ramism, in itself rather a superficial pedagogic method, in Protestant countries like England may perhaps be partly accounted for by the fact that it provided a kind

[7] *Ibid.*, p. 311.

[8] F. Saxl, 'A Spiritual Encyclopaedia of the Later Middle Ages', *Journal of the Warburg and Courtauld Institutes*, V (1942), pp. 82 ff.

[9] See above, pp. 119–21, and Pl. 6.

of inner iconoclasm, corresponding to the outer iconoclasm. Old Grammatica on the portal of some church sculptured with the series of the liberal arts would get the same kind of outer treatment in a rampantly Protestant country as she gets inwardly in Ramism. She would be smashed. In an earlier chapter[10] we suggested that Romberch's encyclopaedic presentation of theological and philosophical sciences and of the liberal arts, to be memorised by corporeal similitudes of them, accompanied by images of notable practitioners of each art, was perhaps a distant echo of the memory of Thomas Aquinas as we see it symbolised in the fourteen similitudes of arts and sciences, accompanied by fourteen practitioners of them, in the fresco of Santa Maria Novella (Pl. I). If we were to imagine something like the figures of that fresco sculptured on some English cathedral or church, the niches would now be, either empty of the destroyed images, or such images as remained would be damaged. So did Ramism inwardly remove the images of the art of memory.

Ramus envisaged his 'dialectical analysis' method as suitable to be used for memorising all subjects, and even for memorising passages of poetry. The first Ramist epitome to appear in print is an analysis of the dialectical order of the complaint of Penelope in Ovid.[11] As Ong has pointed out, Ramus makes quite clear that the object of this exercise is to enable a schoolboy to memorise by this method the twenty-eight lines of Ovid in question.[12] To this it may be added that it is also quite clear that Ramus intends this method to supplant the classical art. Immediately after the epitomised 'dialectical analysis' of the argument of the lines he speaks of that art of memory with places and images which is greatly inferior to his own method, for it uses external signs and images artificially made up, whereas he follows the parts of the composition in a natural way. Hence the dialectical doctrine replaces all other doctrines *ad memoriam confirmandam*.[13] Though one would hesitate to advise schoolboys to construct images of Domitius being beaten up by the Rex family, or of Aesop and Cimber being made up for their parts as memory-for-words cues for their recitation, yet one

[10] See above, p. 121.
[11] P. Ramus, *Dialecticae institutiones*, Paris, 1943, p. 57; reproduced in Ong, *Ramus*, p. 181.
[12] Ong, *Ramus*, p. 194.
[13] *Dialect. inst., ed. cit.*, pp. 57 *verso*–58 *recto*.

also wonders what became in the Ramist method of the musical rhythm of the poem and of its imagery.

Ramus is so constantly aware of the old artificial memory as he replaces it by his 'natural' art that one may almost think of the Ramist method as yet another transformation of the classical art —a transformation which keeps and intensifies the principle of order but does away with the 'artificial' side, the side which cultivated the imagination as the chief instrument of memory.

In considering the reactions of sixteenth-century moderns, like Erasmus, Melanchthon, and Ramus to the art of memory we must constantly bear in mind that the art had reached their times profoundly coloured by the mediaeval transformation through which it had passed. It appeared to them as a mediaeval art, an art belonging to the times of the old architecture and imagery, an art which had been adopted and recommended by the scholastics, an art particularly associated with the friars and their sermons. To the humanist scholar, moreover, it was an art which in the old ignorant times had been wrongly bound up with 'Tullius' as the author of *Ad Herennium*. The humanist educator, enraptured by the elegance of Quintilian, would be inclined to take his attitude to the art as the more purely classical attitude of informed criticism. Erasmus was a humanist in reaction from the 'barbarism' of the Middle Ages. Melanchthon and Ramus were protestants in reaction from scholasticism with which the old art of memory had been associated. Ramus, with his insistence on logical order in memory, is adopting a side of the 'Aristotelianised' scholastic art of memory whilst rejecting its corporeal similitudes, so closely linked with the old didactic method of presenting moral and religious truths through images.

Ramus never obtrudes his religious views in his pedagogical works but he wrote one theological work 'On the Christian Religion' in which he makes very plain what was his attitude to images from the religious point of view.[14] He quotes Old Testament prohibition of images, particularly from the fourth chapter of *Deuteronomy*:—'Take ye therefore good heed unto yourselves; for ye saw no manner of similitude on the day that the Lord spoke unto you in Horeb out of the midst of the fire: Lest ye corrupt your-

---

[14] P. Ramus, *De religione Christiana*, ed. of Frankfort, 1577, pp. 114–15.

selves, and make you a graven image, the similitude of any figure the likeness of male or female . . . And lest thou lift up thine eyes, unto heaven, and when thou seest the sun, and the moon, and the stars, even all the host of heaven, shouldst be driven to worship them . . .' With the old Testament prohibition of graven images, Ramus contrasts Greek idolatrous worship and then goes on to speak of the images in Catholic churches to which the people bow and burn incense before them. It is unnecessary to quote the passage in full for it conforms to the normal type of Protestant propaganda against Catholic images. It places Ramus as sympathetic to the iconoclastic movements which raged during his lifetime in France, England, and the Low Countries; and I would suggest that it is relevant to his attitude to images in the art of memory.

Ramism cannot be entirely identified with Protestantism for it seems to have been popular with some French Catholics, particularly with the Guise family, and was taught to their relative, Mary, Queen of Scots.[15] Nevertheless, Ramus became a Protestant martyr after his death in the Massacre of St. Bartholomew, a fact which certainly had much to do with the popularity of Ramism in England. And there can be no doubt that an art of memory based on imageless dialectical order as the true natural order of the mind goes well with Calvinist theology.

If Ramus and the Ramists were opposed to the images of the old art of memory, what would be their attitude to the art in its occult, Renaissance transformation, with its use of magic, 'graven images' of the stars as memory images ? Their disapproval of the art in this form would surely be even more profound.

Though Ramism is aware of the old art of memory and retains some of its order, whilst discarding places and images, it is in many respects closer to the other type of 'artificial memory' which was not in descent from the rhetoric tradition and which also made no use (in its genuine form) of images. I am speaking, of course, of Lullism. Lullism, like Ramism, included logic in memory for the Lullian Art, as memory, memorised the logical processes of intellect. And another characteristic feature of Ramism, its arrangement or classification of matter in an order descending from 'generals' to 'specials' is a notion implicit in Lullism as it ascends and descends on the ladder of being from specials to generals and from

[15] Howell, *Logic and Rhetoric*, pp. 166 ff.

generals to specials. This terminology is specifically used of memory in Lull's *Liber ad memoriam confirmandam* in which it is stated that memory is to be divided into specials and generals, the specials descending from the generals.[16] In Lullism, the 'generals' are, of course, the principles of the Art, founded on Divine Dignities. The arbitrary manner in which Ramism imposes its 'dialectical order' on every branch of knowledge is strongly reminiscent of Lullism which claims to unify and simplify the whole encyclopaedia by imposing B to K and the procedures of the Art on every subject. Ramism as memory, memorising every subject by the dialectical order of its epitome,[17] is a process akin to Lullism as memory, memorising every subject by memorising the procedures of the Art as done on that subject.

There can be little doubt that the genesis of Ramism owes something to the Renaissance revival of Lullism. Nevertheless there are most profound differences between Ramism and Lullism. Ramism is superficial to child's play compared to the subtleties of Lullism with its attempt to base logic and memory on the structure of the universe.

Ramism as a memory method is clearly moving in an exactly opposite direction from Renaissance occult memory, which seeks to intensify the use of images and of the imagination, seeks even to introduce images into the imageless Lullism. And yet there is a problem here which I can only suggest without attempting to solve it.

It is possible that Giulio Camillo with his occult rhetoric, involving some new and mysterious kind of conflation of logical topics with memory places, involving also an interest in the rhetoric of Hermogenes,[18] was the real initiator of some of the new

[16] Lull, *Liber ad memoriam confirmandam*, ed. Rossi in *Clavis universalis*, p. 262.

[17] The genesis of the Ramist epitome should probably be sought in Lullian manuscripts with their heavily bracketed schemata. Examples of such lay-outs can be seen in Thomas Le Myesier's compendum of Lullism (Paris, Bibl. Nat., Lat. 15450, on which see my article 'The Art of R.L.', p. 172). Such Lullist lay-outs, with their series of brackets (for example the one in Paris, Lat., 15450, f. 99 *verso*) make a very similar impression to the bracketed Ramist epitome, for example the epitome of logic, reproduced in Ong, *Ramus*, p. 202.

[18] See above, pp. 167–8.

rhetorical and methodological movements of the sixteenth century? Johannes Sturm, so important in the new movements, carried on the revival of Hermogenes.[19] And Sturm certainly knew of Giulio Camillo and his Memory Theatre.[20] Sturm was the patron of Alessandro Citolini whose *Tipocosmia* was said to have been 'stolen' from the papers of Camillo's Theatre.[21] If this is true Citolini 'stole' only an encyclopaedic setting out in order of subjects and themes—for that is what the *Tipocosmia* is—but without the images. For there are no images or descriptions of images in the *Tipocosmia*. What I am getting at—in the form of questions or hints for future investigators—is that Camillo might have started on his transcendental or occult level a rhetorical-methodological-memory movement which people like Sturm and Ramus continued, but rationalised by omitting the images.

Leaving aside the undigested and controversial hints in the preceding paragraph, it seems to me certain that Ramus, the Frenchman, would have known of Camillo's Theatre, so famous in France. Since he would certainly have known of it, it may be raised as a possibility that the Ramist dialectical order for memory, descending from 'generals' to 'specials' might have had in it something of a conscious reaction from the occult method of the Theatre, which arranges knowledge under the 'generals' of the planets, from which all the multitude of 'special' things in the world descend.

When we take a look into Ramus's philosophical attitudes, the curious fact emerges that there is a good deal of mysticism behind the apparently intense rationalism of his 'dialectical order'.

[19] See Ong, *Ramus*, pp. 231 ff.

[20] On Sturm and Camillo, see F. Secret, 'Les cheminements de la Kabbale à la Renaissance; le Théâtre du Monde de Giulio Camillo Delminio et son influence', *Rivista critica di storia filosofia*, XIV (1959), pp. 420–1.

[21] Betussi (*Raverta*, ed. Zonta, p. 57) associates Citolini's *Tipocosmia* with Camillo's Theatre. Others make the blunt accusation that Citolini stole from Camillo; for references about this see Liruti, III, pp. 130, 133, 137 ff. The *Tipocosmia* was published at Venice in 1561. Citolini came to England as a Protestant exile with letters of recommendation from Sturm (see L. Fessia, *A. Citolini, esule italiano in Inghilterra*, Milan, 1939–40). The 'poor Italian gentleman' mentioned by Bruno as having had his leg broken by the roughness of the London crowds was Citolini (see G. Bruno, *La Cena de le ceneri*, ed. G. Aquilecchia, Turin, 1955, p. 138).

Ramus's philosophical views can be culled from the first two works in which he enunciated his dialectical method—the *Aristotelicae animadversiones* and the *Dialecticae institutiones*. He seems to envisage the true dialectical principles as deriving from a kind of *prisca theologia*. Prometheus, he says, was the first to open the fountains of dialectical wisdom whose pristine waters eventually reached Socrates. (Compare this with Ficino's *prisca theologia* sequence in which ancient wisdom through a line of successors eventually reaches Plato.[22]) The ancient, true, and natural dialectic was, however, says Ramus depraved and spoiled by Aristotle who introduced artificiality and falsehood into dialectic. Ramus conceives it as his mission to restore the dialectical art to its 'natural' form, its pre-Aristotelian, Socratic and pristine nature. This natural dialectic is the image in the *mens* of the eternal divine light. The return to dialectic is a return to light from shadows. It is a way of ascent and descent from specials to generals, from generals to specials, which is like Homer's golden chain from earth to heaven, from heaven to earth.[23] Ramus repeatedly uses the 'golden chain' image of his system, and in a long passage in the *Dialecticae institutiones* he uses most of the major themes of Renaissance Neoplatonism, including the inevitable quotation of the Virgilian 'Spiritus intus alit', and extols his true natural dialectic as a kind of Neoplatonic mystery, a way of return to the light of the divine *mens* from the shadows.[24]

Viewed from this background of Ramus's thought, the dialectical method begins to lose some of its apparent rationality. It is an 'ancient wisdom' which Ramus is reviving. It is an insight into the nature of reality through which he can unify the multiplicity of appearances. By imposing the dialectical order on every subject the mind can make the ascent and descent from specials to generals

[22] 'Prisca theologia' was the term used by Ficino for the wisdom of ancient sages, such as Hermes Trismegistus. He regarded such 'pristine theology' as a current of wisdom descending from Hermes and others until it eventually reached Plato; see D. P. Walker, 'The *Prisca Theologia* in France'. *Journal of the Warburg and Courtauld Institutes*, XVII (1954), pp. 204 ff.; Yates, *G.B. and H.T.*, pp. 14 ff. Ramus's mind is working on similar lines, though with Prometheus as a pristine dialectician whose wisdom descended to Socrates.

[23] P. Ramus, *Aristotelicae animadversiones*, Paris, 1543, pp. 2 *recto*–3 *verso*.

[24] *Dialect inst.*, ed. cit., pp. 37 ff.; cf. Ong, *Ramus*, pp. 189 ff.

and vice versa. The Ramist method begins to appear almost as mystical a conception as the Art of Ramon Lull, which imposes the abstractions of the Divine Dignities on every subject and thereby makes the ascent and descent. And it begins to appear not dissimilar in aim from Camillo's Theatre which provides the unifying ascent and descent through arrangements of images, or from Bruno's method in *Shadows* of seeking the unifying system by which the mind may return to the light from the shadows.

And, in fact, many were to labour at finding points of contact and amalgamation between all such methods or systems. As we have seen, Lullism was amalgamated with the art of memory; attempts were also made to amalgamate it with Ramism. The search for method by ways infinitely complex and intricate, occult or rational, Lullist, Ramist, and so on, is a major characteristic of the period. And the instigator, the originator, the common root of all this effort after method, so fraught with consequences for the future, is memory. Whoever wishes to probe the origins and growth of methodological thinking should study the history of the art of memory, in its mediaeval transformation, in its occult transformation, memory as Lullism, memory as Ramism. And it may appear when this history is fully written, that the occult transformation of memory was an important stage in the whole process of the search for method.

Whilst, when viewed from a historical distance, all the memory methods are seen to have certain common denominators, when seen at close quarters, or from the point of view of contemporaries, a great gulf separates Peter Ramus from Giordano Bruno. The superficial resemblances are that both claim descent from ancient wisdoms—Ramus from a Socratic pre-Aristotelian wisdom, Bruno from a pre-Greek Egyptian and Hermetic wisdom. Both are violently anti-Aristotelian, though for different reasons. Both make an art of memory the instrument of a reform. Ramus reforms teaching methods by his memory method based on dialectical order. Bruno teaches an occult art of memory as an instrument of a Hermetic religious reform. Ramus discards imagery and the imagination, and drills memory with abstract order. Bruno makes imagery and the imagination the whole key to a significant organisation of memory. Ramus breaks the continuity with the old classical art in its mediaeval transformation. Bruno claims that his occult system is still the art of Tullius, Thomas, and Albertus. The one is a Calvinist pedagogue providing a simplified teaching method; the other a passionate ex-friar using occult memory as a magico-religious technique. Ramus and Bruno stand at opposite poles; they represent totally contrary tendencies of the late Renaissance.

Amongst the 'pedants' whom Bruno attacks at the beginning of *Shadows* for their contempt of the art of memory, we must range, not only the humanist critics, but the Ramists, with their campaign forcibly directed against images in memory. If Erasmus did not think much of Camillo's Theatre, what would Ramus have thought, had he been alive, of Bruno's *Shadows*? The 'arch pedant of France', as Bruno calls Ramus, would certainly have been horrified at Bruno's way of ascent and descent, of reaching the light from the shadows.

Chapter XI

⋄⋄⋄

GIORDANO BRUNO: THE SECRET OF *SEALS*

⋄⋄⋄

I T must have been soon after his arrival in England, early in 1583, that Bruno published the massive volume on memory which I refer to as *Seals*,[1] though it really consists of four items, as follows:

> *Ars reminiscendi*
> *Triginta sigilli*
> *Explanatio triginta sigillorum*
> *Sigillus sigillorum*

The title-page gives no place or date of publication but the book almost certainly appeared early in 1583 and was quite certainly printed by John Charlewood, a London printer.[2] The *Ars reminiscendi* was not a new work but a reprint of the art of memory in *Circe*,[3] published in the preceding year in Paris, where it had followed the terrific incantations of Circe to the seven planets.[4] These incantations, which made the magical character of the following art of memory obvious to Parisian readers (who could also have read the occult *Shadows*) are not included in the reprint published

---

[1] See above p. 201 for the full title. *Seals* is printed in G. Bruno, *Op. lat.*, II (ii), pp. 69–217.

[2] See G. Aquilecchia, 'Lo stampatore londinese di Giordano Bruno', in *Studi di Filologia Italiana*, XVIII (1960), pp. 101 ff.; cf. *G.B. and H.T.*, p. 205.

[3] Bruno, *Op. lat.*, II (i), pp. 211–57.

[4] I have discussed these incantations which are based on those in Agrippa's *De occulta philosophia*, in *G.B. and H.T.*, pp. 199–202.

in England. The English reprint of the *Ars reminiscendi* is however followed by new material, namely the 'Thirty Seals', the 'Explanation of the Thirty Seals', and the 'Seal of Seals'.

If all readers of Bruno's *Shadows* have missed the magical memory system, readers of *Seals* have made even less headway with that work. What are these 'Seals'? As a preliminary to attempting to answer that question I invite the reader to come with me for a page or two to Florence where we will practise the art of memory together.

Agostino del Riccio was a Dominican friar of the convent of Santa Maria Novella in Florence who wrote in 1595 an *Arte delle memoria locale* for the use of 'studious young gentlemen'. This little treatise was never published but the manuscript of it exists in the Biblioteca Nazionale in Florence.[5] It is illustrated by seven drawings which are intended to make clear to the young gentlemen of Florence the principles of the art of memory.

'The King' (Pl. 13a) shows a king who is striking his brow; he represents 'local memory', calling up by this gesture the local memory which is so useful to preachers, orators, students, and all classes of people.[6]

'The First Counsellor' (Pl. 13b) shows a man touching a globe on which are all places—cities, castles, shops, churches, palaces. He represents the first precept of the art, and the friar gives here the usual place rules. He also gives an example of making memory places in the church of Santa Maria Novella in which, beginning from the high altar, you may place there Charity; then continuing round the church you will perhaps place on the altar of the Ciodi, Hope; on the altar of the Gaddi, Faith, then continue to place on all the other chapel altars, on the holy water stoup, on the tombs, and so on, until you come round to the point at which you started.[7] The friar is teaching us the good old fashioned way of using the art, to remember virtues.

[5] Biblioteca Nazionale, II, I, 13. I referred to this manuscript pointing out the similarity of its method to that employed by Bruno in *Seals* in my article 'The Ciceronian Art of Memory', in *Medioevo e Rinascimento, Studi in onore di Bruno Nardi*, Florence, 1955, p. 899. Cf. also Rossi, *Clavis universalis*, pp. 290–1.
[6] Manuscript cited, f. 5.
[7] *Ibid.*, f. 6.

'The Second Counsellor' (Pl. 13c) shows a man surrounded by various objects, including a statue, or rather a bust on a pillar. He represents the precept 'use images'. These can be images of real objects, or imaginary, or we may use figures made by sculptors and artists. Signor Niccolo Gaddi has some fine statues in his gallery which are useful for memory images.[8] After this glimpse of an artistically furnished memory, we are presented with those alphabetical lists which are such a trying feature of the memory treatises. Riccio's lists include mechanical arts, saints, and Florentine families.

'The First Captain or the Straight Line' shows a man with a vertical line passing down his body. On him are to be placed the twelve signs of the zodiac, in accordance with the parts of the body over which they rule, and they are to be remembered on these places as a memory system.[9]

'The Second Captain or the Circular Line' (Pl. 13d) is a man in a circle with legs and arms extended. On the places of this man's body we are to remember the four elements and the eleven heavens: earth, feet; water, knee; air, flank; fire, arm; Luna, right hand; Mercury, fore-arm; Venus, shoulder; Sol, head; Mars, left shoulder; Jupiter, left fore-arm; Saturn, left hand; sphere of fixed stars, left shoulder; christalline sphere, waist; primum mobile, knees; Paradise, under left foot.[10]

In 'The Third Captain or the Transverse Line' (Pl. 13e) twelve small objects are seen, placed on a circle. The friar explains that he memorises these objects on places in the Via della Scala.[11] Those who know Florence will remember that this street still runs into the Piazza Santa Maria Novella. On the Tabernacle in this street he memorises a religious with his cross (see the cross at the top of the circle); on the door of the first house of the row of old houses, he remembers a star; on the door of Jacopo di Borgho's house, a sun; and so on. He also uses the method in a cell of the Dominican fathers, divided into memory places, memorising thereby, for example, that fine conceit of Job on the seven miseries of man.[12]

'The Meal and the Servant' (Pl. 13f) presents a man holding food and drink. Local memory is like eating and drinking. If we ate all our food at once we should have indigestion, so we divide it into separate meals. So we should do with local memory; 'two hundred

[8] *Ibid.*, f. 16.   [9] *Ibid.*, f. 33.   [10] *Ibid.*, f. 35.
[11] *Ibid.*, f. 40 *verso*.   [12] *Ibid.*, f. 40.

notions a day, or two hundred articles of St. Thomas, if we try to memorise them immediately on rising from bed, we shall strain the memory too much.'[13] Therefore take local memory in small doses. Maybe in time we may rise to the heights reached by the famous preacher, Francesco Panigarola, who is said to have used a hundred thousand places.[14]

This friar has not heard of exciting Renaissance transformations of the art of memory. He belongs to the old order of things. Placing his images of virtues on memory places in the church of Santa Maria Novella—once a centre whence the Dominican movement radiated in such force—he is using the technique in the devotional way which, when at the height of its intensity, stimulated the proliferation of virtue and vice imagery. No suspicion need be attached to his use of the zodiac, which is automatically mentioned in memory treatises as a possible system; there is no reason at all why the order of the signs should not be used in a rational way as a memory order. He aims at memorising the order of the spheres, but in a way which, though puerile, is not magical. He is using the traditional Dominican art, memorising by the method pious material, including the *Summa* of Thomas Aquinas. He is an example of the enfeeblement of the art since its great era in the Middle Ages, exhibiting the kind of mentality which is to be found in the late memory treatises.

Why then, do I introduce Fra Agostino del Riccio here? Because his idea of presenting the principles and various techniques of the art through little symbolic pictures, with titles, exactly corresponds to what Bruno does in *Seals*, where, for example, the principle of association is presented as 'The Joiner', or the use of images as 'Zeuxis the Painter'. This is what the *Seals* are, statements of the principles and techniques of the art—but magicised, complicated with Lullism and Cabbalism, blown up into inscrutable mysteries. Bruno was adapting to his own strange purposes a mode of presenting the art which he had learned in his Dominican convent.

The Elizabethan reader who attempted to tackle the curious work which had been published, rather clandestinely (no place or date of publication given) in his country, would presumably begin

[13] *Ibid.*, f. 46.
[14] *Ibid.*, f. 47.

at the beginning with the *Ars reminiscendi*.[15] Continuing to use his terminology of 'subjects' for memory places and 'adjects' for memory images, Bruno gives in this art the classical rules, expanding them very much after the manner of a normal memory treatise.[16] Bruno seems to aim at making a very large number of places. Nothing prevents you when you have been through your house in one part of the city from using (for making memory places in) another house in another part of the city. When you have finished the last of the Roman places, you can connect it with the first of the Parisian places.[17] (One is reminded of Peter of Ravenna's custom of collecting memory places on his travels.[18]) Bruno insists that the images must be striking, and associated with one another. He gives a list of thirty ways of forming images to remind of notions through association[19] (such lists are also given in the normal treatises). He believes that he has a better system for memory for words than Tullius thought of, quoting here from *Ad Herennium* as by Tullius, and thus keeping up the old wrong mediaeval attribution.[20] He recommends as place systems what he calls 'semi-mathematical' subjects,[21] that is diagrammatical figures which are not mathematical in the normal way, but in some other way.

Anyone who had seen a Romberch or a Rossellius would be able to recognise this *Ars reminiscendi* as belonging into a well known genre, that of the memory treatise. But Bruno claims that, although he uses all the old ways, he has some new and better way of using them. This new way is connected with the 'Song of Circe'[22] (presumably the incantations to the planets in *Circe* which are not included with the *Ars reminiscendi* in the English publication). There was therefore some Circaean mystification at the heart of this memory treatise, but what it was exactly the Elizabethan reader might well have been somewhat at a loss to understand. And then he would reach the great barrage of the Thirty Seals, thirty statements of principles and techniques of magic memory, followed by thirty more or less inexplicable 'explanations', some

---

[15] The *Ars reminiscendi* is not given with *Seals* in *Op. lat.*, II (ii) since it had already been printed with *Circe* in *Op. lat.*, II (i), pp. 211–57.
[16] *Op. lat.*, II (i), pp. 221 ff.   [17] *Ibid.*, p. 224.
[18] See above, p. 113.   [19] *Op. lat.*, II (i), pp. 241–6.
[20] *Ibid.*, p. 251. See above, p. 125.
[21] *Ibid.*, pp. 229–31.   [22] *Ibid.*, p. 251.

of which are illustrated with more or less insoluble 'semi-mathe-matical' diagrams. One wonders how many readers ever got through this barrage.

The first seal is 'The Field'.[23] This field is the memory, or the phantasy, the ample folds of which are to be worked upon by the art of places and images. Brief though obscure summaries of the rules are given here, with insistence that images must have power to move through their striking and unusual character. There is also a reference to 'Solyman the Thalmudist' who had a memory system in twelve divisions marked with the names of the patriarchs.

The second Seal is 'The Heaven' (Pl. 14a).[24] So that 'the order and the series of the images of heaven may be engraved' a sphere divided in a certain manner will give places and sites. The descrip-tion of this figure is supplemented by a diagram which is based on the twelve houses of a horoscope. Bruno is using the houses of a horoscope as memory places, or memory rooms, in which the 'images of heaven' will be engraved.

The Seal of 'The Chain'[25] emphasises that memory must pro-ceed from the preceding to what follows as parts of a chain are involved with the preceding and following links. This sounds like association of ideas, as in the Aristotelianising of the memory rules. But in the explanation of this Seal we are told that the chain is really the zodiac, the signs of which run on, the one into the other, and he refers to what he has said about this in *Shadows*, quoting the same Latin poem on the order of the signs which he had quoted there.[26]

It is at this point that we begin to wonder, in a confused way, whether the Seals, or some of them, are really about the memory system in *Shadows*.

The next three Seals are Lullist. The 'Tree' and the 'Wood'[27] are connected with Lull's *Arbor scientiae*, which is mentioned by name, as a wood all the trees of which, representing all knowledge, are rooted in basic principles common to all. The 'Ladder'[28] gives what is actually the third figure of Lull's *Ars brevis* showing

[23] *Op. lat.*, II (ii), pp. 79–80, 121–2.
[24] *Ibid.*, pp. 80, 121–2.
[25] *Ibid.*, pp. 81, 123–4.
[26] *Ibid.*, p. 124; Cf. *Shadows*, *Op. lat.*, II (i), p. 28.
[27] *Op. lat.*, II (ii), pp. 81–2, 124–7.
[28] *Ibid.*, pp. 82, 127–8.

combinations of letters combined on the Lullian wheels. Again we wonder whether these Seals are giving the principle of using Lullian combinatory systems with the astrologised and magicised classical art of memory, as in *Shadows*.

And these wonderings are turned into a certainty in 'Zeuxis the Painter' (Seal 12) who represents the principle of using images in the art of memory. Here we are told that 'the images of Teucer the Babylonian supply me with the indications of three hundred thousand propositions'.[29] And if any more proof is needed of the connection of *Seals* with *Shadows* there is this further remark in 'Zeuxis the Painter':

> Now for the improving of natural memory and the teaching of artificial memory, we know a double picture; the one when we form from strange descriptions images and notae for retaining in memory of which I give examples in the art attached to *De umbris idearum*; the other by feigning as need requires edifices . . . and images of sensible things which will remind us of non-sensible things to be remembered.[30]

The 'double picture' of the two kinds of memory consists, I believe, (1) of the memory based on the astral images such as he gave lists of in *Shadows* and is discussing in *Seals* (2) of the normal classical memory using places in 'edifices'. But in Bruno's systems the techniques even of normal classical memory are never being used normally, but are always galvanised into magical activity through being affiliated to astral systems.

The Seals, though several of them allude to the system in *Shadows*, are not confined to any one system. On the contrary Bruno states that he is trying every possible way; perhaps something for which he is not looking may emerge out of this, as alchemists who do not succeed in making gold sometimes hit on other important discoveries.[31] In the later Seals he is trying variations of astrological arrangements, devices of a Lullist nature (or what he supposes to be Lullist), infiltrations of Cabalist magic in the unending search for a really operative organisation of the psyche. And the search always brings in the tricks of the memory trade, the old techniques of which can be recognised in Seal after Seal, though now presented as occult mysteries. My attitude towards the reader of this book has always been the humane one of trying to spare him

---

[29] *Ibid.*, p. 85.   [30] *Ibid.*, p. 134.   [31] *Ibid.*, p. 129.

the more awful ordeals of memory and I shall therefore not enume-
rate the whole Thirty of the Seals but present only a few selections.

Seal 9 'The Table'[32] describes that interesting form of the
'visual alphabet' which consists of remembering letters by images
of people whose names begin with those letters. Peter of Ravenna,
it will be remembered produced the prize example of this method
by making Eusebius and Thomas change places to help him to
remember ET and TE.[33] Bruno mentions Peter of Ravenna with
admiration in this Seal. Seal 11, 'The Standard',[34] stands for
leading images as standard-bearers for whole groups of things;
thus Plato, Aristotle, Diogenes, a Pyhrronian, an Epicurean, would
serve to indicate not merely those individuals but many notions
having affinity with them. This is the ancient tradition through
which images of notable practitioners of the arts and sciences were
regarded as memory images. Seal 14, 'Daedalus',[35] gives a list of
memory objects to be attached to, or placed on, main images to be
used for organising a cluster of meanings around a main image.
Bruno's memory objects belong into the ancient tradition for such
lists. Seal 15, 'The Numerator'[36] describes how to form images for
numbers with objects whose shapes resemble the numbers. This
was a notion frequently illustrated in the old memory treatises in
which sets of objects-for-numbers are presented together with the
'visual alphabets', or illustrations of sets of objects resembling
letters. Seal 18, 'The Century'[37] arranges groups of a hundred
friends in a hundred places, a valuable example of the classical
precept of making memory images like people we know. Seal 19,
'Squaring the Circle'[38] is based on the inevitable horoscope
diagram. Bruno solves this ancient problem by using a 'semi-
mathematical', that is magical figure as a memory place system.
Seal 21, 'The Potter's Wheel' (Pl. 14b)[39] is again the horoscope
diagram with a bar marked with the initials of the seven planets
revolving within it; this is a very difficult system. Seal 23, 'The
Doctor'[40] uses different kinds of shops, butcher, baker, barber,
and so on, as memory places, as in the method illustrated by one of
the cuts (Pl. 5a) in Romberch's book. But Bruno's shops are not as

[32] *Ibid.*, pp. 83–4, 130–1. [33] See above, p. 119.
[34] *Op. lat.*, II (ii), pp. 84, 132–3. [35] *Ibid.*, p. 139.
[36] *Ibid.*, pp. 86–7, 140–1. [37] *Ibid.*, pp. 87–8, 141.
[38] *Ibid.*, pp. 88, 141–3. [39] *Ibid.*, pp. 90–1, 145–6.
[40] *Ibid.*, pp. 92–3, 147.

straightforward as that. 'The Field and Garden of Circe' (Seal 26)[41] is an extremely magical system, evidently only to be achieved after successful invocation to the seven planets. Here the elemental compounds—hot-moist, hot-dry, cold-moist, cold-dry—mutate and move through places in seven houses to form the changing forms of elemental nature within the psyche. In the 'Peregrinator' (Seal 25),[42] memory images peregrinate through memory rooms, each image drawing from the material memorised in the rooms what it needs. In 'The Cabalistic Enclosure' (Seal 28)[43] the orders of society both ecclesiastical and temporal, from Popes to Deacons and from Kings to Peasants are represented by memory images, ranged in the order of their rank. This was a well-known memory order, often mentioned in the memory treatises as an easily memorised order of figures. But in Bruno's system, the orders perform Cabalistic permutations and combinations among themselves. The last two Seals ('Combiner', 29, and 'Interpreter', 30)[44] are respectively Lullist combinations and Cabalist manipulations of the Hebrew alphabet.

What is this man trying to do? He is working with two sets of ideas, memory and astrology. The memory tradition taught that everything is better remembered through an image, that these images should be striking and emotionally powerful, that they should be linked to one another associatively. Bruno tries to work memory systems based on these principles by linking them to the astrological system, using magically potent images, 'semi-mathematical' or magical places, and the associative orders of astrology. With this he mixes Lullist combinations and Cabalist magic!

The notion of combining memory principles with astral principles is present in Camillo's Theatre. Bruno wants to work this idea out in much more scientific detail. We saw this effort in action in the system in *Shadows*, to which the Seals often allude, but in *Seals* Bruno is trying method after method, system after system in pursuit of his aim. The mind machine analogy again suggests itself. Bruno believes that if he can make a system which gets inside the astrological system, which reflects the permutations and combinations of the changing relations of the planets to the zodiac and their influences on the horoscopal houses, he will be tapping the mechanisms of nature herself to organise the psyche. However, as

[41] *Ibid.*, pp. 95–6, 148–9.   [42] *Ibid.*, pp. 96–7, 150–1.
[43] *Ibid.*, pp. 98–9, 151–2.   [44] *Ibid.*, pp. 100–6, 153–60.

we saw in the last chapter, the view of Bruno's memory systems as magical ancestors of the mind machine is only partially valuable and must not be pressed too far. If we drop the word 'magical' and think of the efforts of an occult memory artist as directed towards drawing out of the psyche combinations of 'archetypal' images we come within range of some major trends of modern psychological thought. However, as with the mind machine analogy, I would not stress a Jungian analogy which might confuse more than it illuminates.

I would prefer to keep within the period and try to think of the period aspects of Bruno's memory attempts. One of these aspects connects with Bruno's anti-Aristotelian philosophy of nature. Speaking of the 'standard bearing' images in the memory as related to the astral groupings of nature, he says:

> All things of nature and in nature, like soldiers in an army, follow leaders assigned to them . . . This Anaxagoras knew very well but Father Aristotle could not attain to it . . . with his impossible and fictitious logical segregations of the truth of things.[45]

This reveals a root of Bruno's anti-Aristotelianism; the astral groupings in nature contradict Aristotle and a man with an astrally based memory cannot think on Aristotelian lines in his natural philosophy. Through the magic of his archetypal memory images he sees the groupings of nature as bound together with magical and associative links.

Or if we think of the Renaissance interpretation of the magic of images we find ourselves within another aspect of Bruno's attitude to memory. We saw that the magic of magic images could be interpreted in the Renaissance as an artistic magic; the image became endued with aesthetic power through being endowed with perfect proportions. We would expect to find that in a highly gifted nature, such as that of Giordano Bruno, the intensive inner training of the imagination in memory might take notable inner forms. And in the discussion of 'Zeuxis the Painter' and of 'Phidias the Sculptor' in the Seals bearing those titles, Bruno reveals himself as a memory artist of the Renaissance.

Zeuxis, the painter, painting the inner images of memory, introduces a comparison of painting with poetry. To painters and poets says Bruno, there is distributed an equal power. The painter

[45] *Ibid.*, p. 133.

excels in imaginative power (*phantastica virtus*); the poet excels in cogitative power to which he is impelled by an enthusiasm, deriving from a divine afflatus to give expression. Thus the source of the poet's power is close to that of the painter.

> Whence philosophers are in some ways painters and poets; poets are painters and philosophers; painters are philosophers and poets. Whence true poets, true painters, and true philosophers seek one another out and admire one another.[46]

For there is no philosopher who does not mould and paint; whence that saying is not to be feared 'to understand is to speculate with images', and the understanding 'either is the fantasy or does not exist without it'.

To come upon the equation of poetry with painting in the context of the images of the art of memory reminds one, that according to Plutarch, it was Simonides, the inventor of the art of memory, who was the first to make this comparison.[47] Bruno is however here recalling the *ut pictura poesis*, the dictum of Horace on which the Renaissance based its theories of poetry and painting. To this he relates the Aristotelian dictum 'to think is to speculate with images'[48] which had been used in the scholastic conflation of Aristotle with 'Tullius' on the classical memory[49] and is often repeated in the memory treatises. And thus, through Zeuxis the Painter who is the painter of images in memory, who stands for the classical rule 'use images', he arrives at the vision of the Poet, the Painter, and the Philosopher as all fundamentally the same, all painters of images in the fantasy, like Zeuxis who paints the memory images, expressed by the one as poetry, by the other as painting, by the third as thought.

'Phidias the Sculptor' stands for the sculptor of the memory, moulding memory statues within.

> Phidias is the former . . . like Phidias the statuary, either moulding in wax, or constructing by addition of a number of small stones, or sculpturing the rough and formless stone as though by subtraction.[50]

The last phrase reminds one of Michelangelo, chiselling at the formless block of marble to release the form which he has seen within it. So also (Bruno would seem to say) does Phidias the sculptor of the fantasy release the forms from the inform chaos of memory.

---

[46] *Ibid., loc. cit.*   [47] See above, p. 28.
[48] 'Intelligere est phantasmata speculari' (*Op. lat.*, II (ii), p. 133).
[49] See above, pp. 70–1.   [50] *Op. lat.*, II (ii), p. 135.

There is something, to my mind, profound in the 'Phidias' Seal, as though in this inner moulding of significant memory statues, this drawing out of tremendous forms by subtraction of the inessential, Giordano Bruno, the memory artist, were introducing us to the core of the creative act, the inner act which precedes the outer expression.

We have rather lost sight of our Elizabethan reader whom we left some pages back wondering whether he could tackle the Thirty Seals. How did he get on? Did he reach 'Zeuxis' and 'Phidias'? If so he would have come upon an exposition of the Renaissance theory of poetry and painting such as had not before been published in England, and he would have found it in the context of the images of occult memory.

What was the philosophy on which the magician, artist, poet, philosopher, based the stupendous effort of the Thirty Seals? That philosophy is given in one phrase which comes in 'The Husbandman' (Seal 8) who is cultivating the field of memory:

> As the world is said to be the image of God, so Trismegistus does not fear to call man the image of the world.[51]

Bruno's philosophy was the Hermetic philosophy; that man is the 'great miracle' described in the Hermetic *Asclepius*; that his *mens* is divine, of a like nature with the star governors of the universe, as described in the Hermetic *Pimander*. In *L'idea del theatro di Giulio Camillo* we were able to trace in detail the basis in the Hermetic writings of Camillo's effort to construct a memory theatre reflecting 'the world', to be reflected in 'the world' of memory.[52] Bruno works from the same Hermetic principles. If man's *mens* is divine, then the divine organisation of the universe is within it, and an art which reproduces the divine organisation in memory will tap the powers of the cosmos, which are in man himself.

When the contents of memory are unified there will begin to appear within the psyche (so this Hermetic memory artist believes) the vision of the One beyond the multiplicity of appearances.

> I was contemplating one knowledge in one subject. For all the principal parts were ordained principal forms . . . and all its secondary forms were joined to the principal parts.[53]

[51] *Ibid.*, pp. 129–30. [52] See above, pp. 145 ff.
[53] *Op. lat.*, II (ii), p. 91. Bruno refers here to the *De auditu kabbalistico.*

254

So we read in 'The Fountain and the Mirror' (Seal 22). The parts are coming together, the secondary parts are joining to the principal parts, the frightful labours of the systems are beginning to bear fruit, and we are beginning to contemplate 'one knowledge in one subject'.

Here is revealed the religious aim of Bruno's memory efforts. We are now ready for the break through to the *Sigillus Sigillorum*, or Seal of Seals, which corresponds to the first visionary part of *Shadows*. In *Shadows* he began with the unified vision and passed down from thence to the unifying processes of the memory system. *Seals* reverses this order, beginning with the memory systems and ending with the 'Seal of Seals'. I can only give an abridged and impressionistic account of this extraordinary discourse.

It begins with claims to divine inspiration. 'These things a divine spirit insinuated into me.'[54] Now that we have followed the life of the celestial gods we are ready to enter the supercelestial circuits. And here he names the famous practitioners of the art of memory in antiquity, Carneades, Cineas, Metrodorus[55] and, above all, Simonides, through whose beneficence all things are sought, found and arranged.[56]

Simonides has been transformed into a mystagogue, one who has taught us how to unify memory on the celestial grade and will now introduce us to the supercelestial world.

All descends from the above, from the fountain of ideas, and to it ascent may be made from below. 'How wonderful would be your work if you were to conform yourself to the opifex of nature . . . if with memory and intellect you understand the fabric of the triple world and not without the things contained therein.'[57] These promises of conformity with the opifex of all nature recall the words in which Cornelius Agrippa describes the Hermetic ascent through the spheres as the experience necessary for the formation of a Magus.[58] It is to this experience that the art of memory, in its apotheosis in the Seal of Seals, has led.

There are remarkable pages on the grades of knowing. Even in

[54] *Ibid.*, p. 161.   [55] *Ibid.*, p. 162.   [56] *Ibid.*, p. 163.
[57] *Ibid.*, p. 165.
[58] On this passage in Agrippa and its influence on Bruno, see *G.B. and H.T.*, pp. 135-6, 239-40.

these extravagant pages, Bruno is still within sight of the memory treatises in which it was quite usual to outline the faculty psychology, that process by which, in the scholastic psychology, images from sense impressions pass from the *sensus communis* through other compartments of the psyche. Romberch, for example, has

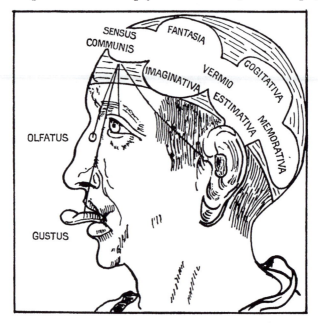

Fig. 9 Diagram of Faculty Psychology. Redrawn from a diagram in Romberch, *Congestorium artificiose memorie*

some pages on the faculty psychology, with many quotations from Thomas Aquinas, and illustrated with a diagram of a man's head opened to show the compartments of the faculties (Fig. 9).[59] Bruno has in mind such a diagram as this, a normal ingredient of the memory treatise, but his argument is directed against the division of the psyche into the compartments of the faculty psychology. These pages of his[60] are a kind of manifesto of the primacy of the

[59] See Romberch, *Congestorium artificiosae memoriae*, pp. 11 ff.; Rosellius, *Thesaurus artificiosae memoriae*, pp. 138 ff. (also with diagram of a man's head showing the faculties). Another treatise which gives the faculty psychology diagram is G. Leporeus, *Ars memorativa*, Paris, 1520 (reproduced in Volkmann, *Ars memorativa*, Pl. 172).

[60] *Op. lat.*, II (ii), pp. 172 ff.

imagination in the cognitive process which he refuses to see as divided among many faculties but as all one. He does distinguish four grades of knowing (influenced here by Plotinus) namely sense, imagination, reason, intellect, but he is careful to open the doors between them by abolishing arbitrary divisions. And in the end he makes it clear that in his view the whole process of cognition is really one, and that it is, fundamentally, an imaginative process.

Looking back now at 'Zeuxis' and 'Phidias' we realise that he has already made these statements in those Seals on the use of images in memory. The understanding either is the fantasy or does not exist without it, he said in 'Zeuxis'. Hence the painter or sculptor of images in the fantasy is the only thinker, and the thinker, the artist, and the poet are all one. 'To think is to speculate with images' Aristotle had said, meaning that the abstracting intellect must work from the images of sense impression. Bruno changes the meaning of the words.[61] There is for Bruno no separate faculty consisting of the abstracting intellect; the mind works only with images, though these images are of different degrees of potency.

Since the divine mind is universally present in the world of nature (continues Bruno in the Seal of Seals)[62] the process of coming to know the divine mind must be through the reflection of the images of the world of sense within the *mens*. Therefore the function of the imagination of ordering the images in memory is an absolutely vital one in the cognitive process. Vital and living images will reflect the vitality and life of the world—and he has in mind both magically vitalised astral images and the living and striking images of the 'Ad Herennian' memory rule[63]—unify the contents of memory and set up magical correspondencies between outer and inner worlds. Images must be charged with affects, and particularly with the affect of Love,[64] for so they have power to penetrate to the core both of the outer and the inner worlds—an extraordinary mingling here of classical memory advice on using emotionally charged images, combined with a magician's use of an emotionally charged imagination, combined again with mystical and religious

<hr/>

[61] On Bruno's confusion of thought about this, see *G.B. and H.T.*, pp. 335–6.

[62] *Op. lat.*, II (ii), pp. 174 ff. Bruno quotes here the Virgilian *mens agitat molem*.

[63] Alluded to in abstruse language, *ibid.*, p. 166.

[64] *Ibid.*, pp. 167 ff.

use of love imagery. We are here within range of Bruno's *Eroici furori* with its love conceits which have power to open 'the black diamond doors' within the psyche.[65]

Finally, in the Seal of Seals, we reach the fifth grade of knowing which Bruno classifies into fifteen 'contractions'.[66] And here he is talking about religious experiences, about good and bad kinds of contemplation, about good and bad kinds of religion, about good 'magical religion' which is the best kind, though it has bad counterfeits or counterparts. I have discussed these passages in my other book,[67] pointing out that Bruno is following Cornelius Agrippa on magical religion, though elaborating Agrippa in more extreme directions. It is now that he makes his dangerous statements. Thomas Aquinas is equated with Zoroaster and Paul of Tarsus as one who had achieved one of the best kinds of 'contractions'.[68] Periods of solitude and retirement are necessary for reaching these. From the desert of Horeb, Moses produced wonders before the Magi of Pharaoh. Jesus of Nazareth did not do his wonderful works until after his conflict with the devil in the desert. Ramon Lull after living the life of a hermit showed himself profound in many inventions. Paracelsus who gloried in the title of hermit was the inventor of a new kind of medicine.[69] Contemplators among the Egyptians, Babylonians, Druids, Persians, Mohammedans, have achieved the higher contractions. For it is one and the same psychic power which operates in low things and in high things, and which has produced all the great religious leaders with their miraculous powers.

And Giordano Bruno presents himself as such a leader, offering a religion, or a Hermetic experience, or an inner mystery cult, the four guides in which are Love by which souls are raised to the divine by a divine *furor*; Art by which one may become joined to the soul of the world; Mathesis which is a magical use of figures; Magic, understood as religious magic.[70] Following these guides we may begin to perceive the four objects, the first of which is Light.[71] This is that primal light of which the Egyptians speak (he means the passage in the Hermetic *Pimander* on the primal light).

[65] Bruno, *Dialoghi italiani*, ed. Aquilechia, p. 969.
[66] *Op. lat.*, II (ii), pp. 180 ff.   [67] *G.B. and H.T.*, pp. 271 ff.
[68] *Op. lat.*, II (ii), pp. 190–1.   [69] *Ibid.*, p. 181.
[70] *Ibid.*, pp. 195 ff.; cf. *G.B. and H.T.*, pp. 272–3.
[71] *Op. lat.*, II (ii), pp. 199 ff.

The Chaldaeans, the Egyptians, the Pythagoreans, the Platonists, all the best contemplators of nature ardently adored that sun, which Plato called the image of the highest God, at whose rising Pythagoras sang hymns, which Socrates saluted in its setting and was seized with ecstacy.

The art of memory has become in Giordano Bruno's occult transformation of it, a magico-religious technique, a way of becoming joined to the soul of the world as part of a Hermetic mystery cult. When the Thirty Seals of memory are broken, this is the 'secret' revealed in the Seal of Seals.

A question naturally arises. Were the thirty Seals with all their impenetrably intricate mnemonic advice a kind of barrier set up to protect the Seal of Seals, to prevent all but the initiated from reaching the core of the book? Did Bruno really believe in the art of memory in these impossible forms in which he expounded it? Or was it a cloak, a device for producing an incomprehensible cloud of words under cover of which he propagated his mystery religion?

Such a thought comes almost as a relief, suggesting as it does an at any rate partially rational explanation of the Seals. According to this theory, the Seals would be meant to be fundamentally incomprehensible presentations of every type of memory technique, occultised, and given this title of *sigilli* with its magical connotations, to provide an impenetrable curtain of mystery intervening between an uninitiated reader and the Seal of Seals. Many readers attempting to study the book from the beginning would throw it aside before they reached the end. Is that what they were meant to do?

Though it is, I think, probable that the motive of concealment does play a part in the arrangement of Bruno's memory books, this is certainly not the only explanation of them. Bruno was undoubtedly genuinely trying to do something which he thought was possible, trying to find the arrangements of significant images which would work as a way of inner unification. The Art 'by which we may become joined to the soul of the world' is one of the guides in his religion. It is not a cloak under which to conceal that religion; it is an essential part of it, one of its main techniques.

Moreover, as we have seen, Bruno's memory efforts are not isolated phenomena. They belong into a definite tradition, the

Renaissance occult tradition to which the art of memory in occult forms had been affiliated. With Bruno, the exercises in Hermetic mnemonics have become the spiritual exercises of a religion. And there is a certain grandeur in these efforts which represent, at bottom, a religious striving. The religion of Love and Magic is based on the Power of the Imagination, and on an Art of Imagery through which the Magus attempts to grasp, and to hold within, the universe in all its ever changing forms, through images passing the one into the other in intricate associative orders, reflecting the ever changing movements of the heavens, charged with emotional affects, unifying, forever attempting to unify, to reflect the great monas of the world in its image, the mind of man. There is surely something which commands respect in an attempt so vast in its scope.

What kind of impression can this extraordinary work have made upon the Elizabethan reader?

He would have known what the art of memory in its more normal forms was like. In the earlier years of the sixteenth century there had been a growing lay interest in the art, as elsewhere. In Stephen Hawes's *Pastime of Pleasure* (1509), Dame Rhetoric describes the places and images, perhaps the first account of the art of memory in English. The 1527 edition of Caxton's *Mirrour of the World* contains a discussion of 'Memory Artyfycyall'. The continental memory treatises spread to England, and an English translation (1548) of the *Phoenix* of Peter of Ravenna was published.[72] In the early Elizabethan period, the memory text-book fashion is represented by William Fulwood's *The Castel of Memorie*,[73] a translation of a treatise by Guglielmo Gratarolo. The third edition of this work (1573) was dedicated to Philip Sidney's uncle, Robert Dudley, Earl of Leicester—an indication that that Italianate nobleman did not exclude memory from his interests. The treatise cites Cicero, Metrodorus (mentioning his zodiacal system) and Thomas Aquinas.

[72] Quotations from Hawes and from Caxton's *Mirrour* on the art of memory, and from Copland's translation of Peter of Ravenna are given in Howell, *Logic and Rhetoric in England*, pp. 86–90, 95–8.

[73] Cf. Howell, p. 143. The first edition of *The Castel of Memorie* was in 1562. It is mainly a medical treatise, like its original, with a section on artificial memory at the end.

But in the Elizabethan world of 1583, the Protestant educational authorities, and probably public opinion generally, were against the art of memory. The influence of Erasmus on English humanism was very strong, and Erasmus, as we have seen, did not encourage the art. The Protestant educationalist, Melanchthon, who was much admired in England, had banished the art from rhetoric. And for the Puritan Ramists, who were extremely powerful and vocal at this time, the imageless 'dialectical order' was the only art of memory.

There would therefore have been strong opposition in influential quarters in England to any attempt to reintroduce the art of memory in its more normal forms. What, then, can have been the reactions to the extreme occult form of the art to be found in *Seals*?

A first impression on an Elizabethan reader attempting to tackle *Seals* might well have been that here was someone come back out of the old Popish past. Both the arts of which this strange Italian spoke, the art of memory and the Art of Lull, were old mediaeval arts, particularly associated with the friars, the one with the Dominicans, the other with the Franciscans. When Bruno came to England, there were no Black Friars wandering in the streets of London choosing places for their memory systems, like Fra Agostino in Florence. The doctors of the modern Oxford and Cambridge were not turning the wheels of the Lullian Art nor memorising its diagrams. The friars had been swept away and their great houses were expropriated or in ruins. The impression of mediaevalism which Bruno and his Art may have given in *Seals* would have been confirmed by the passages in his Italian dialogues, published in the following year, in which he defends the friars of the old Oxford, now despised by their successors, and deplores the destruction of the buildings and foundations of Catholic times in Protestant England.[74]

The art of memory in its mediaeval transformation had formed an integral part of mediaeval civilisation in England, as elsewhere in Europe.[75] The English friars, with their memory 'pictures', had

[74] See *G.B. and H.T.*, pp. 210 ff., etc.; and below, pp. 280–1, 315–6.
[75] On the early memory treatise by Thomas Bradwardine, see above p. 105. There is a rumour that Roger Bacon wrote an *ars memorativa* treatise, but this has not so far been traced (see H. Hajdu, *Das Mnemotechnische Schrifttum des Mittelalters*, Vienna, 1936, pp. 69–70).

certainly practised it.[76] But although Bruno associates himself and his art with the name of Thomas Aquinas, it is obviously not with the mediaeval and scholastic form of the art with which *Seals* is concerned, but with the Renaissance occult form. As we have seen, in Italy the Renaissance form develops out of the mediaeval form and is artistically enshrined in Camillo's Theatre. No such development had taken place in England, so far as I know.

A character who never developed in England, owing to the religious convulsions through which she passed, was the Renaissance friar. When one thinks of Francesco Giorgio, the Venetian Franciscan, infusing Renaissance Hermetic and Cabalist influences into the mediaeval tradition of world harmony in his *De harmonia mundi*,[77] one realises that Renaissance friars such as he never existed in England, unless possibly as characters in plays. The English friar receded into the Gothic past, perhaps lamented by those secretly in sympathy with that past, or feared by the superstitious who doubted what might be the consequences of the destruction of the old magic, but not a contemporary character, like the Jesuit. A stay-at-home Elizabethan Englishman might well never have met a Renaissance friar—until the wild ex-friar, Giordano Bruno, burst suddenly upon the scene with a Hermetic magico-religious, technique developed out of the old arts of memory of the friars.

The only English, or rather Welsh, character who might have acted as some preparation for the arrival of Bruno is John Dee.[78] Dee was saturated in the Renaissance occult influences, and an ardent practitioner, like Bruno, of the magical recipes in Cornelius Agrippa's *De occulta philosophia*. He was also deeply interested in the Middle Ages and a collector of the despised manuscripts of the mediaeval past. Dee was attempting—alone and unaided and without the support of mystical academies such as flourished in Venice —to effect in England that Renaissance transformation of mediaeval traditions which belonged naturally into Italian Renaissance 'Neoplatonism'. Dee may well have been the only representative in sixteenth-century England of the Renaissance revival of Lullism. There were Lullist manuscripts in his library, listed promiscuously

---

[76] See above, pp. 96–9.
[77] See *G.B. and H.T.*, p. 151.
[78] *Ibid.*, p. 148 ff., 187 ff., etc.

with Pseudo-Lullian alchemical works;[79] he no doubt shared the Renaissance assumptions about Lull. And Dee is the kind of person whom one would expect to have been interested in the cognate subject of the art of memory in Renaissance transformations.

Dee's *Monas hieroglyphica*[80] is a sign composed out of the characters of the seven planets. His excitement at his discovery of this composite sign seems incomprehensible. It may be suggested that his *monas* was perhaps, in his eyes, a unified arrangement of significant signs, infused with astral power, which he would believe to have a unifying effect on the psyche, composing it into a *monas* or One, reflecting the *monas* of the world. Though Dee does not use the places and images of the art of memory for this effort, the assumption underlying it may be not dissimilar, as I have suggested earlier,[81] to the assumption made by Camillo when he bases the Theatre on the images and characters of the planets, and to Bruno's assumption that astral images and characters are potent for unifying the memory.

It is therefore possible that those who had been trained under John Dee, and perhaps initiated by him into the Hermetic mysteries of the *monas*, would have had some idea of the kind of thing that Bruno was driving at in his memory systems. We know that Philip Sidney, together with his friends Fulke Greville and Edward Dyer, chose Dee for their teacher in philosophy. It was to Sidney that Bruno addressed himself, dedicating to him two of the works which he published in England; and he twice mentioned Fulke Greville by name. We do not know what Sidney thought of Bruno; no evidence of that from Sidney's side has come down to us. But Bruno himself speaks in terms of passionate admiration of Sidney in his dedications, and he evidently hoped that it was by Sidney and his circle that he would be understood.

Did Sidney wrestle with *Seals* one wonders? Did he get as far as 'Zeuxis', painting the memory images within and expounding the Renaissance theory of *ut pictura poesis*? Sidney himself

[79] There is a copy of Lull's *Ars demonstrativa* transcribed by Dee in the Bodleian (Digby MS. 197). Several Lullian and Pseudo Lullian works are listed in the catalogue of Dee's library; see J.O. Halliwell, *Private Diary of Dr. John Dee and Catalogue of his Library of Manuscripts*, London, Camden Society, 1842, pp. 72 ff.
[80] Reproduced in *G.B. and H.T.*, Pl. 15 (a).
[81] See above, p. 170, note 25.

expounds that theory in his *Defence of Poetrie*—a defence of the imagination against the Puritans—which he may have been writing during the time that Bruno was in England.

As we have seen, *Seals* is very closely related to the two works published in France, *Shadows* and *Circe*. The *Ars reminiscendi* in *Seals* would probably have been reprinted by John Charlewood from a copy of *Circe*, and much of the rest of *Seals* may have been printed from unpublished manuscripts which Bruno had written in France and brought with him to England. He states that the 'Seal of Seals' forms part of his *Clavis Magna*,[82] the work to which he so frequently refers in the books published in France. *Seals* was therefore, in the main, a repetition or an amplification of the 'secret' which Bruno, successor to Giulio Camillo, had brought to a King of France.

The French connection is kept up in the dedication of the book to Mauvissière, the French ambassador at whose house in London Bruno was living.[83] And the new orientation of the 'secret' towards England is shouted aloud in the address to the Vice-Chancellor and doctors of the University of Oxford.[84] For *Seals*, that apotheosis of Renaissance occult memory, was flung at Elizabethan Oxford in an address in which the author describes himself as 'the waker of sleeping souls, tamer of presumptuous and recalcitrant ignorance, proclaimer of a general philanthropy'. It was in no unobtrusive or secretive way that Bruno presented his secret to the Elizabethan public, but in the most provocative way possible, announcing himself as one emboldened and empowered to speak from a non-sectarian standpoint, neither Protestant nor Catholic, one with a new message for the world. *Seals* was the first act of the drama of Bruno's career in England. This is the work which must be studied first, before the dialogues in Italian which he published later, for it represents the mind and the memory of the Magus from whom those works issued. The visit to Oxford, the controversy with the Oxford doctors, the reflection of that controversy in the *Cena de le ceneri* and the *De la causa*, the outline of the Hermetic

---

[82] *Op. lat.*, II (ii), p. 160.

[83] On Bruno's connections with Mauvissière and with Henri III and on his politico-religious mission see *G.B. and H.T.*, pp. 203–4, 228–9 etc.

[84] See *ibid.*, pp. 205–6 where the address to the Oxford doctors in *Seals* is quoted.

moral reform and the announcement of the imminent return of Hermetic religion in the *Spaccio della bestia trionfante*, the mystical ecstacies of the *Eroici furori*—all these future developments are already implicit in *Seals*.

In its setting in Paris, where Camillo's Theatre was remembered, where a mystical King was leading some abstruse kind of ostensibly Catholic religious movement, Bruno's secret had been in an atmosphere more congenial to it than that which it encountered when suddenly thrown, like a bomb, at Protestant Oxford.

Chapter XII

CONFLICT BETWEEN BRUNIAN
AND RAMIST MEMORY

IN 1584 an extraordinary controversy broke out in England about the art of memory. It was waged between an ardent disciple of Bruno and a Cambridge Ramist. This debate may be one of the most basic of all Elizabethan controversies. And it is only now, at the point in the history of the art of memory which we have reached in this book, that one can begin to understand what were the issues at stake, what is the meaning of the challenge which Alexander Dicson[1] threw at Ramism from the shadows of his Brunian art of memory, and why William Perkins angrily retaliated with a defence of the Ramist method as the only true art of memory.

The controversy[2] opens with Dicson's *De umbra rationis*, which is a close imitation of Bruno's *Shadows* (the title of which, *De umbris idearum*, it echoes). This pamphlet, it is hardly a book, is

---

[1] I prefer to keep Dicson's own spelling of his name, rather than modernise it.

[2] The controversy is noticed in J. L. McIntyre, *Giordano Bruno*, London, 1903, pp. 35–6, and D. Singer, *Bruno His Life and Thought*, New York, 1950, pp. 38–40. For new material about the life of Dicson and valuable suggestions about the controversy, see John Durkan, 'Alexander Dickson and S.T.C. 6823', *The Bibliothek*, Glasgow University Library, III (1962), pp. 183–90. Durkan's indication of William Perkins as 'G.P.' is confirmed by the analysis of the controversy in this chapter.

Alexander Dicson was a native of Errol in Scotland, hence the name by which Bruno calls him, 'Dicsono Arelio'. From the traces of him found by Durkan in various state papers it would seem that he was a secret political agent. He died in Scotland about 1604.

dated 1583 on the title-page, but its dedication to Robert Dudley, Earl of Leicester, is dated as having been written 'on the kalends of January'. According to modern dating, therefore, this work was published early in 1584. It elicited the *Antidicsonus* (1584) the author of which styles himself 'G. P. Cantabrigiensis'. That this 'G.P. of Cambridge' was the well known Puritan divine and Cambridge Ramist, William (Guglielmus) Perkins, will become certain in the course of this chapter. With the *Antidicsonus* is bound up another little tract in which 'G.P. of Cambridge' further explains why he is strongly against 'the impious artificial memory of Dicson'. Dicson came to his own defence, under the pseudonym 'Heius Scepsius', with a *Defensio pro Alexandro Dicsono* (1584). And 'G.P.' made another attack, also in 1584, with a *Libellus de memoria*, followed in the same booklet by 'Admonitions to A. Dicson about the Vanity of his Artificial Memory'.[3]

This controversy is waged strictly within the limits of the subject of memory. Dicson puts out a Brunian artificial memory which to Perkins is anathema, an impious art, against which he urges Ramist dialectical order as the only right and moral way of memorising. Our most ancient friend, Metrodorus of Scepsis, plays a prominent part in this Elizabethan fray, for the epithet 'Scepsian' which Perkins hurls at Dicson is proudly adopted by the latter in his defence when he styles himself 'Heius Scepsius'. In Perkins's terminology a 'Scepsian' is one who uses the zodiac in his impious artificial memory. The Renaissance occult memory, in its extreme Brunian form, is at loggerheads with Ramist memory and whilst the controversy is always ostensibly about the two opposed arts of memory, it is at bottom a religious controversy.

---

[3] The full titles of the four works in the controversy are: Alexander Dicson, *De umbra rationis*, printed by Thomas Vautrollier, London, 1583–4; 'Heius Scepsius' (i.e. A. Dicson), *Defensio pro Alexandro Dicsono*, printed by Thomas Vautrollier, London, 1584; 'G. P. Cantabrigiensis', *Antidicsonus* and *Libellus in quo dilucide explicatur impia Dicsoni artificiosa memoria*, printed by Henry Middleton, London, 1584; 'G. P. Cantabrigiensis', *Libellus de memoria verissimaque bene recordandi scientia* and *Admonitiuncula ad A. Dicsonum de Artificiosae Memoriae, quam publice profitetur, vanitate*, printed by Robert Waldegrave, London, 1584.

It is not the least curious feature of the controversy that Dicson's anti-Ramist works are printed by the Huguenot, Vautrollier, who printed the first Ramist works to be published in England (see Ong, *Ramus*, p. 301).

Dicson is enveloped in shadows when we first meet him in the *De umbra rationis,* and they are Brunian shadows. The speakers in the opening dialogues move in a profound night of Egyptian mysteries. These dialogues form the introduction to Dicson's art of memory, in which the loci are called 'subjects' and the images 'adjuvants' or more frequently 'umbra'.[4] Clearly he is using Bruno's terminology. He repeats the 'Ad Herennian' rules for places and images, but muffled in an obscure mystique, after the Brunian manner. The 'umbra' or image is as a shadow of the light of the divine mind which we seek through its shadows, vestiges, seals.[5] The memory is to be based on the order of the signs of the zodiac which are repeated,[6] though Dicson does not repeat the list of the images of the decans. Traces of Bruno's list of inventors are to be discerned in the advice that Theutates may stand for letters; Nereus for hydromancy; Chiron for medicine, and so on;[7] though the full list of Bruno's inventors is not given. Dicson's art of memory is but a fragmentary impression of the systems and expositions of *Shadows* from which it is nevertheless unmistakably derived.

The opening dialogues are the most prominent feature of the work, being nearly as long as the Brunian art of memory which they introduce. They are obviously inspired by those at the beginning of *Shadows.* It will be remembered that Bruno introduces *Shadows* with the conversation between Hermes who produces the book 'on the shadows of ideas' as a way of inner writing; Philothimus who welcomes it as an 'Egyptian' secret; and Logifer, the pedant, whose cackle is likened to animal noises and who despises the art of memory.[8] Dicson varies this personnel slightly. One of his speakers is the same, namely Mercurius (Hermes). The others are Thamus, Theutates, and Socrates.

Dicson has in mind the passage in Plato's *Phaedrus* which I quoted in an earlier chapter,[9] in which Socrates tells the story of the interview between the Egyptian King, Thamus, and the wise Theuth who had just invented the art of writing. Thamus says

---

[4] Dicson, *De umbra rationis,* pp. 38 ff.

[5] *Ibid.,* pp. 54, 62, etc.

[6] *Ibid.,* pp. 69 ff.

[7] *Ibid.,* p. 61.

[8] See above, pp. 202–3, and *G.B. and H.T.,* pp. 192–3.

[9] See above p. 38.

that the invention of writing will not improve memory but destroy it, because the Egyptians will trust in these 'external characters which are not part of themselves' and this will discourage 'the use of their own memory within them'. This argument is closely reproduced by Dicson in the conversation of his Thamus and Theutates.

The Mercurius of Dicson's dialogue is a different character from his Theutates; and this at first seems strange for Mercurius (or Hermes) Trismegistus is usually identified with Thoth-Hermes the inventor of letters. But Dicson follows Bruno in making Mercurius the inventor, not of letters, but of the 'inner writing' of the art of memory. He thus stands for the inner wisdom which Thamus says that the Egyptians lost when external writing with letters was invented. For Dicson, as for Bruno, Mercurius Trismegistus is the patron of Hermetic, or occult, memory.

In the *Phaedrus*, it is Socrates who tells the story of Thamus' reaction to the invention of letters. But in Dicson's dialogue, Socrates has become the cackling pedant, the superficial person who cannot understand the ancient Egyptian wisdom of the Hermetic art of memory. It has been suggested,[10] and I am sure rightly, that this superficial and pedantic Greek is meant as a satire on Ramus. This would fit in with the Ramist *prisca theologia*, in which Ramus is the reviver of the true dialectic of Socrates.[11] Dicson's Socrates-Ramus would be the teacher of a superficial and false dialectical method, whilst his Mercurius is the exponent of a more ancient and better wisdom, that of the Egyptians as represented in the inner writing of occult memory.

Once the origin and meaning of the four speakers is grasped, the dialogue which Dicson puts into their mouths becomes understandable—or at least understandable within its own peculiar terms of reference.

Mercurius says that he sees a number of beasts before him. Thamus says that he sees men, not beasts, but Mercurius insists that these men are beasts in human forms, for the true form of man is the *mens* and these men, through neglecting their true form have fallen into the forms of beasts and come under the 'punishments of matter' (*vindices materiae*). What do you mean by these

[10] By Durkan, *article cited*, pp. 184, 185.
[11] See above, pp. 239–40.

punishments of matter, asks Thamus? To which Mercurius replies:

It is the duodenarius, driven out by the denarius.[12]

This is a reference to the thirteenth treatise of the *Corpus Hermeticum* where is described the Hermetic regenerative experience in which the soul escapes from the domination of matter, described as twelve 'punishments' or vices, and becomes filled with ten powers or virtues.[13] The experience is an ascent through the spheres in which the soul casts off the bad or material influences reaching it from the zodiac (the duodenarius), and ascends to the stars in their pure form, without the contamination of material influences, where it is filled with the powers or virtues (the denarius) and sings the hymn of regeneration. This is what Mercurius means in Dicson's dialogue when he says that the 'duodenarius' of immersion in matter and in beast-like forms is to be driven out by the 'denarius' when the soul becomes filled with divine powers in the Hermetic regenerative experience.

Thamus now describes Theutates as a beast, at which Theutates strongly protests. 'You calumniate, Thamus . . . the use of letters, of mathematics, are these the work of beasts?' Whereupon Thamus replies, closely in the word of Plato's story, that when he was in the city called Egyptian Thebes men were writing in their souls with knowledge, but Theutates has since sold them a bad aid for memory by inventing letters. This has brought in superficiality and quarrelling and made men little better than beasts.[14]

Socrates comes to the defence of Theutates, praising his great invention of letters and defying Thamus to prove that when men knew letters they studied memory less. Thamus then launches a passionate invective against Socrates as a sophist and a liar. He has taken away all criteria of truth, reducing wise men to the level of boys, malicious in disputing; he knows nothing of God and does not seek him in his vestiges and shadows in the *fabrica mundi*; he

---

[12] *De umbra rationis*, p. 5.

[13] *Corpus Hermeticum*, ed. Nock-Festugière, II, pp. 200–9; cf. *G.B. and H.T.*, pp. 28–31.

[14] *De umbra rationis*, pp. 6–8. The insistence on the beast-like forms of men unregenerated by Hermetic experience may have some connection with Bruno's *Circe* in which Circe's magic seems to be interpreted as morally useful by making evident the beast-like characters of men (see *G.B. and H.T.*, p. 202).

can perceive nothing of what is beautiful and good for the soul cannot perceive such things when enclosed in the passions of the body; he encourages such passions, inculcating cupidity and wrath; he is sunk in material darkness, though boasting of superior knowledge:

> for unless the *mens* is present and men are immersed in the bowl (*crater*) of regeneration in vain are they made glorious with commendations.[15]

Here again there is a reference to Hermetic regeneration, to that immersion in the regenerative bowl (*crater*) which is the theme of the fourth treatise of the *Corpus Hermeticum*, 'Hermes to Tat on the Crater or the Monad'.[16]

Socrates makes efforts in self-defence and counter-attack, for example by reproaching Thamus with never having written anything. In view of the theme of the dialogues this line was a mistake. He is crushed by the reply of Thamus that he has written 'in the places of memory',[17] and is dismissed as a vain Greek man.

The presentation of the Greeks as superficial, quarrelsome, and lacking in deep wisdom had a long history behind it, but in the form of a Trojan-Greek antithesis with the Trojans as the wiser and more profound people.[18] Dicson's anti-Greek dialogues are reminiscent of this tradition but with the Egyptians as the representatives of superior wisdom and virtue. In his Greek-Egyptian antithesis Dicson might have been influenced by the sixteenth treatise of the *Corpus Hermeticum* in which King Ammon advises that the treatise should not be translated from Egyptian into Greek which is a vain and empty language and the 'efficacious virtue' of the Egyptian language would be lost by translating it into Greek.[19] He would have known from the Platonic passage which he was using that Ammon was the same god as Thamus. This could have suggested making the Thamus of the Platonic story the opponent of Greek emptiness as typified in Socrates. If Dicson had seen the sixteenth treatise of the *Corpus Hermeticum*

---

[15] *De umbra rationis*, p. 21.
[16] *Corpus Hermeticum*, ed. cit., I, pp. 49–53.
[17] *De umbra rationis*, p. 28.
[18] The Trojan-Greek antithesis is, of course, Virgilian in origin.
[19] *Corpus Hermeticum*, ed. cit., II, p. 232.

in the Latin translation of Ludovico Lazzarelli[20] he might also have seen Lazzarelli's *Crater Hermetis* which describes the passing of a Hermetic regenerative experience from a master to a disciple.[21]

When Mercurius cites passages from the *Hermetica* he is of course quoting supposedly his own works. He is speaking as Mercurius Trismegistus, the teacher of the ancient Egyptian wisdom in the Hermetic writings. And this same Mercurius is he who teaches the 'inner writing' of the occult memory. Bruno's disciple makes abundantly clear what we have already realised from Bruno's own memory works, that the art of memory as he taught it was very closely associated with a Hermetic religious cult. The theme of Dicson's most curious dialogues is that the inner writing of the art of memory represents Egyptian profundity and spiritual insight, carries with it Egyptian regenerative experiences as described by Trismegistus, and is the antithesis of the beast-like manners, the Greek frivolity and superficiality, of those who have not had the Hermetic experience, have not achieved the gnosis, have not seen the vestiges of the divine in the *fabrica mundi*, have not become one with it by reflecting it within.

So strong is Dicson's abhorrence of supposedly Greek characteristics that he even denies that the Greek Simonides invented the art of memory. It was the Egyptians who invented it.[22]

This work may be of importance altogether disproportionate to its size. For Dicson makes it even clearer than Bruno himself does that Brunian memory implied a Hermetic cult. Dicson's art of memory is only an impressionistic reflection of *Shadows*. The important thing in his little work is the dialogues, expanded from the dialogues in *Shadows*, in which there are verbal quotations from the Hermetic regeneration treatises. Here are unmistakable

---

[20] The sixteenth treatise of the *Corpus Hermeticum* was not included in Ficino's Latin translation of the first fourteen treatises which Dicson was probably using. It was first published in the Latin translation of Lazzarelli in 1507. I have suggested (*G.B. and H.T.*, pp. 263–4) that Bruno knew this treatise.

[21] On Lazzarelli's extraordinary *Crater Hermetis*, see Walker, *Spiritual and Demonic Magic*, pp. 64–72; *G.B. and H.T.*, pp. 171–2, etc.

[22] In the art of memory which follows the dialogues, Dicson states that 'he of Chius', that is Simonides of Ceos, is falsely thought to have been the inventor of the art which originally came from Egypt. 'And if it is separated from Egypt it can effect nothing.' He adds that it may have been known to the Druids. (*De umbra rationis*, p. 37).

and strong Hermetic influences of a religious character involved with a Hermetic art of memory.

The probability that Dicson's Socrates is a satirical portrait of Ramus is increased by the fact that the cap fitted and that 'G.P. of Cambridge' was goaded into defence of Ramus and attack on the impious artificial memory of Dicson. In the dedication to Thomas Moufet of his *Antidicsonus*, Perkins states that there are two kinds of arts of memory, one using places and 'umbra', the other by logical disposition as taught by Ramus. The former is utterly vain; the latter is the only true method. Ostentatious memorio-graphers such as Metrodorus, Rossellius, Nolanus, and Dicsonus must be repelled and one must adhere as to a column to the faith of Ramist men.[23]

Nolanus—here is the name that matters. Giordano Bruno of Nola who the year before had flung his *Seals* at Oxford was the real initiator of this debate. Perkins sees him as in alliance with Metrodorus of Scepsis and with Rossellius, Dominican author of a memory treatise. He is also clearly aware of Dicson's connection with Bruno though he makes, so far as I can see, no references in the *Antidicsonus* to Bruno's works on memory, but directs himself solely against the work of the disciple, the *De umbra rationis* of Alexander Dicson.

He says that Dicson's Latin style is obscure and does not smell of 'Roman purity'.[24] That his use of the celestial signs in memory is absurd.[25] That all such nonsense should be thrown out for logical disposition is the sole discipline for memory, as Ramus teaches.[26] That Dicson's soul is blind and in error knowing nothing of the true and the good.[27] That all his images and 'umbrae' are utterly vain for in logical disposition you have a natural power for remembering.

Perkins's arguments are throughout full of reminiscences of Ramus and frequently he quotes verbally from his master, giving references. 'Open your ears', he cries to Dicson, 'and hear the words of Ramus speaking against you, and recognise the immense river of his genius.'[28] He then quotes from the *Scholae dialecticae* on the far superior value for memory of logical disposition as compared

[23] *Antidicsonus*, dedication to Thomas Moufet.
[24] *Ibid.*, p. 17.   [25] *Ibid.*, p. 19.   [26] *Ibid.*, p. 20.
[27] *Ibid.*, p. 21.   [28] *Ibid.*, p. 29.

with the art of memory using places and images;[29] and two passages from the *Scholae rhetoricae*. The first of these is one of Ramus' usual pronouncements on logical order as the basis of memory;[30] the second is another passage comparing Ramist memory to the classical art to the disadvantage of the latter:

> Whatever of art may help the memory is the order and disposition of things, the fixing in the soul of what is first, what second, what third. As to those places and images which are vulgarly spoken of they are inept and rightly derided by any master of arts. How many images would be needed to remember the Philippics of Demosthenes? Dialectical disposition alone is the doctrine of order; from it alone can memory seek aid and help.[31]

The *Antidicsonus* is followed by the *Libellus in quo dilucide explicatur impia Dicsoni artificiosa memoria* in which Perkins goes through the 'Ad Herennian' rules, which Dicson had quoted, opposing to them in detail the Ramist logical disposition. At one point in this somewhat dreary process Perkins becomes very interesting, and indeed unintentionally funny. This is where he is speaking of Dicson's 'animation' of the memory images. Dicson had of course been talking in his obscure Brunian fashion of the classical rule that images must be striking, active, unusual, and able to stir the memory emotionally. Perkins thinks that the use of such images is not only vastly inferior intellectually to logical disposition but is also morally reprehensible, for such images must arouse the passions. And here he mentions Peter of Ravenna who in his book on artificial memory has suggested the use of libidinous images to the young.[32] This must refer to Peter's remarks on how he used his girl friend, Juniper of Pistoia, as an image sure to stimulate his memory since she was so dear to him when young.[33] Perkins holds up Puritan hands of horror at such a suggestion which actually aims at arousing bad affects to stimulate memory. Such an art is clearly not for pious men, but has been made up by impious and confused people who disregard every divine law.

---

[29] *Ibid.*, pp. 29–30. Cf. Ramus, *Scholae in liberales artes*, ed. of Bâle, 1578 col. 773 (*Scholae dialecticae*, lib. XX).

[30] *Antidicsonus*, p. 30. Cf. Ramus, *Scholae*, ed. cit., col. 191 (*Scholae rhetoricae*, lib. I).

[31] *Antidicsonus*, *loc. cit.*; cf. Ramus, *Scholae*, ed. cit., col. 214 (*Scholae rhetoricae*, lib. 3).

[32] *Antidicsonus*, p. 45.   [33] See above, p. 113.

We may here be on the track of a reason why Ramism was so popular with the Puritans. The dialectical method was emotionally aseptic. Memorising lines of Ovid through logical disposition would help to sterilise the disturbing affects aroused by the Ovidian images.

The other work against Dicson by Perkins, published in the same year 1584, is the *Libellus de memoria verissimaque bene recordandi scientia* which is another exposition of Ramist memory with many examples of logical analysis of passages of poetry and prose through which these are to be memorised. In an epistle before the work, Perkins gives a brief history of the classical art of memory, invented by Simonides, perfected by Metrodorus, expounded by Tullius and Quintilian, and in more recent times by Petrarch, Peter of Ravenna, Buschius,[34] Rossellius. What does it all amount to? asks Perkins. There is nothing wholesome or learned in it, but rather it smells of 'some kind of barbarism and Dunsicality'.[35] This is interesting with its use of the word 'Dunsicality', recalling that cry of 'Dunses' used by extreme Protestants against those of the old Catholic order, a word which stimulated the bonfires of Dunsical manuscripts when the Reformers were clearing out the monastic libraries. For Perkins the art of memory has a mediaeval smell; its exponents do not speak with a 'Roman purity'; it belongs to the old times of barbarism and Dunsicality.

The Admonitions to Alexander Dicson which follow run on the same lines as the *Antidicsonus* though with more detailed attention to the 'astronomy' on which Dicson bases memory and which Perkins shows to be false. There is an important reaction against astrology here which deserves careful study. Perkins is making a rational attempt to undermine the 'Scepsian' artificial memory by attacking the astrological assumptions on which it is based. However, the impression of rationality which Perkins makes in these pages is somewhat clouded when we find that the chief reason why it is wrong to use 'astronomy' in memory is because the former is a 'special' art whereas memory as a part of dialectic-rhetoric is a 'general' art.[36] Here Perkins is blindly following the arbitrary Ramist reclassification of the arts.

[34] H. Buschius, *Aureum reminiscendi . . . opusculum*, Cologne, 1501.

[35] *Libellus de memoria*, pp. 3–4 (dedication to John Verner).

[36] The *Admonitiuncula* following the *Libellus* are unpaged. This passage is on Sig. C 8 *verso* of the *Admonitiuncula*.

Towards the end of the Admonitions the matter is summed up in a passage in which Dicson is adjured to compare his artificial memory with the Ramist method. The method records in memory through a natural order, but your artificial memory, Dicson, has been artificially made up by Greeklings. The method uses true places, putting generals in the highest place, subalterns in the middle place, specials in the lowest. But in your art what kind are the places, true or fictitious? If you say that they are true, you lie; if you say that they are fictitious I shall not disagree with you since you thereby cover your art with opprobrium. In the method, the images are clear and distinct and clearly divided, not fugitive shadows as in your art. 'Hence the palm is given to the method over that broken and weak discipline of memory.'[37] The passage is interesting evidence of how the method was developed out of the classical art yet was basically opposed to it on the fundamental point of images. Using the terminology of the classical art, Perkins turns it against the classical art and applies it to the method.

Dicson's *Defensio pro Alexandro Dicsono* is chiefly remarkable for the pseudonym 'Heius Scepsius' under which he published it. The 'Heius' may refer to his mother's maiden name of Hay.[38] The 'Scepsius' is certainly an enrolment under the banner of Metrodorus of Scepsis—and of Giordano Bruno—who use the zodiac in memory.

This controversy abundantly confirms Ong's view that the Ramist method was primarily a method for memorising. Perkins rests his position throughout on the assumption that the Ramist method is an art of memory with which, like Ramus himself, he compares unfavourably the classical art, now to be discarded and superseded. Perkins also confirms the suggestion made in the last chapter that the Brunian type of artificial memory would have looked in Elizabethan England like a mediaeval revival. Dicson's art suggests the past to Perkins, the old bad times of ignorance and Dunsicality.

It is because the opponents think of their respective methods as arts of memory that their warfare is waged entirely in terms of memory. Yet there are obviously other implications in this battle over memory. Both sides think of their respective arts of memory as moral and virtuous, and truly religious, whilst that of their

[37] *Libellus*: *Admonitiuncula*, Sig. E i.
[38] Cf. Durkan, *article cited*, p. 183.

opponent is immoral, irreligious, and vain. Profound Egypt and superficial Greece, or, to put it the other way round, superstitious and ignorant Egypt and reformed Puritan Greece, have different arts of memory. The one is a 'Scepsian' art; the other is the Ramist method.

Proof of the identity of 'G.P.' is found in the fact that in his *Prophetica*, a work published under his own name in 1592, William Perkins makes an attack on the classical art of memory on lines similar to those developed by 'G.P.'. The *Prophetica* has been defined by Howell as the first work by an Englishman which applies the Ramist method to preaching, and Howell also notes that Perkins here ordains that the Ramist method is to be used for memorising sermons, not the artificial memory with places and images.[39] The passage against artificial memory is as follows:

> The artificial memory which consists in places and images will teach how to retain notions in memory easily and without labour. But it is not to be approved (for the following reasons). I. The animation of the images which is the key of memory is impious: because it calls up absurd thoughts, insolent, prodigious and the like which stimulate and light up depraved carnal affections. 2. It burdens the mind and memory because it imposes a triple task on memory instead of one; first (the remembering of) the places; then of the images; then of the thing to be spoken of.[40]

We can recognise in these words of Perkins, the Puritan preacher, the 'G.P.' who wrote against the impious artificial memory of Dicson and who deplored the libidinous images recommended by Peter of Ravenna. The whirligig of time has transformed the mediaeval Tullius, who used to work so hard at forming memorable images of virtues and vices to deter the prudent man from Hell and lead him to Heaven, into a lewd and immoral person deliberately arousing carnal passions with his corporeal similitudes.

Among Perkins's other religious works there is *A Warning against the Idolatrie of the Last Times*, a warning delivered with earnest insistence because 'the remainders of poperie yet sticke in the minds of many.'[41] People are keeping and hiding in their

---

[39] W. S. Howell, *Logic and Rhetoric in England*, pp. 206-7.

[40] W. Perkins, *Prophetica sive de sacra et unica ratione concionandi tractatus*, Cambridge, 1592, Sig. F viii *recto*.

[41] W. Perkins, *Works*, Cambridge, 1603, p. 811.

houses 'idols, that is images that have been abused to idolatrie'[42] and there is the greatest need to see that such idols are given up and all remnants of the former idolatry destroyed wherever this has not yet been done. In addition to urging active iconoclasm, Perkins also warns against the theory underlying religious images. 'The Gentiles said that images erected were elements or letters to knowe God by: so say the Papists, that Images are Laiemens bookes. The wisest among the Gentiles used images and other ceremonies to procure the presence of angels and celestiall powers that by them they might attaine to the knowledge of God. The like doe the Papists with images of Angels and Saints.'[43] But this is forbidden, for 'we may not binde the presence of God, the operation of his spirit, and his hearing of us to any thing, to which God hath not bound himselfe . . . Now God hath not bound himself by any word to be present at images.'[44]

Moreover the prohibition against images applies within as well as without. 'So soone as the minde frames unto it selfe any forme of God (as when he is popishly conceiued to be like an old man sitting in heauen in a throne with a sceptre in his hand) an idol is set up in the minde . . .'[45] This prohibition is to be applied to any use of the imagination. 'A thing faigned in the mind by imagination is an idol.'[46]

We have to picture the controversy between Perkins and Dicson against the background of ruined buildings, smashed and defaced images—a background which loomed ever present in Elizabethan England. We must recreate the old mental habits, the art of memory as practised from time immemorial using the old buildings and the old images reflected within. The 'Ramist man' must smash the images both within and without, must substitute for the old idolatrous art the new image-less way of remembering through abstract dialectical order.

And if the old mediaeval memory was wrong, what of Renaissance occult memory? Occult memory moves in a direction diametrically opposed to Ramist memory, stressing beyond all measure that use of the imagination which the other prohibited, stressing it into a magical power. Both sides think of their own method as the right and religious one, and of their opponents as foolish and wicked. It is with a swelling religious passion that

[42] *Ibid.*, p. 830. [43] *Ibid.*, p. 833. [44] *Ibid.*, p. 716.
[45] *Ibid.*, p. 830. [46] *Ibid.*, p. 841.

Dicson's Thamus inveighs against the disputatious Socrates, who reduces wise men to the level of boys, who does not study the way of the sky, does not seek God in his vestiges and 'umbrae'. As Bruno said when summing up the opposite religious attitude which he found in England:

> They render thanks to God for having vouchsafed to them the light that leads to eternal life with no less fervour and conviction than we feel in rejoicing that our hearts are not blind and dark as theirs are.[47]

Thus in England a battle was joined within memory. There was war in the psyche, and the issues at stake were vast. These issues were not the simple ones of new versus old. Both sides were modern. Ramism was modern. And Brunian and Dicsonian memory were suffused with the Renaissance Hermetic influences. Their arts had more links with the past through the use of images than had the Ramist method. Nevertheless theirs was not the mediaeval art of memory; it was the art in a Renaissance transformation.

These tremendous issues were not presented secretively. On the contrary, they were very much publicised. The sensational controversy between Dicson and Perkins was linked with Bruno's even more sensational *Seals* bombshell and with his controversy with Oxford. Bruno and Dicson between them took on both the universities. Dicson's dispute with a Cambridge Ramist was paralleled by Bruno's dispute with the Aristotelians of Oxford in that visit to Oxford the results of which are reflected in his *Cena de le ceneri* published in 1584, the year of the Dicson-Perkins controversy. Though there were some Ramists in Oxford, it was not a stronghold of Ramism like Cambridge. And the Oxford doctors who objected to Bruno's exposition of Ficinian magic in a context of Copernican heliocentricity were not Ramists, for in the satire on them in the *Cena* they are called Aristotelian pedants. Ramists were, of course, anti-Aristotelian. I have recounted elsewhere the story of Bruno's conflict with Oxford and its reflection in the *Cena*.[48] Here my purpose is only to draw attention to the

---

[47] *Dialoghi italiani, ed. cit.*, p. 47. Bruno says this in the *Cena de le ceneri*, published in 1584.

[48] *G.B. and H.T.*, pp. 205–11, pp. 235 ff., etc.

over-lapping of Bruno's controversy with Oxford with his disciple's contemporary contest with Cambridge.

Bruno reveals in the dedication to the French ambassador of his *De la causa, principio e uno,* also published in this exciting year of 1584, that great commotions were going on around him. He is being persecuted he says by a rapid torrent of attacks, from the envy of the ignorant, the presumption of sophists, the detraction of the malevolent, the suspicion of fools, the zeal of hypocrites, the hatred of barbarians, the fury of the mob—to mention only a few of the classes of opponents which he names. In all this the ambassador has been to him a rock of defence, rising firm out of the ocean and unmoved by the fury of the waves. Through the ambassador he has escaped from the perils of this great tempest and in gratitude he dedicates to him a new work.[49]

The first dialogue of the *De la causa,* though opening with a vision of the sun of the Nolan's new philosophy, is also full of reports of the upheavals. Eliotropio (whose name recalls the heliotrope, the flower which turns towards the sun) and Armesso (possibly a version of Hermes)[50] tell Filoteo, the philosopher (Bruno himself) that there has been much adverse comment on his *Cena de le ceneri.* Armesso hopes that the new work 'may not become the subject of comedies, tragedies, lamentations, dialogues and what not similar to those which appeared a little while ago and obliged you to remain in retirement in the house.'[51] It is being said that he has taken too much upon himself in a country which is not his own. To which the philosopher replies that it is a mistake to kill a foreign doctor because he is trying cures which are unknown to the inhabitants.[52] Asked what gives him this faith in himself, he replies that it is the divine inspiration which he feels within. 'Few people', observes Armesso, 'understand such wares as yours.'[53] It is being said that in the *Cena* dialogues he has poured insult upon a whole country. Armesso thinks that much of his criticism is justified though he is grieved at the attack on Oxford. Whereupon the Nolan makes that retraction of his criticism of the Oxford doctors which takes the form of praise of the friars of mediaeval

[49] *Dialoghi italiani, ed. cit.,* pp. 176–7.
[50] As suggested by D. Singer, *Bruno,* p. 39 note.
[51] *Dialoghi italiani, ed. cit.,* p. 194.
[52] *Ibid.,* p. 201.
[53] *Ibid., loc. cit.*

Oxford whom the men of the present despise.[54] There is thus much inflammatory matter in the dialogue which can have done little to allay the disturbed situation.

Armesso hopes that the speakers in the new dialogues will not cause so much trouble as did those in the *Cena de le ceneri.* He is told that one of the speakers will be 'that clever, honest, kind, gentlemanly and faithful friend, Alexander Dicson, whom the Nolan dearly loves.'[55] And in fact 'Dicsono' is one of the principal speakers in the *De la causa*, which thus not only reflects in its first dialogue Bruno's attacks on Oxford and the troubles they aroused, but also in its four following dialogues recalls Dicson's contemporary adventures with the Cambridge Ramist by introducing 'Dicsono' as a principal speaker and as Bruno's faithful disciple.

Dicsono's presence in the dialogue lends strong point to the remark, not made by him but by another speaker, about the 'archpedant of France'. That this French arch pedant is certainly Ramus is made clear by the words immediately following which describe him as the writer of 'the *Scole sopra le arte liberali* and the *Animadversioni contra Aristotele*',[56] Italian versions of the titles of two of Ramus' most famous works, from which liberal quotation is made by Perkins when confuting the 'impious artificial memory' of Dicson.

As a whole, however, the last four dialogues of *De la causa* are not overtly controversial but yet another exposition of the Nolan's philosophy, that the divine substance may be perceived as vestiges and shadows in matter,[57] that the world is animated by a world soul,[58] that the spiritus of the world may be caught by magical processes,[59] that the matter underlying all forms is divine and cannot be annihilated,[60] that the intellect in man has been called god by Trismegistus and other theologians,[61] that the universe is a shadow through which the divine sun may be perceived, that the secrets of nature may be sought out by a profound magic,[62] that the All is One.[63]

The philosophy is opposed by the pedant Poliinio, but the

[54] *Ibid.*, pp. 209–10; cf. *G.B. and H.T.*, p. 210.
[55] *Dialoghi italiani*, p. 214.
[56] *Ibid.*, p. 260. [57] *Ibid.*, pp. 227–8. [58] *Ibid.*, p. 232.
[59] *Ibid.*, pp. 242 ff. [60] *Ibid.*, pp. 272–4. [61] *Ibid.*, p. 279.
[62] *Ibid.*, p. 340. [63] *Ibid.*, pp. 342 ff.

disciple Dicsono supports his master throughout, asking the right questions for eliciting his wisdom, and earnestly agreeing with all that he says.

Thus in the heated atmosphere of 1584 Bruno himself proclaims Alexander Dicson as his disciple. The excited Elizabethan public is reminded that 'Nolanus' and 'Dicsonus' belong together, that Dicson's *De umbra rationis* is but the voice of Bruno expounding the same mysterious 'Scepsian' art of memory as was to be found in *Shadows* and *Seals* and which belongs with the Nolan's Hermetic philosophy.

Since the art of memory had become such a red-hot subject, it was somewhat daring of Thomas Watson, poet and member of the Sidney circle, to publish in about 1585 or perhaps earlier, a *Compendium memoriae localis*. This seems a perfectly straight exposition of the classical art as a rational mnemotechnic, giving the rules with examples of their own application. And in his preface, Watson is careful to disassociate himself from Bruno and Dicson.

> I very much fear if my little work (*nugae meae*) is compared with the mystical and deeply learned *Sigilli* of the Nolan, or with the *Umbra artificiosa* of Dicson, it may bring more infamy on the author than utility to the reader.[64]

Watson's book shows that the classical art was still popular with poets, and to publish a 'local memory' at this time amounted to taking up a position against Puritan Ramism. He was also perfectly aware, as his preface shows, that Bruno and Dicson were concealing other matters in their arts of memory.

Where did Philip Sidney, the leader of the Elizabethan poetic Renaissance, stand amidst all these controversies? For Sidney, as is well known, was closely identified with Ramism. Sir William Temple, a very prominent member of the Cambridge school, was his friend, and in that same fateful year of 1584 when the 'Scepsians' and the Ramists were at loggerheads over memory, Temple dedicated to Sidney his edition of Ramus's *Dialecticae libri duo*.[65]

---

[64] Thomas Watson, *Compendium memoriae localis*, no date or place of publication, preface. The *S.T.C.* conjectures the date of publication as 1585 and the printer as Vautrollier.
There is a manuscript copy of Watson's work in the British Museum, Sloane 3751.
[65] Cf. Howell, *Logic and Rhetoric in England*, pp. 204 ff.

A very curious problem is raised by the interesting piece of information which Durkan has unearthed in his article on Alexander Dicson. Searching the state papers for references to Dicson, Durkan found this in a letter from Bowes, the English representative at the Scottish court, to Lord Burghley, dated 1592:

> Dickson, master of the art of memory, and sometime attending on
> Mr. Philip Sidney, deceased, has come to court.[66]

It is very striking that Lord Burghley's correspondent knows how best to remind that statesmen (who knew everything) of who Dicson is. A master of the art of memory who formerly attended Philip Sidney. When could Dicson have been in attendance on Sidney? Presumably in those years around 1584 when he made himself conspicuous as a master of the art of memory, and the disciple of that other master of the art, Giordano Bruno.

This scrap of new evidence brings Sidney a little closer to Bruno. If Bruno's disciple was in attendance on him, Sidney cannot have been altogether averse to Bruno himself. We have here for the first time a hint that Bruno had some justification for dedicating to Sidney (in 1585) his *Eroici furori* and his *Spaccio della bestia trionfante*.

How then did Sidney balance himself between influences so opposite as those of the Ramists and of the Bruno-Dicson school of thought? Perhaps both were competing for his favour. There may be some slight evidence for this suggestion in a remark by Perkins in his dedication to Thomas Moufet, who was a member of Sidney's circle, of his *Antidicsonus*. Perkins says in this dedicatory letter that he hopes that Moufet will assist him in repelling the influence of the 'Scepsians' and of the 'School of Dicson'.[67]

The Sidney who was the disciple of John Dee, who allowed Alexander Dicson to be in attendance on him, to whom Bruno felt that he could dedicate his works, does not quite fit with Sidney the Puritan and Ramist, though he must have found some way of

---

[66] *Calendar of State Papers, Scottish*, X (1589–93), p. 626; quoted by Durkan, *article cited*, p. 183.

[67] 'Commentationes autem meas his de rebus lucubrates, tuo inprimis nomine armatas apparer volui: quod ita sis ab omni laude illustris, ut Scepsianos impetus totamque Dicsoni scholam efferuescentem in me atque erumpentem facile repellas'. *Antidicsonus*, Letter to Thomas Moufet, Sig. A 3 recto.

conciliating these opposite influences. No pure Ramist could have written the *Defence of Poetrie*, the defence of the imagination against the Puritans, the manifesto of the English Renaissance. Nor could a pure Ramist have written this Sonnet to Stella:

> Though dusty wits dare scorn astrology,
> And fools can think those lamps of purest light
> Whose numbers, ways, greatness, eternity,
> Promising wonders, wonder do invite
> To have for no cause birthright in the sky
> But for to spangle the black weeds of Night;
> Or for some brawl, which in that chamber hie,
> They should still dance to please the gazer's sight.
> For me, I do Nature unidle know,
> And know great causes great effects procure;
> And know those bodies high reign on the low.
> And if these rules did fail, proof makes me sure,
> Who oft fore-see my after following race,
> By only those two eyes in Stella's face.

The poet is following the way of the sky with religious feeling, like Thamus, the Egyptian king in Dicson's dialogue; he is hunting after the vestiges of the divine in nature, like Bruno in the *Eroici furori*. And if the attitude to the old art of memory with places and images can be taken as a touchstone, Sidney alludes to it in a way which is not hostile. Speaking in the *Defence of Poetrie* of how verse is more easily remembered than prose, he says:

> . . . they that have taught the art of memory have showed nothing so apt for it as a certain room divided into many places, well and throughly known; now that hath the verse in effect perfectly, every word having his natural seat, which seat must needs make the word remembered.[68]

This interesting adaptation of local memory shows that Sidney did not memorise poetry by the Ramist method.

The Nolan left these shores in 1586 but his disciple continued to teach the art of memory in England. I derive this information from Hugh Platt's *The Jewell House of Art and Nature*, published at London in 1592. Platt speaks of 'the Art of Memorie which

---

[68] Sir Philip Sidney, *An Apologie for Poetrie*, ed. E. S. Shuckburgh, Cambridge University Press, 1905, p. 36.

master Dickson the Scot did teach of late years in England, and whereof he hath written a figurative and obscure treatise.'[69] Platt took lessons of Dicson and learned to memorise places in sets of ten with images on them which were to be made lively and active, a process which 'Maister Dickson tearmed to animate the *umbras* (sic) or *ideas rerum memorandarum*'.[70] An example of such an animated 'umbra' was 'Bellona staring with her fierie eies and portraied in all points according to the usual description of the Poets'.[71] Platt found that the method worked up to a point but hardly came up to the expectations raised by his teacher's descriptions of his 'great and swelling art'. He seems to have been taught a simple form of the straight mnemotechnic which he did not know was a classical art but thought was 'Maister Dickson's art'. He was evidently not initiated into Hermetic mysteries.

Dicson's 'figurative and obscure' treatise on memory, with its dialogues in which Hermes Trismegistus quotes from his own works, seems to have had a considerable circulation. It was reprinted with the title *Thamus* in 1597 by Thomas Basson, an English printer settled at Leiden; Basson also reprinted in the same year the *Defensio* by 'Heius Scepsius'.[72] I do not know why Basson was interested in reprinting these works. This printer liked mysteries and was probably a member of the secret sect, the Family of Love.[73] He was a protégé of Sidney's uncle, the Earl of Leicester,[74] to whom the first edition of the 'figurative and obscure' treatise had been dedicated. Henry Percy, ninth Earl of Northumberland owned a copy of *Thamus*;[75] and in Poland it was bound with works by Bruno.[76] Not the least peculiar feature in the career of this strange book is that the Jesuit, Martin Del Rio, in his book against magic published in 1600, commends as 'not without salt and acumen the *Thamus* of Alexander Dicson which Heius

[69] Platt, *Jewell House*, p. 81.

[70] *Ibid.*, p. 82.

[71] *Ibid.*, p. 83.

[72] See J. Van Dorsten, *Thomas Basson 1555–1613*, Leiden, 1961, p. 79.

[73] *Ibid.*, pp. 65 ff.

[74] *Ibid.*, pp. 16 ff.

[75] Manuscript catalogue at Alnwick Castle of the library of the ninth Earl of Northumberland.

[76] See A. Nowicki, 'Early Editions of Giordano Bruno in Poland', *The Book Collector*, XIII (1964), p. 343.

Scepsius defends against the attack of a Cambridge man in the edition published at Leiden.'[77] Why was the Egyptian 'inner writing' of the art of memory as taught by Dicson worthy of Jesuit commendation, whereas the master from whom he learned it was burned at the stake?

In the Venetian Renaissance, Giulio Camillo had raised his Memory Theatre in the sight of all, though it was a Hermetic secret. In the peculiar circumstances of the English Renaissance, the Hermetic form of the art of memory perhaps goes more underground, becoming associated with secret Catholic sympathisers, or with existing secret religious groups, or with incipient Rosicrucianism or Freemasonry. The Egyptian king, with his 'Scepsian' method opposed to the method of Socrates, the Greek, may provide a clue through which some Elizabethan mysteries would take on a more definite historical meaning.

We have seen that the debate within the art of memory hinged on the imagination. A dilemma was presented to the Elizabethans in this debate. Either the inner images are to be totally removed by the Ramist method or they are to be magically developed into the sole instruments for the grasp of reality. Either the corporeal similitudes of mediaeval piety are to be smashed or they are to be transposed into vast figures formed by Zeuxis and Phidias, the Renaissance artists of the fantasy. May not the urgency and the agony of this conflict have helped to precipitate the emergence of Shakespeare?

[77] Martin Del Rio, *Disquisitionum Magicarum, Libri Sex*, Louvain, 1599–1600, ed. of 1679, p. 230.

Chapter XIII

❖◇❖

GIORDANO BRUNO: LAST
WORKS ON MEMORY

❖◇❖

WHEN Bruno arrived back in Paris in 1586, having crossed the Channel with Mauvissière, the French ambassador who had protected him from tumults in England, he found conditions much less favourable to his secret than they had been two years earlier when he had dedicated *Shadows* to Henri III.[1] Now Henri was almost powerless in the face of the extreme Catholic reaction, led by the Guise faction and supported by Spain. Paris was a city of fears and rumours on the eve of the Wars of the League which would drive the King of France from his throne.

In this troubled and dangerous town, Bruno did not fear to confront the doctors of Paris with his anti-Aristotelian philosophy. The address given by Bruno's disciple, Jean Hennequin (a French Alexander Dicson speaking for the Master) to the doctors of the university summoned to hear him in the Collège de Cambrai[2] follows very similar lines to the address which Bruno represents himself (in the *Cena de le ceneri*) as having given to the Aristotelian doctors at Oxford. The speech in the Collège de Cambrai opposes the philosophy of the living universe, infused with the divine life, the philosophy of gnosis or insight into the divinity of nature, to the deadness and emptiness of the Aristotelian physics.

At the same time, Bruno published a book called *Figuratio*

---

[1] On Bruno's second visit to Paris, see *G.B. and H.T.*, pp. 291 ff.

[2] *Camoeracensis Acrotismus*, in G. Bruno, *Op. lat.*, I (i), pp. 53 ff. Cf. *G.B. and H.T.*, pp. 298 ff.

Aristotelici physici auditus[3] which teaches how to memorise the physics of Aristotle through a series of mythological memory images which are to be placed on a curious looking place system. Memorising the physics of Aristotle by the artificial memory evidently belonged into the Dominican tradition because Romberch, in that useful memory Congestion of his, tells the following story:

> A young man, almost ignorant of this art (of memory), depicted on walls some rather inane little figures through which he could go through in order the *De auditu physico* of Aristotle; and though his simulachra did not accord very well with the matter, they helped him to remember it. If such weak aids yet help memory, how much more will it be helped if its foundation is improved by use and exercise.[4]

Here is the exact title which Bruno uses for a compendium of Aristotelian physics, *De auditu physico*, and here is a friar recounting how it might be memorised by the artificial memory, which is what Bruno purports to be doing.

I say advisedly 'purports to be doing', for there is something peculiar here. Why does he want us to memorise the dead and empty Aristotelian physics? Why are we not urged to draw into memory the living powers of the divine universe through magically animated images? And it may be that this is what the book is really about. Mythological figures are to be used as the memory images, the Arbor Olympica, Minerva, Thetis as matter, Apollo as form, the 'superior Pan' as nature, Cupid as motion, Saturn as time, Jupiter as the prime mover, and so on.[5] Such forms as these, animated with the magic of divine proportions, would contain Bruno's philosophy, would themselves be the imaginative means of grasping it. And when we see that the place system[6] on which the images are to be placed (Pl. 14c) is one of those horoscope-like diagrams such as are to be seen in *Seals* we realise that the images are supposed to be magically animated, magically in contact with cosmic powers. And indeed the connection with *Seals* is stated at

[3] *Op. lat.*, I (iv), pp. 129 ff. The book is published at Paris 'ex Typographia Petri Cheuillot, in vico S. Ioannis Lateranensis, sub Rosa rubra', and is dedicated to Piero Del Bene, Abbot of Belleville. On the significance of this dedication, see *G.B. and H.T.*, pp. 303 ff.

[4] Romberch, *Congestorium artificiose memorie*, pp. 7 *verso*–8 *recto*.

[5] *Op. lat.*, I (iv), pp. 137 ff.

[6] *Ibid.*, p. 139.

the beginning of the *Figuration*, where the reader is told to turn to the Thirty Seals and choose from them what suits him, perhaps the Seal of the Painter, perhaps that of the Sculptor.[7]

The memory system by which the physics is to be 'figured' is in itself a contradiction of the physics. The book is a Seal, the counterpart of his anti-Aristotelian attack on the Parisian doctors, just as, in England, *Seals* was the counterpart of his attack on the Oxford doctors. Zeuxis or Phidias, painting or sculpturing tremendous and significant images within the memory, represent Bruno's way of understanding the living world, of grasping it through the imagination.

When Bruno left Paris he wandered through Germany to Wittenberg where he wrote several books, amongst them the *Torch of the Thirty Statues*, henceforth to be referred to as *Statues*. Though almost certainly written at Wittenberg about 1588, this work which is an unfinished fragment, was not published in Bruno's lifetime.[8] In *Statues*, Bruno is doing what he advised the reader of the *Figuration* to do. He is using the Seal of Phidias the Sculptor. These towering mythological Statues sculptured within by the Michelangelesque memory artist do not merely express or illustrate Bruno's philosophy. They *are* his philosophy, showing forth the power of the imagination to grasp the universe through images. The series begins with the 'infigurable' concepts after which come the figured Statues.

Within this series, Bruno presents his philosophical religion, his religious philosophy. The infigurable ORCUS or ABYSS signifies the infinite desire and need for the divine infinity, the thirst for the infinite,[9] as in Bruno's *De l'infinito universo e mondi*. The figurable APOLLO as he rides by, standing naked in his chariot, his head nimbed with solar rays, is the MONAD or the ONE,[10] the central sun towards which all Bruno's unifying efforts are directed. SATURN follows, brandishing his sickle, as the Beginning or Time.

[7] *Ibid.*, p. 136.
[8] The *Lampas triginta statuarum* was copied by Bruno's disciple, Jerome Besler, at Padua in 1591, and is one of the collection of writings in the Noroff manuscript first published in the edition of the Latin works in 1891 (*Op. lat.*, III, pp. I ff.) Cf. *G.B. and H.T.*, pp. 307 ff.
[9] *Op. lat.*, III, pp. 16 ff.
[10] *Ibid.*, pp. 63–8.

PROMETHEUS, devoured by the vulture, is the *Causa efficiens*[11] (these three Statues contain the theme of Bruno's *De la causa, principio, e uno*). SAGITTARIUS, the archer of the zodiac, bending his bow, is the direction of the intention towards an object[12] (as in the mystical aspirations of Bruno's *De gli eroici furori*). COELIUS signifies the natural goodness as expressed in the order of nature, the symmetry of the stars, the natural order of heaven directed towards a good end,[13] Bruno's search in the *fabrica mundi* for the vestiges of the divine. VESTA signifies moral goodness, that which tends to the good of human society, Bruno's insistence on social ethics and philanthropy. Through VENUS and her son CUPID we seek the unifying force of love, the living spiritus of the living world,[14] as in Bruno's religion of Love and Magic.

MINERVA is an important Statue. She is the *mens*, the divine in man reflecting the divine universe. She is memory and reminiscence, recalling the art of memory which was the discipline of Bruno's religion. She is the continuity of human reason with divine and demonic intelligences, representing Bruno's belief in the possibility of establishing such communications through mental images. By the LADDER OF MINERVA we rise from the first to the last, collect the external species in the internal sense, order intellectual operations into a whole by art,[15] as in Bruno's extraordinary arts of memory.

I have reduced *Statues* to the barest minimum, giving little impression of the impact of the work and of the intense visualisation of the figures with their attributes. This is one of the most impressive of Bruno's writings, in which he can be so clearly seen living out his conviction that the Poet, the Philosopher, and the Artist, are all one. In the introduction, he states that he is not innovating in this work but reviving something of very great antiquity, calling back again

> . . . the use and form of ancient philosophies and of the earliest theologians who used not so much to veil the arcana of nature in types and similitudes as to declare and explain them digested in a series and more easily accomodated to memory. We easily retain a sensible, visible, imaginable statue, we commend easily to the work

---

[11] *Ibid.*, pp. 68–77. [12] *Ibid.*, pp. 97–102.
[13] *Ibid.*, pp. 106–11. [14] *Ibid.*, pp. 151 ff.
[15] *Ibid.*, pp. 140–50.

of memory fabulous fictions; therefore (through them) we shall be able without difficulty to consider and retain mysteries, doctrines, and disciplinary intentions . . . as in nature we see vicissitudes of light and darkness so also there are vicissitudes of different kinds of philosophies. Since there is nothing new . . . it is necessary to return to these opinions after many centuries.[16]

There are three lines of thinking in this passage which Bruno has amalgamated into one.

It alludes first of all to the theory of the myths and fables of the ancients as containing within them truths of natural and moral philosophy. The Renaissance text-book which explained in handy form the natural and moral truths contained in the myths was, of course, the *Mythologia* of Natalis Comes. Bruno certainly knew Comes' work and is drawing on it in *Statues*, though the philosophy in the Statues is his own philosophy. He believes that he is drawing out of the myths the true ancient philosophy which he is reviving.

But Bruno introduces memory into his theory of mythology. He reverses the usual statement, that the ancients concealed arcana in the myths, when he says that, on the contrary, they declared and explained truths through the myths in order to make them more easily remembered. Then comes an echo of Thomist and Dominican theory about the art of memory, that the 'sensibilia' are more easily retained in memory than the 'intelligibilia' and that therefore we may use in memory the 'corporeal similitudes' advised by Tullius because these will help us to direct spiritual intentions towards intelligible things. Bruno's Dominican training has impressed the Thomist theorising of the art of memory towards religious and spiritual intentions most deeply on his mind. The Statues are all said to contain 'intentions'; they express not only the natural and moral truth but the intention of the soul towards it. Though Bruno's theory and practice of memory was radically different from that of Thomas Aquinas, it was only out of the religious use of the image in memory that the Brunian type of transformation of the art of memory into the discipline of his religion could have taken place.

Finally, when Bruno speaks of vicissitudes of light and darkness and of the light now returning with him, he always means the

---

[16] *Ibid.*, pp. 8–9.

Hermetic or 'Egyptian' philosophy and the magical religion of the Egyptians who, as described in the Hermetic *Asclepius*, knew how to make statues of the gods through which to draw down celestial and divine intelligences. The memory statues are intended to have in them this magical power, applied inwardly. There are many magical and talismanic touches in the descriptions of them.[17] Camillo interpreted the magic of the statues of the *Asclepius* as a magic of artistic proportion, and so, perhaps, we may think of Phidias the Sculptor as a 'divine' artist of the Renaissance as he moulds in Bruno's memory the great figures of the gods.

The *Statues* would thus have for Bruno a three-fold power; as ancient and true statements in mythological form of the ancient and true philosophy and religion which he believes that he is reviving; as memory images containing within them intentions of the will towards grasping these truths; as artistically magic memory images through which the Magus believes that he puts himself in contact with 'divine' and demonic intelligences'.

As a Brunian memory system, *Statues* belongs recognisably within the whole complex of the memory works. It confirms the interpretation of the *Figuration of Aristotle* as containing within its memory system the refutation of the Aristotelian philosophy which it is supposed to memorise,[18] for many of the mythological figures of the *Figuration* are the same as those in *Statues*.

The Thirty Statues are, I believe, supposed to be revolved on Lullian combinatory wheels. The system, when completed (as already mentioned the manuscript is incomplete) would have represented one of Bruno's frightful efforts to combine the classical art of memory with Lullism by putting images, instead of letters, on the combinatory wheels. Bruno wrote several Lullian works whilst at Wittenberg with which the Thirty Statues probably connect,[19] for it is noticeable that in *Statues* Bruno is using concepts taken from the *principia* and *relata* of Lullism. A revolving system using thirty mythological figures is given

[17] See *G.B. and H.T.*, p. 310.

[18] There may here be an interesting anticipation of Francis Bacon's use of mythology as a vehicle for conveying an anti-Aristotelian philosophy; see Paolo Rossi, *Francesco Bacone*, Bari, 1957, pp. 206 ff.

[19] The titles of these works, *De lampade combinatoria lulliana* and *De progressu et lampade venatoria logicorum* obviously connect with the title *Lampas triginta staturum*. Cf. *G.B. and H.T.*, p. 307.

in *Shadows* (the Lycaon to Glaucus series)[20] which is probably the germ out of which the more ambitious system of *Statues* developed.

The *Figuration* and *Statues* are not full Brunian memory treatises. They are examples of how to use the Seals Zeuxis the Painter or Phidias the Sculptor by basing memory on mythological images which (1) contain the Brunian philosophy; (2) upon which imagination and will are directed with strong intentions; (3) which are believed to be astralised or magicised into images which, like the magic statues of the *Asclepius*, will attract celestial or demonic powers into the personality.

William Perkins was absolutely right in seeing the Bruno-Dicson artificial memory in a context of Catholic versus Protestant attitude to images. For whilst Bruno, the heretical Magus of Memory could (and did) develop out of pious mediaeval use of the images of the art of memory, the Protestant inner and outer iconoclasm arrested the possibility of any such development.

Bruno's last book on memory was the last work which he published, just before he returned to Italy, to the prisons of the Inquisition and eventual death at the stake. The invitation sent to him from Venice by the man who wished to learn his memory secrets precipitated this return. In this book, therefore, Bruno is propounding his memory secrets for the last time. The book is called *De imaginum signorum et idearum compositione*[21] and will henceforth be referred to as *Images*. It was published at Frankfort in 1591, but was probably mainly written in Switzerland, perhaps at the castle near Zurich of Johann Heinrich Hainzell, an occultist and alchemist with whom Bruno stayed for a time and to whom the book is dedicated.

The book is in three parts. The third and last part consists of 'Thirty Seals'. As in *Seals*, published eight years previously in England, Bruno is here listing various types of occult memory systems. Many of these are the same as in the English *Seals* with the same titles, but these latest Seals are, if possible, even more obscure than the earlier ones. The Latin verses in which some of them are described have affinities with the Latin poems which

---

[20] *Op. lat.*, II (i), pp. 107. See above, p. 222, note 63.
[21] *Op. lat.*, II (iii), pp. 85 ff. Cf. *G.B. and H.T.*, pp. 325 ff.

Bruno had recently published at Frankfort.[22] There may be new developments in these latest Seals, particularly in the elaboration of pseudo-mathematical, or 'mathesistical', place systems. A great difference between these German Seals and the English Seals is that they do not lead up to a 'Seal of Seals' revealing the religion of Love, Art, Mathesis, and Magic as the English series did. It seems to have been only in England that Bruno made that revelation so explicitly in a printed work.

The Thirty Seals published in Germany, with their connections with the Latin poems published in Germany, would form a vital point of departure for the study of Bruno's influence in Germany, just as the English Seals, with their connections with the Italian dialogues published in England, are vital for his influence in England. This book is mainly directed towards his influence in England and I therefore do not attempt further discussion here of the Thirty Seals in the third part of *Images*. Something must be said, however, of the first two parts of the book in which Bruno grapples once again with his eternal problem of images and presents a new memory system.

The first part is an art of memory in which (as in the arts in *Shadows* and *Circe*, the latter reprinted in *Seals*) Bruno goes through the 'Ad Herennian' rules but in a yet more mystifying form than hitherto. Moreover he now speaks, not of an art but of a method. 'We institute a method, not about things but about the significance of things.'[23] He begins with rules for images; different ways of forming memory images; images for things and images for words; that images must be lively, active striking, charged with emotional affects so that they may pass through the doors of the storehouse of memory.[24] Egyptian and Chaldaean mysteries are hinted at, yet beneath all the verbiage the memory treatise structure is clearly visible. I think that he is mainly using Romberch. When in the chapter on 'images for words' he says that the letter O may be represented by a sphere; the letter A by a ladder or compasses; the letter I by a column,[25] he is simply

---

[22] The *De immenso, innumerabilibus et infigurabilibus*; the *De triplici minimo et mensura*; the *De monade numero et figura*. The imagery in these poems connects with *Statues* and *Images* in ways too complex to begin to investigate here.

[23] *Op. lat.*, II (iii), p. 95.

[24] *Ibid.*, p. 121.   [25] *Ibid.*, p. 113.

describing in words one of the visual alphabets illustrated by Romberch.

He then passes to rules for places (this is the wrong order, rules for places should come first) and here also the memory treatise foundation is obvious. Sometimes he breaks into Latin verse which sounds most impressive but which Romberch helps one to construe.

> Complexu numquam vasto sunt apta locatis
> Exiguis, neque parva nimis maiora receptant.
> Vanescit dispersa ampla de sede figura,
> Corporeque est modico fugiens examina visus.
> Sint quae hominem capiant, qui stricto brachia ferro
> Exagitans nihilum per latum tangat et altum.[26]

What can this mean? It is the rule that memory *loci* should not be too large nor too small, with the addition in the last two lines of Romberch's advice that a memory locus should not be higher nor wider than a man can reach, the rule which Romberch illustrates (see Fig. 3).

In association with the art of memory in this first part of *Images* Bruno presents an architectural memory system of terrible complexity. By an 'architectural' system I mean that this is a system using sequences of memory rooms in each of which memory images are to be placed. The architectural form is, of course, the most normal form of the classical art of memory but Bruno is using it in a highly abnormal way in which the distribution of the memory rooms is involved with magical geometry and the system is worked from above by celestial mechanics. There are twenty-four 'atria' or rooms each divided into nine memory places with images on them. These 'atria' with their nine divisions are illustrated in diagrammatical form on pages of the text. There are also fifteen 'fields' in the system, each divided into nine places; and thirty 'cubicles', which bring the system within range of the 'thirty' obsession.

One has to get hold of the general idea that everything in this lower world is supposed to be memorised through the images in these atria, fields, and cubicles. Everything in the physical world is to be here, all plants, stones, metals, animals, birds, and so on (Bruno

[26] *Ibid.*, p. 188.

makes use for his encyclopaedic classifications of the alphabetical lists to be found in the memory text books). Also every art, science, invention known to man, and all human activities. Bruno states that the atria and fields which he teaches how to erect will include all things which can be said, known, or imagined.

A large order! But we are used to this kind of thing. This is an encyclopaedic memory system like the one in *Shadows* in which all the contents of the world, all arts and sciences known to men, were supposed to be included on the wheels surrounding the central wheel with its celestial images. Neither I nor the reader are Magi, but we can at least get hold in a general way of the idea that all the material which—in the system of *Shadows*—was shown on the inventors' wheel and the other wheels surrounding the central magic images wheel is now distributed in a system of memory rooms. This is an architectural 'Seal' full of correspondences, associative orders, which are both mnemonic and astral.

But where is the celestial system through which alone an encyclopaedic occult memory like this could work? The celestial system is in the second part of *Images*.

In this second part[27] there appear before us twelve tremendous figures or 'principles' which are said to be the causes of all things, under the 'ineffable and infigurable Optimus Maximus'. These are JUPITER (with Juno), SATURN, MARS, MERCURY, MINERVA, APOLLO, AESCULAPIUS (with Circe, Arion, Orpheus), SOL, LUNA, VENUS, CUPID, TELLUS (with Ocean, Neptune, Pluto). These are the celestial ones, the great statues of the cosmic gods. With these main figures, Bruno arranges large numbers of talismanic or magic images, presumably to assist in drawing their powers into the psyche. I have analysed this series and its associated images in my other book,[28] pointing out that Bruno is here applying the Ficinian talismanic magic to memory images, probably with the idea of drawing particularly strong Solar, Jovial, and Venereal influences into the personality of the kind of Magus which he aspires to be. These figures form the celestial system of *Images*, inner statues magically assimilated to the influences of the stars.

How are the two systems in *Images*—the memory rooms of the first part and the celestial figures of the second part—to be combined?

[27] *Ibid.*, pp. 200 ff.
[28] See *G.B. and H.T.*, pp. 326 ff.

Probably a diagram (Pl. 14d) is the 'Seal' which expresses the system as a whole. It represents, we are told, the arrangement of the twenty-four atria, the memory rooms each with their loci filled with images. Each individual atrium, and the plan of the atria as a whole, is said to have a relationship to the four points of the compass. The circle surrounding the square plan of the memory rooms represents, I believe, the heavens. On it would be inscribed the celestial figures and images, the round celestial system animating, organising, unifying, the infinite detail of the contents of the lower world memorised in the places and images of the system of memory rooms.

This diagram should, then, represent the memory building of the system in *Images* as a whole, a round building representing the heaven with a square lay-out inside it, a building reflecting the upper and the lower worlds in which the world as a whole is remembered from above, from the unifying, organising, celestial level. Perhaps this system carries out the suggestion in Seal 12 of *Seals*, where Bruno says that 'he knows a double picture' for memory,[29] one the celestial memory with astral images, the other by 'feigning as need requires edifices'. This system would be using the 'double picture' simultaneously, combining the round celestial system with the square system composed of the memory rooms.

We now notice the lettering on the central circle of the diagram, which is nowhere explained in the text (and which is not reproduced accurately in the nineteenth-century edition of this work). Perhaps we are becoming bewitched or bemused but do the letters on that circle begin to read as 'Alta Astra'? Is this the memory temple of an astral religion?

A very much simpler use of classical architectural memory adapted to a Renaissance use is to be discerned in Campanella's City of the Sun. The *Città del Sole*[30] is, of course, primarily a Utopia, the description of an ideal city, the religion of which is a solar or astral cult. The city is round, with a round temple in its centre on which are said to be depicted all the stars of heaven with

[29] See above, p. 249

[30] The *Città del Sole* was written by Campanella in about 1602 when he was in the prisons of the Inquisition in Naples. It was first published in a Latin version in 1623. On the City of the Sun and its affinities with Bruno's ideas, see *G.B. and H.T.*, pp. 367 ff.

their relationships to things here below. The houses of the city are arranged as circular walls, or *giri*, concentric with the central circle in which is the temple. On these walls are said to be depicted all mathematical figures, all animals, birds, fishes, metals, and so on; all human inventions and activities; and on the outermost circle or wall are statues of great men, great moral and religious leaders and founders of religions. This is the kind of encyclopaedic lay-out of a universal memory system, with a 'celestial' organising basis, with which Bruno has made us very familiar. And Campanella repeatedly stated that his City of the Sun, or perhaps some model of it, could be used for 'local memory', as a very quick way of knowing everything 'using the world as a book'.[31] Clearly the City of the Sun when used as 'local memory' would be a fairly simple Renaissance memory system, one in which the classical principle of memorising places in buildings has been adapted to world-reflecting uses, after the Renaissance manner.

The City of the Sun, which is a Utopian city based on an astral religion, when used as a memory system may be usefully compared with Bruno's systems, both the one in *Shadows* and the one in *Images*. It is much simpler than Bruno's systems because static in a City (as Camillo's system is static in a Theatre) and does not attempt Bruno's awful complexities. Nevertheless if we compare the 'Alta Astra' on the round central altar of the *Images* system with the round temple at the centre of the City of the Sun, certain basic similarities between 'local memory' as conceived by Bruno and Campanella, both of whom were trained in the Dominican convent at Naples, may become apparent.

'To think is to speculate with images', says Bruno again in *Images*,[32] misinterpreting Aristotle as he had done in *Seals*. Nowhere is his overwhelming preoccupation with the imagination more apparent than in this his last work which contains the most painfully complex of all his systems and his last thoughts about images. Working with two traditions about the use of images, the mnemonic tradition and the talismanic or magical tradition, he is

---

[31] See Tommaso Campanella, *Lettere*, ed. V. Spampanato, Bari, 1927, pp. 27, 28, 160, 194 and L. Firpo, 'Lista dell'opere di T. Campanella', *Rivista di Filosofia*, XXXVIII (1947), pp. 213–29. Cf. Rossi, *Clavis universalis*, p. 126; *G.B. and H.T.*, pp. 394–5.

[32] *Op. lat.*, II (iii), p. 103; Cf. *G.B. and H.T.*, p. 335.

struggling within his own frame of reference with problems which are still unsolved, within any frame of reference.

'On the composition of images, signs, and ideas'; this is the title of the book, and Bruno is using 'ideas' in the sense of magical or astral images, the sense in which he used it in *Shadows*. In the first part of *Images* he discusses and composes memory images, using the memory tradition rules; in the second part he discusses and composes 'ideas', talismanic images, effigies of the stars as magicised 'statues', trying to make images which will act as conveyors of cosmic powers into the psyche. In these labours he as it were both 'talismanises' mnemonic images and introduces mnemonic aspects into talismans as he 'composes' the latter to suit his purposes. The two traditions about imparting power into images—the memory tradition that images must be emotionally striking and able to move the affects, and the magical tradition of introducing astral or cosmic powers into talismans—fuse in his mind as he toils at the composing of images, signs, and ideas. There is genius in this book, as of a being of great brilliance working at a white heat of intensity at a problem which he believes to be more important than any other, the problem of how to organise the psyche through the imagination.

The conviction that it is within, in the inner images which are nearer to reality than the objects of the outer world, that reality is grasped and the unified vision achieved, underlies the whole. Seen in the light of an inner sun, the images merge and fuse into the vision of the One. The religious impulse which moves Bruno in his stupendous memory efforts is nowhere more apparent than in *Images*. Tremendous is the force of the 'spiritual intentions' which he directs upon his inner images, and this force is a legacy from the mediaeval transformation of the classical art of memory, however strangely changed in this its latest Renaissance transformation into an Art which is one of the disciplines of a Hermetic or 'Egyptian' religion.

Bruno may have had time to give some memory lessons in Padua and Venice after his return to Italy, but when he disappeared into the prisons of the Inquisition in 1592 his wandering career was over. It strikes one as rather curious, though it may be only a coincidence, that when Bruno was eclipsed another memory teacher arose who wandered through Belgium, Germany, and

France. Though neither Lambert Schenkel nor his disciple Johannes Paepp were of the same calibre as Giordano Bruno, they are worthy of attention as post-Brunian memory teachers who knew something about Bruno's version of artificial memory.

Lambert Schenkel[33] (1547 to *circa* 1603) was a rather celebrated person in his day, who attracted attention by public exhibitions of his powers of memory and by his published works. His origins appear to have been in the Catholic Low Countries; he studied at Louvain and his first book on memory, *De memoria*, was published at Douai in 1593, which would seem to give it the approval of that intensely Catholic centre of Counter-Reformation activities.[34] However, doubts about Schenkel seem to have arisen and he was later accused of magic. He charged fees for his lessons and the aspirer after learning the secrets of memory was obliged to consult him personally, for the full secrets were not, so he said, revealed in his books.

Schenkel's chief work on memory is his *Gazophylacium*, published at Strasburg in 1610 and in a French translation at Paris in 1623.[35] It is mainly based on his earlier *De memoria* though with elaborations and additions.

With the *Gazophylacium* we are in the stream of the Romberch and Rossellius type of memory text-book, and Schenkel is very consciously trying to attach himself to the Dominican memory tradition through his constant quotations from Thomas Aquinas as the great expert on memory. He gives a long history of the art of memory in the first part of the book, mentioning all the usual names, Simonides of course, Metrodorus of Scepsis, Tullius, and so on, and in modern times Petrarch, and so on, adding to the usual lists of modern names many others whom he connects with proficiency in memory, among them Pico della Mirandola. Schenkel gives references for his statements and his

[33] On Schenkel, see the article in *Biographie universelle, sub. nom.*, and in the *Encyclopaedia Britannica*, article 'Mnemonics'; Hajdu, *Das Mnemotechnische Schrifftum des Mittelalters*, pp. 122–4; Rossi, *Clavis universalis*, pp. 128, 154–5, 250 etc.

[34] There seems to have been a good deal of interest in a revival of the art of memory in the Catholic Low Countries, judging by the impassioned oration in favour of the art of Simonides made at Louvain in 1560 and published as N. Mameranus, *Oratio pro memoria et de eloquentia in integrum restituenda*. Brussels, 1561.

[35] L. Schenkel, *Le Magazin des Sciences*, Paris, 1623.

book can indeed be recommended as rather valuable to the modern historian of the art of memory who, if he cares to look up Schenkel's references, may be led to a good deal of useful material.

What Schenkel teaches appears to be in no way unusual; it is basically the classical art, with long sections on places, giving diagrams of rooms containing memory places, and long sections on images. It could be a rational mnemotechnic which Schenkel is teaching though in the elaborated forms in which it had become involved in the memory treatises. But he is very obscure and he mentions some rather suspect authors, such as Trithemius.

Schenkel had a disciple and imitator, one Johannes Paepp. The works on memory of this Paepp are deserving of rather careful attention because he plays a rôle which may be vulgarly described as letting the cat out of the bag. He, as he describes it, 'detects Schenkel' or reveals the secret of the occult memory hidden in Schenkel's books. This purpose is stated in the title of his first book, *Schenkelius detectus: seu memoria artificialis hactenus occultata*, published at Lyons in 1617. And he continued the good work of 'detecting Schenkel' in two subsequent publications.[36] The tell-tale Paepp mentions a name which Schenkel never mentions, Jordanus Brunus,[37] and the secret which he reveals seems to be somewhat of a Brunian nature.

Paepp has been a careful student of Bruno's works, particularly of *Shadows* from which he quotes several times.[38] And his long lists of magic images to be used as memory images are very reminiscent of those in *Images*. Arcane philosophical mysteries, says Paepp, are contained in the art of memory.[39] There is nothing of the strange philosophical and visual power of Bruno in his little books, but he gives in a curious passage one of the clearest indications that I have found of how the texts on classical and scholastic memory could become applied to Hermetic contemplation of the order of the universe.

---

[36] *Eisagoge, seu introductio facilis in praxim artificiosae memoriae*, Lyons, 1619; and *Crisis, iani phaosphori, in quo Schenkelius illustratur*, Lyons, 1619.

[37] Paepp's mentions of Bruno are noted by Rossi, *Clavis universalis*, p. 125 (quoting an article by N. Badaloni). See also Rossi, 'Note Bruniane', *Rivista critica di storia della filosofia*, XIV (1959) pp. 197–203.

[38] *Eisagoge*, pp. 36–113; *Crisis*, pp. 12–13 etc.

[39] *Schenkelius detectus*, p. 21.

After quoting from the *Summa* (II, 2, 49) of Thomas Aquinas the famous treatment of memory, and emphasising what Thomas says of order in memory, he immediately follows on to a quotation from 'the fifth sermon of Trismegistus in Pimander'. He is using Ficino's *Pimander*, his Latin translation of the *Corpus Hermeticum*, the fifth treatise of which is on 'God who is both apparent and inapparent'. It is a rhapsody on the order of the universe as a revelation of God and on the Hermetic experience in which, through contemplation of this order, God is revealed. Next he passes to a quotation from the *Timaeus*, and thence to Cicero in *De oratore* on placing in order as the best aid to memory, and to *Ad Herennium* (which he still assumes to be by Cicero) on the art of memory as consisting in an order of places and images. Finally he returns to the rule of Aristotle and Thomas that frequent meditation helps memory.[40] The passage shows a transition from the places and images of the artificial memory to the order of the universe ecstatically perceived as a religious experience by 'Trismegistus'. The sequence of quotations and ideas here shows the thought-sequence through which the places and images of the Tullian and Thomist artificial memory became a technique for imprinting the universal world order on memory. Or, in other words, how the techniques of artificial memory turned into the magico-religious techniques of the occult memory.

It is a secret of the Renaissance which Paepp is still revealing in the early seventeenth century, for the fifth treatise of Trismegistus is quoted in Camillo's *L'Idea del Theatro*.[41] But it has reached him via Giordano Bruno.

Schenkel and his indiscreet disciple confirm what we have already guessed, that memory teaching with an occult side passed on with it might well become the vehicle for propagating a Hermetic religious message, or a Hermetic sect. They also show us, by contrast, what genius and power of imagination Bruno infused into material which, when treated by a Schenkel or a Paepp, sinks back to the memory treatise level. Gone now are the visions of a great Renaissance artist sculpturing within the memory statues, infusing philosophic power and religious insight into the figures of his vast cosmic imagination.

---

[40] *Crisis*, pp. 26–7.
[41] See above, p. 153. It is also alluded to by Alexander Dicson.

What are we to make of the extraordinary sequence of Giordano Bruno's works on memory? They all belong closely together, are all interlocked with one another. *Shadows* and *Circe* in France, *Seals* in England, the *Figuration* on the second visit to France, *Statues* in Germany, *Images* the last published work before the fatal return to Italy—are they all traces of the passage through Europe of a prophet of a new religion transmitting messages in a code, the memory code? Was all the intricate memory advice, were all the various systems, barriers erected to confuse the uninitiated but indicating to the initiated that behind all this there was a 'Seal of Seals', a Hermetic sect, perhaps even a politico-religious organisation?

I have drawn attention in my other book to the rumour that Bruno was said to have founded a sect in Germany called the 'Giordanisti',[42] suggesting that this might have something to do with the Rosicrucians, the mysterious brotherhood of the Rosy Cross announced by manifestos in the early seventeenth century in Germany, about which so little is known that some scholars argue that it never existed. Whether or not there is any connection between the rumoured Rosicrucians and the origins of Free-masonry, first heard of as an institution in England in 1646 when Elias Ashmole was made a mason, is again a mysterious and unsettled question. Bruno, at any rate, propagated his views in both England and Germany, so his movenents might conceivably be a common source for both Rosicrucianism and Freemasonry.[43] The origins of Freemasonry are wrapped in mystery, though supposed to derive from mediaeval guilds of 'operative' masons, or actual builders. No one has been able to explain how such 'operative' guilds developed into 'speculative' masonry, the symbolic use of architectural imagery in masonic ritual.

These subjects have been the happy hunting-ground of wildly imaginative and uncritical writers. It is time that they should be investigated with proper historical and critical methods and there are signs that that time is approaching. In the preface to a book on the genesis of Freemasonry it is stated that the history of masonry ought not to be regarded as something apart but as a branch of social history, a study of a particular institution and the ideas underlying it 'to be investigated and written in exactly the same

[42] See *G.B. and H.T.*, pp. 312–13, 320, 345, 411, 414.
[43] See *ibid.*, pp. 274, 414–16.

way as the history of other institutions'.[44] Other more recent books on the subject have been moving in the direction of exact historical investigation, but the writers of such books have to leave as an unsolved question the problem of the origin of 'speculative' masonry, with its symbolic use of columns, arches, and other architectural features, and of geometrical symbolism, as the frame-work within which it presents a moral teaching and a mystical outlook directed towards the divine architect of the universe.

I would think that the answer to this problem may be suggested by the history of the art of memory, that the Renaissance occult memory, as we have seen it in Camillo's Theatre and as it was fervently propagated by Giordano Bruno, may be the real source of a Hermetic and mystical movement which used, not the real architecture of 'operative' masonry, but the imaginary or 'specula-tive' architecture of the art of memory as the vehicle of its teachings. A careful examination of the symbolism, both of Rosicrucianism and of Freemasonry, might eventually confirm this hypothesis. Such an investigation does not belong within the scope of this book, though I will point to some indications of the lines on which it might be conducted.

The supposedly Rosicrucian manifesto or *Fama* of 1614 speaks of mysterious *rotae* or wheels, and of a sacred 'vault' the walls, ceiling and floor of which was divided into compartments each with their several figures or sentences.[45] This could be something like an occult use of artificial memory. Since for Freemasonry there are no records until much later, the comparison here would be with masonic symbolism of the late seventeenth and eighteenth centuries and particularly, perhaps, with the symbolism of that branch of masonry known as the 'Royal Arch'. Some of the old prints, banners, and aprons of Royal Arch masonry, with their designs of arches, columns, geometrical figures and emblems,[46] look as though they might well be in the tradition of occult memory.

---

[44] Douglas Knoop and G. P. Jones, *The Genesis of Freemasonry*, Manchester University Press, 1947, preface, p.v.

[45] *Allgemeine und General Reformation der gantzen weiten Welt. Beneben der Fama Fraternitas, dess Löblichen Ordens des Rosencreutzes*, Cassel, 1614, English translation in A. E. Waite, *The Real History of the Rosicrucians*, London, 1887, pp. 75, 77.

[46] See the illustrations in Bernard E. Jones, *Freemasons' Book of the Royal Arch*, London, 1957.

That tradition would have been entirely forgotten, hence the gap in the early history of masonry.

The advantage of this theory is that it provides a link between later manifestations of the Hermetic tradition in secret societies and the main Renaissance tradition. For we have seen that Bruno's secret had been a more or less open secret in the earlier Renaissance when Camillo's Theatre was such a widely publicised phenomenon. The secret was the combination of the Hermetic beliefs with the techniques of the art of memory. In the early sixteenth century this could be seen as belonging naturally into a Renaissance tradition, that of the 'Neoplatonism' of Ficino and Pico as it spread from Florence to Venice. It was an example of the extraordinary impact of the Hermetic books on the Renaissance, turning men's minds towards the *fabrica mundi*, the divine architecture of the world, as an object of religious veneration and a source of religious experience. In the later sixteenth century, the more troubled age in which Bruno passed his life, the pressures of the times, both political and religious, may have been driving the 'secret' more and more underground, but to see in Bruno only the propagator of a secret society (which he may have been) would be to lose his full significance.

For his secret, the Hermetic secret, was a secret of the whole Renaissance. As he travels from country to country with his 'Egyptian' message Bruno is transmitting the Renaissance in a very late but a peculiarly intense form. This man has to the full the Renaissance creative power. He creates inwardly the vast forms of his cosmic imagination, and when he externalises these forms in literary creation, works of genius spring to life, the dialogues which he wrote in England. Had he externalised in art the statues which he moulds in memory, or the magificent fresco of the images of the constellations which he paints in the *Spaccio della bestia trionfante*, a great artist would have appeared. But it was Bruno's mission to paint and mould within, to teach that the artist, the poet, and the philosopher are all one, for the Mother of the Muses is Memory. Nothing comes out but what has first been formed within, and it is therefore within that the significant work is done.

We can see that the tremendous force of image-forming which he teaches in the arts of memory is relevant to Renaissance imaginative creative force. But what of the frightful detail with which he expounds those arts, the revolving wheels of the *Shadows* system charged, not in general but in detail, with the contents of the worlds of nature and of man, or the even more appalling accumulations of memory rooms in the system in *Images*? Are these systems erected solely as vehicles for passing on the codes or rituals of a secret society? Or, if Bruno really believed in them, surely they are the work of a madman?

There is undoubtedly, I think, a pathological element in the compulsion for system-forming which is one of Bruno's leading characteristics. But what an intense striving after method there is in this madness! Bruno's memory magic is not the lazy magic of the *Ars notoria*, the practitioner of which just stares at a magical *nota* whilst reciting magical prayers. With untiring industry he adds wheels to wheels, piles memory rooms on memory rooms. With endless toil he forms the innumerable images which are to stock the systems; endless are the systematic possibilities and they must all be tried. There is in all this what can only be described as a scientific element, a presage on the occult plane of the preoccupation with method of the next century.

For if Memory was the Mother of the Muses, she was also to be the Mother of Method. Ramism, Lullism, the art of memory—all those confused constructions compounded of all the memory methods which crowd the later sixteenth and early seventeenth centuries—are symptoms of a search for method. Seen in the context of this growing search or urge, it is not so much the madness of Bruno's systems as their uncompromising determination to find a method which seems significant.

At the end of this attempt to make a systematic study of Bruno's works on memory, I would emphasise that I do not claim to have fully understood them. When later investigators have discovered more about the almost unknown and unstudied subjects with which this book attempts to deal, the time will be ripe for reaching a fuller understanding of these extraordinary works, and of the psychology of occult memory, than I have been able to achieve. What I have tried to do, as a necessary preliminary for understanding, is to attempt to place them in some kind of a historical context. It was the mediaeval art of memory, with its religious and ethical associations, which Bruno transformed into his occult systems which seem to me to have, possibly, a triple historical relevance. They may be developing Renaissance occult memory in the direction of secret societies. They certainly still contain the full Renaissance artistic and imaginative power. They presage the part to be played by the art of memory and Lullism in the growth of scientific method.

But no historical net, no examination of trends or influences, no psychological analysis, may ever quite serve to catch or to identify this extraordinary man, Giordano Bruno, the Magus of Memory.

Chapter XIV

THE ART OF MEMORY AND BRUNO'S ITALIAN DIALOGUES

THE art of memory as he conceived it is inseparable from Bruno's thought and religion. The magical view of nature is the philosophy which makes possible the magical power of the imagination to make contact with it, and the art of memory as transformed by Bruno was the instrument for making this contact through the imagination. It was the inner discipline of his religion, the inner means by which he sought to grasp and unify the world of appearances. Moreover, as in Camillo's theatre the occult memory was thought of as giving magical power to the rhetoric, so Bruno aspired to infuse his words with power. He wished to act upon the world as well as to reflect it, as he poured forth in poetry or prose his Hermetic philosophy of nature and the Hermetic or 'Egyptian' religion which he associated with it and of which he prophesied in England the imminent return.

We would therefore expect to find that the patterns of the occult memory as we have studied them in the memory works will be traceable in all Bruno's writings, and particularly in those for which he is most widely known—that fascinating series of dialogues in Italian[1] which he wrote in the house of the French ambassador in London, surrounded by the tumults which he so vividly describes.

---

[1] As mentioned above (see p. 294) I am excluding discussion of Bruno's Latin poems, published in Germany, which ought also to be examined in relation to his memory systems, using the version of the 'Thirty Seals' which he published in Germany.

308

In the *Cena de le ceneri* or 'Ash Wednesday Supper', published in England in 1584, is reflected Bruno's visit to Oxford and his clash with the Oxford doctors over his Ficinian or magical version of Copernican heliocentricity.[2] The dialogues have a topographical setting which takes the form of a journey through the streets of London. The journey appears to begin from the French embassy, which was situated in Butcher Row, a street running into the Strand at about the point where the Law Courts now stand, and to be directed towards the house of Fulke Greville who is said to have invited Bruno to expound his views on heliocentricity. From the description of the journey, its objective seems to be situated near Whitehall.[3] Bruno and his friends are supposed to be making their way from the embassy to the house where the mysterious 'Ash Wednesday Supper', which gives its title to the book, was to take place.

John Florio and Matthew Gwinne[4] call for Bruno at the embassy, later than he expected them, and they all start off after sunset through the dark streets. When they reach the main street (having come down Butcher Row into the Strand) they decide to turn off it towards the Thames and to continue the journey by boat. After shouting 'Oars' for a long time they succeed in hailing two elderly boatmen in an ancient, leaking boat. There are difficulties over the fare but eventually the boat starts with its passengers and proceeds extremely slowly. Bruno and Florio enliven the journey by singing verses from Ariosto's *Orlando furioso*. 'Oh feminil ingegno' chants the Nolan, followed by a rendering by Florio of 'Dove senze me, dolce mia vita' which he sang 'as though thinking of his loves'.[5] The boatmen now insisted on their landing though they were nowhere near their destination. The party found themselves in a dark and dirty lane enclosed by high walls. There was nothing for it but to struggle on, which they did, cursing the while. At last they reached again 'la grande ed ordinaria strada' (the

[2] See *G.B. and H.T.*, pp. 235 ff.
[3] Greville's house was really in Holborn. It has been suggested that he might have been lodging near Whitehall, or that Bruno was really thinking of the palace; see W. Boulting, *Giordano Bruno*, London, 1914, p. 107.
[4] Bruno, *Dialoghi italiani*, ed. Aquilecchia, pp. 26–7. The two who call for Bruno are explicitly stated in the first version of this passage to have been Florio and Gwinne; see Bruno, *La cena de le ceneri*, ed. G. Aquilecchia, Turin, 1955, p. 90 note.
[5] *Dialoghi italiani*, pp. 55–6.

Strand) only to find that they were close to the point from which they had originally started down towards the river. The boating interlude had got them nowhere. There was now some thought of giving up the whole expedition, but the philosopher remembered his mission. The task with which he is faced, though hard, is not impossible. 'Men of rare spirit who have in them something of the heroic and the divine, will climb the hill of difficulty and wring from harsh circumstances the palm of immortality. And though you may never reach the winning post nor gain the prize, cease not to run the race.'[6] They therefore decided to persevere and began to make their way along the Strand towards Charing Cross. They now encountered rough crowds, and at 'the pyramid near the mansion where three streets meet' (Charing Cross) the Nolan received a blow to which he ironically replied 'Tanchi, maester', the only English words he knew.

At last they arrive. Curious incidents occur but they are eventually seated. At the head of the table was an unnamed knight (probably Philip Sidney); Greville was on Florio's right and Bruno was on his left. Next to Bruno was Torquato, one of the doctors with whom he was to dispute; the other, Nundinio, sat facing him.

The journey is far from clear; the account of it is interrupted whilst Bruno expounds his new philosophy, his Hermetic ascent through the spheres to a liberated vision of a vast cosmos, and his interpretation of Copernican heliocentricity in a manner very different from that of Copernicus himself, who, being 'only a mathematician', did not realise the significance of his discovery. At the 'Supper' Bruno debates with the two 'pedant' doctors as to whether or not the Sun is at the centre; there are mutual misunderstandings; the 'pedants' become vindicative and the philosopher is extremely rude. The last word is with the philosopher who maintains against Aristotle, and with Hermes Trismegistus, that the earth moves because it is alive.

Bruno afterwards told the Inquisitors that this 'Supper' really took place at the French embassy.[7] Was the journey through the streets and waterways of London then entirely imaginary? I would put it in this way. The journey is something in the nature of an occult memory system through which Bruno remembers the

---

[6] *Ibid.*, p. 63.
[7] *Documenti della vita di Giordano Bruno*, ed. Spampanato, p. 121.

themes of the debate at the 'Supper'. 'To the last of the Roman places you may add the first of the Parisian places', he says in one of his memory books.[8] In the *Cena de le ceneri*, he is using 'London places', the Strand, Charing Cross, the Thames, the French embassy, a house in Whitehall, on which to remember the themes of a debate about the Sun at a Supper, themes which certainly have occult significances relating in some way to the return of magical religion heralded by the Copernican Sun.

Just before Bruno begins his account of the 'Supper' and the events leading up to it, he calls on Memory to aid him:

> And thou, Mnemnosyne mine, who art hidden beneath the thirty seals and immured within the dark prison of the shadows of ideas, let me hear thy voice sounding in my ear.
>
> Some days ago there came two messengers to the Nolan from a gentleman of the court. They informed him that this gentleman was very desirous of having some conversation with him in order to hear his defence of the Copernican theory and of other paradoxes included in his new philosophy.[9]

And then begin the expositions of Bruno's 'new philosophy' combined with the confused account of the journey to the 'Supper' and of the debate there with the 'pedants' about the Sun. The invocation to the Mnemosyne of *Seals* and *Shadows* at the beginning of the whole story seems to prove my point. Whoever wishes to know what kind of rhetoric proceeded from the occult memory, let him read the *Cena de le ceneri*.

And this magical rhetoric has exerted an extraordinary influence. Much of the legend of Bruno, the martyr for modern science and the Copernican theory, Bruno bursting out of mediaeval Aristotelian trammels into the nineteenth century, rests on the rhetorical passages in the *Cena* on the Copernican Sun and on the Hermetic ascent through the spheres.

The *Cena de le ceneri* affords an example of the development of a literary work out of the procedures of the art of memory. For the *Cena* is, of course, not a memory system; it is a set of dialogues with lively and well characterised interlocutors, the philosopher, the pedants, and others, and in which these people take part in a story, the journey to the Supper and what happened when they arrived. There is satire in the work; and comic incidents. There is,

---

[8] See above, p. 247.   [9] *Dialoghi italiani*, p. 26.

above all, drama. Bruno wrote a comedy, the *Candelaio* or 'Torch Bearer' when in Paris, and he had distinct dramatic gifts which he felt stirring within him when in England. We can thus see in the *Cena* how the art of memory could as it were develop into literature; how the streets of memory places could become populated with characters, could become the backcloth for a drama. The influence of the art of memory on literature is a practically untouched subject. The *Cena* affords an example of a work of imaginative literature the connection of which with the art of memory is undoubted.

Another interesting feature is the use of allegory within a mnemonic setting. Making their way along the memory places towards a mystical objective, the seekers meet with many impediments. They try to save time by taking an old creaking boat; this only brings them back to where they started, and in a worse case, struggling between high walls in a dark and miry lane. Back in the Strand they persevere towards Charing Cross, butted and buffeted by insensitive crowds of animal-like people. And when they do at last arrive at the Supper there is a lot of formality about where they are to sit. And the pedants are there, arguing about the Sun, or is it about the Supper? There is in the *Cena* something which reminds one of the obscure struggles of the people in Kafka's world, and that is the kind of level on which these dialogues should be read. And yet such modern parallels may be misleading; for in the *Cena* we are in the Italian Renaissance where people burst easily into love lyrics from Ariosto; and the memory places are places in Elizabethan London, where dwell mysterious knightly poets who seem here to be presiding over a very mysterious gathering.

One reading of the allegory in the occult memory places might be that the old decaying Noah's Ark of a boat was the Church which landed the pilgrim between the walls of an unsatisfactory convent, whence he escaped feeling himself entrusted with a heroic mission, only to find that the Protestants, with their Supper, were even more blind to the rays of the returning Sun of magical religion.

The irascible Magus displays his failings in this book. He is annoyed, not only with the 'pedants' but also with Greville's treatment of him, though he has nothing but praise for Sidney, that famous and cultured knight, who is 'well known to me, first by reputation when I was in Milan and France, and now, since I have been in this country, through having met him in the flesh.'[10]

This was the book which aroused the storms of protest which obliged Bruno to stay within the embassy, under the ambassador's protection.[11] And in the same year his disciple, Dicsono, was having his tussle with the Ramist. What sensations in the memory places of Elizabethan London! Though there were no genuine Black Friars making places in London on which to memorise the *Summa* of Thomas Aquinas, like Fra Agostino in Florence,[12] a heretical ex-Friar was using the ancient technique in his most extraordinary version of the Renaissance occult transformation of the art of memory.

The *Cena* ends with curious mythological adjurations addressed to those who have criticised it. 'I address all of you together, calling upon some in the name of Minerva's shield and spear, upon others in that of the noble issue of the Trojan horse, upon others by the venerable beard of Aesculapius, upon others by Neptune's trident, upon others by the kicks which the horses gave to Glaucus, and asking all so to conduct yourselves in future that we may be able to write better dialogues about you, or hold our peace.'[13] Those who had been admitted to the mysteries of some mythological memory 'Seal' might have been able to understand what all this was about.

In the dedication to Philip Sidney of his *De gli eroici furori* (1585) Bruno states that the love poetry in this work is not addressed to a woman but represents heroic enthusiasms directed towards a religion of natural contemplation. The pattern of the work is formed by a succession of about fifty emblems which are described in poems and discussed in commentaries on the poems. The images are mostly Petrarchan conceits about eyes and stars, arrows of Cupid,[14] and so on, or *impresa* shields with devices on them. These images are strongly charged with emotion. Read in the context of

[10] *Ibid.*, p. 69. [11] See above, p. 280. [12] See above, pp. 245–6.
[13] *Dialoghi italiani*, p. 171.
[14] Cf. my article 'The Emblematic Conceit in Giordano Bruno's *De gli eroici furori* and in the Elizabethan Sonnet Sequences', *Journal of the Warburg and Courtauld Institutes*, VI (1943), pp. 101–21; and *G.B. and H.T.*, pp. 275. There is now a new English translation of the *Eroici furori* by P. E. Memmo, University of North Carolina Press, 1964, with preface.

the many passages in the memory works on the need for magic memory images to be charged with affects, and particularly with the affect of love, we begin to see the love emblems of the *Eroici furori* in a new context, not, of course, as a memory system, but as traces of the memory methods in a literary work. Particularly when the series leads up towards the end to a vision of Circe the enchantress do we begin to feel ourselves within the familiar patterns of Bruno's mind.

A question may be asked here. Did the persistent tradition which associated Petrarch with memory include some view of the conceits as memory images? Such images after all contain the 'intentions' of the soul towards an object. At any rate, Bruno is using the conceits with strong intentions, as imaginative and magical means of achieving insight. A connection with *Seals* of this litany of love images is suggested by a reference to the 'contractions' or religious experiences described in the Seal of Seals.[15]

This book shows the Philosopher as Poet, pouring out the images of his memory in poetic form. The recurring poems on Actaeon, who hunts after the vestiges of the divine in nature until he is himself hunted and devoured by his dogs, express a mystical identification of subject with object, and the wildness of the chase, amidst the woods and waters of contemplation, after the divine object. Here, too, there appears a vast vision of Amphitrite, embodying like some great memory statue, the enthusiast's imaginative grasp of the monas or the One.

The plan of Bruno's *Spaccio della bestia trionfante*, published in England in 1585 and dedicated to Sidney, is based on the images of the forty-eight constellations of the sky, the northern constellations, the zodiac, and the southern constellations. I have elsewhere suggested that Bruno may have been using the *Fabularum liber* of Hyginus, with its account of the forty-eight constellation images and the mythology associated with them.[16] Bruno uses the order of the constellations as the ground plan of his sermon on virtues and vices. The 'Expulsion of the Triumphant Beast' is the expulsion of vice by virtue, and in his long sermon on this text Bruno describes in detail how to each of the forty-eight constel-

---

[15] *Dialoghi italiani*, p. 1091; cf. *G.B. and H.T.*, p. 281.
[16] *G.B. and H.T.*, p. 218.

lations virtues are triumphantly mounting whilst opposite vices descend, vanquished by virtues in the great reform of the heavens.

Johannes Romberch, the Dominican author of the memory text-book of which we have found so much evidence that it was very well known to Bruno, mentions that the *Fabularum liber* of Hyginus provides an easily memorised order of memory[17] places. It gives you, thinks Romberch, a fixed order which can be usefully used as a memory order.

Virtues and vices, rewards and punishments—were not these the basic themes of the sermons of the old friars? Romberch's advice about using Hyginus on the order of the constellations as a memory order, if adopted by a preaching friar, might have been used for memorising a sermon on virtues and vices. When Bruno in the dedication of the *Spaccio* to Sidney lists the ethical themes which he is attaching to the forty eight constellations[18] might not this have brought to mind a type of preaching very different from that now current in Elizabethan England? And such an evocation of the past would be underlined by the constant attacks in the *Spaccio* on the modern pedants who despise good works, an obvious allusion to the Calvanist emphasis on justification by faith. When Jove calls on some future Herculean deliverer to rid Europe of the miseries which afflict it, Momus adds:

It will be sufficient if that hero puts an end to that idle sect of pedants, who, without doing good according to divine and natural law, consider themselves and want to be considered religious men pleasing to the gods, and say that to do good is good, and to do ill is wicked. But they say it is not by the good that is done, or by the evil that is not done, that one becomes worthy and pleasing to the gods, but rather it is by hoping and believing according to their catechism. Behold, oh gods, if there ever existed ribaldry more open than this . . . The worst is that they defame us, saying that this (religion of theirs) is an institution of the gods; and it is with this that they criticise effects and fruits, even referring to them with the title of defects and vices. Whereas nobody works for them and they work for nobody (because their only labour is to speak ill of works), they, at the same time, live on the works of those who have

[17] Romberch, *Congestorium artificiose memorie*, p. 25 *recto*. See above, pp. 116–17.

[18] *Dialoghi italiani*, pp. 561 ff.; *The Expulsion of the Triumphant Beast*, trans. A. D. Imerti, Rutgers University Press, 1964, pp. 69 ff.

laboured for others rather than for them, and who for others have instituted temples, chapels, lodgings, hospitals, schools, and universities. Wherefore they are outright thieves and occupiers of the hereditary wealth of others who, if they are not perfect nor as good as they should be, will not be, however (as are the first), perverse and pernicious to the world, but rather will be necessary to the republic, will be experts in the speculative sciences, students of morality, solicitous of augmenting zeal and concern for helping one another and of upholding society (for which all laws are ordained) by proposing certain rewards to benefactors and threatening certain punishments to delinquents.[19]

This was the kind of thing that could not be said openly in Elizabethan England, save by someone safe in the French embassy under diplomatic protection. And in the context of the sermon on virtues and vices, memorised on the constellations, it must have been pretty clear that the ex-friar's sermon had an application to the teachings of the Calvanist 'pedants' and to the destruction which they had wrought upon the works of others. Bruno prefers to such doctrines the moral laws which the ancients taught. As a close student of the *Summa* of Thomas Aquinas he would of course know the use made of 'Tullius' and other ancient writers on ethics in the Thomist definitions of the virtues and vices.

Nevertheless, the *Spaccio* is very far from being the sermon of a mediaeval friar on virtues and vices, rewards and punishments. The personified powers of the soul who conduct the reform of the heavens are JUPITER, JUNO, SATURN, MARS, MERCURY, MINERVA, APOLLO with his magicians Circe and Medea and his physician Aesculapius, DIANA, VENUS and CUPID, CERES, NEPTUNE, THETIS, MOMUS, ISIS. These figures perceived inwardly in the soul are said to have the appearance of statues or pictures. We are in the realms of the occult memory systems based on magically animated 'statues' as memory images. I have discussed in my other book[20] the close relationship of the speakers in the *Spaccio* to the twelve principles on which the memory system of *Images* is based, and the further study of Bruno's other works on memory made in the present book brings out even more clearly that the statuesque reforming gods of the *Spaccio* belong into the context of the occult

[19] *Dialoghi italiani*, pp. 623–4; *The Expulsion*, trans. Imerti, pp. 124–5. Cf. *G.B. and H.T.*, p. 226.
[20] *G.B. and H.T.*, pp. 326 ff.

memory systems. Their reform, though based on moral laws, virtues and vices as they conceive them, includes the return of 'Egyptian' magical religion of which there is a long defence,[21] with a long quotation from the *Asclepius* on how the Egyptians knew how to make statues of the gods into which they drew down celestial powers. The Lament in the *Asclepius* for the suppression of the divine Egyptian magical religion is also quoted in full. Bruno's moral reform is thus 'Egyptian' or Hermetic in quality and the association of this side of it with the old virtue and vice preaching results, in a most curious way, in a new ethic—an ethic of natural religion and a natural morality through the following of natural laws. The virtue and vice system is related to the good and bad sides of planetary influences, and the reform is to make the good sides triumph over the bad and to emphasise the influence of good planets. Hence there is to result a personality in which Apollonian religious insight combines with Jovial respect for moral law; the natural instincts of Venus are refined into a complexion 'more gentle, more cultivated, more ingenious, more perspicacious, more understanding';[22] and a general benevolence and philanthropy is to replace the cruelties of the warring sects.

The *Spaccio* is an independent work of imaginative literature. Its dialogues may be read straightforwardly for their bold and strange treatment of many themes, for their curious humour and satire, for the dramatic treatment of the story of this reforming council of the gods, for their many touches of Lucianic irony. Nevertheless the structure of a Brunian memory system can be clearly perceived underlying the work. In his usual way he has taken a system from the memory text-books, the use of Hyginus on the order of the constellations as a memory order, and has 'occultised' it into a 'Seal' of his own. His intense concern with the actual images of the constellations can be clearly seen to belong into his magical modes of thinking as we have found them in his books on memory.

It is therefore, I think, justifiable to say that the *Spaccio* represents the type of celestial rhetoric which goes with a Brunian occult memory system. The speeches, listing the epithets describing the good sides of the influences of the planetary gods, would be

---

[21] *Ibid.*, pp. 211 ff.

[22] On echoes of the *Spaccio* in Berowne's speech on love in Shakespeare's *Love's Labour's Lost*, see *G.B. and H.T.*, p. 356.

supposed to be infused with planetary power, like the oratory emanating from Camillo's memory system. The *Spaccio* is the magical sermon of the ex-friar.

In the heated atmosphere surrounding Bruno's controversy with the Oxford doctors and the controversy of his disciple with the Cambridge Ramist, the *Spaccio* would not have been read in the calm and detached spirit with which the modern student approaches it. Its 'Scepsian' memory system would surely have been clearly visible to all in view of the recent controversies. The anxieties of William Perkins must have been considerably increased by the dedication of such a work as this to Sidney. The 'Egyptian' lengths to which 'Scepsians' like Nolano and Dicsono might go were indeed made evident in the *Spaccio*. Yet to some this strange work might have come as a blinding revelation of an imminent universal Hermetic religious and moral reform, presented in the splendid imagery of some great Renaissance work of art, painted and sculptured within by the memory artist.

The Italian dialogues with their underlying memory Seals would refer the reader back to *Seals* as the operative Brunian work, the one which opened his whole campaign in England and made the art of memory a crucial issue. The reader of *Seals* who had penetrated to the Seal of Seals might hear the Italian dialogues poetically, see them artistically, and understand them philosophically, as sermons on the religion of Love, Art, Magic, and Mathesis.

Such were the influences emanating from the strange occupant of the French embassy during the years 1583 to 1586. These were the crucial years, the germinal years, for the inception of the English poetic Renaissance, ushered in by Philip Sidney and his group of friends. It was to this circle that Bruno addressed himself, dedicating to Sidney the two most significant dialogues, the *Eroici furori* and the *Spaccio*. In words strangely prophetic of his future fate, he speaks of himself in the *Spaccio* dedications:

> We see how this man, as a citizen and servant of the world, a child of Father Sun and Mother Earth, because he loves the world too much, must be hated, censured, persecuted and extinguished by it. But, in the meantime, may he not be idle or badly employed while awaiting his death, his transmigration, his change. Let him today present to Sidney the numbered and arranged seeds of his moral philosophy . . .[23]

[23] *The Expulsion of the Triumphant Beast*, trans. Imerti, p. 70.

(Numbered and arranged indeed they are, as in a celestial memory system.) Nor do we now have to rely only on the dedications for evidence of the significance of Bruno in Sidney's circle; we have seen how the issues associated with the 'Scepsians', Nolano and Dicsono, in their controversies with Aristotelians and Ramists seem to hover around Sidney. Sidney's inseparable friend, Fulke Greville, figures as host at the mysterious Supper, and is mentioned in the *Spaccio* dedication as 'that second man who, after your (i.e. Sidney's) first good offices, extended and offered to me the second'.[24] Surely Bruno's impact on England must have been the supreme experience of these years, a sensation closely associated with the leaders of the English Renaissance.

And what of the influence of this impact on him who was to be the supreme manifestation of this very late Renaissance? Shakespeare was nineteen when Bruno came to England and twenty-two when he left it. We do not know in what year Shakespeare came to London and began his career as actor and playwright; we only know that it must have been some time before 1592 when he was already well established. Amongst the scraps of evidence or rumour about Shakespeare there is one which connects him with Fulke Greville. In a book published in 1665 it is said of Greville that

> One great argument for his worth, was his respect for the worth of others, desiring to be known to posterity under no other notions than of Shakespeare's and Ben Johnson's Master, Chancellor Egerton's Patron, Bishop Overall's Lord, and Sir Philip Sidney's friend.[25]

It is not known when, or in what way, Greville may have been Shakespeare's master. But it is likely that Shakespeare may have known Greville for they both came from Warwickshire;[26] Greville's family seat was near Stratford-on-Avon. When the young man from Stratford came to London it is therefore possible that he might have had access to Greville's house and circle, where he might have learned to know what it meant to use the zodiac in artificial memory, like Metrodorus of Scepsis.

[24] *Ibid.*, p. 70
[25] David Lloyd, *Statesmen and Favourites of England since the Reformatiom*, 1665; quoted in E. K. Chambers, *William Shakespeare*, Oxford, 1930, II, p. 250.
[26] See T. W. Baldwin, *The Organisation and Personnel of the Shakespearean Company*, Princeton, 1927, p. 291 note.

❖◇❖

Chapter XV

THE THEATRE MEMORY SYSTEM
OF ROBERT FLUDD

❖◇❖

D URING the period of the English Renaissance, the Hermetic influences were at their height in Europe, but no full-scale treatment of Hermetic philosophy by an Englishman was published until the reign of James I. Robert Fludd[1] is one of the best-known of Hermetic philosophers, and his numerous and abstruse works, many of them beautifully illustrated with hieroglyphic engravings, have been attracting a good deal of attention in recent years. Fludd was in the full Renaissance Hermetic Cabalist tradition as it had descended from Ficino and Pico della Mirandola. He was saturated in the *Corpus Hermeticum,* which he read in Ficino's translation, and in the *Asclepius,* and it is hardly an exaggeration to say that quotations from the works of 'Hermes Trismegistus' are to be found on nearly every page of his works. He was also a Cabalist, in descent from Pico della Mirandola and Reuchlin, and so closely does Fludd seem to represent the Renaissance occult tradition that I have elsewhere used some of the engraved illustrations in his works, with their diagrammatic presentations of his outlook, to clarify the earlier Renaissance synthesis.[2]

But Fludd lived in times when the Renaissance modes of Hermetic and magical thinking were under attack from the rising

---

[1] On Fludd's life and works, see the article in the *Dictionary of National Biography,* and J. B. Craven, *Doctor Robert Fludd,* Kirkwall, 1902. Fludd was actually of Welsh descent.

[2] See *G.B. and H.T.,* Pls. 7, 8, 10, 16, and pp. 403 ff.

a   b

c   d

e   f

13   Pictures illustrating the Principles of the Art of Memory
From Agostino del Riccio, *Arte della memoria locale*, 1595,
Biblioteca Nazionale, Florence (MS. II, 1, 13) (pp. 244-6)

generation of seventeenth-century philosophers. The authority of the *Hermetica* was weakened when Isaac Casaubon, in 1614, dated them as having been written in post-Christian times.[3] Fludd totally ignored this dating and continued to regard the *Hermetica* as the actual writings of the most ancient Egyptian sage. His passionate defence of his beliefs and outlook brought him into active conflict with the leaders of the new age. His controversies with Mersenne and with Kepler are famous, and in these controversies he appears in the character of a 'Rosicrucian'. Whether or not the Rosicrucians actually existed, it is a fact that the manifestos announcing the existence of a brotherhood of the Rosy Cross aroused immense excitement and interest in the early years of the seventeenth century. In his earliest works, Fludd announced himself a disciple of the Rosicrucians and became identified by the general public with the mysterious and invisible brotherhood and its elusive aims.

We have always found that the Hermetic or occult philosopher is likely to be interested in the art of memory, and Fludd is no exception to this rule. Coming as he does so very late in the Renaissance, at a time when the Renaissance philosophies are about to give way before the rising movements of the seventeenth century, Fludd erects what is probably the last great monument of Renaissance memory. And, like its first great monument, Fludd's memory system takes a theatre as its architectural form. Camillo's Theatre opened our series of Renaissance memory systems; Fludd's Theatre will close it.

Since, as will be suggested in the next chapter, Fludd's memory system may have a rather breath-taking importance as a reflection —distorted by the mirrors of magic memory—of Shakespeare's Globe Theatre, I hope that the reader will bear with my painstaking efforts in this chapter to break the last of the Seals of Memory with which I shall confront him.

The memory system is to be found in the work which is Fludd's most characteristic and complete presentation of his philosophy. It has the cumbrous title *Utriusque Cosmi, Maioris scilicet et Minoris, metaphysica, physica, atque technica Historia*. The 'greater and lesser worlds' which this history claims to cover are the great

---

[3] See *ibid.*, pp. 399 ff. The book in which Casaubon dated the *Hermetica* was dedicated to James I.

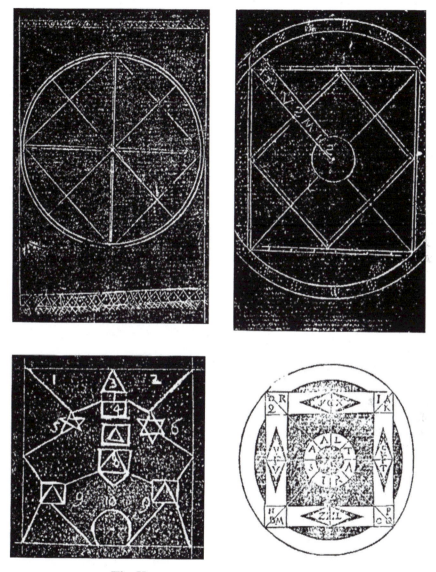

14a ABOVE LEFT   The Heaven

14b ABOVE RIGHT   The Potter's Wheel

'Seals' from Bruno's *Triginta Sigilli* etc. London, 1583 (pp. 248, 250)

14c LEFT   Memory system from Bruno's *Figuratio Aristotelici physici auditus* (*Figuration of Aristotle*), Paris, 1586 (p. 288)

14d Memory system from Bruno's *De imaginum compositione*, Frankfort, 1591 (p. 297)

world of the macrocosm, the universe, and the little world of man, the microcosm. His views on the universe and on man are supported by Fludd with many quotations from 'Hermes Trismegistus' in *Pimander* (that is, Ficino's Latin translation of the *Corpus Hermeticum*) and in the *Asclepius*. With his magico-religious Hermetic outlook he unites Cabalism, thus completing the world-view of the Renaissance Magus more or less as we found it many years earlier in Camillo's Theatre.

This monumental work was published by John Theodore de Bry at Oppenheim in Germany in parts.[4] The first part of the first volume (1617), the one on the macrocosm, opens with two extremely mystical dedications, the first to God, the second to James I as God's representative on earth. The second volume, on the microcosm, came out in 1619 with a dedication to God in which the Deity is defined with many quotations from Hermes Trismegistus. There is now no mention of James I, but since in the

---

[4] Robert Fludd, *Utriusque Cosmi Maioris Scilicet et Minoris, Metaphysica, Physica atque Technica Historia.*

Tomus Primus. De Macrocosmi Historia in duos tractatus divisa.

De Metaphysico Macrocosmi et Creaturum illius ortu etc., Oppenheim, Aere Johan-Theodori de Bry. Typis Hieronymi Galleri, 1617.

De Naturae Simia seu Technica Macrocosmi Historia, Oppenheim, Aere Johan-Theodori de Bry. Typis Hieronymi Galleri, 1618.

Tomus Secundus. De Supernaturali, Naturali, Praeternaturali et Contranaturali Microcosmi Historia . . . Oppenheim, Impensis Johannis Theodori de Bry, typis Hieronymi Galleri, 1619.

Sectio I. Metaphysica atque Physica . . . Microcosmi Historia.

Sectio II. Technica Microcosmi Historia.

De praeternaturali utriusque mundi historia, Frankfort, typus Erasmeri Kempferi, sumptibus Johan-Theodori de Bry, 1621.

(To this volume there is attached at the end a reply by Fludd to Kepler, entitled *Veritatis proscenium* etc.)

From this setting-out of the complex publication of the work, it can be seen that *Tomus Primus*, on the macrocosm, was published in two parts in 1617 and 1618; *Tomus Secundus*, on the microcosm, was published in 1619 (the Frankfort publication of 1621 was a later part of this volume). John Theodore de Bry, the publisher of the whole series, was the son of Theodore de Bry (who died in 1598) whose publishing and engraving business he inherited. John Theodore de Bry is stated on the title-pages of *Tomus Primus* to be responsible for the engravings ('aere Johan-Theodori de Bry'), but this is not stated on the title-pages of *Tomus Secundus*. The engraved title-page of *De Naturae Simia* (1618) is signed 'M. Merian sculp.'. Matthieu Merian was John Theodore de Bry's son-in-law and a member of the firm.

dedication of the first volume he was very closely associated with the Deity, presumably his presence is still implied in the dedication of the second volume to the Deity alone. It is almost as though Fludd calls on James in these dedications as Defender of the Hermetic Faith.

At about this time we know that Fludd was appealing very specially to James to support him against the attacks of his enemies. A manuscript in the British Museum, of probably about 1618, contains a 'Declaration' by Robert Fludd about his printed works and his views addressed to James.[5] He defends both himself and the Rosicrucians as harmless followers of divine and ancient philosophies, mentions the dedication of the *Macrocosm* to James, and appends testimonials from foreign scholars about the value of his writings. The dedication to James of the work, the second volume of which contains the memory system, thus belongs to a period of his life when he felt himself to be under attack and wished very particularly to enlist the support of the King.

Fludd was living in England at the time when he wrote this and other works, yet he did not publish this or his other works in England. This fact was noted as detrimental by one of his enemies. In 1631, a certain Dr. William Foster, an Anglican parson, attacked Fludd's Paracelsan medicine as magical, alluded to the fact that Marin Mersenne had called him a magician, and insinuated that it was because of his reputation as a magician that he did not publish his works in England. 'I suppose this to be one cause why he hath printed his bookes beyond the Seas. Our Universities and our Reverend Bishops (God bee thanked) are more cautelous than to allow the Printing of Magical books here.'[6] In his reply to Foster (with whom he said that he did not differ in religion) Fludd took up the references to his controversy with Mersenne. 'Mersenne has accused me of magic, and Foster wonders how King James allowed me to live and write in his

---

[5] Robert Fludd, 'Declaratio brevis Serenessimo et Potentissimo Principe ac Domine Jacobo Magnae Britanniae . . . Regi', British Museum, MS. Royal 12 C ii.

[6] William Foster, *Hoplocrisma-Spongus: or A Sponge to wipe away the Weapon-Salve*, London, 1631. The 'weapon-salve' was an ointment recommended by Fludd which Foster states to be dangerously magical, and Paracelsan in origin.

kingdom.'[7] Fludd says that he was able to convince King James of the innocency of his works and intentions (alluding probably to the 'Declaration') and points to the fact that he dedicated a book to James (alluding certainly to the dedication of the *Utriusque Cosmi . . . Historia*) as evidence that there was nothing wrong with them. And he firmly rejected Foster's explanation of why he sent his works beyond the seas to be printed. 'I sent them beyond the Seas because our home-borne Printers demanded five hundred pounds to print the first volume and to find the cuts in copper; but beyond the Seas it was printed at no cost of mine, and that as I would wish . . .'[8] Though Fludd published a good many books with engraved illustrations beyond the seas, this remark almost certainly refers particularly to the *Utriusque Cosmi . . . Historia*, both volumes of which are illustrated with a remarkable series of engravings.

The illustrations of his works was very important to Fludd for it was part of his purpose to present his philosophy visually or in 'hieroglyphics'. This aspect of Fludd's philosophy came out in his controversy with Kepler, when the mathematician taunted him with his 'pictures' and 'hieroglyphs', with his use of number 'after the Hermetic fashion', as compared with the genuinely mathematical diagrams in Kepler's own works.[9] Fludd's pictures and hieroglyphics are often extremely complicated and it would matter very much to him that they should correspond accurately with his complicated text. How did Fludd communicate to the publisher and engraver in Germany his wishes about the illustrations?

If Fludd needed a trusty emissary to carry his text and materials for the illustrations to Oppenheim, there was one at hand in Michael Maier. This man, who had belonged to the circle of the Emperor Rudolph II, certainly believed in the existence of Rosicrucians and believed that he was himself one of them. It is said

[7] *Dr. Fludd's Answer unto M. Foster, or The Squesing of Parson Foster's Sponge ordained for him by the wiping away of the Weapon-Salve*, London, 1631, p. 11.

[8] *Ibid.*, pp. 21–2. *The Squesing of Parson Foster's Sponge*, the only book which Fludd published in England, was evidently regarded as a work of more than local interest and belonging into the great international controversies of the day, for a Latin version of it was published at Gouda in 1638 (R. Fludd, *Responsum ad Hoplocrisma-Spongum M. Fosteri Presbiteri*, Gouda, 1638).

[9] See *G.B. and H.T.*, pp. 442–3.

to have been he who persuaded Fludd to write his *Tractatus Theologo-Philosophicus*, dedicated to the Brothers of the Rosy Cross, and published by De Bry at Oppenheim.[10] Moreover, it is said to have been Maier who took this work of Fludd's to Oppenheim to be printed.[11] Maier came and went a good deal between England and Germany and at about this time he was having works of his own printed by De Bry at Oppenheim.[12] There was therefore an emissary, Maier, who might have taken Fludd's materials for the illustrations of the *Utriusque Cosmi . . . Historia* to Oppenheim in order that the book might be published 'as I would wish', as he says was done.

The point is of some importance for the Theatre memory system is illustrated and the problem will arise (in the next chapter) as to how far one of these illustrations can be depended on as reflecting a real stage in London.

To resume this brief introduction to the *Utriusque Cosmi . . . Historia*, it may be said that this book is in the Renaissance Hermetic-Cabalist tradition; that it taps the tradition at the time of the 'Rosicrucian' furore; that its dedication attempts to enlist James I as defender of the tradition; that liaison between Fludd in England and the publisher in Germany could have been effected through Michael Maier or through channels of communication between the De Bry firm and England established during the earlier publishing enterprises.

In view of this significant historical situation of the book, it is significant to find that it contains an occult memory system, a memory 'Seal', the complexity and mystery of which are worthy of Bruno himself.

---

[10] See J. B. Craven, *Count Michael Maier*, Kirkwall, 1910, p. 6.

[11] See Craven, *Doctor Robert Fludd*, p. 46.

[12] Maier's *Atalanta fugiens*, with its remarkable illustrations, was published by John Theodore de Bry at Oppenheim in 1617; his *Viatorum hoc est de montibus planetarum* was published by the same firm in 1618.

It should be added that channels of business communication between the De Bry firm and England may well have been established by the elder De Bry (Theodore de Bry) who published in *America* engravings after the drawings of John White. Theodore de Bry visited England in 1587 to collect materials and illustrations for his publications of voyages of discovery. See P. Hulton and D. B. Quinn, *The American Drawings of John White*, London, 1964, I, pp. 25–6.

Fludd treats of the art of memory in the second volume of his *History of the Two Worlds*, the one on man as microcosm, where he gives what he calls 'the technical history of the microcosm' by which he means the technich or arts used by the microcosm. The contents of this part are usefully set out in visual form at the beginning of it. Homo, the microcosm, has above his head a triangular glory marking his divine origin; below his feet is a monkey, Fludd's favourite symbol of the art by which man imitates, or reflects, nature. The segments of the circle show the arts or technics about to be treated, and which are in fact treated in this order in the following chapters. They are:—Prophecy, Geomancy, Art of Memory, Genethliology (the art of horoscope making), Physiognomics, Chiromancy, Pyramids of Science. The art of memory is designated by five memory *loci* with images on them. The context in which we see the art of memory here is instructive; its places and images are next door to the horoscope diagram, marked with the signs of the zodiac. Other magical and occult arts are in the series which also includes prophecy, suggesting mystical and religious connotations, and the pyramids which are Fludd's favourite symbol of up and down movement, or interaction between the divine or the spiritual and the terrestrial or the corporeal.

The chapter on 'the science of spiritual memorising which is vulgarly called *Ars Memoriae*'[13] is introduced by a picture illustrating this science (Pl. 15). We see a man with a large 'eye of imagination' in the fore part of his head; and beside him five memory loci containing memory images. Five is Fludd's favourite number for a group of memory places, as will appear later, and the diagram also illustrates his principle of having one main image in a memory room. The main image is an obelisk; the others are the Tower of Babel, Tobias and the Angel, a ship, and the Last Judgment with the damned entering the mouth of Hell—an interesting relic in this very late Renaissance system of the mediaeval virtue of remembering Hell by the artificial memory. These five images are nowhere explained or referred to in the following text. I do not know whether they are intended to be read allegorically—the obelisk as an Egyptian symbol referring to the 'inner writing' of the art which will overcome the confusions of

[13] *Utriusque Cosmi . . . Historia*, Tomus Secundus, sectio 2, pp. 48 ff.

326

Babel and conduct its user under angelic guidance to religious safety. This may be over fanciful, and in the absence of any explanation by Fludd it is better to leave them unexplained.

After some of the usual definitions of artificial memory, Fludd devotes a chapter[14] to explaining the distinction which he makes between two different types of art, which he calls respectively the 'round art (*ars rotunda*)', and the 'square art (*ars quadrata*).'

> For the complete perfection of the art of memory the fantasy is operated in two ways. The first way is through *ideas*, which are forms separated from corporeal things, such as spirits, shadows (*umbrae*), souls and so on, also angels, which we chiefly use in our *ars rotunda*. We do not use this word 'ideas' in the same way that Plato does, who is accustomed to use it of the mind of God, but for anything which is not composed of the four elements, that is to say for things spiritual and simple conceived in the imagination; for example angels, demons, the effigies of stars, the images of gods and goddesses to whom celestial powers are attributed and which partake more of a spiritual than of a corporeal nature; similarly virtues and vices conceived in the imagination and made into shadows, which were also to be held as demons.[15]

The 'round art', then, uses magicised or talismanic images, effigies of the stars; 'statues' of gods and goddesses animated with celestial influences; images of virtues and vices, as in the old mediaeval art, but now thought of as containing 'demonic' or magical power. Fludd is working at a classification of images into potent and less potent such as was Bruno's constant preoccupation.

The 'square art' uses images of corporeal things, of men, of animals, of inanimate objects. When its images are of men or of animals, these are active, engaged in actions of some kind. The 'square art' sounds like the ordinary art of memory, using the active images of *Ad Herennium* and perhaps 'square' because using buildings or rooms as places. These two arts, the round and the square, are the only two possible arts of memory, states Fludd.

> Memory can only be artificially improved, either by medicaments, or by the operation of the fantasy towards *ideas* in the round art, or through images of corporeal things in the square art.[16]

---

[14] *Ibid.*, p. 50.   [15] *Ibid., loc. cit.*   [16] *Ibid.*, pp. 50–1.

The practice of the round art, though it is quite different from the art with the 'ring of Solomon' of which Fludd heard rumours at Toulouse (and which must have been blackly magical), demands nevertheless, he says, the assistance of demons (in the sense of daemonic powers not of demons in Hell) or the metaphysical influence of the Holy Spirit. And it is necessary that 'the fantasy should concur in the metaphysical act.'[17]

Many people, continues Fludd, prefer the square art because it is easier, but the round art is infinitely the superior of the two. For the round art is 'natural' using 'natural' places and is naturally adapted to the microcosm. Whereas the square art is 'artificial' using artificially made up places and images.

Fludd then devotes a whole, fairly long chapter, to a polemic against the use of 'fictitious places' in the square art.[18] To understand this we must remind ourselves of the age long distinction, stemming from *Ad Herennium* and the other classical sources between 'real' and 'fictitious' memory places. 'Real' places are real buildings of any kind used for forming places in the normal way in the mnemotechnic. 'Fictitious' places are imaginary buildings or imaginary places of any kind which the author of *Ad Herennium* said might be invented if not enough real places were available. The distinction between 'real' and 'fictitious' places went on for ever in the memory treatises with much elaborate glossing on these themes. Fludd is very much against the use of 'fictitious' buildings in the square art. These confuse memory and add to its task. One must always use real places in real buildings. 'Some who are versed in this art wish to place their square art in palaces fabricated or erected by invention of the imagination; that this opinion is inconvenient we will now briefly explain.'[19] So opens the chapter

[17] *Ibid.*, p. 51. The extremely magical art of memory of which Fludd has heard at Toulouse sounds like the *ars notoria*. Fludd might possibly be referring to Jean Belot who had been publishing in France earlier in the century works on chiromancy, physiognomy, and the art of memory (on Belot, see Thorndike, *History of Magic and Experimental Science*, VI, pp. 360–3). Belot's highly magical artificial memory, in which he mentions Lull, Agrippa, and Bruno, is reprinted in the edition of his *Oeuvres*, Lyons, 1654, pp. 329 ff. The art of memory by R. Saunders (*Physiognomie and Chiromancie . . . whereunto is added the Art of Memory*, London, 1653, 1671) is based on that of Belot and repeats his mention of Bruno. Saunders dedicated his book to Elias Ashmole.

[18] *Utriusque Cosmi . . . Historia*, II, 2, pp. 51–2.

[19] *Ibid.*, p. 51.

against the use of fictitious places in the square art. It is an important chapter for, if true to these strongly held views against fictitious places, the buildings which Fludd will use in his memory system will be 'real' buildings.

Having laid down his distinction between the *ars rotunda* and the *ars quadrata* and the different kinds of images to be used in each, and having made clear his view that the *ars quadrata* must always use real buildings, Fludd now arrives at the exposition of his memory system.[20] This is a combination of the round and the square. Based on the round heavens, the zodiac and the spheres of the planets, it uses in combination with these, buildings which are to be placed in the heavens, buildings containing places with memory images on them which will be, as it were, astrally activated by being organically related to the stars. We have met this kind of thing before. In fact the idea is exactly the same as that in Bruno's *Images*,[21] where he used sets of *atria* or rooms, cubicles, and 'fields', crammed with images, and activated by being organically affiliated to his 'round' art, the images in which were gods and goddesses to whom celestial influences were attributed. Bruno had also laid down the distinction between what Fludd calls the 'round' and the 'square' arts in his *Seals* published in England thirty-six years before Fludd's work.[22]

The striking and exciting feature of Fludd's memory system is that the memory buildings which are to be placed in the heavens in this new combination of the round and the square arts, are what he calls 'theatres'. And by this word 'theatre' he does not mean what we should call a theatre, a building consisting of a stage and an auditorium. He means a stage. The truth of this statement that the 'theatre' which Fludd illustrates is really a stage, will be amply proved later. It will, however, be useful to state it here in advance before starting on the memory system.

The 'common place' of the *ars rotunda*, states Fludd, is 'the ethereal part of the world, that is the celestial orbs numbered from the eighth sphere and ending in the sphere of the moon.'[23] This statement is illustrated by a diagram (Pl. 16) showing the eighth sphere, or zodiac, marked with the signs of the zodiac, and

[20] *Ibid.*, pp. 54 ff.   [21] See above, pp. 295 ff.
[22] See above, p. 249.
[23] *Utriusque Cosmi . . . Historia*, II, 2, p. 54.

enclosing seven circles representing the spheres of the planets, and a circle representing the sphere of the elements at the centre. This represents, say Fludd, a 'natural' order of memory places based on the zodiac, and also a temporal order through the movement of the spheres in relation to time.[24]

On either side of the sign Aries, two small buildings are shown. They are tiny 'theatres', or stages. These two 'theatres', in this actual form with two doors at the back of the stage, are never illustrated again nor referred to in the text. An occult memory system always has many unexplained *lacunae* and I do not understand why Fludd never afterwards mentions these two 'theatres'. I can only suppose that they are placed here on the cosmic diagram as a kind of advance statement of the principle of this memory system, which will use 'theatres', buildings containing memory *loci* after the manner of the *ars quadrata*, but placed on the great common place of the *ars rotunda*, that is placed in the zodiac.

Exactly facing the diagram of the heavens, on the next page of the book, there is an engraving of a 'theatre' (Pl. 17). The diagram of the heavens and the picture of the 'theatre' are placed on opposite pages in such a manner that, when the book is closed, the heavens cover the theatre. This theatre, as already stated, is not a complete theatre but a stage. The wall facing us, as we gaze at it, is its *frons scaenae*, containing five entrances, as in the classical *frons scaenae*. This is, however, not a classical stage. It is an Elizabethan or Jacobean multilevel stage. Three of the entrances are on ground level; two are arches, but the central one can be closed by heavy hinged doors which are shown half open. The other two entrances are on an upper level; they open on to a battlemented terrace. In the centre, as a very noticeable feature of this stage, there is a kind of bay window, or an upper chamber or room.

This picture of a 'theatre' or stage is introduced by Fludd with the following words:

---

[24] If this, the basic diagram for the *ars rotunda*, is compared with the design on the title-page of the first volume of the *Utriusque Cosmi . . . Historia*, we see there the temporal revolution visually depicted through the rope wound round macrocosm and microcosm which Time is pulling. We can also understand by comparison with this picture, in which the microcosm is represented within the macrocosm, why the 'round' art of memory is the 'natural' one for the microcosm.

> I call a theatre (a place in which) all actions of words, of sentences, of particulars of a speech or of subjects are shown, *as in a public theatre in which comedies and tragedies are acted.*[25]

Fludd is going to use this theatre as a memory place system for memory for words and memory for things. But the theatre itself is like 'a public theatre in which comedies and tragedies are acted.' Those great wooden theatres in which the works of Shakespeare and others were played were technically known as 'public theatres'. In view of Fludd's strong convictions about the undesirability of using 'fictitious places' in memory, can we assume that this is a real stage in a public theatre which he is showing us?

The chapter containing the illustration of the theatre is headed 'The description of the eastern and western theatres' and it appears that there are to be two of these theatres, the one 'eastern' and the other 'western', identical in plan but different in colour. The eastern theatre is to be light, bright and shining, since it will hold actions belonging to the day. The western theatre will be dark, black and obscure, belonging to the night. Both are to be placed in the heavens, and refer, presumably, to the day and night 'houses' of the planets. Is there to be an eastern and a western theatre for each of the signs of the zodiac? Are they to be placed as we see those two little stages on each side of Aries on the plan, but not only with one sign but all round the heavens? I rather think so. But we are in the realms of occult memory and it is not easy to follow how these theatres in the heavens are supposed to work.

The closest comparison for this system is Bruno's system in *Images* in which elaborate arrangements of memory rooms containing places for memory images (as in what Fludd calls the 'square' art) are affiliated to a 'round' or celestial system. Similarly (or so I believe) Fludd's 'theatres' are memory rooms which are to be affiliated to the round heavens by being placed in the zodiac. If he intends that two such 'theatres' are to be placed with each sign, then the 'theatre' which he illustrates would be one of twenty-four identical memory rooms. The 'eastern' and 'western' or day and night theatres introduce time into a system which is attached to the revolution of the heavens. It is of course a highly occult or magical system, based on belief in the macrocosm-microcosm relationship.

[25] *Utriusque Cosmi . . . Historia*, II, 2, p. 55.

On the bay window of the 'theatre' are inscribed the words THEATRUM ORBI. Since Fludd and the highly educated engraver certainly knew Latin it seems difficult to believe that this can be a mistake for THEATRUM ORBIS. I suggest therefore (though with diffidence) that the dative case is intentional and that the inscription means, not that this is a 'Theatre of the World' but one of the 'theatres' or stages to be placed with or in the world, that is in the heavens shown on the opposite page.

'Each of the theatres will have five doors distinct from one another and about equidistant, the use of which we will explain later'[26] says Fludd. Thus the five doors or entrances seen in the picture of the 'theatre' are confirmed by the text which states that the theatres have five doors. There is agreement between picture and text about this. The use of the five doors in the theatres which Fludd explains later is that they are to serve as five memory *loci*, which stand in a relationship with five columns to which they are said to be opposite.[27] The bases of these five columns are shown in the foreground of the picture of the 'theatre'. One is round, the next square, the central one is hexagonal, and then come another square one and another round one. 'There are to be feigned five columns, distinguished from one another by shape and colour. The shapes of the two at each extremity are circular and round; the middle column will have the figure of a hexagon; and the intermediary ones will be square.'[28] Here again the picture corresponds with the text, for the picture shows the bases of columns of these shapes and arranged in this order.

These columns, continues Fludd, are of different colours, corresponding to 'the colours of the doors of the theatres opposite to them'. These doors are to be used as five memory *loci* and are to be distinguished from one another by being remembered as different in colour. The first door will be white, the second red, the third green, the fourth blue, the fifth black.[29] The correspondence

[26] *Ibid.*, *loc. cit.*

[27] *Ibid.*, p. 63.

[28] 'His pratis oppositae fingantur quinque columnae, quae itidem debent figura & colore distingui; Figura enim duarum extremarum erit circularis & rotunda, mediae autem columna habebit figuram hexagoneam, & quae his intermedia sunt quadratam possidebunt figuram' (*Ibid*, p. 63). Though he speaks of 'fields' (*prata*) here, he is thinking of the five doors as memory fields or places.

[29] *Ibid.*, *loc. cit.*

between the doors and the columns is perhaps indicated in the picture of the 'theatre' by the geometrical forms shown on the battlemented terrace. I do not understand how these correspondencies are supposed to work in detail, though it is clear that the main central door on ground level would correspond to the main central column in the shape of a hexagon, and the other four doors to the four circular and square columns.

With this set of ten places, five doors and five columns, in all the 'theatres', Fludd is proposing to remember things and words in his magical memory system. Though he does not mention the rules of *Ad Herennium* in connection with the doors and the columns he certainly has these in mind. The doors are spaced to form suitable memory places. The columns are of different shapes so that they may not be too much alike and confuse the memory. The notion of remembering memory *loci* as of different colours as an additional help for distinguishing between them is not in *Ad Herennium* but is often advised in the memory treatises.

The system works through being hitched to the stars, or rather to the 'principle ideas' as Fludd calls them in a chapter on the relation of the planets to the signs of the zodiac.[30] This chapter gives the celestial basis of the system; and it is immediately followed by the chapter on the five doors and five columns in the memory theatres. The heavens work together with the theatres, and the theatres are in the heavens. The 'round' and the 'square' art are united to form a memory 'Seal', or an occult memory system of extreme complexity. Fludd never uses the word 'Seal', but his memory system is undoubtedly of a Brunian type.

Two other 'theatres' (Pl. 18a, b) are illustrated in Fludd's text. These are not multilevel stages like the main theatres but more like rooms with one wall left out so that the spectator looks into them. They have a matching connection with the main theatres through the battlements on their walls which are of a similar design to the battlements on the terraces of the main theatres. These subsidiary theatres are also to be used as memory rooms. One has three doors and the other five; in the one with five doors there is a similar system of columns, indicated by their bases, and working in connection with the doors, as in the main theatres. These subsidiary theatres connect with the main theatres and through them with the heavens.

[30] *Ibid.*, p. 62.

333

We have spoken of the 'places' in Fludd's system; the main 'common place' is the heavens with which are connected the theatres as memory rooms. What about the second aspect of memory, 'images'? What does Fludd have to say about these?

For his basic or celestial images he used talismanic or magic images such as Bruno uses on the central wheel of *Shadows*. The images of the signs of the zodiac and the characters of the planets are shown on the plan of the heavens, but not images of decans, planets, houses, and so on. We can however gather that Fludd was thinking on the lines of such images when in his chapter on 'the order of the principle ideas through the spheres of the planets' he analyses the progression of Saturn through the zodiac, giving different images of Saturn in different signs, and says that the same may be done with other planets.[31] These would be the celestial or magically operative images to be used in the 'round' part of the system.

After this chapter on images of the 'principle ideas' comes one on 'less principal images' which are to be put in the theatres, on the doors and the columns. These are the images to be used in the 'square' part of the art. They are to be formed in accordance with the rules for striking images in *Ad Herennium*, from which Fludd quotes, but as it were magicised in this magical system. Amongst the sets of five images to be used in the theatres are Jason holding the golden fleece, Medea, Paris, Daphne, Phoebus. Another set is Medea collecting magic herbs, to be put on the white door; Medea killing her brother on the red door; and Medea in other aspects on the other three doors.[32] There is another set of five Medea images;[33] also some Circe images. The magic of these sorceresses must have been very helpful to the system.

Like Bruno, Fludd is deeply involved in the complexities of the old memory treatises which survive in the midst of the magic and add to its obscurity. Lists of names or things in alphabetical order of the type so dear to writers like Romberch and Rossellius are given, but now made mysterious through their involvement in an occult art. Amongst such lists as given by Fludd are all the main mythological figures, and also lists of virtues and vices—the latter reminding us of mediaeval artificial memory in the midst of the extraordinary farrago.

[31] *Ibid., loc. cit.*   [32] *Ibid.*, p. 65.   [33] *Ibid.*, p. 67.

Fludd indeed makes very clear his attachment to the old memory treatise tradition by including illustrated specimens of 'visual alphabets'.[34] The visual alphabet was a sort of sign manual of the old memory treatises. Probably already adumbrated by Boncompagno in the thirteenth century, we have met it again and again in Publicius, Romberch, Rossellius, and so on.[35] Bruno though he never actually illustrates a visual alphabet, frequently refers to them or describes them in words.[36] Fludd's visual alphabets show that, like Bruno, he would think of his extraordinary memory 'Seal' as still in continuity with the old memory tradition.

To sum up, Fludd's memory system appears to me to be very like one of Bruno's systems. There is the same terrific effort towards a detailed attempt to use the principles of the art of memory in association with the heavens to form a total world-reflecting system. Besides the general plan of the whole thing, many smaller points remind one of Bruno. Fludd uses the terms 'cubicles' and 'fields' of memory places, terms often used by Bruno. He does not, however, appear to be using Lullism,[37] nor does he harp on 'thirty' like Bruno. The Brunian system which appears to me closest to Fludd's system is the one in *Images* where there is a similar attempt to use a very complex series of memory rooms in association with the heavens. For Bruno's *atria* as memory rooms, Fludd substitutes his 'theatres' as memory rooms, as the architectural or 'square' side of a system used in conjunction with the 'round' heavens.

This 'theatre' or stage with its five doors to be used as five memory places is the leading motif of the whole system. We can see it adumbrated in the introductory illustration (Pl. 15) of the man seeing with the eye of imagination five memory places with their five images.

Fludd himself gives the impression that he learned his art of memory in France. In his earlier years he had travelled in several European countries and had spent some time in the south of

---

[34] He also gives sets of visual images for numbers, again an old tradition. Examples of memory places with images for numbers on them are given in the section 'De Arithmetica Memoriali' in the first volume of the book (*Utriusque Cosmi . . . Historia*, I, 2, pp. 153 ff.).

[35] See above, pp. 118 ff. [36] See above, pp. 250, 294–5.

[37] Though Lull appears as a memory image representing alchemy (*Utriusque Cosmi . . . Historia*, II, 2, p. 68).

France. In a section on the art of geomancy in the *Utriusque Cosmi . . . Historia* he says that he practised geomancy at Avignon in the winter of 1601–2, afterwards leaving that city for Marseilles where he instructed the Duc de Guise and his brother 'in the mathematical sciences'.[38] To the same period of Fludd's life in the south of France must refer the account which he gives at the beginning of the section on the art of memory of how he first became interested in this art at Nîmes; then further perfected himself in it at Avignon; and when he went to Marseilles to teach the Duc de Guise and his brother 'the mathematical sciences', he also taught those noblemen the art of memory.[39]

Fludd may therefore have heard of Camillo's Theatre and of Bruno's works when in France. But *Seals* had been published in England, and Dicsono had taught the art of memory in London long after Bruno's departure. There could therefore have been a tradition of Brunian memory descending in England and reaching Fludd that way.

And one wonders whether an immediate influence on Fludd's memory system may have come from a work published in London in 1618, that is one year before the publication, in 1619, of the part of the *Utriusque Cosmi . . . Historia* which contains the memory system. This was the *Mnemonica; sive Ars reminiscendi* by John Willis,[40] in which a memory system formed sets of identical 'theatres' is described. Willis illustrates one of his 'theatres', or 'repositories' as he also calls them (Fig. 10). It is a building on one

---

[38] *Utriusque Cosmi . . . Historia*, I, 2, pp. 718–20. An English translation of the passage is given by C. H. Josten, 'Robert Fludd's theory of geomancy and his experiences at Avignon in the winter of 1601 to 1602', *Journal of the Warburg and Courtauld Institutes*, XXVII (1964), pp. 327–35. This article discusses the theory of geomancy given by Fludd in *Utriusque Cosmi . . . Historia*, II, 2, pp. 37 ff., where it comes immediately before his treatment of the art of memory, with which it may be usefully compared.

[39] *Ibid.*, II, 2, p. 48.

[40] John Willis, *Mnemonica; sive Ars Reminiscendi: e puris artis naturae- que fontibus hausta . . .* London, 1618. An English translation of part of the work was published by the author three years later (John Willis, *The Art of Memory*, London, 1621). And an English translation of the whole work appeared in 1661 (John Willis, *Mnemonica: or The Art of Memory*, London, printed and are to be sold by Leonard Sowersby, 1661). Long extracts from the 1661 publication are given by G. von Feinaigle, *The New Art of Memory*, London, 1813 (third edition), pp. 249 ff.

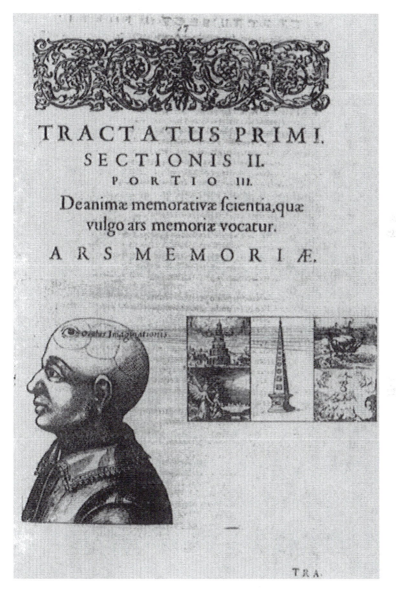

15   First page of the *Ars memoriae* in Robert Fludd's *Utriusque Cosmi . . . Historia*, Tomus Secundus, Oppenheim, 1619 (pp. 326-7)

C A P.   IX.

De loco communi artis rotundæ, deóque eius partitione in proprit locís pre vocabulorum recordatione.

Locus communis artis rotundæ est pars mundi ætherea, scilicet orbes cœlestes, numerando ab octava sphæra, & finiendo in sphæra Lunæ. Partitionem autem eius *dupliciter* facimus; *unam* scilicet *ratione loci & ordinis* qua eum naturaliter primum secundùm Zodiaci distinctionem in duodecim æquales partes distribuimus, quas signa cœlestia Astrologi vocaverunt; *Alteram verò ratione temperis,* in qua fit subdivisio: Nam, quia primum mobile, cursum suum raptum uno die naturali perficit (ab oriente nempe in occidentê) idcirco quælibet diei hora respondet quinque Zodiaci gradibus, quod quidem spatium est dimidia signi pars. Signi autem longitudo debet ad motum Solis quantitate unius horæ diei. Peracto Zodiaco vel octava sphæra incipiendo cum cœlo Saturni & sic io cæteris peripheria cœli medii versus sphæram ignis descendendo, ut in figura sequenti explicatur.

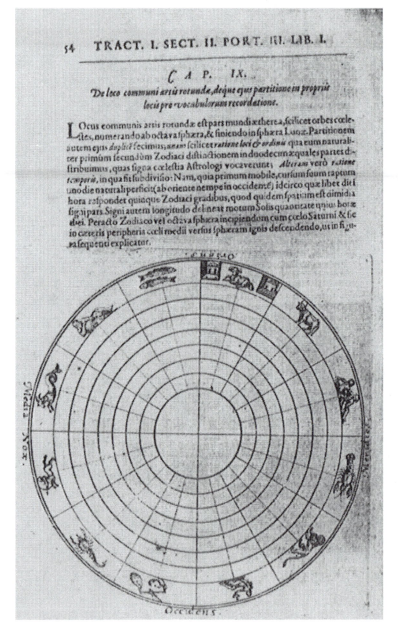

16   The Zodiac
From Robert Fludd's *Ars memoriae* (pp. 329-30, 347)

level, with the front wall omitted, so that one looks into it, and divided into two halves by a column near the back wall. This division gives Willis two memory rooms in which he memorises *loci*. The repositories or theatres are to be imagined as of different colours to distinguish them in memory; and the memory images

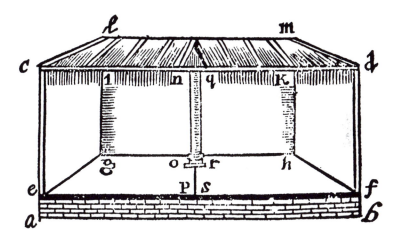

Fig. 10 Memory Theatre or Repository. From J. Willis, *Mnemonica,*
1618

should have something in them to remind of the colour of the theatre to which they belong. Willis gives the following examples of images to be used in a 'golden' theatre to remind a man of business which he has to do in a market town:

> The first business he thinks upon, is to enquire the price of seed wheat in the market. Let him therefore suppose in the first place or roome of the first Repositorie, that he seeth diuers men standing together with sacks of corne . . . and that on the nearer side of the stage, he seeth a country man clad in russet, with a paire of high shooes on, pouring wheate out of a sacke into a bushell, the eares or handles whereof are of pure gold; that by this supposition the Idea may haue the colour of the Repositorie, which is gold, attributed to it . . .
>
> The second business is to procure mowers to cut down medow grasse. Let therefore be supposed in the second place of the first Repositorie, 3 or foure husbandly men to be whetting their sithes,

Luci itaque temporales sunt duplices, cùm alius sit orientalis, qui scilicet in eodem signo orientalem mundi plaga in respicit, atque huncc locum theatro albo impleri imaginabimur: Alius verò occidentalis, sive occidentalis figni portio, in qua ponetur theatrum quoddam nigrum, de quo posteà dicemus.

CAP. X.

De theatri orientalis & occidentalis descriptione.

Theatrum appello illud, in quo omnes vocabolorum, sententiarum, particularum orationis seu subjectorum actiones tanquam in theatro publico, ubi comcædiæ & tragcædiæ aguntur, demonstrantur. Hujusmodi theatrorum speciem unam in puncto orientis sitam esse imaginabimini, quæ realis seu corporea, sed quasi vapore æthereo consideranda est: Sicque illa theatri umbra similitudinibus spirituum agentium repleta. Primum ergo theatrum habebit colorem album, lucidum & splendidum, præ se ferens diem, diurnasque actiones. Quare in oriente collocabitur, quia Sol ab Oriente se attollens diem incipit, claritatemque mundo pollicetur: Secundum verò fingetur imbutum colore nigro, fusco & obscuro: illudque in Occidente positum imaginaberis, quia Sol in Occidente existens noctem & obscuritatem brevi venturam denunciat Quodlibet autem horum theatrorum habebit quinque portas ab invicem distinctas, & ferè æquidistantes, quarum usus posteà demonstrabimus.

17 The Theatre
From Robert Fludd's *Ars memoriae* (pp. 330 ff., 346 ff.)

18a ABOVE Secondary Theatre
18b BELOW Secondary Theatre
From Robert Fludd's *Ars memoriae* (pp. 333, 353-4)

the blades whereof are of gold, agreeable to the colour of the Repositorie . . . The relation which this Idea hath unto the former, is in respect of situation, because both Ideas are placed upon the stage of the first Repositorie . . .[41]

This seems a perfectly rational use of the art as a straight mnemotechnic; it might work very well as an inner shopping list, when, as the author says 'we are destitute of the aid of Paper, Ink, or Table-Books'.[42] The similarity to Fludd's use of sets of 'theatres' with columns in them as memory rooms is however striking; also the emphasis on differentiating memory places by remembering them as of different colours. And there might even be a humble origin for Fludd's marvellous Day and Night theatres in the zodiac in Willis's advice that 'things charged in Memory by day, are to be deposited at least before sleep; things charged by night are to be deposited immediately after sleep'.[43]

It was Bruno's custom to take a rational memory system and 'occultise' it into a magical system; we have seen him doing that again and again. Possibly this is what Fludd did to Willis's sets of what he calls 'theatres' as memory rooms; he occultised them into magical activity by affiliating them to the zodiac. Alternatively, when we remember how at about the same time in France, Paepp was 'detecting' Schenkel,[44] detecting in his apparently rational expositions of the art of memory an occult undercurrent, we may wonder whether there was more than meets the eye in Willis's *Mnemonica*. I cannot solve this little problem but it had to be mentioned because the fact that an art of memory using sets of 'theatres', or stages, as memory rooms was published in England the year before the publication of Fludd's system is somewhat significant, suggesting as it does that it may not have been solely through his travels abroad that Fludd had heard of the art of memory.

At any rate, Fludd's memory system seems to take us back many years to the time of the great controversies centred on Metrodorus of Scepsis and the use of the zodiac in artificial memory, with all that that implied. Had William Perkins been still alive when Fludd's book was published he would surely have recognised in it the 'impious artificial memory' of a 'Scepsian'.

---

[41] Willis, *The Art of Memory*, 1621 translation, pp. 58–60.
[42] Willis, *The Art of Memory*, 1661 translation, p. 28.
[43] *Ibid.*, p. 30.   [44] See above, pp. 301–2.

Mersenne, in one of his attacks on Fludd, said that Fludd's two worlds rested on unproven 'Egyptian' teaching (that is teaching in the *Hermetica*) that man contains the world, and on the statement of 'Mercurius' (in the *Asclepius*) that man is a great miracle and like to God. Mersenne correctly seized here on the Hermetic basis of Fludd's two worlds.[45] It is because Fludd's man as microcosm potentially contains the world that he can reflect it within. Fludd's occult art of memory is an attempt to reproduce or re-create the macrocosm-microcosm relationship by establishing, or composing, or making conscious in the memory of the micro-cosm the world which he contains, which is the image of the macro-cosm, which is the image of God. The effort to do this by manipulating the stars in man through astralised images in the occult version of the art of memory is the basis of all Bruno's Herculean efforts, which Fludd is copying.

Yet, though Bruno and Fludd both operate their occult memory systems from Hermetic philosophies, those philosophies are not identical. Fludd's outlook is that of the earlier Renaissance, in which the 'three worlds' or stages of the whole creation—the elemental world, the celestial world, and the supercelestial world—are Christianised by identifying the supercelestial world with the Christianised angelic hierarchies of Pseudo-Dionysius. This allows a placing of Christianised angelic and Trinitarian apex, as it were, to the whole system. Camillo belongs into this outlook. His 'Theatre of the World' connects beyond the stars with sephiroth and angels which in the mind of a Christian Renaissance Hermetic philosopher are identified with Christian angelic hierarchies which are the image of the Trinity.

Bruno who rejected the Christian interpretation of the *Hermetica* and wished to return to a pure 'Egyptian' religion, dismissed what he called the 'metaphysical' apex of the system. For him there is beyond the celestial world a supercelestial One, or an intellectual Sun, which it is his object to reach through its manifestations or vestiges in nature and through grouping and unifying these through their images in memory.

One of Fludd's illustrations expresses in visual form the reflection of the three worlds within the mind and memory of the microcosm. He shows a man who is first taking in sense impressions from the

[45] Marin Mersenne, *Quaestiones celeberrimae in Genesim*, Paris, 1623, cols. 1746, 1749. Cf. *G.B. and H.T.*, p. 437.

339

sensible world or *mundus sensibilis* through his five senses. Next he is dealing with these within as images or 'umbra' in a *mundus imaginabilis*. In the discussion in the text of this *mundus imaginabilis* Fludd includes in it the reflection of the images of the zodiac and of the stars.[46] The microcosm at this stage is unifying the contents of memory on the celestial level. Then the diagram passes to the *mens*, to the intellectual world where a vision is received of the nine celestial hierarchies and of the Trinity. Finally the diagram comes to the seat of memory, at the back of the head, which receives all three worlds into itself.

For Bruno, the intellectual sun arrived at by the *mens* through the unifying process would not have this Christian and Trinitarian aspect. And further, Bruno would abolish, and does abolish in *Seals*, the divisions of the 'faculty psychology' which Fludd here partially retains, the passage of material from sense impression through the various 'faculties' thought of as separate compartments within the psyche. For Bruno there is but one power and one faculty which ranges through all the inner world of apprehension, namely the imaginative power or the imaginative faculty which passes immediately through the gates of memory and is one with memory.[47]

Thus Fludd as Hermetic philosopher and Hermetic psychologist does not speak with quite the same voice as Bruno. It is indeed probable that the Hermetic tradition which reached Fludd was not so much the form of it imported by Bruno as that already established in England by John Dee. Fludd has a strong interest in mechanics and in machines (regarded in the Hermetic tradition as a branch of magic)[48] which had been characteristic of Dee but was not characteristic of Bruno. Dee was also closer to the original Christianised and Trinitarian form of the tradition, which Bruno discarded, but which is still present in Fludd.

[46] *Utriusque Cosmi . . . Historia*, II, pp. 205 ff.

[47] See above, pp. 256–7. There is a similar rejection of faculty psychology in Campanella's *Del senso delle cose e delle magia* (ed A. Bruers, Bari, 1925, p. 96) in a passage where Campanella, in this as in so many other respects close to Bruno, accuses the faculty psychology of 'making many souls out of one indivisible soul'.

Fludd's psychology is, however, a fully Renaissance one in its insistence on the prime importance of imagination.

[48] See *G.B. and H.T.*, pp. 147 ff.

Nevertheless, in his Hermetic memory system Fludd was influenced by Bruno, in itself a proof that it was Bruno more than any other who developed the art of memory as a Hermetic art. In spite of the differences between Fludd and Bruno as Hermetic philosophers, Fludd's memory Seal presents us with fundamentally the same problems as those with which we have tried to grapple in Bruno. We can more or less grasp in a general way the nature of the effort made in such a system, but the detail defeats us. Is it pure madness to place twenty-four memory theatres in the zodiac? Or is it a madness potentially leading to method? Or is such a system the Seal or secret code of a Hermetic sect or society?

It is easier to turn to the historical aspect of the problem and to see Fludd's system as the recurrence of a pattern which seems to run through the Renaissance. We saw it first in the Memory Theatre which Giulio Camillo brought as a secret to a King of France. We saw it again in the Memory Seals which Bruno carried from country to country. We see it finally in the Theatre Memory System in the book which Fludd dedicated to a King of England. And this system contains, as a secret hidden within it, factual information about the Globe Theatre.

It may be that the interest aroused by this extraordinary fact will direct intensive research by many scholars upon these problems with which I have struggled alone, and that the nature and meaning of Renaissance occult memory will become clearer in the future than it is to me.

Chapter XVI

FLUDD'S MEMORY THEATRE
AND THE GLOBE THEATRE

HE great wooden public theatres which could hold thousands of people and which had housed the drama of the English Renaissance were still standing in Fludd's time and still in use. The original Globe Theatre, erected on the Bankside in 1599, which was the home of the Lord Chamberlain's company of actors to which Shakespeare belonged and for which he wrote his plays, had been burned down in 1613. The Globe was at once rebuilt on the same foundations and on the same lines as its predecessor though more magnificent. This new playhouse was said to be 'the fairest that ever was in England'.[1] James I contributed a considerable amount towards the cost of the rebuilding.[2] This was to be expected since he had taken the Lord Chamberlain's company under his protection and they were now known as the King's Men.[3] The King would naturally take an interest in the rebuilding of the theatre of his own company of players.

There has been great interest in recent years in attempted reconstructions of Elizabethan and Jacobean playhouses, and in particular of the Globe, with its associations with Shakespeare.[4]

[1] E. K. Chambers, *Elizabethan Stage*, Oxford University Press (first edition 1923, revised edition 1951), II, p. 425.

[2] *Ibid., loc. cit.*

[3] *Ibid.*, pp. 208 ff.

[4] The basic information is given in Chambers, *Elizabethan Stage*, II, Book IV 'The Play-Houses'. Amongst the numerous studies are J. C. Adams, *The Globe Playhouse*, Harvard, 1942, 1961; Irwin Smith, *Shakes-*

The visual evidence for doing so is scanty; in fact it consists mainly of one rough sketch of the interior of the Swan theatre, the famous De Witt drawing (Pl. 19), which has been pored over by experts for every scrap of information which it may contain. It may not be very accurate, and it is a copy of De Witt's original sketch (which does not exist). Nevertheless it is the best piece of visual evidence so far available about the interior of a public theatre and all reconstructions take their departure from it. On the foundation of the De Witt drawing, of contracts for theatre buildings, and of analysis for stage directions in the plays, the modern reconstructions of the Globe have been built up. The situation is however not satisfactory. The De Witt drawing is of the Swan, not of the Globe; the building contracts are for the Fortune and the Hope,[5] not for the Globe. No visual evidence about the interior of the Globe has been used for none has been supposed to exist. Visual evidence about its exterior has been drawn from early maps of London in which an object, said to represent the Globe, can be seen on Bankside.[6] These maps give conflicting evidence as to whether the building was round or polygonal.

Nevertheless much progress in understanding of what the Globe may have been like has been made. We know that the back wall of the stage was formed by the wall of the 'tiring house', the building within which the actors changed clothes, kept properties, and so on. This tiring house wall had three levels. On the lowest level, giving on to the stage, were doors or openings thought to be probably three in number, perhaps a central door flanked by two side entrances. One of these doors may have opened to display an inner stage. On the second level was a terrace, much used for

[5] Printed in Chambers, *Elizabethan Stage*, II, pp. 436 ff., 466 ff.
[6] Details from the maps which show the Globe are reproduced in Irwin Smith, *Shakespeare's Globe Playhouse*, Plates 2–13.

---

peare's Globe Playhouse*, New York, 1956, London, 1963 (based on the Adams reconstruction); C. W. Hodges, *The Globe Restored*, London, 1953; A. M. Nagler, *Shakespeare's Stage*, Yale, 1958; R. Southern, 'On Reconstructing a Practicable Elizabethan Playhouse', *Shakespeare Survey*, XII (1959), pp. 22–34; Glynn Wickham, *Early English Stages*, II, London, 1963; R. Hosley, 'Reconstitution du Théâtre du Swan' in *Le Lieu Théâtral à la Renaissance*, ed. J. Jacquot, Centre National de la Recherche Scientifique, Paris, 1964, pp. 295–316.

sieges and fights, which could have been battlemented since 'battlements' are mentioned in theatre documents and in plays.[7] There was also somewhere on this upper level a room, called 'the chamber', and windows. Above this level again there was a third tier, and the 'huts' containing stage machinery. The stage, with its back wall or *frons scaenae* formed by the tiring house wall, was raised on a platform and jutted out into the 'yard', an open space in the unroofed theatre where stood the 'groundlings', that part of the audience who paid a small sum for standing room. Those who could afford seats were accommodated in the galleries which ran round the building. This general lay-out can be seen in the De Witt drawing of the Swan; there is the stage with its back wall formed of the wall of the tiring house jutting out into the yard; and there are the surrounding galleries. We see on the stage here only two hinged doors on ground level and no evidence of any door opening to disclose an inner stage. On the upper level there is no 'chamber', and no windows, but only a gallery which appears to contain spectators but which might also have sometimes been used by actors. But the stage which we are looking at in this drawing is not the stage of the Globe.

One feature which has come out clearly in the reconstructions is that in these theatres part of the stage had a covering which projected from the tiring house wall and was supported by columns or 'posts' as they were called.[8] Two such columns or posts can be seen on the stage in the De Witt drawing supporting such a covering. Only the inner part of the stage was protected in this way; the outer stage, as can be seen in the De Witt drawing, was uncovered. It is known that the underside of this covering was painted to represent the heavens. In the Adams reconstruction of the Globe the ceiling of the inner stage cover is shown as painted with the signs of the zodiac, with some other vaguely arranged stars within the circle of the zodiac.[9] Naturally this is a modern attempt to reconstruct the ceiling; no specimen of these painted theatrical heavens has survived. They would certainly not have shown a vaguely decorative sky indiscriminately sprinkled with stars. They would have been representations of the zodiac with its

[7] Chambers, *Elizabethan Stage*, I, pp. 230-1; III, pp. 44, 91, 96; IV, p. 28.
[8] *Ibid.*, II, pp. 544-5; III, pp. 27, 38, 72, 108, 141, 144.
[9] Irwin Smith, *Shakespeare's Globe Playhouse*, Plate 31.

twelve signs of the spheres of the seven planets within it, perhaps fairly simple representations, or perhaps sometimes more elaborate.[10] This part of the furnishing of a theatre was called in the contracts and elsewhere 'the heavens';[11] sometimes it was referred to as 'the shadow'.[12]

In an article published in 1958, the late Richard Bernheimer reproduced the engraving of the *Theatrum Orbi* from Fludd's book. From his remarks about it I quote the following:

> That the illustration portrays a structure of generally Elizabethan type, though an unusual one stylistically, is apparent at first glance. Shakespearians will recognise the presence of a lower and an upper stage, of two entrance doors flanking an inner stage, of battlements fitted for scenes of siege, and of a bay window, out of which Juliet might lean to drink in the honeyed words of her swain: all things which none has ever seen, although they have been postulated by research into stage directions and allusions in dramatic texts.[13]

Bernheimer saw something, saw things which, as he says, no modern eye has seen though we know from the plays that they must have existed. Unfortunately, he spoiled this brilliant intuition by making basic mistakes in his interpretation of the engraving and of Fludd's text.

The first mistake was that Bernheimer took the engraving to represent a whole theatre, a very small theatre with boxes at the sides for the audience rather like those in a sixteenth-century

---

[10] The so-called *English Wagner Book* of 1592, which Chambers thought of some value as evidence about the English theatre, describes a magical theatre in which were posts and a tiring house and which was adorned 'with the heavenly firmament, and often spotted with golden teares which men callen Stars. There was lively portrayed the whole Imperiall Army of the faire heavenly inhabitants' (Chambers, *Elizabethan Stage*, III, p. 72).

[11] Chambers, *Elizabethan Stage*, II, pp. 466, 544–6, 555; III, pp. 30, 75–7, 90, 108, 132, 501.

[12] For example in the Fortune contract; Chambers, II, pp. 437, 544–5.

[13] Richard Bernheimer, 'Another Globe Theatre', *Shakespeare Quarterly*, IX (Winter 1958), pp. 19–29.

Perhaps I may be allowed to mention that it was I who drew Professor Bernheimer's attention to the Fludd engraving when he was collecting theatre material at the Warburg Institute in 1955. I had then myself no idea of any connection between the engraving and the Globe.

tennis court; whereas the engraving does not represent a whole theatre. It represents a stage, or rather part of a stage.

The second mistake was that Bernheimer, not having served a tough apprenticeship on Brunian memory 'Seals', was naturally baffled by the 'round' and the 'square' arts. He saw that Fludd was saying a great deal about the 'round' and he thought that this meant that he was saying that the building shown in the engraving was round. Since there is nothing round about the building shown in the engraving, Bernheimer leaped to the conclusion that the engraving bore no relation to the text. He assumed that the German printer had used some print which he had by him to illustrate Fludd's obscure mnemonics, a print (entirely imagined by Bernheimer) representing a small theatre somewhere in Germany which had been rigged up in a tennis court and given some Elizabethan features to make a visiting company of English actors feel more at home. By inventing this myth, Bernheimer allowed his remarkable observation about the Shakespearean character of the stage shown in the engraving to evaporate into nothing. The curious way in which he muffled and destroyed what he had intuitively seen accounts, I suppose, for the fact that the Globe reconstructors seem to have taken no notice of his article and its illustration.

Now if Fludd uses, as he states that he does, a 'real' public theatre for the stages of his world memory system (Bernheimer overlooked this statement) what could be more suitable than the Globe, the most famous of the London public theatres and the very name of which suggests the world? Moreover, since his first volume was dedicated to James I, would it not have been a good way of keeping up that monarch's interest in the second volume to allude in the memory system to the newly rebuilt Globe, towards the erection of which James had largely contributed and which was the theatre of his own company of players, the King's men?

The only features in the engraving of the *Theatrum Orbi* which Fludd mentions in his text and of which he makes use in his mnemonics are the five doors or entrances on the stage wall and the five columns 'opposite' to them of which the bases only are shown in the engraving. He never mentions in the text nor uses in the mnemonics the other features so clearly depicted in the engraving —the bay window, the battlemented terrace, the side walls with

346

those openings in their lower part. And though the *cinque portae* on the stage wall are constantly mentioned—are in fact the basis of the scheme of the five memory *loci*—he never specifies the differences between the *cinque portae* which are shown in the engraving, never says that the central one has those great hinged doors which we see half opening to disclose an inner room. What would be the object of showing all these features in the engraving, which he does not use nor mention in the text about the mnemonics, unless they were 'real' features of a 'real' stage to which he wanted to make allusion?

Moreover, 'real' stages contained the feature which is the basis of the *ars rotunda*, the 'heavens' painted on the underside of the cover of the inner stage. Let us once more open the volume and gaze at the diagram of the heavens on the left-hand page which, when the book is closed, covers the stage shown on the right-hand page. Does this arrangement not only refer to the magic mnemonics, in which stages like this are placed right and left of the signs of the zodiac all round the heavens, but also refer to the arrangement of a 'real' theatre? Once one begins to think on these lines one is on the road which leads to understanding of the relationship of the engraving of the *Theatrum Orbi* to the Globe theatre.

The engraving represents that part of the stage of the Globe which would be covered by the stage 'heavens'.

What we are seeing as we look straight ahead to the back wall is the tiring house wall at the Globe, not the whole of it but only the two lower levels; the ground level with the three entrances; the second level with the terrace and the chamber. We do not see the third level *because we are under the heavens* which are projecting invisibly above us from below the third tier of the tiring house wall.

There are five entrances to this stage; three are on ground level, a large central door opening to display an inner room, and two other entrances flanking it; and there are two entrances on the upper level. These are the *cinque portae* used as memory *loci* in the memory system. But Fludd is not using 'fictitious places'; he is using 'real places'. Those five entrances are real, placed as they were placed on the real stage of the Globe. And the projecting bay window is real; it is the window of the upper 'chamber' with a real battlemented terrace on either side of it.

But what about the side walls of the stage shown in the engraving

347

with those box-like apertures near their bases? These side walls close the stage in and make it impossible as an acting space visible from a whole theatre. And what about the five columns, of which only the bases are shown, and which, if really in the positions shown, would impossibly obstruct an audience's view of the stage from the front?

My explanation of these features is that they are distortions of the real stage introduced for mnemonic purposes. Fludd wanted a 'memory room' within which to practise his mnemonics with the five doors and the five columns. He wanted this 'memory room' to be based on a real stage but closed at the sides to form an enclosed 'memory theatre', perhaps rather like one of Willis's memory theatres or repositories. To see the real stage of the Globe behind the engraving, one has therefore to remove the side walls.

These side walls make a curious impression. They look somehow structurally impossible as though there were insufficient support for their upper expanses above the boxes. And they do not fit on properly to the end wall, for they cut off bits of the battlements of the terrace. They look flimsy as compared with the solidity of the end wall. They are to be swept away as unreal mnemonic distortions of the real stage. Nevertheless these imaginary side walls show a feature of the 'real' theatre, namely the boxes or 'gentlemen's rooms', occupied by persons of rank and friends of the actors, which were situated in the galleries on either side of the stage.[14]

The five columns are also unreal, introduced for the purposes of the mnemonics. Fludd himself says that they are 'feigned'.[15] Nevertheless, they too have a 'real' aspect for they are situated on the line on which there would be on the real stage, not five, but two columns or 'posts' rising to support the 'heavens'.

Once these fundamental points have been grasped—that the engraving shows the tiring house wall at the Globe from below the 'heavens' and that the stage has been distorted into a memory room—we can, by combining the Fludd engraving with the De Witt drawing, cause the stage of the Globe to appear out of the magic memory system.

In the sketch of the stage of the Globe as revealed by Fludd (Pl. 20) the mnemonic distortions are cleared away. The impossible

[14] *Elizabethan Stage*, II, p. 531.   [15] See above, p. 332.

side walls are removed and two columns or 'posts' rise to support the 'heavens' above. The columns are copied from those in the 'Temple of Music' in the first volume of the *Utriusque Cosmi . . . Historia.* The 'heavens' show the zodiac and spheres of the planets, as in the diagram facing the memory theatre, but the signs of the zodiac are shown by their characters only. No attempt has been made to represent their images, and this is but a skeletal outline of what the painted 'heavens' at the Globe may have been like. The 'gentlemen's rooms' or boxes are shown in their proper place, in the galleries on either side of the stage. Instead of being distorted into a 'memory room', the stage is now clearly seen projecting from the tiring house wall into the yard, open at the sides, and with posts supporting the heavens over the inner stage.

If this sketch is compared with the De Witt drawing it can be seen to be in agreement with it in the essentials of tiring house wall, projecting stage, posts, and galleries for the audience. The only difference—and it is a very big one—is that it shows us, not the stage of the Swan, but the stage of the Globe.

The Fludd engraving thus becomes a document of major importance for the Shakespearean stage. It would be of course the second Globe, the one rebuilt after the fire of 1613 of which Fludd wished to remind James I in this extremely complex way. It was in the first Globe that many of Shakespeare's plays had been acted. He died in 1616, only three years after the burning of the first Globe. But the new theatre used the foundations of the old one and it is generally assumed that the stage and interior of the old Globe were pretty exactly reproduced in the new one. I have not disguised the fact that the Fludd engraving shows us the stage of the second Globe in the distorting mirrors of magic memory. But the sketch clears away what I believe to be the main distortions. Fludd meant to use a real 'public theatre' in his memory system; he says so, repeatedly emphasising that he is using 'real' and not 'fictitious' places. And what he shows us about the stage of the Globe we either know was there, or has been conjectured to be there, though the exact configuration of entrances chamber, and terrace, has not been known.

Fludd shows us that there were five entrances to the stage, three on ground level and two on the upper level giving on to the terrace. And this solves a problem which has worried some scholars who have thought that there ought to be more than three entrances but there did not seem to be room for any more on ground level. Chambers suggested that there ought to be five entrances, corresponding to the five entrances in the *frons scaenae* of the classical stage.[16] The classical stage was of course on one level. Here we see the classical theme of the five entrances of the *frons scaenae* transposed to the multilevel *frons scaenae* formed by the tiring house wall of the Globe where there are three entrances below and two above. It is an extremely satisfying solution of the problem and one which suggests that, notwithstanding the battlements and bay window, there may have been some classical and Vitruvian elements in the design of the Globe.

The question of the 'inner stages' is one which has much exercised scholars. An extreme form of the 'inner stage' theory was put forward by Adams who thought that there was a large 'inner stage' opening in the centre on ground level and an 'upper inner stage' immediately above it. This emphasis on inner stages is now rather unfashionable but Fludd shows great hinged doors opening in the centre to display something, and immediately above them he shows the 'chamber'. The only alteration or emendation of Fludd's engraving which is made in the sketch is the suggestion that the front of the bay window (part of which is taken up in the engraving by the title) might have opened in two ways, either as windows opening whilst the lower part was closed, or the whole folding right back. The bay window could then be used either for window scenes (the windows opening separately from the doors as a whole) or when the doors were fully opened an 'upper inner stage' would be displayed. Such lower and upper inner stages could have extended right through the tiring house to the back of the building where windows would have lighted them from the back.

The position of the chamber as shown by Fludd solves what has been one of the major problems of Shakespearean staging. It has been known that there was a terrace on the upper level which was thought to run right across it, and known also that there was an upper chamber. It has been thought that this chamber was placed behind the terrace which with its railings or balusters (or rather, as we now see, its battlements) would obscure the view into the chamber.[17] Fludd shows us that the terrace ran *behind* the front

[16] *Elizabethan Stage*, III, p. 100.

[17] See the discussion of this problem in Irwin Smith, *Shakespeare's Globe Playhouse*, pp. 124 ff.

part of the chamber which projected beyond it over the main stage. The terrace as it were passed *through* the chamber which could be entered from it on either side (entrances which could be curtained off when the whole chamber was being used as an upper inner stage). No one has thought of this solution of the chamber and terrace problem which is obviously the right one.

The corbelled projecting window over a great gate was a familiar feature of Tudor architecture. An example at Hengrave Hall (1536) shows corbelled projecting windows in a gatehouse with battlements.[18] The gatehouse has been said to be a chief feature of English great houses of the sixteenth century;[19] it was a descendant of the fortified and battlemented gatehouses of earlier times and often retained the battlements. Another example of a gatehouse-like entrance to a great house with projecting corbelled window above it is Bramshill, Hants (1605–12)[20] which with its three entrances and terrace on either side of the corbelled window is reminiscent of the stage shown by Fludd. These comparisons are introduced to suggest that the stage wall revealed to us by Fludd has something of the attributes of the gatehouse or entrance to a great contemporary mansion, yet it could easily turn into the battlemented and fortified entrance to town or castle. I also make these comparisons in order to point out that in both the examples mentioned the corbel under the projecting window over the gate comes down to the top of the gate, which makes one wonder whether the central door or gate shown in the Fludd engraving is too small and ought to be extended up to the base of the corbel, as suggested in the sketch.

Bernheimer thought he saw German influence in the corbel under the bay window in the engraving.[21] In view of the English examples here cited it is perhaps unnecessary to suppose this, though the possibility of some influence on the engraving at the German end of the publication cannot be entirely excluded.

The final touch to the stage architecture in Fludd's engraving is

[18] See John Summerson, *Architecture in Britain 1530 to 1830* (Pelican History of Art), London, 1953, Plate 8.

[19] *Ibid.*, p. 13.

[20] *Ibid.*, Plate 26.

[21] *Article cited*, p. 25.

added by the fashionable Italianate effect of 'rustication' shown on the walls (this is roughly reproduced in the sketch). We know that the great wooden public theatres were covered with painted canvas. The effect here shown must be rather similar to that created for a wooden banqueting house erected at Westminster in 1581 which had walls 'closed with canuas, and painted all the out-sides of the same most artificiallie with a worke called rustike, much like to stone'.[22] One wonders whether the imitation 'rustic work' which Fludd shows was one of the expensive improvements made in the second Globe. The use of the rustication with battlements and bay window gives an extraordinarily hybrid effect to the whole, but shows once again that the illusion aimed at was that of a great modern mansion, which yet could be easily switched to present the sterner aspect of fortified castle or town.

Though mnemonic distortions, German influences, and the splendours of the second Globe may come to some extent between Fludd's engraving and Shakespeare's original theatre, there can be no doubt that this Hermetic philosopher has shown us more of it than we have ever seen before. Fludd is in fact the only person who has left us any visual record at all of the stage on which the plays of the world's greatest dramatist were acted.

We can therefore begin to people this stage with scenes. There are the doors on ground level for the street scenes, doors at which people knock, at which they talk in the 'threshold' scenes. There is the 'penthouse', formed by the projecting bay window, which affords shelter from the rain. There are the battlemented walls of city or castle with projecting bastion (entered by defenders from the terrace) and under it the great city or castle gate, all ready for historical scenes of siege or battle. Or, if we are in Verona, there is the House of Capulet with its lower room where they prepared the banquet and its upper chamber from the window of which Juliet leaned 'on such a night as this'. Or, if we are at Elsinore, there are the ramparts on which Hamlet and Horatio were conversing when Hamlet saw the Ghost. Or if we are in Rome, there is the rostrum from which Mark Antony addressed friends, Romans, citizens, on the stage below. Or if we are in London, there is the upper room of the Boar's Head Tavern in Eastcheap.

[22] Chambers, *Elizabethan Stage*, I, p. 16 note.

19 The De Witt Sketch of the Swan Theatre
Library of the University of Utrecht (pp. 343, 348-9)

Or if we are in Egypt, chamber and terrace are dressed to hold the monument in which Cleopatra died.[23]

We have now to direct our gaze on the other two 'theatres' (Pl. 18a, b) which Fludd illustrates in his memory system. These are one level stages, one having five entrances, the other, three entrances. The one with five entrances has bases of imaginary columns opposite to them, after the manner of the main theatre. These subsidiary theatres were to be used in the memory system with the main theatre with which, as we noted before, they have a matching relationship through the battlements on their walls similar to those on the terrace. These theatres are also covered with canvas painted to resemble, in one case stone walls, in the other case, wooden walls of which the carefully jointed timbers are shown.

Here I must interpolate that the memory treatises often advise that memory places are better remembered if they are remembered as made of different materials.[24] Fludd has distinguished between his memory theatres by making the main one of 'rustic work' and the subsidiary ones of plain stone blocks and wooden beams respectively. Nevertheless, as always, Fludd insists that these secondary theatres too are 'real' and not fictitious places. One is labelled as 'the figure of a true theatre'.[25] The subsidiary theatres are therefore, like the main one, not only magic memory theatres but reflections of something 'real' or true seen at the Globe.

Shakespearean scholars have puzzled as to how localities were indicated on the main stage. A case in point is that of the Capulet orchard which had walls which Romeo leaped in order to come under Juliet's window. Chambers suggested that he must have had a wall to leap and pointed to many other scenes, such as those showing camps of rival armies, which seem to demand differentiation by walls or some kind of divisions. He conjectured that possibly scenic constructions resembling walls were brought on to

[23] The plays alluded to here, though some of them may have been first produced at other theatres than the Globe were all, almost certainly, played at some time at the Globe. Shakespearean drama was also, of course, played at the court and, after 1608, at the Blackfriars theatre.

[24] For example Romberch, *Congestorium artificiosae memoriae*, pp. 29 *verso–30 recto*; Bruno, *Op. lat.*, II, ii, p. 87 (*Seals*).

[25] 'Sequitur figura vera theatri', *Utriusque Cosmi . . . Historia*, II, 2, p. 64.

20 Sketch of the stage of the Globe Theatre based on Fludd (pp. 348 ff.)

the stage.[26] And numerous references to 'battlements' as scenic units have been collected from theatre documents by Glynn Wickham.[27]

I suggest that Fludd's two subsidiary memory theatres reflect such scenic constructions, or screens, resembling battlemented walls. They would be made of light wooden frames covered with painted canvas and easily moveable. Fludd makes a very important revelation about such constructions by showing that they had entrances and so could be used for playing scenes in which entrances and exits are made. They could have been placed before-hand on the stage to provide for scenes required by a play which were not playable with the facilities provided by the main *frons scaenae*. For example, extra scenes representing the Capulet orchard and the Friar's cell—which was in the country, to which his visitors made their way and entered by a door—would be required for *Romeo and Juliet*. Or take the case of the camps of rival armies between which the scenes change so rapidly in *Richard III*; the problem of how such scenes were staged is solved if we can think of constructions such as Fludd's subsidiary theatres being used for the rival camps.

Again, Fludd has shown us something for which no visual evidence has hitherto existed. That he makes his battlemented subsidiary theatres match the main theatre with its battlemented terrace suggests that these scenic constructions were thought of as an integral part of the stage as a whole. This revelation, like his revelation of the relationship between terrace and chamber, may make it possible to understand the changes of scene in Shakespeare's plays more clearly than ever before.

Does Fludd, who tells us so much about the stage, have nothing to tell us about the shape and plan of the Globe Theatre as a whole? I believe that if one sets about it carefully and methodically one can draw out of Fludd's evidence sufficient information to enable one to draw a plan of the whole theatre, not of course a detailed architect's plan showing position of staircases and the like, but a plan of the basic geometrical forms used in the construction of the theatre. I believe that Fludd gives information about the plan of the theatre as a whole in two ways: first through the shapes

[26] *Elizabethan Stage*, III, pp. 97-8.
[27] *Early English Stages*, II, pp. 223, 282, 286, 288, 296, 305, 319.

of the five column bases which he mentions; and secondly through his strong insistence that there were five entrances to the *frons scaenae*.

The five column bases shown in the engraving of the *Theatrum Orbi* are round, square, hexagonal, square, round. Those are their shapes, not only as shown in the engraving but as stated in the text.

The only visual evidence about the external shape of the Globe is to be found, as already mentioned, in those early maps of London in which small representations of the theatre are shown on Bankside. In some maps the Globe is indicated as a polygonal building; in others as a round building. Poring over the indistinct forms shown on the maps Adams believed that he could detect eight sides on one of them, and he therefore based his elaborate reconstruction of the Globe on an octagon. Others have preferred the round Globe theory. The evidence of the maps is really quite inconclusive.

We do however possess a statement by an eyewitness about the shape of the Globe, though some scholars have thought it unreliable. Dr. Johnson's friend, Hester Thrale, lived in the mideighteenth century near the site of the Globe which had been demolished in 1644, under the Commonwealth, but of which some remains could still be seen in her time, remains which she describes as a 'black heap of rubbish'. Mrs. Thrale took a romantic interest in the old theatre about which she makes this statement: 'There were really curious remains of the old Globe Playhouse, which, though hexagonal in form without, was round within.'[28]

Encouraged by Mrs. Thrale, I believe that Fludd is stating through the shapes of the five column bases the geometrical forms used in the construction of the Globe, namely the hexagon, the circle, and the square.

Let us now ponder on the fact on which Fludd insists so strongly, namely that there were five entrances to the stage shown in his engraving. Fludd's evidence about this very satisfactorily solves the problem raised by Chambers, that the Globe stage ought to have had five entrances, like the classical theatre. It did have five entrances, not as in the classical stage all on ground level, but three on ground level and two above—an adaptation of the five

[28] Quoted by Chambers, *Elizabethan Stage*, II, p. 428.

entrances of the classical stage to a multilevel theatre. In spite of the basic difference from the classical stage, due to the multilevel stage, do the five entrances at the Globe nevertheless suggest Vitruvian and classical influence on its design?

In the Roman theatre as described by Vitruvius the position of the *frons scaenae*, of the five entrances to the stage, and of the seven gangways leading to the seats in the auditorium, are determined by four equilateral triangles inscribed within a circle. These four triangles are shown in Palladio's reconstruction of the Vitruvian theatre illustrated by a diagram in Barbaro's commentary on Vitruvius (Pl. 9a), first published in 1556.[29] Here we see how the base of one triangle determines the line of the *frons scaenae* whilst its apex points to the main gangway in the auditorium. Three triangle apices determine the positions of the three main entrances or doors in the *frons scaenae*. Two other triangle apices determine the two entrances to the stage from the sides. Six other triangle apices determine six gangways in the auditorium (the main central one making the seventh, determined by the triangle the base of which determined the position of the *frons scaenae*). Vitruvius likens these four triangles to the triangles inscribed by astrologers within the zodiac to form the *trigona* of the signs (triangles connecting related signs of the zodiac with one another).[30] The classical stage was thus planned in accordance with the *fabrica mundi*, to reflect the proportions of the world. May we not assume that the Globe theatre, with its 'heavens' over part of the stage, would also have been planned in accordance with the *fabrica mundi*, as was the classical stage, and that the four triangles inscribed within a circle would have played a part in determining its *frons scaenae* and gangways?

The attempt here made to draw a suggested plan of the Globe works on the assumption that this theatre was an adaptation of the Vitruvian theatre. It would have to be an adaptation, for the stage of this theatre, unlike that of the classical theatre, was not all on one level; and the galleries of its auditorium also consisted of super-

[29] Some modern authorities interpret Vitruvius as saying that the triangles are inscribed within the circle of the orchestra. Palladio, in this diagram, interprets him as saying that the triangles are inscribed within the circle of the whole theatre. We follow Palladio's diagram which might have been known to the designers of the Globe.

[30] See above, pp. 170–1.

imposed galleries, not of the rising graded seating of the classical theatre.

The other assumption made in drawing the plan is that Fludd gives information that the basic geometrical forms used in the construction of the Globe were the hexagon, the circle, and the square.

And thirdly, the plan utilises dimensions given in the contract for the building of the Fortune theatre.[31] The Fortune contract has always been a main source for Globe reconstructors because it states in two places that certain of its specifications are to be like what has been done at the Globe. This contract is, however, a confusing document from the point of view of the Globe reconstructor because (1) the Fortune was a square theatre and so cannot have been exactly like the Globe; (2) its statements are often vaguely phrased, and it is not at all clear, to my mind at least, which parts of it are being made like the Globe. Nevertheless the dimensions which it specifies cannot be ignored. The Fortune contract gives a dimension of 43 feet for the stage which is to 'extend to the middle of the yard'; and a dimension of 80 feet for the size of the square of which the theatre is formed, with an inner square of 55 feet arrived at by the subtraction of the width of the galleries. The plan of the Globe here attempted keeps the dimension of 43 feet for the stage, but increases the total dimension of 80 feet given for the square Fortune to a dimension of 86 feet for the diameter of the circle formed by the outer wall of the galleries in this theatre, which we believe was round within and hexagonal without.

The new plan of the Globe (Fig. 11) is based on a hexagon as the external form of the theatre. Within the hexagon is inscribed a circle (the outer wall of the galleries). Within the circle are inscribed four triangles; the base of one gives the position of the *frons scaenae*; its apex points to the opposite part of the auditorium; six other triangle apices point towards other parts of the auditorium. On the inner circle, which marks the boundary between the galleries and the yard, seven openings are indicated, opposite the apices of the seven triangles. These, it is suggested, mark gangways between seats in the galleries whose positions are determined by the triangles, like the gangways in a classical theatre. Two such entries, marked 'ingressus' can be seen in the

---

[31] Printed in Chambers, *Elizabethan Stage*, II, pp. 436 ff.

De Witt drawing (Pl. 19); it is possible that these were not actual entrances to the lower gallery which may have been more probably entered from the back, like the upper galleries, but they would mark the significant seven points at which there were seven gangways between the seats.

Three other triangle apices determine the position of the three

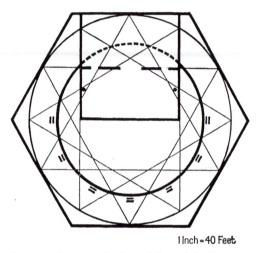

1 Inch = 40 Feet

Fig. 11 Suggested Plan of the Globe Theatre

doors on ground level in the *frons scaenae*, as in the classical theatre. But there is a deviation from the classical theatre in that the remaining two triangle apices do not mark entrances; in the classical theatre they would mark side entrances to the stage, but at the Globe the other two entrances to the stage were on the upper level, immediately above the two entrances flanking the main entrance on ground level. Thus the five entrances at the Globe needed only three triangle apices to mark their positions. It is a deviation from the classical theatre due to the multilevel stage.

The square includes both tiring house and stage, and is bounded at the back by the outer hexagonal wall. Since there were acting areas within the tiring house it may perhaps be said that the square is the stage as a whole. The part of it in front of the *frons scaenae* is a rectangle jutting out into the middle of the yard. The front of the stage is on the diameter of the yard, just as the proscenium of the classical stage was on the diameter of the orchestra. The two round

358

'posts' indicate the point at which the stage cover, or 'heavens', ends. These column bases, actually marking the real 'posts', also indicate which part of the theatre is shown in the Fludd engraving.

No attempt is made to suggest the position of door or doors into the theatre nor any architectural details at all. It is simply a plan of basic geometrical forms. But I believe that the Vitruvian zodiacal triangles and Fludd's symbolic geometry may be safer and more stable guides to the basic plan of the Globe than the indistinct maps and indistinct contracts on which reconstructions have hitherto been based.

It is very interesting to realise how closely the Globe comes out as an adaptation of Vitruvius. If this plan is compared with the Palladian plan of the Vitruvian theatre (Pl. 9a) it can be seen that both plans have to solve the problem of placing a stage and a stage building in relation to a circle, and they solve it in much the same way. Except that the Globe seats its audience in superimposed galleries and the Globe has a multilevel stage. Also the hexagonal outline of the Globe enables it to get in a square, which is just not obtainable within the circle of the Vitruvian theatre plan.

This square is highly significant, for it relates the Shakespearean theatre to the temple and the church. In his third book on temples, Vitruvius describes how the figure of a man with extended arms and legs fits exactly into a square or a circle. In the Italian Renaissance, this Vitruvian image of Man within the square or the circle became the favourite expression of the relation of the microcosm to the macrocosm, or, as Rudolf Wittkower puts it, 'invigorated by the Christian belief that Man as the image of God embodied the harmonies of the Universe, the Vitruvian figure inscribed in a square and a circle became a symbol of the mathematical sympathy between microcosm and macrocosm. How could the relation of Man to God be better expressed . . . than by building the house of God in accordance with the fundamental geometry of square and circle?'[32] This was the preoccupation of all the great Renaissance architects. And it was evidently the preoccupation of the designers of the Globe Theatre.

The old theory of the inn yard as the ancestor of the wooden theatres of the English Renaissance begins to seem singularly

[32] Rudolf Wittkower, *Architectural Principles in the Age of Humanism*, London, Warburg Institute, 1949, p. 15.

inadequate,[33] though it may still account for some things, perhaps for the galleries, and for the use of the word 'yard' for the orchestra. The very attempt to build large theatres in wood shows classical influence, for Vitruvius states that many of the 'public theatres' in Rome were built of wood.[34] And the remarks of foreign visitors when surveying the many London public theatres indicate that they saw classical influence in them. De Witt speaks of the 'amphitheatres' of London.[35] A traveller who visited London in 1600 says that he saw an English comedy in a theatre 'constructed in wood after the manner of the ancient Romans'.[36] And the design of the Globe as revealed by Fludd seems to suggest a knowledge, not only of Vitruvius, but also of interpretations of Vitruvius in the Italian Renaissance.

The first of the wooden theatres of the English Renaissance was the 'Theater' which was built by James Burbage in 1576 in Shoreditch.[37] The 'Theater' was the prototype of all the new style wooden theatres. Moreover it was particularly associated with the origins of the Globe, for timber from the 'Theater' was carried across the river and used in the building of the first Globe on Bankside in 1599.[38] If we are to look for influences from the Italian Renaissance revival of Vitruvius on the origins of the Globe, these should be available before 1576, when the 'Theater' was built. As well as Shute's book on architecture (1563) a source in England of such influences would have been the Hermetic philosopher John Dee, the teacher of Philip Sidney and his circle.

In the year 1570 (that is six years before the building of the 'Theater') a very important book was printed by John Day in London. It was the first English translation of Euclid made by H. Billingsley, citizen of London.[39] The translation is preceded

[33] The inn yard theory is already on the way out; see Glynn Wickham, *Early English Stages*, II, pp. 157 ff.

[34] *De architectura*, Lib. V, cap. V, 7.

[35] Chambers, *Elizabethan Stage*, II, p. 362. Cf. also the passage quoted from *Holland's Leaguer* where the Globe, the Hope, and the Swan are described as 'three famous Amphytheators' (*ibid.*, p. 376).

[36] *Ibid.*, p. 366.

[37] *Ibid.*, pp. 384 ff.

[38] *Ibid.*, p. 399. The 'Theater' is also associated with the Globe in that it was the theatre chiefly used by the Lord Chamberlain's men, Shakespeare's company, before the building of the Globe.

[39] ' *The Elements of the Geometrie of the most ancient Philosopher Euclide of Megara, Faithfully (now first) translated into the Englishe toung, by*

by a very long preface in English by John Dee,[40] in which Dee surveys all the mathematical sciences, both from the point of view of Platonic and mystical theory of number and also with the purpose of being of practical utility to artisans. In this preface Dee makes many quotations from Vitruvius. When discussing Man as the 'Lesse World' he says 'looke in Vitruuius', referring in the margin to the first chapter of Vitruvius's third book,[41] which is the chapter in which the Vitruvian man within the square and the circle is described. And in the part of this preface on architecture, Dee gives the Vitruvian theory of architecture as the noblest of the sciences and of the architect as the universal man who must be familiar, not only with the practical and mechanical aspects of his profession, but with all other branches of knowledge. Moreover, Dee is here using, not only 'Vitruuius the Romaine' but also 'Leo Baptista Albertus, a Florentine'. Relying on both Vitruvius and Alberti, Dee sees perfect architecture as immaterial. 'The hand of the Carpenter is the Architectes Instrument', carrying out what the architect 'in minde and Imagination' determines. 'And we may prescribe in mynde and Imagination the whole formes, all materiall stuffe beyng secluded.'[42]

It seems strange that this preface by Dee, with its enthusiastic references to the ideals of the revival of Vitruvius in the Italian Renaissance, has been so little noticed. Perhaps this neglect is to be attributed to the prejudice against Dee as an 'occult philosopher'. I understand, however, that R. Wittkower will include Dee in his forthcoming book on English architectural theory.

Dee gives no details of architectural plans but when discussing music as one of the sciences which the architect must know he

[40] On the quotation from Pico della Mirandola in this preface see *G.B. and H.T.*, p. 148.

[41] *Elements of the Geometrie*, Preface, sig. c iiii, *recto*. In the immediately following sentences, Dee urges the reader to 'Looke in *Albertus Durerus, De Symmetria humani Corporis*. Looke in the 27 and 28 Chapters, of the second booke, *De occulta Philosophia*.' In these books of the *De occulta philosophia*, Agrippa gives the Vitruvian figures of the man within the square and the circle.

[42] Preface, sig. d iii, *recto*.

H. Billingsley, Citizen of London . . . With a very fruitfull Praeface made by M. I. Dee . . ' Imprinted at London by Iohn Daye (the preface is dated February 3rd, 1570).

mentions one feature of the ancient theatre, those mysterious musical sound-amplifiers which Vitruvius says were placed under the seats:

> And Musike he (the architect) must nedes know: that he may haue understanding, both of Regular and Mathematicall Musike . . . Moreouer, the Brasen Vesels, which in Theatres, are placed by Mathematicall order . . . under the steppes . . . and the diuersities of the soundes . . . are ordered according to Musicall Symphonies & Harmonies, being distributed in ye Circuites, by Diatessaron, Diapente, and Diapason. That the conuenient voyce, of the players sound, when it come to these preparations, made in order, there being increased: with yt increasing, might come more cleare & pleasant, to ye eares of the lokers on.[43]

With this poetic passage on the musical voices of the players we may be near to the genesis of the Shakespearean type of theatre. For James Burbage was a carpenter by trade. When he came to build his 'amphitheatre' would he not have been likely to use this translation of Euclid, in the preface of which was this musical evocation of the ancient theatre, and the description of how 'the hand of the carpenter' carries out the ideal forms in the mind of the architect?

A vast subject is opened up here, and one at which I can only hint in a brief paragraph. Dee is giving in this preface the Renaissance theory of number; he has in view practical applications of the mathematical sciences, and addresses himself to artisans. These subjects were excluded from the universities, a fact to which Dee frequently refers in the preface. Hence it would come about that it would devolve on an artisan, a carpenter like James Burbage, to introduce the true Renaissance architecture of the Elizabethan age, the wooden theatre architecture. Was it also Burbage (perhaps with the advice of Dee) who adapted Vitruvius by combining the classical theatre with a heritage from the mediaeval religious theatre, the multilevel stage?[44] It was this adaptation which made of

---

[43] *Ibid.*, sig. d iii *verso*. Cf. Vitruvius, Lib. V, cap V.

[44] Another mediaeval survival in the Shakespearean theatre would be those secondary theatres which Fludd shows, used to indicate simultaneously different localities, after the manner of the mediaeval 'mansions'.

The Shakespearean theatre, as now understood, becomes one of the most interesting and powerful of Renaissance adaptations of the Vitruvian theatre (on which see R. Klein and H. Zerner, 'Vitruve et le théâtre de la

the Shakespearean theatre a marvellous synthesis of the immediate contact between players and audience of the classical theatre with a hint of the hierarchy of spiritual levels expressed in the old religious theatre.

Though the first Globe would have carried on traditions begun by the first 'amphitheatre', it was a new theatre, and generally regarded as the best and most successful of the theatres. It was the theatre of which Shakespeare was joint owner; it is even conceivable that he might have had some influence on its design. And the Globe (judging by Fludd's reflection of the second Globe) shows that the Shakespearean theatre was not an imitation but an adaptation of Vitruvius. Apart from the change on the *frons scaenae* from a classical building to a battlemented and bay-windowed mansion, there was the basic change introduced by the multilevel stage. The old religious theatre showed a spiritual drama of the soul of man in relation to the levels of Hell, Purgatory, and Paradise. A Renaissance theatre like the Globe also expressed the spiritual drama, but in relation to the changed Renaissance outlook which approached religious truth through the world, through the *fabrica mundi*.

The Shakespearean theatre was a splendid theatre, an adaptation of Vitruvius superior to the picture stage within the proscenium arch, which lost the true Vitruvian qualities. Yet the picture stage theatre would supplant the Globe type of theatre for centuries, had indeed already supplanted it when the Fludd engraving was

---

Renaissance italienne' in *Le Lieu Théâtral à la Renaissance*, ed. J. Jacquot, Centre National de la Recherche Scientifique, 1964, pp. 49–60).

Evidence could, I think be gathered from Dee's Preface that he knew Daniele Barbaro's commentary on Vitruvius, the book which contains Palladio's reconstruction of the Roman theatre (Pl. 9a). When speaking of Vitruvius's dedication of his work to Augustus, Dee adds 'in whose daies our Heauenly Archemaster was borne' (Preface, sig. d iii *recto*). Barbaro, at the beginning of his commentary (p. 2 in the edition of Venice, 1567) dwells on the universal peace of the Augustan age 'in which time Our Lord Jesus Christ was born'.

It may be of significance that, according to Anthony à Wood (*Athenae Oxonienses*, London, 1691, cols. 284–5) Billingsley was assisted in his mathematical work on Euclid by an Austin Friar named Whytehead who had been expelled from his convent in Oxford in the time of Henry VIII and lived in Billingsley's house in London. In the background of this circle, there was thus an expert on number and its symbolic meaning surviving from the old pre-Reformation world.

published. Fludd was old-fashioned in his taste in theatres, for the picture stages introduced at Court by Inigo Jones in 1604 were beginning to make the Globe look out of date by 1619.

'All the world's a stage.' Fludd teaches us to reconsider those familiar words. No one has ever guessed that the designers of that vanished wooden building were skilled in the subtleties of cosmological proportion. Though Ben Jonson doubtless knew this for when surveying the charred remains of the first Globe, after the fire, he exclaimed, 'See the World's ruins!'[45]

'The belief in the correspondence of microcosm and macrocosm, in the harmonic structure of the universe, in the comprehension of God through mathematical symbols . . . all these closely related ideas which had their roots in antiquity and belonged to the undisputed tenets of mediaeval philosophy and theology, acquired new life in the Renaissance and found visual expression in the Renaissance church.'[46] Rudolf Wittkower is discussing the use of the round form for churches in the Renaissance. He quotes from Alberti, who believed that the round form was the form most beloved by nature, as was proved by her own creations, and that nature was the best teacher for 'nature is God'.[47] Alberti recommended nine basic forms for churches, amongst them the hexagon, the octagon, the decagon, and the dodecagon, all figures determined by the circle.[48] The designers of the Globe chose the hexagon for their religious theatre.

One more fact does Fludd tell us, namely how the World Theatre faced in relation to the points of the compass. These are marked on the diagram of the 'heavens' (Pl. 16) facing the engraving of the stage—'Oriens' is at the top of it, 'Occidens' at the bottom. When these 'heavens' cover the stage, we learn that the stage was at the east end of the theatre, like the altar in a church.

Thoughts occur to one of the possibility of using Fludd's revelations, not only for the understanding of the actual staging of Shakespeare's plays, but also for an interpretation of the relative spiritual significance of scenes played on different levels. Is the

[45] Quoted by Chambers, *Elizabethan Stage*, II, p. 422.
[46] R. Wittkower, *Architectural Principles in the Age of Humanism*, p. 27.
[47] *Ibid.*, p. 4.
[48] See the diagrams, *ibid.*, p. 3; and for Serlio's plan for a hexagonal church, *ibid.*, Plate 6.

Shakespearean stage a Renaissance and Hermetic transformation of the old religious stage? Are its levels (there was a third level above the 'heavens' about which Fludd gives no information) a presentation of the relation of the divine to the human seen through the world in its threefold character? The elemental and sub-celestial world would be the square stage on which man plays his parts. The round celestial world hangs above it, not as astrologically determining man's fate but as the 'shadow of ideas', the vestige of the divine. Whilst above the 'heavens' would be the super-celestial world of the ideas which pours its effluxes down through the medium of the heavens, and whither ascent is made by the same steps as those of the descent, that is through the world of nature.

Perhaps scenes of higher spiritual significance in which the shadows are less dense are scenes which were played high. Juliet appeared to Romeo in the chamber. Cleopatra died high in her Egyptian monument. Prospero once appeared 'on the top', invisible to the actors on the stage below the 'heavens' but visible to the audience.[49] It is not known whether *The Tempest* was first performed at the Globe or at Blackfriars, the theatre arranged in the building of the old convent of the Dominicans which the King's company of players acquired in 1608. But the Blackfriars theatre no doubt had a 'heavens', so whether Prospero was first seen 'on the top' at Blackfriars or at the Globe, his appearance would be singularly impressive as the apotheosis of the benevolent Magus who had risen beyond the shadows of ideas to the supreme unifying vision.

At the close of this chapter, I wish to emphasise that I regard its contents as only a first attempt to utilise material which has not hitherto been available for the reconstruction of the Shakespearean type of theatre. This material consists, first of all, of the engravings in Fludd's memory system, and secondly of the use of Dee's preface to Billingsley's Euclid as evidence that it was Dee (and not Inigo Jones) who was the first 'Vitruvius Britannicus', and that therefore Vitruvian influences were available to the designers of the first Elizabethan Theatre and its successors. The chapter will certainly be scrutinised and criticised by experts, and in this way the subject will no doubt be advanced further than I have been able to take it. There is much more actual research to be

[49] *The Tempest*, III, iii; cf. Irwin Smith, *Shakespeare's Globe Playhouse*, p. 140.

done, particularly on the German end of the publication of Fludd's work (which may throw light on the engraver of the theatre), and on Vitruvian influences in both Dee and Fludd.

I have had to compress the chapter as much as possible lest this book, which is about the history of the art of memory, should lose its bearings. Yet this chapter had to be in this book, because it is only in the context of the history of the art of memory that the relationship of Fludd's memory system to a real theatre can be understood. It is in strict pursuance of the history of the art of memory that we have found ourselves introduced into the Shakespearean theatre. To whom do we owe this extraordinary experience? To Simonides of Ceos and Metrodorus of Scepsis; to 'Tullius' and Thomas Aquinas; to Giulio Camillo and Giordano Bruno. For unless we had travelled on our long journey with the art of memory down the ages, though we might have seen something exciting in the Fludd engraving (as Bernheimer did) we could not have understood it. It is with the tools forged in following the history of the art of memory that we have been able to excavate the Globe theatre from its hiding place in Fludd's *Utriusque Cosmi . . . Historia.*

It has been well and truly hidden there for three and a half centuries. And here the question arises which has always baffled us in studying Bruno's memory Seals. Were these fantastic occult memory systems deliberately made impossible and inscrutable in order to hide a secret? Is Fludd's system of the twenty-four memory theatres in the zodiac an elaborate casket deliberately contrived to conceal his allusion to the Globe theatre from all but the iniated, of whom we must suppose that James I was one?

As I have said before, I think that although the Renaissance Hermetic tradition was becoming more and more of a secret in the late Renaissance, the occult memory system is not to be entirely accounted for as a cipher. The occult memory belongs into the Renaissance as a whole. It was the Renaissance on the Hermetic side as a whole, the secret of its inner stimulus to the imagination, which Giordano Bruno brought with him to England, and I would see in Bruno's visit and in the 'Scepsian' controversies aroused by his *Seals* a basic factor in the formation of Shakespeare. I would also suggest that the two native Hermetic philosophers, John Dee and Robert Fludd, ought not to be excluded from the attention of those interested in the English Renaissance. It may be because they have been excluded that the secret of Shakespeare has been missed.

The revelation of the Globe within the last of the Seals of Memory would be incomprehensible and unbelievable if presented without preparation, yet it has an intelligible historical context within the history of the art of memory, and it is this which alone concerns us in the concluding pages of this chapter.

Camillo's Theatre is in many ways analogous to Fludd's Theatre system. There is in both cases a distortion of a 'real' theatre for the purposes of a Hermetic memory system. Camillo distorts the Vitruvian theatre by transferring the practice of decorating with imagery the five entrances to its stage to the seven times seven imaginary gates which he erects in the auditorium. Fludd stands with his back to the auditorium and looking towards the stage, loading with imaginary imagery its five doors, used as memory *loci*, and distorting the stage for his mnemonic purposes by crushing it into a memory room. In both cases there is a distortion of a real theatre, though the distortions are of a different kind.

Camillo's Theatre rises in the midst of the Venetian Renaissance and is immediately derivative from the movement initiated by Ficino and Pico. It arouses immense admiration and interest and seems to belong naturally with those powerful manifestations of the creative imagination which we see at that stage in the Italian Renaissance. Admired by Ariosto and Tasso, its architectural form was related to the neoclassical architecture out of which was soon to develop a significant 'real' theatre, the Teatro Olimpico. Fludd's Theatre memory system arises within a philosophy which is very closely derivative from the earlier Renaissance tradition. And it uses the type of theatre which had housed the supreme achievement of a very late Renaissance. When we meditate as best we can on this comparison, it begins to seem after all historically right that Fludd's Hermetic memory system should reflect the Globe.

The question to which I can give no clear or satisfactory answer is: What was the occult memory? Did the change from forming corporeal similitudes of the intelligible world to the effort to grasp the intelligible world through tremendous imaginative exercises such as those to which Giordano Bruno devoted his life really stimulate the human psyche to a wider range of creative imaginative achievement than ever before? Was this the secret of the Renaissance and does the occult memory represent that secret? I bequeath this problem to others.

❖◦❖

Chapter XVII

THE ART OF MEMORY AND THE GROWTH OF SCIENTIFIC METHOD

❖◦❖

IT HAS been the purpose of this book to show the place of the art of memory at the great nerve centres of the European tradition. In the Middle Ages it was central, with its theory formulated by the scholastics and its practice connected with mediaeval imagery in art and architecture as a whole and with great literary monuments such as Dante's *Divine Comedy*. At the Renaissance its importance dwindled in the purely humanist tradition but grew to vast proportions in the Hermetic tradition. Now that we are already in the seventeenth century in the course of our history will it finally disappear, or survive only marginally and not at the centre? Robert Fludd is a last outpost of the full Renaissance Hermetic tradition. He is in conflict with representatives of the new scientific movement, with Kepler and Mersenne. Is his Hermetic memory system, based on the Shakespearean Globe Theatre, also a last outpost of the art of memory itself, a signal that the ancient art of Simonides is about to be put aside as an anachronism in the seventeenth century advance?

It is a curious and significant fact that the art of memory is known and discussed in the seventeenth century not only, as we should expect, by a writer like Robert Fludd who is still following the Renaissance tradition, but also by the thinkers who are turning in the new directions, by Francis Bacon, by Descartes, by Leibniz. For in this century the art of memory underwent yet another of its transformations, turning from a method of memorising the encyclopaedia of knowledge, of reflecting the world in memory, to an aid for investigating the encyclopaedia and the world with the object of discovering new knowledge. It is fascinating to watch how, in the trends of the new century, the art of memory survives as a factor in the growth of scientific method.

In this concluding chapter, which comes as a postscript to the main part of the book, I can only briefly indicate the importance of the art of memory in this new rôle. Insufficient though it is, this chapter must be attempted because in the seventeenth century the art of memory is still in a significant position in a major European development. Our history which began with Simonides must not end before Leibniz.

The word 'method' was popularised by Ramus. We saw in an earlier chapter[1] that there is a close connection between Ramism and the art of memory and that this alone might suggest a connection between the history of memory and the history of method. But the word was also used of Lullism and Cabalism which flourished in the Renaissance in close association with memory. To give one example out of the many which might be cited, there is the 'circular method' for knowing everything described by Cornelius Gemma in his *De arte cyclognomica*[2] which is a compound of Lullism, Hermetism, Cabalism, and the art of memory. This work may have influenced Bruno who also calls his procedures a 'method',[3] and the use of this word for modes of thinking which would seem to have little connection with the new mathematical method was widely prevalent in the seventeenth century as the following anecdote will illustrate.

When the members of a small private academy in Paris assembled for their first meeting, about the year 1632, the subject of their deliberations was 'method'. The conference began with a highly abbreviated reference to the 'method of the Cabbalists' who from the archetypal world descend to the intellectual world and thence to the elemental world; the members then passed to an equally rapid characterisation of the 'method of Ramon Lull', based on divine attributes; and thence to what they described as 'the method of ordinary philosophy'. In the published account of

[1] See above, pp. 231 ff.
[2] Cornelius Gemma, *De arte cyclognomica*, Antwerp, 1569.
[3] See above, p. 294.

their transactions these efforts are summed up under the title 'De la méthode'.[4] The very few pages in which these large subjects are dismissed are unworthy of attention save as an indication of how little surprise would have been aroused by the title *Discours de la méthode* of the book published five years later by Descartes.

Amongst the numerous 'methods' circulating in the early seventeenth century, the art of memory was prominent and so also was the art of Ramon Lull. These two great mediaeval arts, which the Renaissance had tried to combine, turn into methods in the seventeenth century and play their part in the methodological revolution.[5]

Francis Bacon had a very full knowledge of the art of memory and himself used it.[6] There is indeed in Aubrey's life of Bacon one of the few evidences of the actual design of a building for use in 'local memory'. Aubrey says that in one of the galleries in Bacon's house, Gorhambury, there were painted glass windows 'and every pane with severall figures of beast, bird and flower: perhaps his Lordship might use them as topiques for locall use'.[7] The importance which Bacon attached to the art of memory is shown by the fact that it figures quite prominently in the *Advancement of Learning* as one of the arts and sciences which are in need of reform, both in their methods and in the ends for which they are

[4] *Recueil général des questions traitées és Conférences du Bureau d'Adresse*, Lyons, 1633–66, I, pp. 7 ff. On this academy at the 'Bureau d'Adresse', run by Théophraste Renaudot, see my *French Academies of the Sixteenth Century*, p. 296.

[5] The useful book by Neal W. Gilbert, *Renaissance Concepts of Method* (Columbia, 1960) discusses the classical sources of the word and contains valuable pages on 'art' and 'method'. The 'Renaissance concepts of method' discussed are, however, chiefly Ramist and Aristotelian. The 'methods' with which this next chapter is concerned are not mentioned.

I would think that Ong is probably right (*Ramus, Method and the Decay of Dialogue*, Cambridge, Mass., 1958, pp. 231 ff.) in stressing the importance of the revival of Hermogenes in drawing attention to the word 'method'. This revival was fostered by Giulio Camillo (see above, p. 168, note 19, p. 238.

[6] On Bacon and the art of memory, see K. R. Wallace, *Francis Bacon on Communication and Rhetoric*, North Carolina, 1943, pp. 156, 214; W. S. Howell, *Logic and Rhetoric in England*, Princeton, 1956, p. 206; Paolo Rossi, *Francesco Bacone*, Bari, 1957, pp. 480 ff., and *Clavis universalis*, 1960, pp. 142 ff.

[7] John Aubrey, *Brief Lives*, ed. O. L. Dick, London, 1960, p. 14.

used. The extant art of memory could be improved, says Bacon, and it should be used, not for empty ostentation, but for useful purposes. The general trend of the *Advancement* towards improving the arts and sciences and turning them to useful ends is brought to bear on memory, of which, says Bacon, there is an art extant 'but it seemeth to me that there are better precepts than that art, and better practices of that art than those received'. As now used the art may be 'raised to points of ostentation prodigious' but it is barren, and not used for serious 'business and occasions'. He defines the art as based on 'prenotions' and 'emblems', the Baconian version of places and images:

> This art of memory is but built upon two intentions; the one prenotion, the other emblem. Prenotion dischargeth the indefinite seeking of that we would remember, and directeth us to seek in a narrow compass, that is, somewhat that hath congruity with our place of memory. Emblem reduceth conceits intellectual to images sensible, which strike the memory more; out of which axioms may be drawn better practique than that in use . . .[8]

Places are further defined in the *Novum Organum* as the

> order or distribution of Common Places in the artificial memory, which may be either Places in the proper sense of the word, as a door, a corner, a window, and the like; or familiar and well known persons; or anything we choose (provided they are arranged in a certain order), as animals, herbs; also words, letters, characters, historical personages . . .[9]

Such a definition as this of different types of places comes straight out of the mnemonic text-books.

The definition of images as 'emblems' is expanded in the *De augmentis scientiarum:*

> Emblems bring down intellectual to sensible things; for what is sensible always strikes the memory stronger, and sooner impresses itself than the intellectual . . . And therefore it is easier to retain the image of a sportsman hunting the hare, of an apothecary ranging his boxes, an orator making a speech, a boy repeating verses, or a player acting his part, than the corresponding notions of invention, disposition, elocution, memory, action.[10]

[8] F. Bacon, *Advancement of Learning*, II, xv, 2; in *Works*; ed. Spedding, III, pp. 398–9.
[9] *Novum Organum*, II, xxvi; Spedding, I, p. 275.
[10] *De augmentis scientiarum*, V, v; Spedding, I, p. 649.

Which shows that Bacon fully subscribed to the ancient view that the active image impresses itself best on memory, and to the Thomist view that intellectual things are best remembered through sensible things. Incidentally, this acceptance of images in memory shows that Bacon, though influenced by Ramism, was not a Ramist.

It was therefore roughly speaking the normal art of memory using places and images which Bacon accepted and practised. How he proposed to improve it is not clear. But amongst the new uses to which it was to be put was the memorising of matters in order so as to hold them in the mind for investigation. This would help scientific enquiry, for by drawing particulars out of the mass of natural history, and ranging them in order, the judgment could be more easily brought to bear upon them.[11] Here the art of memory is being used for the investigation of natural science, and its principles of order and arrangement are turning into something like classification.

The art of memory has here indeed been reformed from 'ostentatious' uses by rhetoricians bent on impressing by their wonderful memories and turned to serious business. And amongst the ostentatious uses which are to be abolished in the reformed use of the art Bacon certainly has in mind the occult memories of the Magi. 'The ancient opinion that man was a microcosmus, an abstract or model of the world, hath been fantastically strained by Paracelsus and the alchemists', he says in the *Advancement*.[12] It was on that opinion that 'Metrodorian' memory systems such as that of Fludd were based. To Bacon such schemes might well have seemed 'enchanted glasses' full of distorting 'idola', and far from that humble approach to nature in observation and experiment which he advocated.

Nevertheless though I would agree with Rossi that the Baconian reform of the art of memory would on the whole preclude occult memory, yet Bacon is an elusive character and there is a passage in the *Sylva Sylvarum* in which he introduces the art of memory in a context of the use of the 'force of the imagination'. He tells a story of a card trick which was worked by the force of the imagination of the juggler, by which he 'bound the spirits' of the onlooker

[11] *Partis Instaurationis Secundae Delineatio et Argumentum*; Spedding, III, p. 552. Cf. Rossi, *Clavis*, pp. 489 ff.
[12] *Advancement*, II, x, 2; Spedding, III, p. 370.

to ask for a certain card. As a commentary òn this card trick through 'force of imagination' comes the following:

> We find in the art of memory, that images visible work better than other conceits: as if you would remember the word *philosophy*, you shall more surely do it by imagining that such a man (for men are best places) is reading upon Aristotle's Physics; than if you should imagine him to say, *I'll go study philosophy*. And therefore this observation would be translated to the subject we now speak of (the card trick): for the more lustrous the imagination is, it filleth and fixeth better.[13]

Though he is exploring the subject scientifically, Bacon is profoundly imbued with the classical belief that the mnemonic image has power through stirring the imagination, and he connects this with 'force of imagination' tricks. This line of thought was one of the ways through which the art of memory became an adjunct of the magician in the Renaissance. Bacon is evidently still seeing such connections.

Descartes also exercised his great mind on the art of memory and how it might be reformed, and the mnemonic author who gave rise to his reflections was none other than Lambert Schenkel. In the *Cogitationes privatae* there is the following remark:

> On reading through Schenkel's profitable trifles (in the book *De arte memoria*) I thought of an easy way of making myself master of all I discovered through the imagination. This would be done through the reduction of things to their causes. Since all can be reduced to one it is obviously not necessary to remember all the sciences. When one understands the causes all vanished images can easily be found again in the brain through the impression of the cause. This is the true art of memory and it is plain contrary to his (Schenkel's) nebulous notions. Not that his (art) is without effect, but it occupies the whole space with too many things and not in the right order. The right order is that the images should be formed in dependence on one another. He (Schenkel) omits this which is the key to the whole mystery.
>   I have thought of another way; that out of unconnected images should be composed new images common to them all, or that one image should be made which should have reference not only to the one nearest to it but to them all—so that the fifth should refer to the

---

[13] *Sylva sylvarum*, Century X, 956; Spedding, II, p. 659.

first through a spear thrown on the ground, the middle one through a ladder on which they descend, the second one through an arrow thrown at it, and similarly the third should be connected in some way either real or fictitious.[14]

Curiously enough, Descartes's suggested reform of memory is nearer to 'occult' principles than Bacon's, for occult memory does reduce all things to their supposed causes whose images when impressed on memory are believed to organise the subsidiary images. Had Descartes consulted Paepp on 'detecting' Schenkel[15] he would have known of this. The phrase about the 'impression of the cause' through which all vanished images can be found might easily be that of an occult memory artist. Of course Descartes is certainly not thinking on such lines but his brilliant new idea of organising memory on causes sounds curiously like a rationalisation of occult memory. His other notions about forming connected images are far from new and can be found in some form in nearly every text-book.

It seems unlikely that Descartes made much use of local memory which, according to quotations in Baillet's *Life*, he neglected to practise much in his retreat and which he regarded as 'corporeal memory' and 'outside of us' as compared with 'intellectual memory' which is within and incapable of increase or decrease.[16] This singularly crude idea is in keeping with Descarte's lack of interest in the imagination and its functioning. Rossi suggests, however, that the memory principles of order and arrangement influenced Descartes, as they did Bacon.

Both Bacon and Descartes knew of the art of Lull to which they both refer in very derogatory terms. Discussing false methods in the *Advancement*, Bacon says:

There hath been also laboured and put into practice a method, which is not a lawful method, but a method of imposture; which is, to deliver knowledges in such a manner, as men may speedily come to make a show of learning who have it not. Such was the travail of Raymundus Lullus in making that art which bears his name . . .[17]

[14] Descartes, *Cogitationes privatae* (1619–1621); in *Œuvres*, ed. Adam and Tannery, X, p. 230. Cf. Rossi, *Clavis*, pp. 154–5.

[15] See above, p. 301.

[16] Descartes, *Œuvres, ed. cit.*, X, pp. 200, 201 (fragments from the *Studium bonae mentis, circa* 1620, preserved in quotation in Baillet's *Life*).

[17] *Advancement*, II, xvii, 14; Spedding, III, p. 408.

And Descartes in the *Discours de la méthode* is equally severe on the Lullian art which serves but to enable one 'to speak without judgment of those things of which one is ignorant'.[18]

Thus neither the discoverer of the inductive method, which was not to lead to scientifically valuable results, nor the discoverer of the method of analytical geometry, which was to revolutionise the world as the first systematic application of mathematics to the investigation of nature, have anything good to say of the method of Ramon Lull. Why indeed should they? What possible connection can there be between the 'emergence of modern science' and that mediaeval art, so frantically revived and 'occultised' in the Renaissance, with its combinatory systems based on Divine Names or attributes. Nevertheless the Art of Ramon Lull had this in common with the aims of Bacon and Descartes. It promised to provide a universal art or method which, because based on reality, could be applied for the solution of all problems. Moreover it was a kind of geometrical logic, with its squares and triangles and its revolving combinatory wheels; and it used a notation of letters to express the concepts with which it was dealing.

When outlining his new method to Beeckman, in a letter of March 1619, Descartes said that what he was meditating was not an *ars brevis* of Lull, but a new science which would be able to solve all questions concerning quantity.[19] The operative word is, of course, 'quantity', marking the great change from qualitative and symbolic use of number. The mathematical method was hit upon at last, but in order to realise the atmosphere in which it was found we should know something of those frenzied pre-occupations with arts of memory, combinatory arts, Cabalist arts, which the Renaissance bequeathed to the seventeenth century. The occultist tide was receding and in the changed atmosphere the search turns in the direction of rational method.

In the transference of Renaissance modes of thinking and procedures to the seventeenth century a considerable part was played by the German, Johann-Heinrich Alsted (1588–1638), encyclopaedist, Lullist, Cabalist, Ramist, and the author of the *Systema*

[18] *Discours de la méthode*, part II; *Œuvres, ed. cit.*, VI, p. 17.

[19] *Œuvres, ed. cit.*, X, pp. 156–7. Cf. my article, 'The Art of Ramon Lull', *Journal of the Warburg and Courtauld Institutes*, XVII (1954), p. 155.

mnemonicum,[20] a vast repertoire on the art of memory. Like Bruno and the Renaissance Lullists, Alsted believed that the pseudo-Lullian *De auditu kabbalistico* was a genuine Lullian work,[21] which facilitated his assimilation of Lullism to Cabalism. Alsted describes Lull as a 'mathematician and Cabalist'.[22] He defines method as the mnemonic instrument which proceeds from generals to specials (a definition of course, also influenced by Ramism) and he calls the Lullian circles places corresponding to the places of the art of memory. Alsted is a Renaissance encyclopaedist, and a man of the Renaissance, too, in his efforts to fuse every kind of method in the search for a universal key.[23]

Yet he, too, is affected by the reaction against Renaissance occultism. He wished to free Lullism from the idle dreams and fancies with which it had been contaminated and to return to the purer doctrine as taught by Lavinheta. In the preface, dated 1609, to his *Clavis artis Lullianae* he inveighs against commentators who have defaced the divine art with their falsehoods and obscurities, mentioning by name Agrippa and Bruno.[24] Yet Alsted published one of Bruno's manuscripts (not, it is true, a Lullian one) after his death.[25] There seems to be a movement going on in the Alstedian circle, in which Bruno is remembered, towards a reformed version of those procedures which Bruno had so extravagantly stimulated on a wildly Hermetic plane. A full study of Alsted might reveal that the seeds which Bruno had sown during his travels in Germany had germinated but were bringing forth fruits more suited to

[20] J.-H. Alsted, *Systema mnemonicum duplex . . . in quo artis memorativae praecepta plene et methodice traduntur*, Frankfort, 1610.

[21] *Systema mnemonicum*, p. 5; quoted by Rossi, *Clavis*, p. 182. The influential *De auditu kabbalistico* (on which see above, pp. 189, 197, 209) may have helped to propagate the word 'method' which is used in its preface (*De auditu kabbalistico* in R. Lull, *Opera*, Strasburg, 1598, p. 45).

[22] See T. and J. Carreras y Artau, *Filosofía Cristiana de los siglos XIII al XV*, Madrid, 1943, II, p. 244.

[23] One of his works is entitled *Methodus admirandorum mathematicorum novem libris exhibens universam mathesim*, Herborn, 1623. See Carreras y Artau, II, p. 239.

[24] J.-H. Alsted, *Clavis artis Lullianae*, Strasburg, 1633, preface; See Carreras y Artaus, II, p. 241; Rossi, *Clavis*, p. 180.

[25] The *Artificium perorandi*, written by Bruno at Wittenberg in 1587, was published by Alsted at Frankfort in 1612. See Salvestrini-Firpo, *Bibliografia di Giordano Bruno*, Florence, 1958, numbers 213, 285.

the new age. But it would require a whole book to investigate the vast output of Alsted.

Another interesting example of the emergence of a more rational method from Renaissance occultism is afforded by the *Orbis pictus* of Comenius (first edition in 1658).[26] This was a primer for teaching children languages, such as Latin, German, Italian, and French, by means of pictures. The pictures are arranged in the order of the world, pictures of the heavens, the stars and celestial phenomena, of animals, birds, stones and so on, of man and all his activities. Looking at the picture of the sun, the child learned the word for sun in all the different languages; or looking at the picture of a theatre,[27] the word for a theatre in all the languages. This may seem ordinary enough now that the market is saturated with children's picture books, but it was an astonishingly original pedagogic method in those times and must have made language-learning enjoyable for many a seventeenth-century child as compared with the dull drudgery accompanied by frequent beatings of traditional education. It is said that the boys of Leipzig in the time of Leibniz were brought up on 'the picture book of Comenius' and Luther's catechism.[28]

Now there can be no doubt that the *Orbis pictus* came straight out of Campanella's *City of the Sun*,[29] that Utopia of astral magic in which the round central Sun temple, painted with the images of the stars, was surrounded by the concentric circles of the walls of the city on which the whole world of the creation and of man and his activities was represented in images dependent on the central causal images. As has been said earlier, the *City of the Sun* could be used as an occult memory system through which everything could be quickly learned, using the world 'as a book' and as 'local memory'.[30] The children of the Sun City were instructed by the Solarian priests who took them round the City to look at the

---

[26] *Orbis sensualium pictus*, Nuremberg, 1658. This is not the same work as Comenius's earlier language primer, the *Janua linguarum*. Comenius was a pupil of Alsted.

[27] Reproduced in Allardyce Nicoll, *Stuart Masques and the Renaissance Stage*, London, 1937, fig. 113.

[28] See R. Latta, introduction to Leibniz's *Monadology*, Oxford, 1898, p. 1.

[29] See Rossi, *Clavis*, p. 186.

[30] See above, p. 298.

pictures, whereby they learned the alphabets of all languages and everything else through the images on the walls. The pedagogic method of the highly occult Solarians, and the whole plan of their City and its images, was a form of local memory, with its places and images. Translated into the *Orbis pictus*, the Solarian magic memory system becomes a perfectly rational, and extremely original and valuable, language primer. It may be added that the Utopian city described by Johann Valentin Andreae—that mystery man whom rumour connected with the manifestos of the Rosicrucians—is also decorated all over with pictures which are used for instructing youth.[31] However, Andreae's *Christianopolis* was also influenced by the *City of the Sun*, which was thus probably the ultimate source of the new visual education.

One of the pre-occupations of the seventeenth century was the search for a universal language. Stimulated by Bacon's demand for 'real characters' for expressing notions[32]—characters or signs which should be really in contact with the notions they expressed— Comenius worked in this direction and through his influence a whole group of writers—Bisterfield, Dalgarno, Wilkins and others —laboured to found universal languages on 'real characters'. As Rossi has shown, these efforts come straight out of the memory tradition with its search for signs and symbols to use as memory images.[33] The universal languages are thought of as aids to memory and in many cases their authors are obviously drawing on the memory treatises. And it may be added that the search for 'real characters' comes out of the memory tradition on its occult side. The seventeenth-century universal language enthusiasts are translating into rational terms efforts such as those of Giordano Bruno to found universal memory systems on magic images which he thought of as directly in contact with reality.

Thus Renaissance methods and aims merge into seventeenth-century methods and aims and the seventeenth-century reader did not distinguish the modern aspects of the age so sharply as we do.

[31] J. V. Andreae, *Reipublicae Christianopolitanae Descriptio*, Strasburg, 1619; English translation by F. E. Held, *Christianopolis, an Ideal State of the Seventeenth Century*, New York and Oxford, 1916, p. 202. On Andreae and Campanella, see *G.B. and H.T.*, pp. 413–14.

[32] In *The Advancement of Learning*, II, xvi, 3; Spedding, III, pp. 399–400. Cf. Rossi, *Clavis*, pp. 201 ff.

[33] See Rossi's valuable survey of the 'universal language' movement in its relation to the art of memory in *Clavis*, chapter VII, pp. 201 ff.

For him, the methods of Bacon or of Descartes were just two more of such things. The monumental *Pharus Scientiarum*[34] published in 1659 by the Spanish Jesuit, Sebastian Izquierdo, is an interesting example of this.

Izquierdo makes a survey of those who have worked towards the founding of a universal art. He gives considerable space to the 'circular method' or *Cyclognomica* of Cornelius Gemma (if anyone ever tries to understand the Cyclognomic Art which may be historically important, Izquierdo might help); thence he passes to the *Novum Organum* of Francis Bacon, to the art of Ramon Lull, and the art of memory. Paolo Rossi has written valuable pages on Izquierdo[35] in which he points out the importance of the Jesuit's insistence on the need for a universal science to be applied to all the sciences of the encyclopaedia; for a logic which should include memory; and for an exact procedure in metaphysics to be modelled on the mathematical sciences. There may be an influence of Descartes on the last-named project, but it is also apparent that Izquierdo is thinking on Lullian lines and along the lines of the old efforts to combine Lullism with the art of memory. He insists that Lullism must be 'mathematicised' and in fact he gives pages and pages in which, for the Lullian combinations of letters, combinations of numbers have been substituted. Rossi suggests that this is a presage of Leibniz's use of the principles of the *combinatoria* as a calculus. Athanasius Kircher, a more famous Jesuit, also urged the 'mathematicising' of Lullism.[36]

When one sees in the pages of Izquierdo influences from Bacon, and perhaps from Descartes, working side by side with Lullism and the art of memory, and how the mathematical trend of the century is working amongst the older arts, it becomes more and more apparent that the emergence of seventeenth-century methods should be studied in the context of the continuing influence of the arts.

But it is Leibniz who affords by far the most remarkable example of the survival of influences from the art of memory and from Lullism in the mind of a great seventeenth-century figure. It

[34] Sebastian Izquierdo, *Pharus Scientiarum ubi quidquid ad cognitionem humanam humanitatis acquisibilem pertinet*, Leyden, 1659.

[35] Rossi, *Clavis*, pp. 194–5.

[36] A. Kircher, *Ars magna sciendi in XII libros digesta*, Amsterdam, 1669. Cf. Rossi, *Clavis*, p. 196.

is, of course, generally known that Leibniz was interested in Lullism and wrote a work *De arte combinatoria* based on adaptations of Lullism.[37] What is not so well known, though it has been pointed out by Paolo Rossi, is that Leibniz was also very familiar with the traditions of the classical art of memory. In fact, Leibniz's efforts at inventing a universal calculus using combinations of significant signs or characters can undoubtedly be seen as descending historically from those Renaissance efforts to combine Lullism with the art of memory of which Giordano Bruno was such an outstanding example. But the significant signs or characters of Leibniz's 'characteristica' were mathematical symbols, and their logical combinations were to produce the invention of the infinitesimal calculus.

Amongst Leibniz's unpublished manuscripts at Hanover there are references to the art of memory, mentioning in particular Lambert Schenkel on the subject (this is the memory writer also mentioned by Descartes) and another well-known memory treatise, the *Simonides Redivivus* of Adam Bruxius published at Leipzig in 1610. Following indications given by Couturat, Paolo Rossi has drawn attention to this evidence from the manuscripts that Leibniz was interested in the art of memory.[38] There is also plenty of evidence of this in the published works. The *Nova methodus discendae docendaeque jurisprudentia* (1667) contains long discussions of memory and the art of memory.[39] *Mnemonica*, says Leibniz, provides the matter of an argument; *Methodologia* gives it form; and *Logica* is the application of the matter to the form. He then defines *Mnemonica* as the joining of the image of some sensible thing to the thing to be remembered, and this image he calls a *nota*. The 'sensible' *nota* must have some connection with the thing to be remembered, either because it is like it, or unlike it, or connected with it. In this way words can be remembered, though this is very difficult, and also things. Here the mind of the great Leibniz is moving on lines which take us straight back to *Ad*

[37] See L. Couturat, *La logique de Leibniz*, Paris, 1901, pp. 36 ff.; and below, pp. 381–3.

[38] See L. Couturat, *Opuscules et fragments inédits de Leibniz*, Hildesheim, 1961, p. 37; Rossi, *Clavis*, pp. 250–3. These references to mnemonics are found in Phil. VI.19 and Phil. VII.B.III.7 (unpublished Leibniz manuscripts at Hanover).

[39] Leibniz, *Philosophische schriften*, ed. P. Ritter, I (1930), pp. 277–9.

Herennium, on images for things, and the harder images for words; he is also recalling the three Aristotelian laws of association so intimately bound up with the memory tradition by the scholastics. He then mentions that things seen are better remembered than things heard, which is why we use *notae* in memory, and adds that the hieroglyphs of the Egyptians and the Chinese are in the nature of memory images. He indicates 'rules for places' in the remark that the distribution of things in cells or places is helpful for memory and names as mnemonic authors to be consulted about this, Alsted and Frey.[40]

This passage is a little memory treatise by Leibniz. I am inclined to think that the figure on which a number of visual emblems are disposed on the title-page of the *Disputatio de casibus in jure* (1666)[41] is intended to be used as a local memory system for remembering law suits (a thoroughly classical use of the art of memory) and many other indications of Leibniz's knowledge of the tricks of the memory trade could no doubt be unearthed. One which I have noticed is the remark (in a work of 1678) that the *Ars memoriae* suggests a way of remembering a series of ideas by attaching them to a series of personages, such as patriarchs, apostles, or emperors[42]—which takes us back to one of the most characteristic and time-honoured of the memory practices which had grown up around the classical rules.

Thus Leibniz knew the memory tradition extremely well; he had studied the memory treatises and had picked up, not only the main lines of the classical rules, but also complications which had grown up around these in the memory tradition. And he was interested in the principles on which the classical art was based.

Of Leibniz and Lullism much has been written, and ample evidence of the influence upon him of the Lullist tradition is afforded by the *Dissertatio de arte combinatoria* (1666). The opening diagram in this work,[43] in which the square of the four elements is associated with the logical square of opposition, show his grasp of Lullism as a natural logic.[44] In the prefatory pages he mentions modern Lullists, among them Agrippa, Alsted, Kircher, and not

[40] J. C. Frey, *Opera,* Paris, 1645–6 contains a section on memory.
[41] *Philosophische schriften,* ed. Ritter, I, p. 367.
[42] Couturat, *Opuscules,* p. 281.
[43] *Philosophische schriften,* ed. Ritter, I, p. 166.
[44] See above, p. 178.

omitting 'Jordanus Brunus'. Bruno, says Leibniz, called the Lullian Art a 'combinatoria'[45]—the word which Leibniz himself is using of his new Lullism. He (Leibniz) is interpreting Lullism with arithmetic and with the 'inventive logic' which Francis Bacon wanted to improve. There is already here the idea of using the 'combinatoria' with mathematics which, as we have seen, had been developing in Alsted, Izquierdo, and Kircher.

In this new mathematical-Lullist art, says Leibniz, *notae* will be used as an alphabet. These *notae* are to be as 'natural' as possible, a universal writing. They may be like geometrical figures, or like the 'pictures' used by the Egyptians and the Chinese, though the new Leibnizian *notae* will be better for 'memory' than these.[46] In the other context in which we have already met the Leibnizian *notae* these were quite definitely connected with the memory tradition, and were something like the images demanded by the classical art. And here, too, they are connected with memory. It is perfectly clear that Leibniz is emerging out of a Renaissance tradition—out of those unending efforts to combine Lullism with the classical art of memory.

The *Dissertatio de arte combinatoria* is an early work of Leibniz's, written before his sojourn in Paris (1672–6) during which he perfected his mathematical studies, learning from Huyghens and others of all the recent advances in the higher mathematics. It was from this work that he was to make his own advances, and into that history belongs the emergence of the infinitesimal calculus, which Leibniz arrived at apparently quite independently of Isaac Newton who was working on similar lines at the same time. About Newton, I have nothing to say, but the context in which the infinitesimal calculus emerges in Leibniz belongs into the history traced in this book. Leibniz himself said that the germ of his later thinking was in the *Dissertatio de arte combinatoria*.

As is well known, Leibniz formed a project known as the 'characteristica'.[47] Lists were to be drawn up of all the essential notions of thought, and to these notions were to be assigned symbols or 'characters'. The influence of the age-long search since

---

[45] *Philosophische schriften,* ed. Ritter, I, p. 194. Leibniz refers to the preface of Bruno's *De Specierum scrutinio,* Prague, 1588 (Bruno, *Op. lat.,* II (ii), p. 333).

[46] *Philosophische schriften,* ed. Ritter, I, p. 302. Cf. Rossi, *Clavis,* p. 242.

[47] Couturat, *Logique de Leibniz,* pp. 51 ff.; Rossi, *Clavis,* pp. 201 ff.

Simonides, for 'images for things' on such a scheme is obvious. Leibniz knew of the aspirations so widely current in the time for the formation of a universal language of signs or symbols[48] (the schemes of Bisterfield and others) but such schemes, as has already been mentioned, were themselves influenced by the mnemonic tradition. And the 'characteristica' of Leibniz was to be more than a universal language; it was to be a 'calculus'. The 'characters' were to be used in logical combinations to form a universal art or calculus for the solution of all problems. The mature Leibniz, the supreme mathematician and logician, is obviously still emerging straight out of Renaissance efforts for conflating the classical art of memory with Lullism by using the images of the classical art on the Lullian combinatory wheels.

Allied to the 'characteristica' or calculus in Leibniz's mind was the project for an encyclopaedia which was to bring together all the arts and sciences known to man. When all knowledge was systematised in the encyclopaedia, 'characters' could be assigned to all notions, and the universal calculus would eventually be established for the solution of all problems. Leibniz envisaged the application of the calculus to all departments of thought and activity. Even religious difficulties would be removed by it.[49] Those in disagreement, for example, about the Council of Trent would no longer go to war but would sit down together saying, 'Let us calculate.'

Ramon Lull believed that his Art, with its letter notations and revolving geometrical figures, could be applied to all the subjects of the encyclopaedia, and that it could convince Jews and Mohammedans of the truths of Christianity. Giulio Camillo had formed a Memory Theatre in which all knowledge was to be synthesised through images. Giordano Bruno, putting the images in movement on the Lullian combinatory wheels, had travelled all over Europe with his fantastic arts of memory. Leibniz is the seventeenth-century heir to this tradition.

Leibniz tried to interest various potentates and academies in his projects but without success. The encyclopaedia was never drawn up; the assignment of the 'characters' to the notions was never completed; the universal calculus was never established. We are reminded of Giulio Camillo who was never able to complete the

[48] Couturat, *Logique de Leibniz*, pp. 51 ff.; Rossi, *Clavis*, pp. 201 ff.
[49] Couturat, *Logique*, p. 98, and cf. the article Leibniz in *Enciclopedia Filosofica* (Venice, 1957).

stupendous Memory Theatre which met with only partial and insufficient support from the King of France. Or of Giordano Bruno, feverishly trying memory scheme after memory scheme, until he met his death at the stake.

Yet Leibniz was able to bring some parts of his total scheme to fruition. He believed that the advances that he had made in mathematics were fundamentally due to his having succeeded in finding symbols for representing quantities and their relations. 'And indeed', says Couturat, 'there is no doubt that his most famous invention, that of the infinitesimal calculus, arose from his constant search for new and more general symbolisms, and that, inversely, this invention confirmed him in his opinion of the capital importance for the deductive sciences of a good characteristic.'[50] Leibniz's profound originality, continues Couturat, consisted in representing by appropriate signs, notions and operations for which no notation had hitherto existed.[51] In short, it was through his invention of new 'characters' that he was able to operate the infinitesimal calculus, which was but a fragment, or a specimen, of the never completed 'universal characteristic'.

If, as has been suggested, Leibniz's 'characteristica' as a whole comes straight out of the memory tradition, it would follow that the search for 'images for things', when transferred to mathematical symbolism, resulted in the discovery of new and better mathematical or logico-mathematical, notations, making possible new types of calculation.

It was always a principle with Leibniz in his search for 'characters' that these should represent as nearly as possible reality, or the real nature of things, and there are several passages in his works which throw an illuminating light on the background of his search. For example, in the *Fundamenta calculi ratiocinatoris*, he defines 'characters' as signs which are either written, or delineated, or sculptured. A sign is the more useful the closer it is to the thing signified. But Leibniz says that the characters of the chemist or of the astronomers, such as John Dee put forward in his *Monas*

[50] Couturat, *Logique*, p. 84.
[51] *Ibid.*, p. 85. Cf. also Couturat's note in *Opuscules*, p. 97: 'Quelle que soit la valeur de cet essai d'une caractéristique nouvelle, il faut, pour le juger équitablement, se rappeler que c'est de cette recherche de signes appropriés qu'est né l'algorithme infinitésimal usité universellement aujourd'hui'.

hieroglyphica, are not of use, nor the figures of the Chinese and the Egyptians. The language of Adam, by which he named the creatures, must have been close to reality, but we do not know it. The words of ordinary languages are imprecise and their use leads to error. What alone are best for accurate enquiry and calculation are the *notae* of the arithmeticians and algebraists.[52]

The passage, and there are others similar to it, shows Leibniz conducting his search, moving meditatively in the world of the past amongst the magic 'characters', the signs of the alchemists, the images of the astrologers, of Dee's monas formed of the characters of the seven planets, of the rumoured Adamic language, magically in contact with reality, of the Egyptian hieroglyphs in which truth was hidden. Out of all this he emerges, like his century emerging from the occultism of the Renaissance, finding the true *notae,* the characters nearest to reality in the symbols of mathematics.

Yet Leibniz knew that past very well, and was perhaps even guarding against suspicions that his 'universal characteristic' might be too closely connected with it when he speaks of his project as an 'innocent magia' or a 'true Cabala'.[53] At other times he will present it very much in the language of the past, as a great secret, a universal key. The introduction to the 'arcana' of his encyclopaedia states that here will be found a general science, a new logic, a new method, an *Ars reminiscendi* or Mnemonica, an *Ars Characteristica* or Symbolica, an *Ars Combinatoria* or Lulliana, a Cabala of the Wise, a Magia Naturalis, in short all sciences will here be contained as in an Ocean.[54]

We might be reading the lengthy title-page of Bruno's *Seals,*[55] or the address in which he introduced the doctors of Oxford to those mad magic memory systems, which led up to the revelation of the new religion of Love, Art, Magic, and Mathesis. Who would guess from these clouds of old style bombast that Leibniz really

[52] Leibniz, *Opera philosophica* ed. J. E. Erdman, Berlin, 1840, pp. 92–3. There is a very similar text in *Philosophische schriften,* ed. C. J. Gerhardt, Berlin, 1880, VII, pp. 204–5.
On Leibniz's interest in the 'lingua Adamaica', the magical language used by Adam in naming the creatures, see Couturat, *Logique,* p. 77.
[53] Leibniz, *Sämtliche Schriften und Briefe,* ed. Ritter, Series I, Vol. II, Darmstad, 1927, pp. 167–9; quoted by Rossi, *Clavis,* p. 255.
[54] *Introductio ad Encyclopaediam arcanam,* in Couturat, *Opuscules,* pp. 511–12. Cf. Rossi, *Clavis,* p. 255.
[55] See above, p. 201.

had found a Great Key? The true Clavis, he says, in an essay on the 'characteristica', has hitherto not been known, hence the ineptitudes of magic with which books are full.[56] The light of truth has been lacking which only mathematical discipline can bring.[57]

Let us turn back now and gaze once more at that strange diagram (Pl. 11) which we excavated from Bruno's *Shadows*, where the magic images of the stars revolving on the central wheel control the images on other wheels of the contents of the elemental world and the images on the outer wheel representing all the activities of man. Or let us remember *Seals* where every conceivable memory method known to the ex-Dominican memory expert is tirelessly tried in combinations the efficacy of which rests on the memory image conceived of as containing magical force. Let us read again the passage at the end of *Seals* (which can be paralleled from all Bruno's other memory books) in which the occult memory artist lists the kinds of images which may be used on the Lullian combinatory wheels, amongst which figure prominently signs, *notae*, characters, seals.[58] Or let us contemplate the spectacle of the statues of gods and goddesses, assimilated to the stars, revolving, both as magic images of reality and as memory images comprehending all possible notions, on the wheel in *Statues*. Or think of the inextricable maze of memory rooms in *Images*, full of images of all things in the elemental world, controlled by the significant images of the Olympian gods.

This madness had a very complex method in it, and what was its object? To arrive at universal knowledge through combining significant images of reality. Always we had the sense that there was a fierce scientific impulse in those efforts, a striving, on the Hermetic plane, after some method of the future, half-glimpsed, half-dreamed of, prophetically foreshadowed in those infinitely intricate gropings after a calculus of memory images, after arrangements of memory orders in which the Lullian principle of movement should somehow be combined with a magicised mnemonics using characters of reality.

'Enfin Leibniz vient', we may say, paraphrasing Boileau. And

[56] Leibniz, *Philosophische schriften*, ed. C. J. Gerhardt, Berlin, 1890, VII, p. 184.

[57] *Ibid.*, p. 67 (*Initia et specimena scientiae novae generalis*).

[58] Bruno, *Op. lat.*, II (ii), pp. 204 ff.

looking back now from the vantage point of Leibniz we may see Giordano Bruno as a Renaissance prophet, on the Hermetic plane, of scientific method, and a prophet who shows us the importance of the classical art of memory, combined with Lullism, in preparing the way for the finding of a Great Key.

But the matter does not end here. We have always hinted or guessed that there was a secret side to Bruno's memory systems, that they were a mode of transmitting a religion, or an ethic, or some message of universal import. And there was a message of universal love and brotherhood, of religious toleration, of charity and benevolence implied in Liebniz's projects for his universal calculus or characteristic. Plans for the reunion of the churches, for the pacification of sectarian differences, for the foundation of an 'Order of Charity', form a basic part of his schemes. The progress of the sciences, Leibniz believed, would lead to an extended knowledge of the universe, and therefore to a wider knowledge of God, its creator, and thence to a wider extension of charity, the source of all virtues.[59] Mysticism and philanthropy are bound up with the encyclopaedia and the universal calculus. When we think of this side of Leibniz, the comparison with Bruno is again striking. The religion of Love, Art, Magic, and Mathesis was hidden in the Seals of Memory. A religion of love and general philanthropy is to be made manifest, or brought about, through the universal calculus. If we delete Magic, substitute genuine mathematics for Mathesis, understand Art as the calculus, and retain Love, the Leibnizian aspirations seem to approximate strikingly closely— though in a seventeenth-century transformation—to those of Bruno.

A 'Rosicrucian' aura clings to Leibniz, a suggestion often vaguely raised, and dismissed without examination or discussion of the many passages in Leibniz's works in which he mentions 'Christian Rosenkreuz', or Valentin Andreae, or refers, directly or indirectly, to the Rosicrucian manifestos.[60] It is impossible to

[59] Couturat, *Logique de Leibniz*, pp. 131–2, 135–8, etc.

[60] That Leibniz was a Rosicrucian is, however, firmly acepted by that excellent scholar, Couturat: 'On sait que Leibniz s'etait affilié en 1666 à Nürnberg à la société secrète des Rose-Croix' (*Logique de Leibniz*, p. 131, note 3). Leibniz himself may hint that he was a Rosicrucian (*Philosophische Schriften*, ed. Ritter, Vol. I (1930), p. 276). The rules for his

investigate this problem here, but it is a possible hypothesis that the curious connections between Bruno and Leibniz—which undoubtedly exist—might be accounted for through the medium of a Hermetic society, founded by Bruno in Germany, and afterwards developing as Rosicrucianism. The 'Thirty Seals' which Bruno published in Germany.[61] and their connections with the Latin poems published in Germany, would be the starting-point for such an investigation at the Bruno end. And the enquiry from the Leibniz end would have to await the full publication of Leibniz manuscripts and the clearing up of the present unsatisfactory situation concerning the edition of the works. We shall therefore no doubt have to wait a long time for the solution of this problem.

The standard histories of modern philosophy, which repeat after one another the idea that the term 'monad' was borrowed by Leibniz from Bruno, omit as quite outside their purview any mention of the Hermetic tradition from which Bruno and other Hermetic philosophers of the Renaissance took the word. Though Leibniz as a philosopher of the seventeenth century has moved into another atmosphere and a new world, the Leibnizian monadology bears upon it the obvious marks of the Hermetic tradition. The Leibnizian monads, when they are human souls having memory, have as their chief function the representation or reflection of the universe of which they are living mirrors[62]—a conception with which the reader of this book will be thoroughly familiar.

A detailed comparison of Bruno with Leibniz, on entirely new lines, might be one of the best approaches to the study of the emergence of the seventeenth century out of the Renaissance Hermetic tradition. And such a study might demonstrate that all that was most noble in the religious and philanthropic aspirations of seventeenth-century science was already present, on the Hermetic plane, in Giordano Bruno, transmitted by him in the secret of his arts of memory.

    *   *   *   *   *

[61] See above, p. 294.

[62] Leibniz, *Monadology*, trans. R. Latta, Oxford, 1898, pp. 230, 253, 266 etc.

---

projected Order of Charity (Couturat, *Opuscules*, pp. 3–4) are a quotation from the Rosicrucian *Fama*. Other evidence from his works could be adduced, but the subject needs more than a fragmentary treatment.

I have chosen to end my history with Leibniz, because one must stop somewhere, and because it may be that here ends the influence of the art of memory as a factor in basic European developments. But there were many survivals in later centuries. Books on the art of memory continued to appear, still recognisably in the classical tradition, and it is unlikely that the traditions of occult memory were lost, or ceased to influence significant movements. Another book could probably be written carrying the subject on into later centuries.

Though this book has tried to give some account of the history of the art of memory in the periods covered, it should not be regarded as in any sense a complete or final history. I have used only a fraction of the material available, or which might be made available by further research, for the study of this vast subject. The serious investigation of this forgotten art may be said to have only just begun. Such subjects do not have behind them, as yet, an apparatus of organised modern scholarship; they do not belong into the normal curricula and so they are left out. The art of memory is a clear case of a marginal subject, not recognised as belonging to any of the normal disciplines, having been omitted because it was no one's business. And yet it has turned out to be, in a sense, everyone's business. The history of the organisation of memory touches at vital points on the history of religion and ethics, of philosophy and psychology, of art and literature, of scientific method. The artificial memory as a part of rhetoric belongs into the rhetoric tradition; memory as a power of the soul belongs with theology. When we reflect on these profound affiliations of our theme it begins to seem after all not so surprising that the pursuit of it should have opened up new views of some of the greatest manifestations of our culture.

I am conscious as I look back of how little I have understood of the significance for whole tracts of history of the art which Simonides was supposed to have invented after that legendary disastrous banquet.

INDEX

Abel, 220
Abraham, 220
Academies, in Paris, 207, 369; in
 Naples, 205; in Venice, 134, 156,
 157 (74), 158, 166–9, 201, 262
Achilles, 30
Actaeon, 314
Adam, language of, 385
Ad Herennium, main source for
 classical art of memory, 1–17, 23,
 25, 30, 40–1, 43; transmission of
 to Middle Ages, 26, 50, 52–8;
 known as Second Rhetoric of
 Tullius, 20–1, 54–6; conflated
 with Aristotle's *De memoria et
 reminiscentia* by the scholastics,
 20–1, 32–3, 62 ff.; later memory
 tradition based on, 26, 89–90, 99,
 103, 105–9, 199, 223, 233, 247,
 268, 274, 294, 302, 327–8, 333–4,
 380–1, etc.; Lull and, 185, 192–3,
 195 (38); humanists and, 125–6,
 236
Adonis, 164
Aelian, 28
Aesculapius, 296, 313, 316
Aesop (actor), 65–6, 235
Agamemnon, 14
Agrippa, Henry Cornelius, 102, 124,
 157–8, 206–7, 214–15, 255, 258,
 262, 328 (17), 361, 364, 376, 381
Alamanni, Luigi, 133
Alaric, 50
Alberti, L. B., 136 (27), 361, 364
Albertus Magnus, and the art of
 memory, xii, 20–1, 32, 57, 60–70,
 72, 76, 84–6, 90, 97, 99, 104, 110,
 174, 185, 202–5, 230, 242, 368,
 381
Alchemy, 190–1, 197, 209, 224, 249,
 263, 335 (37), 372, 385
Alcuin, 53–4
Alsted, Johann-Heinrich, 375–7,
 381–2
Ammon, *see* Thamus
Amphitrite, 226, 228, 314
Amphitheatres, 130–1, 133, 360
Anaxogoras, 221, 226, 252
Andreae, Johann Valentin, 378, 387
Angels, 148, 150, 339–40
Ammianus Marcellinus, 28

Annius of Viterbo, 149 (56)
Anselm, 175
Apollas Callimachus, 27 (1)
Apollo, 138, 143, 153–4, 164, 168,
 225, 288–9, 296, 316, 327, 334
Apollodorus, 27 (1)
Apollonius of Tyana, 42–3
Aquinas, Thomas, and the art of
 memory, xii, 20–1, 32, 57, 60,
 70–81;
 his influence in the memory
 tradition, 82 ff., 92, 94, 99, 101–3,
 106, 107 (3), 110, 114–15, 120–1,
 123–4, 165, 174, 185, 192–3,
 202–5, 230, 233, 235, 242, 246,
 256, 258, 260, 262, 291, 300, 302,
 313, 316, 366, 368, 372, 381;
 condemnation of *Ars notoria*, 43,
 204;
 representation of in Chapter
 House of Santa Maria Novella,
 Florence, 79–80, 94, 100, 121,
 164, 223, 235, 244;
 see Aristotle, Similitudes
Archimedes, 45, 164, 221
Argus, 152–3
Aries, sign of the zodiac, 40–1, 182,
 197, 330, 331;
 and the memory image in *Ad
 Herennium*, 41, 68–9
Arion, 296
Ariosto, 134, 169, 309, 312, 367
Aristotle, his allusions to Greek
 mnemonics, 31–5;
 theory of memory and
 reminiscence, 32–6, 44;
 the *De memoria et reminiscentia*
 conflated with *Ad Herennium*
 by the scholastics, 32, 35, 61 ff.;
 Thomist-Aristotelian influence in
 the later memory tradition, 83,
 87, 106, 115, 160, 185, 192–3, 195
 (38), 202, 204, 206, 233, 236, 253,
 257, 298, 302, 381;
 the *Physics* memorised by the art
 of memory, 287–9;
 Anti-Aristotelianism (Bruno and
 Ramus), 240–1, 252, 279, 287,
 289, 292, 310–11, 319;
 see also 61, 150, 164, 223, 370 (5)
Ars dictaminis, 57–60, 89 (22)

INDEX

Theatres, as memory systems, xi,
37–8, 129–59, 206, 320–41
Thebes, Egypt, 38, 270
Themistocles, 17, 103
Theodectes, 44
Theodore of Gaza, 107 (4)
Thetis, 288, 316
Theutates, 268–70
'Thirty', Bruno's use of, 210–12,
219, 225, 227, 229, 244, 247, 254,
259, 295, 335
Thomas Aquinas, see Aquinas
Thoth (Theuth), 38, 220, 268–9
Thrale, Hester, 355
Tiraboschi, Girolamo, 135
Tiro, 15 (16)
Titian, 162, 164, 206
Tobias and the Angel, 326
Tommai, Petrus, see Peter of
Ravenna
Topics, logical, and memory places,
31, 232, 238
Toscanus, J. M., 135
Toulouse, France, 328
Tree diagrams, 184, 186–7, 190,
248
Triangle, 182–3, 197, 375
Trigona (zodiac), 170, 356
Trinity, the, 49, 151, 153, 174, 176,
178–9, 181–3, 188, 210, 229–30,
339, 340
Triptolemus, 28
Trismegistus, see Hermes
Trismegistus
Trithemius, 167, 211, 301
Trojans, 271, 313

Universal language, 378, 382–3
Utopias, 297–8, 377–8
Ut pictura poesis, 28, 253–4, 263–4

Valla, Lorenzo, 125, 164
Vautrollier, Thomas, 267 (3)
Venice, Camillo's Theatre, 129–59;
and the Venetian Renaissance,
160–72;
see also 55, 82, 110, 189–201, 203,
262, 286, 293, 299, 305, 367 and
Academies
Venus, 24, 143–4, 149, 154, 163,
290, 296, 316–17
Vesta, 98, 290
Vicenza, Italy, 165 (12), 171

Victorines, the, 175
Vienna, 109
Viglius Zuichemus, letters to
Erasmus, 130–4, 144, 157–8, 166,
203
Virgil, 16, 95, 206, 240, 271 (18)
Virtues and vices, definitions of,
20–1, 54, 57, 61–2, 67, 73–4, 78–9
84–5, 86–8;
personifications of as memory
images, xii, 30, 48, 55, 59–60,
89–90, 92–4, 98–100, 102–3, 120,
187, 193, 244, 277, 314–17, 327,
334
Visual alphabets, and memory
inscriptions, 118–20, 123–4, 163,
206, 250, 294–5, 335
Vitruvius, 136–7, 170–2, 350, 356,
359–63, 365–7
Vulcan, 30, 143, 164

Wax imprints, mental images
compared to, 6–7, 19, 23, 32,
35–6, 51, 87
Weczdorff, Jodocus, 114 (25)
White, John 325 (12)
Whytehead (Austin Friar), 363
Wilkins, J., 378
Willis, John, 336–8, 348
Wittenberg, Germany, 289, 292,
376 (25)
Wood, Anthony à, 363 (44)
Worlds, three, 143, 148, 150, 165,
339–40, 365, 369

Xenophanes, 221

Zeuxis, representing memory
images, 28, 164, 246, 249, 252–3,
257, 286, 289, 293
Zodiac, 170–1, 187, 190, 270, 340,
344–5, 347, 349, 356, 366;
use of in the art of memory, 23–4,
39–40, 42, 69, 101, 116, 122,
140–1, 146, 208, 212–14, 217, 224,
226, 245–6, 248, 251, 267–8, 276,
314, 326, 329–31, 333–4, 338,
340, see Decans, Metrodorus of
Scepsis
Zohar, the, 147, 149, 177
Zoroaster, 164, 208, 219, 258
Zuichemus, see Viglius Zuichemus
Zurich, Switzerland, 293

Printed in the USA/Agawam, MA
January 14, 2011

556116.069